A Histor  **s in**

Volume III – Ben Het: 1969

Kenard Ventu,

thanks for your service.

Caribou squadrons hauled over 1,000,000 passengers and nearly 100,000 tons of cargo in 1969 as "Vietnamyzation" of the war began. The siege at Ben Het foretold what would happen at Dak Seang in 1970. Heroes flying the Mighty Boo earned 4 Silver Stars, 253 DFC's and 4 "one day" Air Medals.

Pat Hanover

E. Patrick Hanavan, Jr.
12402 Winding Branch
San Antonio, TX 78230-2770

First Printing

Books in this series:
Vol. I – The First Year: 1966-1967 (published 17 Aug 2012)
Vol. II – Tet Offensive: 1968 (published 27 Aug 2013)
Vol. III – Ben Het: 1969 (published 6 Aug 2014)
Vol. IV – Dak Pek and Dak Seang: 1970
Vol. V – Vietnamization: 1971-1972

Col. Hanavan relates an historic tale that isn't covered anywhere else. The Canadian-built Caribou (C-7A) was in the USAF inventory of active aircraft only 6 years. In that time, it was the only airplane that could deliver the goods to tiny Special Forces camps on hilltops and in jungles with reliable precision. Several Caribou crews died completing that mission. I flew the Caribou in 1967-68 during the '68 Tet offensive during the highest casualty year of the war. This is the best-researched book on the war that I've seen. If you're interested in how beans and bullets got to the Green Berets, then you have to read Hanavan's true story.

Col. Dick Besley, 535th TAS, Vung Tau, 1967-1968

I flew Caribous from Vung Tau and CamRanh Bay airbases. I loved flying the STOL airplane, which never gave me a problem. Col Hanavan's books on this subject are so detailed and filled with personalities from the operation. All of the problems and solutions involved in setting up a new Air Force wing in-country, while maintaining a wartime operational tempo, are wonderfully described in the first two volumes. I can't wait for Volumes 3 and 4 to be published.

Maj. Richard Davidson, 536th TAS, Vung Tau, 1969-1970

I was a crew chief on the Caribou aircraft at Phu Cat in Vietnam. This book brought back a lot memories from that time and place. I look forward to hearing from Bou guys from that time and place.

William Troy, 537th TAS, Phu Cat, 1967-1968

I am a veteran of the Vietnam War, where I was a crew member on the Caribou during the time frame described in Volume 2. Many memories here, good and bad.

MSgt. Jerry York, 537th TAS, Phu Cat, 1967-1968

I was a USAF engine mechanic on the Caribou, trained by the 601st Field Training at Ft. Benning, GA. Caribou Airlines is a MUST read for those of us that were there. If being interested in what it takes to start, from the ground up, this is your book to read. It is very factual and informative, covering the good, the bad, and the ugly. We were very proud of the things we all accomplished for the Caribou, with the Army and the USAF.

Sgt. Bob Cummings, 459th TAS, Phu Cat, 1966

A must read for Vietnam War buffs!. Col. Hanavan tells the story of the Bou as it was. I flew the C-7A throughout Vietnam. His stories and accounts of the operation are accurate. He has given an excellent account of what happened and how it happened.

Marty Hillman, 459th TAS, Phu Cat, 1967-1968

Caribou Airlines is a must read for anyone interested in what it takes to start, from the ground up, a USAF Tactical Airlift Wing in a combat zone. The personal stories included give the reader a sense of the dedication to duty, the hard work, the long hours, and the danger involved in accomplishing a very critical mission under less than desirable conditions. The short unimproved runways, mountainous terrain, and enemy fire make for some exciting reading. Because of some very dedicated maintenance personnel, the planes were patched up overnight, and the crews got up the next day and did it all again.

Senior Master Sgt. Kenneth Synco, 537th TAS, Phu Cat, 1969

The books are very impressive, well written, and expertly researched. I started reading and was overwhelmed with the technical and military-air jargon. You guys had your own language. Both books will be read cover to cover. Thank you for your service!

Carl Maggio, High school classmate of the author
Member of the 1951 American Legion national championship baseball team

Dedication

This history is dedicated to the thousands of Airmen, Soldiers, Sailors, Marines, and Coast Guardsmen who fought bravely in Southeast Asia during the Vietnam War, especially to my brothers who flew, maintained, and supported the C-7A Caribou, our beloved "Bou."

It is also dedicated to the families of those military personnel. They showed their courage, dedication, and perseverance while their loved ones were in harm's way in far away places. In many respects, they were heroes, just as were their loved ones.

> To the airmen – Sierra Hotel!
> To the soldiers – Hoo Rah!
> To the sailors – Bravo Zulu!
> To the marines – Semper Fi!
> To the coasties – Bravo Zulu!

As of 2014, five memorial benches honoring our fallen brothers had been installed: one each at The National Museum of the USAF in Dayton, OH; the Museum of Aviation in Warner Robins, GA; the Air Mobility Command Museum at Dover AFB, DE; the Air Force Enlisted Heritage Hall at the Gunter Annex of Maxwell AFB, AL; and the Travis Heritage Museum at Travis AFB, CA.

Foreword

Having been thoroughly captured by Volumes I and II of this great series, I was really excited to have the opportunity to review the manuscript for Volume III. This Volume covers the period both Colonel Hanavan, the author, and I, as a young Captain and Squadron Maintenance Officer, were there as part of "the Caribou nation" to live the first run of this piece of U.S. Air Force history.

As in the first two volumes, Col. Hanavan's skills and patience as a researcher and distiller of facts and statistics combine with his adeptness as a story-teller to bring to life the story of the Caribou in Vietnam. It is the story of American airmen at war – the operators, the maintainers, and those who were the support structure that made it all work so successfully. It is the story of how we prepared ourselves, how we lived day to day and of how we still took time to reach out and relate to the local Vietnamese populations on a personal level.

Especially important, this is the story of the lifeline made possible for the U.S. Army Special Forces and Vietnamese fighters in the remotest and often most contested places that could not have been sustained so ably without this exceptional aircraft and the great people who either flew them into the face of danger or kept them ready to go.

This Volume will rekindle memories for everyone on both ends of the Caribou lifeline. But, for aircraft maintenance crews, it will especially bring back a sense of appreciation for what our aircrews faced every day while bringing in critical supplies by landing on roads or barely prepared "landing strips" in the remotest corners of Vietnam.

Summaries of damaged aircraft recoveries in this period at forward bases will especially bring back memories of how, in just doing the mission, our aircraft were operated near the limits routinely, resulting in over-boosted engines and the need for over-the-wing engine changes that took us to places few non-aircrew airmen expected to visit. As a result, we too experienced a taste of life in the forward outposts and a real appreciation for the importance of the support lifeline we were for the Army Special Forces.

For those of us who have wondered if anyone will ever again read or use the unit history reports we so dutifully prepared each year, this series is your answer. When expertly researched and distilled, and then combined with first hand insights and powerful personal stories – history indeed comes alive!

Great job, Pat, on three in a row!!

John M Nowak
Lieutenant General, USAF (Ret.)
USAF Deputy Chief of Staff, Logistics
458 TAS, Squadron Maintenance Officer, July 1968 - August 1969

The Author

Pat Hanavan graduated from the United States Naval Academy in 1958. Midshipman Hanavan received the Marine Corps Association Prize in 1958 for the best research paper on operational or doctrinal aspects of ground, air, or amphibious operations, *Peleliu Pushover*.

He and Alicia, his wife of 55 years, raised four children (Patrick III, Cynthia, Michael, and Theresa). During his 20 years in the United States Air Force, he was a pilot, research and development engineer, maintenance officer, and logistics officer. His USAF assignments included the 55th Weather Reconnaissance Squadron, the 6570th Aerospace Medical Research Laboratory, Aeronautical Systems Division, the 535th Tactical Airlift Squadron and the 483rd Tactical Airlift Wing in Vietnam, the Space and Missile Systems Organization, Headquarters Air Force Systems Command, Warner Robins Air Logistics Center, and San Antonio Air Logistics Center.

He worked on manned extravehicular operations for the Gemini and Manned Orbiting Laboratory space programs from 1964-1965. The Ohio Society of Professional Engineers recognized him as its Young Engineer of 1966.

Pat flew the C-7A Caribou as an Instructor Pilot in the 535th Tactical Airlift Squadron at Vung Tau, Republic of Vietnam (RVN), during the Tet Offensive of 1968 and was then assigned as the Quality Control Officer and Chief Test pilot for the 483rd Tactical Airlift Wing at Cam Ranh Bay, RVN. During his Vietnam tour, he flew over 600 hours in the C-7A Caribou. Colonel Hanavan retired from the USAF in 1978 and transitioned to industry and academia.

Dr. Hanavan received a Ph.D. in Engineering from the University of California at Los Angeles while on active duty in the Air Force. From 1979-1990 he was a member of the faculty at The University of Texas at San Antonio. Then he worked at the Software Engineering Institute from 1990-1995. His engineering and management consulting work took him to many countries, including France, Australia, China, England, Canada, Italy, Holland, Korea, and Singapore.

He is a registered Professional Engineer in Software Engineering (Texas) and in Aeronautical Engineering (Ohio). He has been a member of the National Society of Professional Engineers since 1965 and is a Life Senior Member of the Institute of Electrical and Electronics Engineers, a Senior Member of the Association for Computing Machinery, and a senior member of the American Institute of Aeronautics and Astronautics.

Pat has been a member of the C-7A Caribou Association since 2003 and serves as its President, newsletter editor, and historian.

Preface

Caribou Airlines is a comprehensive history of USAF C-7A operations in Vietnam. It is about the aircrews, crew chiefs, maintenance officers, line chiefs, maintainers, phase inspection personnel, specialty shop personnel, supply personnel, personal equipment specialists, administration and operations personnel, commanders, staff personnel, etc. – all those who made it possible to deliver the troops, guns, ammunition, rations, beer, soda, equipment, animals, etc. to the hundreds of bases throughout the battlefields of Vietnam. The 483rd Tactical Airlift Wing and its squadrons were not an airline, *per se*, but they were tasked with supporting Army and Marine units and other customers with air landed and air dropped supplies using pre-defined, emergency, and opportune sorties to front line locations where the supplies were needed.

Some books about airpower during the Vietnam War mention the C-7A Caribou, either when it was operated by the United States Army or by the United States Air Force. Ray Bowers allotted only 24 pages of his 806 page book, *Tactical Airlift*, to the Caribou, so the book could not delve deeply into the history of the Caribou, its missions, and its men during the Vietnam War. Colonel Wilbert T. Turk told about his time as Commander of the 483rd Tactical Airlift Wing in 1968 and 1969 in *Hangar Flying With Grandpa*. Colonel Steve N. Pisanos told about his time with the Caribou as Squadron Commander of the 457th Tactical Airlift Squadron (1967-1968) in *The Flying Greek*. The Caribou was the focal point for Daryle D. McGinnis in his Vietnam novel, *A Waterfall In A War*.

In 2009, my search for the names and accomplishments of Caribou personnel during the Vietnam War led me to the Air Force Historical Research Agency (AFHRA) at Maxwell AFB, AL. There I found a wealth of information in the quarterly histories of the 483rd Tactical Airlift Wing and its squadrons from 1967-1972, including the early days when Air Force personnel were integrated into the Army Aviation Companies that were using the Caribou to support Army units in Vietnam. From July through December 1966, Air Force personnel flew with Army crews and worked alongside their Army counterparts in maintenance and supply activities supporting the Caribou.

Research at the AFHRA uncovered over 22,000 7th Air Force (7 AF) Special Orders during the time period from 1 July 1967 through 31 March 1972. These orders included 2 Air Force Crosses, 35 Silver

Stars, 1184 Distinguished Flying Crosses, 14 Airman's Medals, 7 Air Medals for single day missions, and 43 Purple Hearts. This is a significant number of awards for flying squadrons dedicated to delivering passengers and cargo to their customers. The history of the Military Advisory Command, Vietnam (MACV); newsletters of the C-7A Caribou Association; and personal stories of the men directly involved with Caribou operations provided additional perspective.

The audience for this book is broad. It includes USAF personnel involved with the C-7A, Army and USMC personnel supported by the Caribou squadrons, and anyone interested in how tactical airlift into fields as narrow as 50 feet wide and 1000 feet long was done using the remarkable and beloved Bou.

While working on the Caribou history, I discovered instances of inconsistency in applying the rules for awards. When you read the citation for some award in the text, you might think to yourself, "I did something similar, but I didn't get a Silver Star or DFC." Many of you, rightfully, may have that thought. We did the job because it was there to be done and the troops on the ground needed our support. It's as simple as that.

All Caribou personnel deserve to be recognized and to have their story told. Crew chiefs, personal equipment specialists, supply clerks, line chiefs, engine mechanics, instrument technicians, command post personnel, phase dock personnel, administration specialists – all did extraordinary things … everyone played a vital part in the success of the Caribou units.

This book echoes the words of Lt. Col. Oliver L. North, USMC, "Theirs is a story that deserves to be told!"

Acknowledgements

I am grateful for the assistance of many people who helped me in my endeavor to write *Caribou Airlines*. I want to thank the personnel of the Air Force Historical Research Agency (AFHRA) at Maxwell AFB, AL. Dr. Charles O'Connell, Director, and Archangelo ("Archie") DiFante granted me access to the voluminous holdings of the Agency. Sylvester ("Sly") Jackson and Juan Rackley patiently pulled the large number of volumes of unit histories, special orders, and microfilm which were essential for my research. Tammy Horton and Lee Morris welcomed me warmly on my many trips to AFHRA. Without their help, this book would have been impossible to write.

My gratitude goes to the members of the C-7A Caribou Association who generously shared their remembrances of flying Caribou missions in Vietnam. Many of them wrote stories of their missions, frustrations, and high jinks while assigned to the 483rd Tactical Airlift Wing.

Special thanks are due to my daughter and editor exraordinaire, Cindy McElver, for her meticulous reading of the manuscript and many useful suggestions about improvements. It doesn't hurt to have an English major in the family. My son, Patrick, checked the manuscript and found typos no one else found. Thanks to him also for his exceptional job well done and suggestions.

There are other friends, Peter Bird and Dave Hutchens, to thank for their willingness to plow through the manuscript. Peter is my expert on desktop publishing tools, photographs, fonts, styles, etc. His editing and suggestions were extraordinary in making this book readable and consistent. Peter also gave permission to use his Caribou picture for the cover of the book.

Most of all, I want to give special thanks to Alicia, my wife, who has always been there for me. I thank her for patiently and diligently proofing many versions of the manuscript. She has been my eagle-eyed proof-reader of both technical writings, training materials, and stories for the past 56 years. She spots things that others frequently miss. Without her, this book would be woefully inadequate in language, grammar, and punctuation. To her, I give my love and gratitude beyond measure.

Washing the Mighty Bou (Copyright © 2014 Bill Craig)

"Where's That Oil Leak?" (Copyright © 2014 Bill Craig)

Tactical Airlift

The decision to build the de Havilland Canada DHC-4 Caribou was made in 1956, the object being to develop an aircraft combining the load-carrying capability of the Douglas DC-3 with the Short Take-off and Landing (STOL) performance of the L-20A Beaver and U-1A Otter, both from de Havilland Canada. The Canadian army placed an order for two and the U.S. Army followed with five, the U.S. Secretary of Defense waiving a restriction which limited the U.S. Army to fixed wing aircraft with an empty weight less than 5000 lbs.

The prototype flew in July 1958,[1] its high wing having a characteristic center-section with marked anhedral.[2] The rear door was designed as a ramp for items weighing up to 6700 lbs. In the troop-carrying role, up to 32 soldiers could be carried. The Caribou served with the Royal Canadian Air Force (RCAF) as the CC-108 and with the U.S. Army as the AC-1 (1962 designation CV-2A). As a result of its evaluation of the first five aircraft, the U.S. Army adopted the Caribou as standard equipment and placed orders for 159.

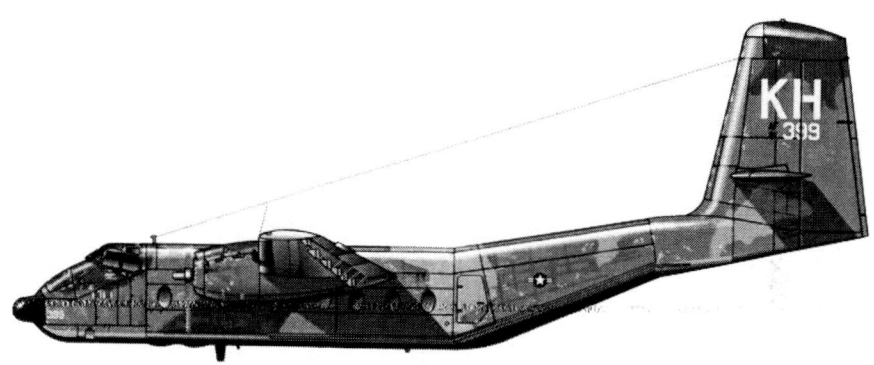

The second batch of aircraft was designated CV-2B. Following tension on the border between China and India, the U.S. Army handed over two Caribous to the Indian Air Force in early 1963. In January 1967, the 134 Caribous still in service with the U.S. Army were transferred to U.S. Air Force charge as C-7A transports. The aircraft was a general sales success and examples flew not only with air forces throughout the world, but also with civil operators. In Canadian service, the Caribou was replaced by the DHC-5 Buffalo and surplus examples were sold to a number of nations including Colombia, Oman,

C-7A Caribou

deHavilland of Canada

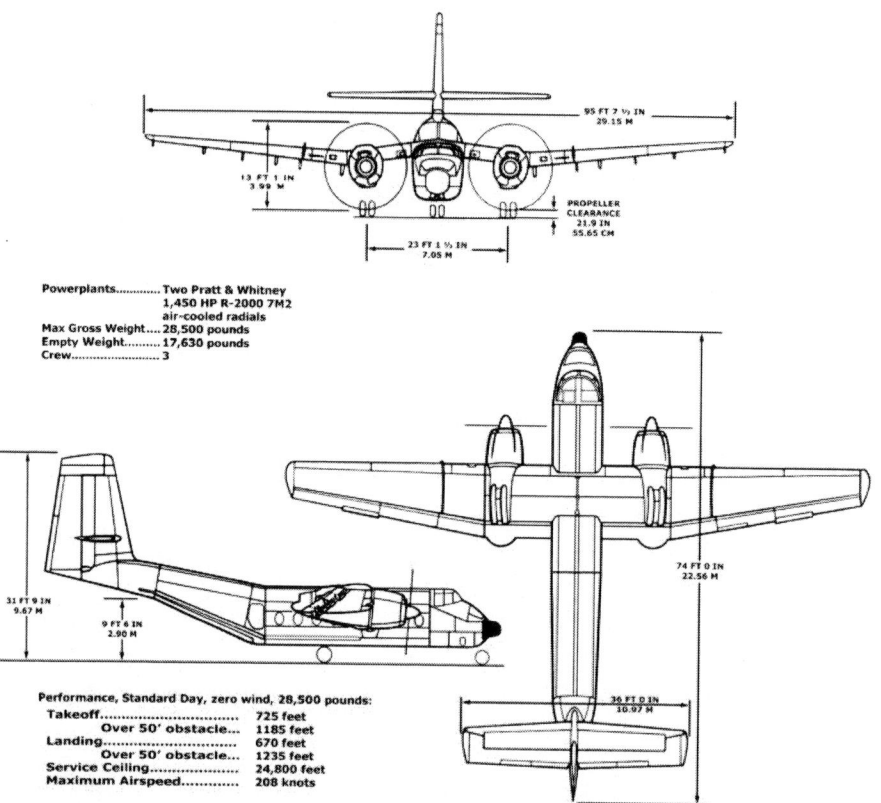

Powerplants.............. Two Pratt & Whitney
1,450 HP R-2000 7M2
air-cooled radials
Max Gross Weight.... 28,500 pounds
Empty Weight.......... 17,630 pounds
Crew........................ 3

Performance, Standard Day, zero wind, 28,500 pounds:

Takeoff.................................	725 feet
Over 50' obstacle...	1185 feet
Landing.................................	670 feet
Over 50' obstacle...	1235 feet
Service Ceiling....................	24,800 feet
Maximum Airspeed..............	208 knots

and Tanzania. Many of the Canadian aircraft had been loaned to the United Nations, seeing extensive international service. Production ended in 1973. The DHC-4A model supplanted the DHC-4 on the production line from aircraft number 24. The two models are very similar apart from the later model's increase in weight, maximum take-off weight of the DHC-4 being 26,000 lbs. Total production was 307.

The C-7A Caribou has short field landing and takeoff capability. It can carry, on average, 5000 pounds of general cargo or about 32 passengers, somewhat fewer passengers if they are fully combat ready. The Caribou can also be utilized to carry litters. It was basically designed for close, front line support into short, rough surfaced landing strips.

The C-7A was described in the history reports of the 483rd TAW. "The de Havilland C-7A is an all-metal, land-based monoplane. The mission is to provide transportation or cargo for delivery by parachute or by landing. The airplane can be used as a tactical transport carrying 32 ground troops or 25 paratroops and equipment, and can readily be converted for aeromedical evacuation or aerial delivery missions. When used as an ambulance, the airplane can carry 20 litters. The C-7A can land and take off on runways as short as 1000 feet, and can be used on most forward airstrips."

T.O. 1-C-7A-1, 1 October 1970, page 1-26:

"A double-slotted full-span type wing flap system is actuated by pressure supplied from the normal hydraulic system to a wing flap actuator in the cargo compartment roof; movement is then transmitted from the actuator through mechanical linkage to the flaps. Operation of the wing flaps is controlled by the wing flap selector lever in the flight compartment, through an internal follow-up valve, which allows the flaps to be positioned at any point within flap range.

Movement of the flaps is indicated on the wing flap position indicator in the flight compartment. Since the ailerons droop with the lowering of the flaps, the range of aileron movement varies in accordance with the position of the flaps. Movement of the flaps is also mechanically transferred to the horizontal stabilizer so that it trims automatically throughout the full flap range. Wing flaps are held mechanically in the UP position, and hydraulically in all other positions."

The STOL performance of the Caribou is largely due to the full-span-double-slotted flap system. A slotted flap has a gap between the flap and the wing, forcing high pressure air from below the wing and over the flap, helping the airflow remain attached to the flap. This increases lift compared to a split flap. Lift across the entire chord of the primary airfoil is greatly increased as the velocity of air leaving the trailing edge is increased to that of the higher-speed, lower-pressure air flowing around the leading edge of the slotted flap. Any flap that allows air to pass between the wing and the flap is considered to be a slotted flap. The slotted flap was developed at Handley-Page in the 1920's. Some flap systems, e.g., the C-7A Caribou, use multiple slots to boost the effect even more.

Full-span Double-slotted (Fowler) Flaps of the C-7A
(Copyright © 2014 Peter Bird)

DOUBLE-SLOTTED FOWLER FLAP

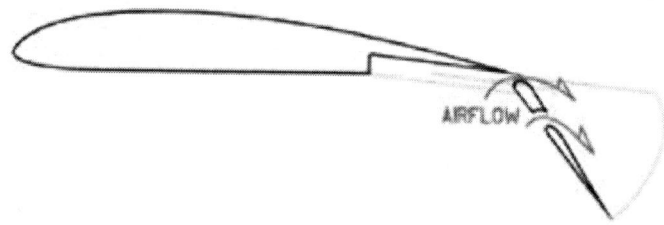

End Notes: Tactical Airlift

[1] George Neal, de Havilland Canada test pilot, made the first flight of the prototype DHC-4 Caribou on July 30, 1958 at Downsview Airport, the location of the Toronto Aerospace Museum. He retired in 1983 as Director of Flight Operations of de Havilland Canada. On November 21, 2008 Mr. Neal celebrated his 90th birthday.

[2] Downward inclination of an aircraft wing in relation to the lateral axis

[3] *483rd Tactical Airlift Wing History: 1967* (available at the Air Force Historical Research Agency, Maxwell AFB, AL)

[4] *USAF Airlift Activities in Support of Operations in South Vietnam, Jan 1965-Mar 1968. Corona Harvest Report, January 1973*

Table of Contents

South Vietnam

Tactical Situation

During 1969, the number of American troops fighting the war had peaked and begun to decline. The maximum was 549,000 early in the year, declining to 434,000 in the spring of 1970. There was no Khe Sanh or Tet offensive. The American withdrawal had begun in earnest. During his last year in office, President Lyndon B. Johnson had outlined a strategy that looked to eventual reductions in American strength, fewer American casualties, and greater South Vietnamese participation in fighting the enemy. This disengagement, as well as the means of enlarging South Vietnam's combat role, now became the principal concerns of President Richard M. Nixon, who launched his administration by attempting to formulate his own policy for Southeast Asia.[1]

President Nixon asked General Earle G. Wheeler, Chairman of the Joint Chiefs of Staff, for a study on "the feasibility and utility of war and quarantining Cambodia against the receipt of supplies and equipment for … the North Vietnamese forces operating in and from Cambodia against South Vietnam." [2] General Creighton W. Abrams, Commander of the U. S. Military Assistance Command, Vietnam, advocated B-52 strikes against the Central Office for South Vietnam (COSV), a communist headquarters believe located in the Fishhook region of Cambodia, which directed enemy activity in South Vietnam.

After the 14 March rocket attacks on Saigon, Nixon launched OPERATION MENU, the bombing of the Cambodia bases. Combat Skyspot radars were used to direct the release of bombs. William Beecher of the New York Times reported that raids had begun on "Viet Cong and North Vietnamese supply dumps and base camps in Cambodia" several weeks after the start of OPERATION MENU.[3] Prince Norodom Sihanouk of Cambodia ignored the attacks and North Vietnam was also silent. During the 14 months of OPERATION MENU, B-52's flew 3,875 sorties against six North Vietnamese Army (NVA) base areas in Cambodia, dropping more than 100,000 tons of bombs.

Designed to "enhance the vital interests of our country, to stimulate increased self-defense awareness and self-reliance for the Government of South Vietnam, and sustain the support of the American public," the program of withdrawing U.S. troops and turning the war over to the South Vietnamese was labeled "de-Americanization" at first. Secretary of Defense, Melvyn R. Laird, objected to the term because it emphasized the American departure without reflecting the increasing importance of better trained and more formidably equipped South Vietnam-

1

ese combat forces. He proposed "Vietnamization" which promptly received Presidential Approval.[4]

USAF General John P. Mc Connell, acting Chairman of the Joint Chiefs of Staff, proposed three conditions essential to successful Vietnamization. He told the Security Council that "the reductions should not place the remaining American forces at any tactical disadvantage, should not result in abandonment of equipment the South Vietnamese could not use, and should not be completed until South Vietnamese units were able to take over their nation's defense." [5]

A barrage fell on Bien Hoa on 23 February. It destroyed two Air Force aircraft on the ground, damaged eight others, and served to signal an abortive ground attack. Air Force F-100's and F-4's, directed by Forward Air Controllers (FACs) joined South Vietnamese planes and U.S. Army helicopters in ending the threat to the base. Enemy forces closing in on Long Binh, near Bien Hoa, encountered similar resistance. Bien Hoa was the only Air Force base subjected to an infantry assault, but shells, rockets, or small arms fire struck Phan Rang, Pleiku, Phu Cat, Da Nang, Cam Ranh Bay, and several lesser airfields used by American airmen.

Also in February, the North Vietnamese directed their fire against the outpost at Ben Het, within howitzer range of Base Area 609 in Cambodia. The shelling continued into early March when the enemy advanced on the camp using Soviet-designed amphibious light tanks. The attack was essentially a probe of the defenses of the highlands, rather than a serious attempt to overwhelm Ben Het. The NVA effort served mainly as a prelude to further action later in the year.

During May, coinciding with a spring offensive, North Vietnamese tanks, infantry, and artillery again massed near Ben Het, which lay within 10 miles of the meeting point of the borders of South Vietnam, Cambodia, and Laos. The signs of an impending attack on Ben Het laid urgency to the interdiction of roads and trails in the vicinity of the camp. By the end of June, air strikes and seasonal rains reduced the motor traffic in the area by some 90 percent, according to intelligence estimates.

Morning fog plagued Ben Het and afternoon thunderstorms drowned the region. Targeting for B-52 strikes around Ben Het became increasingly difficult as the siege wore on. Friendly outposts and patrols disappeared from the hills around the camp, depriving planners of a useful source of information. Instead of probing NVA positions and locating targets for air strikes, Col. Nguyen Ba Lien pulled his troops back into the camp itself or the nearby headquarters town of

Dak To. He yielded control of the ridges that overlooked Ben Het and enemy antiaircraft crews took advantage of the absence of threats on the ground and set up their weapons to cover the approaches to the airstrip. At the beginning of June, the C-7A's supplying the camp could no longer land to unload. Later, the Caribous either parachuted their cargo from medium altitude or flew over the runway at an altitude of a few feet and released a chute that snatched heavily laden pallets out of the aircraft.

Escorts of fighter-bombers flew in support of the Caribous to suppress enemy fire. For much of the siege, a FAC met the approaching cargo planes and escorted them, spaced 50 minutes apart, over the camp, while two F-4's stood by to attack any antiaircraft battery the FAC might spot. North Vietnamese gunners scored hits on six C-7A's and wounded three crewmen during the first three weeks of June. Mission planners increased the number of strike aircraft, made sure that fighters and FACs arrived a few minutes before the transports, and adjusted the tactics used by the Caribous and their escorts.

The siege of Ben Het ended on 2 July, when the North Vietnamese relaxed their pressure after some 1800 tactical sorties had been flown in defense of the camp. The number of B-52 sorties in defense of Ben Het totaled about 800. Gunships, AC-47's and AC-119G's, averaged not quite two sorties each night, firing more than 500,000 rounds into the hills overlooking the camp. Sorties by Caribous averaged four per day, delivering more than 200 tons of cargo during the battle.

From Ben Het, the enemy turned his attention to Bu Prang and Duc Lap, Special Forces camps in southern II Corps, across the border from Base Area 740. Aerial defense of the two camps began in late October. When the enemy broke contact in mid-December, Air Force tactical fighters had dropped 3,000 tons of bombs and B-52's dropped five times that weight. By 1 December, General Abrams was seeking permission for the B-52's to hit targets in the area west of Bu Prang that was claimed by both South Vietnam and Cambodia.

Secretary of State, Henry Kissinger, issued a directive for the first reduction in U.S. strength since 1963. A large contingent of 25,000 troops was set for departure on 1 July. After President Nixon visited Saigon in July, he directed that 37,000 more troops depart Vietnam by the end of the year, making a total of 62,00 for 1969. Budgetary considerations and withdrawal of U.S. forces reduced the level of aerial activity in South Vietnam. The number of B-52 sorties ranged from 1,400 to 1,800 per month with a monthly average of 1,650 and a limit of 19,000 for 1969.

The budget-based ceiling imposed on tactical sorties during the fall of 1969 applied only to American aerial endeavors. It did not affect the Vietnamese Air Force or the Royal Australian Air Force.

In October, a Moratorium Day around the U.S. drew crowds varying from a few thousand in some cities to over 100,000 in others. By the end of 1969, the Third Marine Amphibious Force (III MAF) was gone from South Vietnam.

The brief chronology in Appendix II illustrates the nature of 1969 on the battlefield and the military and civilian planning of the year.

End Notes: Tactical Situation

[1] *The JCS and the War In Vietnam, 1969-1970*, pp. 5-7
[2] Message from Director of the Joint Staff to General Nazzaro, Acting CINCPAC and General Abrams, dated 230107Z January 1969, Subject: Cambodia
[3] *New York Times*, May 8, 1969, pg. 1
[4] Kissinger, *White House Years*, pg. 272
[5] Message from Gen. Goodpaster to General Abrams, dated 282219Z March 1969

Col. Wilbert T. Turk, Commander, 483 TAW

483rd Tactical Airlift Wing [1]

The mission of the 483rd Tactical Airlift Wing (483 TAW) at Cam Ranh Bay Air Base was "to provide intra-theater airlift in support of all free world military, civic actions, civilian forces and units engaged in combat, combat support, logistics, and civic assistance in the Republic of Vietnam (RVN). To accomplish this through air-land and aerial delivery of personnel and supplies in conformance with established MACV (Military Assistance Command Vietnam) priorities for employment of C-7A aircraft and to perform other airlift missions as directed by Commander, 834th Air Division (834 AD)." [2]

The Wing continued to employ the specified user system, no longer new to Air Force airlift operations, but still unique to the Caribous. That system was designed and agreed upon during the transfer of the C-7A to the USAF from the United States Army to assure a specified number of aircraft to a given unit. Although the aircraft were centrally controlled by the Wing, they were dedicated to a specified unit. This contrasted with the Common User Airlift service employed elsewhere in the Air Force.

The specified user system was effective. It permitted both the 483 TAW and the user to plan and coordinate movement requirements and Air Operations. The system produced a very high utilization rate of the Wing's aircraft. Specified users served by the Wing included: Military Assistance Command Thailand (MACTHAI) / Joint United States Military Assistance Group (JUSMAG); Military Assistance Command Vietnam (MACV); Traffic Management Agency (TMA); United States Army Republic of Vietnam (USARV); I Field Forces Vietnam (IFFV); II Field Forces Vietnam (IIFFV); First Air Cavalry Division (1 Cav); Third Marine Amphibious Force (III MAF); 5th Special Forces Group (5SFG); and Civil Operations and Rural Development Support (CORDS).

Elements of the 483 TAW remained tenant organizations at all operating locations. Wing relations with host units [3] at Vung Tau Army Airfield, Phu Cat Air Base, and Cam Ranh Bay Air Base continued to be excellent, as were the relations with host units at the Forward Operating Locations (FOL).

To accomplish these missions, the Wing and its units were authorized a total of 351 officers and 1314 enlisted personnel in the first quarter. Of these authorizations, 335 officers and 1383 enlisted personnel were assigned. Forty-five civilian personnel were authorized, but only 38 were assigned. Total manning was 1710 authorized and 1756 assigned. The Wing was authorized 95 C-7A aircraft, 85 were possessed, and 76 were Combat Ready.[4]

The Wing consisted of the Headquarters, the 457th Tactical Airlift Squadron (457 TAS), the 458 TAS, and the 483rd Consolidated Aircraft Maintenance Squadron (483 CAMS) located at Cam Ranh Bay; the 459 TAS and the 537 TAS located at Phu Cat Air Base; and the 535 TAS, the 536 TAS, and the 6483rd Tactical Group Provisional (6483 TGP) located at Vung Tau Air Base.[5]

Col. Wilbert T. Turk continued as Commander of the 483 TAW in the first and second quarters. Col. Keith L. Christensen continued as Wing Vice-Commander, Col. Leslie J. Greenwood as Deputy Commander for Operations (DCO), and Lt. Col. William A. Ulrich as Deputy Commander for Materiel (DCM).

On 1 February, the Second Anniversary Party was held at Cam Ranh Bay. The "fete" was delayed to avoid conflict with parties on New Year's day. Honored guests included Lt. Gen. Peers, U.S. Army, who gave the commemorative address and Maj. Gen. Burl William McLaughlin, 834AD Commander, who made the commemorative remarks. Other guests included Col. Harold R. Aaron, 5SFG Commander, and Capt. James Henderson, United States Naval Air Facility Commander. Col. Turk set the tone as Master of Ceremonies.

On 15 February, Lt. Col. Ralph L. Peters assumed command of the 483 CAMS. On 19 February, Lt. Col. Edward J. Thielen assumed command of 457 TAS, relieving Lt. Col. Donald L. Flood.[6]

In the second quarter, Col. Christensen continued as Wing Vice-Commander, Col. Greenwood as DCO, Lt. Col. Ulrich as DCM, and Lt. Col. James W. Buckley, Jr. as Commander of the 6483 TGP.

The Wing enjoyed 100 percent manning in April and May, and 93 percent manning in June. At the end of the quarter, the Wing was authorized 351 officers, 1303 airmen, and 46 civilians and there were 327 officers, 1323 airmen, and 43 civilians assigned. The Wing was authorized 95 C-7A aircraft, 95 were assigned, 89 were possessed, and 81 were Combat Ready.

Numerous distinguished visitors honored the Wing by visits during the second quarter. Col. Turk gave briefings on the mission of the Wing to the Secretary of the Air Force, Dr. Robert C. Seamans; the Vice Chief of Staff, USAF, General John D. Ryan; the Commander-in-Chief, PACAF, General Joseph J. Nazzaro; and the Commander, 5SFG, Col. Harold A. Aaron.

The Wing had 99 percent manning in July, 100 percent manning in August, and 96 percent manning in September. Although some areas were overmanned and others undermanned, there were no major problems. The Wing was authorized 350 officers, 1313 airmen, and 42 civilians and there were 313 officers, 1310 airmen, and 44 civilians assigned. Included in the Wing totals was the manning for the 483 CAMS, the 483 CAMS Operating Location A (OLAA) at Phu Cat, the 483 CAMS Operating Location B (OLAB) at Vung Tau, and the 6483 TGP at Vung Tau. The manning for the 483 CAMS was 8 officers and 304 airmen of which there were 7 officers and 321 airmen assigned. The manning for 483 CAMS OLAA was 3 officers and 229 airmen of which there were 3 officers and 212 airmen assigned. The manning for 483 CAMS OLAB was 3 officers and 189 airmen of which there were 2 officers and 183 airmen assigned. The manning for the 6483 TGP was one officer and one was assigned.

The Wing was authorized 96 C-7A aircraft, 94 were assigned, 89 were possessed, and 81 were Combat Ready on 1 July. On 30 September the authorization was 96 C-7A aircraft, 94 were assigned, 88 were possessed, but only 76 were Combat Ready.

On 4 September, Col. Christensen assumed command of the Wing[7] and Col. Turk returned to the U.S. In his farewell letter to the Wing on 30 August, he remarked (in part):

> "The performance of each of you has been phenomenal. As a result of your achievements, the Wing has reached new highs in operational effectiveness and mission accomplishment. I extend to each of you my personal thanks and appreciation for your splendid contributions to your squadron, the Wing, and the entire Air Force effort in SEA. I am proud of your accomplishments and I know you share in this pride.
>
> I wish each of you continued success and good luck during the remainder of your tour in RVN. Most importantly, I wish you a safe return home and a joyous reunion with your loved ones at the end of your tour.
>
> It has been an honor and a privilege to serve as your Wing Commander the past year. No Air Force Officer could expect a more satisfying assignment during his military career."

Col. Abbott C. Greenleaf assumed duties as Wing Vice Commander. Col. Roger P. Larivee assumed duties as DCO and Lt. Col. Jean L. Coover assumed duties as Assistant DCO. Lt. Col. James W. Thompson assumed duties of Assistant DCM. Lt. Col. Moses J. McKeithan assumed duties as Executive Officer. Col. John J. Koehler commanded the 6483 TGP.

Some distinguished visitors honored the Wing by visits during the third quarter. Col. Christensen gave briefings on the mission of the Wing to the Vice Commander-in-Chief, PACAF, Lt. Gen. James V. Edmundson during his visit on 21-22 July and to General Joseph J. Nazzaro, Commander-in-Chief, PACAF during his visit from 8-11 September, who commented favorably on the performance of the Wing.

In the fourth quarter, Col. Alfred S. Hess assumed duties as DCM, Lt. Col. Harold J. Brennen assumed duties as Assistant DCM, and Capt. David J. Blanchard assumed duties as Chief of Logistics/Plans.

The Wing was authorized 350 officers, 1297 airmen, and 42 civilians and there were 299 officers, 1181 airmen, and 39 civilians assigned. Included in the Wing totals was the manning for the 483 CAMS, the 483 CAMS OLAA at Phu Cat, the 483 CAMS OLAB at Vung Tau, and the 6483 TGP at Vung Tau. The manning for the 483 CAMS was 8 officers and 298 airmen of which there were 9 officers and 270 airmen assigned. The manning for the 483 CAMS OLAA was 3 officers and 225 airmen of which there were 4 officers and 204 airmen assigned. The manning for the 483 CAMS OLAB was 3 officers and 189 airmen of which there were 3 officers and 188 airmen assigned. The manning for the 6483 TGP was one officer and one was assigned.

At the beginning of the quarter, the Wing was authorized 96 C-7A aircraft, 94 were assigned, 88 were possessed, and 76 were Combat Ready. At the end of the quarter, only 82 aircraft were possessed and 68 were Combat Ready.

Operations

Effective 1 January 1969, there was a reorganization within the Deputy Commander for Operations (DCO) activity which resulted in a net loss of one officer position and seven Airman positions.[8] In March, the Wing Commander's position (Brig. Gen.), Air Force Specialty Code (AFSC) 0002, in the Command Section was redesignated as a Colonel position, AFSC 0066.[9]

Effective on 15 March, the 6483rd Tactical Group Provisional (TGP) was activated at Vung Tau Army Airfield.[10] With this activation, one Colonel position was transferred from the Wing Headquarters Operations Staff to be used for a command position in the TGP.[11] Lt. Col. James W. Buckley, Jr. assumed duties as Commander of the 6483 TGP, effective 18 March.[12] Concomitantly, the 535 TAS, the 536 TAS, and Operating Location B (OLAB) were attached to the 6483 TGP for command-and-control.[13] The expressed purpose of this reorganization was to free the commanders of the Tactical Airlift Squadrons to [concentrate on] problems of command and supervision as employed in a conventional Air Force Wing. The Air Force operation at Vung Tau had resembled the outmoded Air Force Group organization and, consequently, should have been authorized a combat support function to provide necessary Air Base support and services for the two tactical squadrons and the 483 CAMS OLAB.

The Wing had contemplated the reorganization of the support function at Vung Tau as early as October 1968. The Wing proposal, submitted to PACAF in January of 1969, was different from the organization finally directed.[14] This proposal from the 483 TAW through the 834AD had been forwarded by 7AF to PACAF for appropriate action.

The type of missions flown by the C-7A included: routine cargo, support of Special Forces and other free world forces in Vietnam, medical evacuations, emergency re-supply, tactical emergencies, combat essential missions, radio relays for the 1Cav, numerous daily air drops of paratroopers, ammunition, building supplies, petroleum-oil-lubricants (POL), general cargo, rations, and such oddities as live cows, pigs, chickens, and fresh produce. The livestock and fowl were in support of ARVN troops due to the lack of refrigeration in the field.

In the first quarter, it became apparent to the Wing that its mission sites at Tan Son Nhut (call sign "Blinker"), Nha Trang ("Law Alpha"), and Pleiku ("Blite") duplicated the functions and responsibilities assigned to Airlift Control Elements (ALCEs) of the 834AD. Therefore, it was recommended by the Wing that the mission sites be phased out.[15] The recommendation was approved by the 834AD.

At the beginning of the quarter, 144 crews were authorized, "formed," and available, but only 93 crews were Combat Ready. At the end of the quarter, 144 crews were authorized, 144 were "formed," and 128 were available, but only 105 crews were Combat Ready. Because of the normal one year tour of duty in Southeast Asia (SEA), continual upgrading of newly arrived crew members remained a persistent requirement. A total of 62 Aircraft Commanders, 68 Copilots, and 50 Flight Engineers were upgraded during the quarter. In addition, 34 Aircraft Commanders were upgraded, 10 to Flight Examiner and 24 to Instructor Pilot. Nineteen Flight Engineers were upgraded, 6 to Flight Examiner Flight Engineer and 13 to Instructor Flight Engineer.

In the 457 TAS, 3 pilots were upgraded to Flight Examiner, 4 to Instructor Pilot, 9 to Aircraft Commander, 11 to First Pilot, and 11 to Copilot. In the 458 TAS, 3 pilots were upgraded to Flight Examiner, 4 to Instructor Pilot, 12 to Aircraft Commander, 12 to First Pilot, and 12 to Copilot. In the 459 TAS, 1 pilot was upgraded to Flight Examiner,

4 to Instructor Pilot, 6 to Aircraft Commander, 9 to First Pilot, and 13 to Copilot. In the 535 TAS, 3 pilots were upgraded to Instructor Pilot, 6 to Aircraft Commander, 12 to First Pilot, and 8 to Copilot. In the 536 TAS, 2 pilots were upgraded to Flight Examiner, 7 to Instructor Pilot, 17 to Aircraft Commander, 12 to First Pilot, and 8 to Copilot. In the 537 TAS, 1 pilot was upgraded to Flight Examiner, 2 to Instructor Pilot, 12 to Aircraft Commander, 14 to First Pilot, and 16 to Copilot. No Flight Engineers were upgraded to Flight Examiner, one was upgraded to Instructor, and 7 completed their initial qualification.

In the 458 TAS, 2 Flight Engineers were upgraded to Flight Examiner, 2 were upgraded to Instructor, and 10 completed their initial qualification. In the 459 TAS, 1 Flight Engineer was upgraded to Flight Examiner, 1 was upgraded to Instructor, and 9 completed their initial qualification. In the 535 TAS, 1 Flight Engineer was upgraded to Flight Examiner, 2 were upgraded to Instructor, and 8 completed their initial qualification. In the 536 TAS, 1 Flight Engineer was upgraded to Flight Examiner, 3 were upgraded to Instructor, and 8 completed their initial qualification. In the 537 TAS, 1 Flight Engineer was upgraded to Flight Examiner, 4 were upgraded to Instructor, and 8 completed their initial qualification.

Normally, 48 missions were scheduled daily and distributed among the users as follows: 1 to USARV, 7 to IFFV, 7 to IIFFV, 4 to III MAF, 1 to MACTHAI, 5 to IV CORPS, 8 to 5SFG, 8 to 1Cav, 5 to MACV, and 2 to CORDS.[16] A 49th mission was flown daily to move support personnel and equipment between the three operating bases at Phu Cat, Cam Ranh Bay, and Vung Tau. Additional Wing missions were generated on an "as required" basis in order to support dedicated user missions which had incurred maintenance delays enroute. This concept of operations provided responsive, reliable, and effective airlift while conserving 'one-of-a-kind' maintenance personnel and equipment.

When possible, mission fragging normally tasked Wing units at one of the three bases, whichever was closest to the user's area of operations. As a rule, unit aircraft deployed and redeployed daily from their home stations. Thus, trained personnel, equipment, and supplies were concentrated and highly effective. The three home bases were relatively secure and no aircraft were damaged or lost to enemy action at these bases during the quarter.

Numerous Forward Air Controller (FAC) only and FAC/fighter support missions were flown at Song Be (V-30), Duc Phong (V-269), Katum (V-287), Bu Krak (V-176), and Tien Phuoc (V-239). These support missions were flown to preclude the threat of enemy fire on Caribou aircraft using those fields at various times throughout the quarter.

The flying hour and crew duty costs involved in positioning/depositioning the aircraft daily to and from the user's area of work was considered a worthwhile investment, ensuring both aircrew and aircraft safety. The aircraft remained at forward bases only when battle damage or other flying safety constraints prevented their return to one of the three home stations. Command-and-control procedures to quickly repair and/or replace mission aircraft undergoing excessive maintenance delays were used to maintain responsiveness to and reliability for the user.

PACAF allocated 30,336 flying hours quarterly to the 483 TAW. An over-fly of two percent (606 hours) was authorized during each of the first three fiscal quarters of 1969. Dedicated user requirements continued to require 49 missions daily. In March, with a projected over-fly of 1290 hours, authority was granted to over-fly the program by the 1290 hours. In the first quarter, the allocation was over-flown by 1213.1 hours.

The majority (4,366) of the 4,435 missions flown were air-landed missions. There were only 69 airdrop missions flown during the quarter, as compared with more than three times that number flown in the last quarter of 1968. Only six missions designated as a priority higher than routine were flown. This was less than half those flown during the previous quarter. There were 3 Combat Essential missions flown in January, 2 in February, and 1 in March. There were 31 airdrop sorties flown in January, carrying 59.8 tons of cargo. In February, there were 21 airdrop sorties flown, carrying 39 troops and 36.2 tons of cargo. In March, there were 17 airdrop sorties flown, carrying 34.7 tons of cargo.

Initial launch reliability was 98.2 percent in January, 99.3 percent in February, and 99.3 percent in March, making 98.9 percent for the quarter. There were 28 initial delays in January, 10 in February, and 10 in March, for a total of 48. There were 36.2 chargeable initial delay hours in January, 7.5 in February, and 9.9 in March, for a total of 53.6. Enroute reliability was 98.2 percent in January, 98.3 percent in February, and 98.5 percent in March, making 98.3 percent for the quarter.

At the beginning of the second quarter, 144 crews were authorized and 128 were "formed," but only 117 crews were Combat Ready. At the end of the quarter, 144 crews were authorized and 138 were "formed," but only 127 crews were Combat Ready.

The previously designated 48 missions were scheduled daily and distributed among the users as follows: 1 to USARV, 7 to IFFV, 7 to

IIFFV, 4 to III MAF, 1 to MACTHAI, 5 to IV CORPS, 8 to 5SFG, 8 to 1Cav, 5 to MACV, and 2 to CORDS. The 49th mission continued as a support mission for the Wing.

The majority of the 4,471 missions flown were air-landed missions, although airdrop sorties increased sharply to 199. This was due mostly to support of the besieged Special Forces Camp at Ben Het (V-179). There was also a sharp increase in high-priority missions to 57 (1 Tactical Emergency, 41 Emergency Resupply, and 15 Combat Essential) as compared with 6 in the first quarter. The Ben Het support accounted for most of the increase. In April, there was one Tactical Emergency mission and one Combat Essential mission. In May, there were two Emergency Resupply missions and one Combat Essential mission. In June, there were 39 Emergency Resupply missions and 13 Combat Essential missions.

The 537 TAS, staging from Pleiku (V-4), routinely provided exclusive fixed-wing logistical airlift for Ben Het, where airdrops began on 3 January. Aircrews always strove for minimum ground time as the airfield was a favorite mortar target for the enemy. An increase in this activity was noted in May, with several intended air-landed sorties turned away by Special Forces advisors due to incoming rounds. Airland operations were continued throughout the month despite several aircraft encountering mortar explosions while off-loading equipment and personnel. The airfield was closed in early June due to further increased enemy activity and runway damage. About the same time, the main supply route from Kontum (V-15) became very hazardous and frequently was closed to truck convoys. Aerial delivery of supplies, beginning on 3 June, was central to survival of the camp throughout the siege which ended "officially" on 30 June, but Caribou support continued into July. The problem of resupply was further complicated by a postage-stamp size drop zone (100 yards by 200 yards), intensive automatic weapons ground fire, and the seasonally adverse weather conditions. The high tonnage required daily brought an immediate evaluation aimed at using C-123 or C-130 aircraft to reduce the sorties and thus the exposure rate in the extremely hazardous conditions. It was determined that only the C-7A could do the drop into the limited landing area and small drop zone.

Supported by Forward Air Controller-directed fire suppression missions, a total of 86 air drops were made, delivering over 200 tons of ammunition, POL, rations, water, and medical supplies. Every load was on-target and 100 percent recoverable. The majority of these missions (77) were flown by crews of the 537 TAS. An additional eight were flown by the 457 TAS and 458 TAS.

After a change in concept from fighter escort to fire suppression, FAC-directed fighter support (A-1E, A-37, F-4, F-100) played a great part in reducing battle damage and casualties. Until this change, eight Caribous were hit, but all were able to make a safe recovery to the staging base at Pleiku (V-4). Three 537 TAS aircrew members were awarded the Purple Heart for injuries received on 13 June from bullet fragments or shrapnel while flying the *Soul* 455 mission. Maj. Delbert D. Lockwood received facial wounds from bullet fragments. 1/Lt. William F. Quinn, Jr. received fragments in his right leg.[17] TSgt. John E. White was wounded in the right arm by shrapnel. A total of 2 Silver Stars, 25 DFCs, 3 Purple Hearts, and 7 Air Medals were awarded to C-7A crews for their heroic actions in supporting Ben Het.

Initial launch reliability was 99.5 percent in April, 99.4 percent in May, and 99.9 percent in June, making 99.6 percent for the quarter. There were 7 initial delays in April, 9 in May, and 1 in June, for a total of 17. There were 4.8 chargeable initial delay hours in April, 7.6 in May, and 0.7 in June, for a total of 13.1. Enroute reliability was 98.6 percent in April, 98.6 percent in May, and 99.0 percent in June, making 98.7 percent for the quarter. There were 218 enroute delays in April, 214 in May, and 141 in June, for a total of 573.

At the beginning of the third quarter, 144 crews were authorized and 140 were "formed," but only 127 crews were Combat Ready. At the end of the quarter, 144 crews were authorized and 129 were "formed," but only 125 crews were Combat Ready.

The one year tour length continued to make upgrade training essential to the successful accomplishment of the mission. During the third quarter, a total of 74 Aircraft Commanders, 55 First Pilots, 66 Copilots, and 31 Flight Engineers were upgraded. In addition, 50 Aircraft Commanders were further upgraded, 11 to Flight Examiner and 29 to Instructor Pilot. Twenty-seven fully qualified Flight Engineers were upgraded, 7 to Flight Examiner Flight Engineer and 20 to Instructor Flight Engineer.

The previously designated 48 missions remained unchanged and were scheduled daily and distributed among the users as follows: 1 to USARV, 7 to IFFV, 7 to IIFFV, 4 to III MAF, 1 to MACTHAI, 5 to IV CORPS, 8 to 5SFG, 8 to 1Cav, 5 to MACV, and 2 to CORDS. The 49th mission continued as a support mission for the Wing.

As in the two previous quarters, when possible, the daily mission fragmentation orders normally tasked Wing units at one of the three bases (Phu Cat, Cam Ranh Bay, Vung Tau) whichever was closest to the user's area of operations. As a rule, unit aircraft deployed and redeployed daily from their home stations. Thus, trained personnel, equipment, and supplies were concentrated and highly effective. The three home bases were relatively secure and no aircraft had been lost to enemy action at these stations, although nine aircraft were superficially damaged at Cam Ranh Bay when a rocket impacted in the parking area on 4 September.

The majority of the 4,494 missions flown were air-landed missions. A total of 303 airdrop sorties were flown for a 50 percent increase over the second quarter. This increase was attributed to the monsoon weather conditions in the Delta which made several airfields unusable for air-land operations.

High-priority missions remained at approximately the same level, i.e., 52 in the third quarter compared with 57 in the second quarter. In July, there were 17 Emergency Resupply missions and 4 Combat Essential missions. In August, there were 19 Emergency Resupply missions and 6 Combat Essential missions. In September, there were 6 Combat Essential missions. There were 115 airdrop sorties flown in July, carrying 236 troops and 212 tons of cargo. In August, there were 112 airdrop sorties flown, carrying 552 troops and 166 tons of cargo. In September, there were 76 airdrop sorties flown, carrying 68 troops and 154 tons of cargo.

Numerous FAC only and FAC/fighter support missions were flown at An Hoa (V-257), Ben Het (V-179), Dong Ha (V-22), Duc Hoa (V-200), LZ Gerber, Hon Quan (V-133), Katum (V-287), Loc Ninh (V-31), Plei Djereng (V-285), Quang Ngai (V-23), Tra Bong (V-112), and Truc Giang (V-14). These were flown to reduce the threat of enemy fire on C-7A aircraft using those fields.

Initial launch reliability was 99.8 percent in July, 99.7 percent in August, and 99.8 percent in September, making 99.4 percent for the quarter. There were 4 initial delays in July, 5 in August, and 17 in September, for a total of 26. There were 3.4 chargeable initial delay hours in July, 7.3 in August, and 14.5 in September, for a total of 26.2 hours. Enroute reliability was 98.4 percent in July, 98.9 percent in August, and 98.4 percent in September, making 98.6 percent for the quarter. There were 223 enroute delays in July, 160 in August, and 204 in September, for a total of 587. These delays accumulated 344.6 hours in July, 257.1 hours in August, and 349.1 hours in September, for a total of 950.8.

In the fourth quarter, the Wing continued to employ the specific user system, still unique to the Caribous. However, due to a redistribution of the daily missions flown by the Wing, several missions that were previously dedicated to specified users were given to the Traffic Management Agency (TMA) of MACV for Common and Service Airlift Support. In some instances, these missions supported the same user, but were controlled by MACV.

The specified users served by the 483 TAW included: Military Assistance Command Thailand (MACTHAI); Joint United States Military Assistance Group (JUSMAG); Military Assistance Command Vietnam (MACV); United States Army, Republic of Vietnam (USARV); I Field Forces Vietnam (IFFV); II Field Forces Vietnam (IIFFV); First Air Cavalry Division (1Cav); Third Marine Amphibious Forces (III MAF); and 5th Special Forces Group (5SFG).

The Wing began, on a trial basis, a new concept of operations. The purpose was to eliminate a portion of the Wing's non-productive flying time. It involved dedicated user missions shuttling out of Bien Hoa (V-2) each day. By having two of these missions remain overnight at Bien Hoa and launch from there the following day, a saving of approximately 5.6 flying hours per day was realized. This operational concept was being evaluated as the quarter ended to determine if it had accomplished its objectives.

The designated 49 missions were scheduled daily and distributed among the users as follows: 6 to IFFV, 14 to IIFFV, 4 to III MAF, 2 to MACTHAI, 4 to IV CORPS, and 19 to MACV/TMA (including 8 to 1Cav, 8 to 5SFG, 2 to CORDS, and 1 to 483 TAW fragged by MACV). The 49th mission continued as a support mission for the Wing, but fragged by MACV.

The Caribou squadrons played a vital role in the resupply of the Special Forces Camps Bu Dop-Bu Krak area while the camps were experiencing the pressure of the winter offensive.

High-priority missions were only 39 in the fourth quarter compared to 57 in the second quarter and 52 in the third quarter. This reflected the changing nature of the war on the battlefield. In October, there were 12 Combat Essential missions. In November, there were 15 Combat Essential missions. In December, there were 12 Combat Essential missions. In October, there were 67 airdrop sorties flown, carrying 221 troops and 101 tons of cargo. In November, there were 56 airdrop sorties flown, carrying 59 troops and 104 tons of cargo. In December, there were 43 airdrop sorties flown, carrying 25 troops and 60 tons of cargo.

The initial launch reliability numbers were significantly poorer than for the first three quarters of 1969. Initial launch reliability was

97.8 percent in October, 98.7 percent in November, and 97.8 percent in December, making 98.1 percent for the quarter. There were 33 initial delays in October, 19 in November, and 33 in December, for a total of 85. There were 40 chargeable initial delay hours in October, 22 in November, and 51 in December, for a total of 1,122 hours. Enroute reliability was 98.4 percent in October, 98.3 percent in November, and 98.3 percent in December, making 98.3 percent for the quarter. There were 227 enroute delays in October, 199 in November, and 223 in December, for a total of 649. These delays accumulated 465 hours in October, 423 hours in November, and 354 hours in December, for a total of 1,342.

At the beginning of the quarter, 144 crews were authorized and 129 were "formed," but only 125 crews were Combat Ready. At the end of the quarter, 144 crews were authorized and 121 were "formed," but only 114 crews were Combat Ready.

The PACAF flying hour program for the second quarter of Fiscal Year 1969 allotted 30,336 flying hours to the 483 TAW. In the past, the Wing overflew the flying hour program by some 800-1200 hours per quarter. In the fourth quarter, the Wing was able to remain within the flying hour program with no sacrifice of mission reliability or service to the user [sic].

The IG team from 7AF inspected the Wing from 18 to 26 November. The Wing was given an overall rating of "Satisfactory."

Training and Stan-Eval

In the first quarter, security training received increased emphasis due to the increased threat situation during the Tet season. All personnel were re-briefed on the local threat situation, sabotage/espionage reporting procedures, and alert instructions. A quarterly security inspection was conducted in accordance with Air Force Regulation 205-1. The security program within the Wing was considered satisfactory.

Sixty-two quarterly no-notice flight checks of squadron aircrews were completed by the Stan/Eval team: 12 in the 535 TAS, 11 in the 536 TAS, 11 in the 537 TAS, 11 in the 457 TAS, 9 in the 458 TAS, and 8 in the 459 TAS. The "C-7A Master Question File, dated 1 Feb 69"[18] was published and distributed to all squadrons. The Pilots Standardization Review Panel was held at Cam Ranh Bay on 20 March. On 22 March, the Flight Engineer Review Panel was held at Cam Ranh Bay. The minutes of both reviews were combined, published, and distributed.[19]

After a thorough study, the total time requirements for Aircraft

Commander upgrade were revised. The revision brought the total time requirements in line with current C-123 and PACAFM 51-27 requirements. The new requirements were summarized in tabular form:

Flying Experience Required to Upgrade to Aircraft Commander			
Experience Level	Total Flying Hours	C-7A Flying Hours	In-country Flying Hours
A	1500	60	75
B	1400	145	75
C	1300	230	75
D	1200	315	75
E	1100	400	75
F	1000	485	75
G	900	560	75
H	850	600	75

The Stan/Eval team published several charts to assist aircrew members: an Ammunition Compatibility Chart, dated 4 January 1969; a Crosswind Component Normal/Short-Field Landing Chart, dated 1 February 1969; a Safe Single Engine Chart, dated February 1969; and a Landing Roll Computation Chart (undated). The team also recommended that operation into six Type I airfields (as short as 1000 feet and as narrow as 50 feet) be restricted to Flight Examiners, Instructor Pilots, and pilots designated by the Squadron Commander who have demonstrated sustained proficiency for six months in-country. The recommendation was made a Wing Policy. The designated restricted airfields were: Dak Pek (V-42), Bu Krak (V-176), Plei Me (V-218), Tra Bong (V-112), Ha Thanh (V-204), and Ha Tien South (V-273).

TSgt. Carl S. Taft, the Wing Stan/Eval Flight Engineer who left on emergency leave, was replaced by MSgt. Victor C. Doyle. On 1 February, Maj. Richard M. Lantz was assigned, bringing the section to authorized strength.

In the second quarter, the normal one year tour of duty in SEA drove a persistent requirement to upgrade newly arrived crew members. During the quarter, 70 Aircraft Commanders, 71 First Pilots, 91 Copilots, and 44 Flight Engineers were upgraded. In addition, 31 Aircraft Commanders received further upgrading: 8 to Flight Examiner and 23 to Instructor Pilot. Twenty-one Flight Engineers received further upgrading: 8 to Flight Examiner Flight Engineer and 13 to Instructor Flight Engineer.

The On the Job Training (OJT) program for Flight Engineers advanced in the second quarter. A Phase Test for the AFSC 435X0 Specially Training Standard was developed, printed, and distributed to each squadron. The Career Development Course for non-panel Flight Engineers became available in May. All squadrons ordered them at that time and the squadrons at Vung Tau received the first copies in June. The number of Flight Engineers in OJT continued to taper off as most new engineers being assigned to the Wing were qualified panel engineers.

The Stan/Eval team completed 66 quarterly no-notice flight checks of squadron aircrews, 11 in each squadron. In April, the 834AD convened a joint C-7A/C-123 conference at Tan Son Nhut Air Base.[20] Wing Chiefs of Stan/Eval and representatives of squadron Stan/Eval sections attended. Differences in methods of operation and tactics were discussed and evaluated to the mutual benefit of both the C-7A and the C-123 Wings. The Pilots Standardization Review Panel for the second quarter was held at Cam Ranh Bay on 3 July. On 30 July, the Flight Engineer Review Panel for the second quarter was held at Cam Ranh Bay. The minutes of both reviews were combined, published, and distributed.[21] C-7A Standardization Guide for aircrew members, dated 1 July 1969, was revised, published, and distributed.

The following items were published by the Wing Stan/Eval to assist aircrew members:
1. *483 TAW Refuel/Defuel Checklist*, 15 June 1969
2. Passenger briefing cards in both English and Vietnamese
3. 483 TAW Supplement 1 to PACAFM 51-27, 15 May 1969
4. 483 TAW Supplement 1 to PACAFM 55-27, 30 June 1969
5. 483 TAW Supplement 1 to 834AD Manual 60-1, 15 April 1969

On 2 June, a revised Instructor Pilot Upgrade Program was put into effect with the following minimum flying hour requirements: total pilot time of 1000 hours and total C-7A Aircraft Commander time of 100 hours. Final authorization to commence upgrade training for an individual pilot required the approval of the Wing Commander. The minimum flying time qualification for Instructor Pilots had to be reduced from the previous requirement of 1500 hours to 1000 hours because of an overall reduction of pilot experience within the Wing.

Lt. Col. James R. Osborn, Chief of Stan/Eval, completed his tour and was replaced by Maj. Joseph W. Stokes.

In the third quarter, the Wing experienced the first quarter of Flight Engineer manning at full authorized strength. The quality of Flight Engineer personnel remained extremely high with 91 percent of the input being panel-qualified Flight Engineers (AFSC 43570C). The posture on 1 July was composed of 152 Flight Engineers (AFSC 435X0), 1 Flight Engineer qualified Flight Mechanic (AFSC 431X0), and 11 Loadmasters (AFSC 607X0) qualified as Flight Engineers, for a total of 164 Flight Engineer qualified personnel. On 30 September, the manning was composed of 145 Flight Engineers (AFSC 435X0) and 8 Loadmasters (AFSC 607X0) qualified as Flight Engineers. This slight over-manning helped the Wing spread the Date of Estimated Return from Overseas (DEROS) of Flight Engineers throughout the year and eliminate the critical shortage previously experienced during the October through December time periods.

Quarterly formal evaluation visits to each squadron by Wing Stan/Eval were discontinued. They were replaced by semi-annual staff assistance visits by a team consisting of representatives from the Wing Stan/Eval, Safety, Training, and Life Support offices. One visit was made to the 535 TAS and the 536 TAS at Vung Tau. Particular attention was given to training records, Crew Information Files, maintenance of USAF Forms 846, and life support equipment. Spot checks were administered to 11 aircrews. No-notice spot checks were administered to four crews of the 458 TAS.

The third quarter Flight Engineer Standardization Review Panel Conference was held at Cam Ranh Bay on 22 September. A workshop group comprised of representatives from each squadron and Wing Stan/Eval was convened on 24 September to review and establish a new Stan/Eval Guide. The third quarter Pilots Standardization Review Panel Conference was held at Cam Ranh Bay on 25 September. The minutes of both conferences were combined, published, and distributed.[22]

The following items were published by the Stan/Eval Division to assist aircrew members:
1. Aircraft Commander Briefing Card
2. Change 1 to 483 TAW Supplement 1 to PACAFM 55-27, 21 Aug 1969
3. 483 TAW Supplement 1 to 834AD Manual 60-1, 15 Sep 1969
4. Change 1 to 483 TAWR 55-2, 20 Sep 1969
5. 483 TAW Supplement 1 to PACAFR 55-25, 20 Sep 1969

Many recommended changes to T.O. 1-C-7A-1 were sent to the 834AD for a major command review conference. On 17 August, an extra training mission per week was authorized for each squadron. This additional training mission was designed to provide additional landing and emergency procedures training for Copilots. When Copilots were not available, Aircraft Commanders were scheduled for additional training.[23]

Capt. Charles E. Hardie of the 457 TAS was assigned to Wing Stan/Eval. MSgt. Doyle returned to the U.S. and was replaced by SMSgt. Joseph W. Grimsley from the 537 TAS.

In the fourth quarter, upgrading totaled 83 to Aircraft Commander, 76 to Copilot, and 41 to qualified Flight Engineer. The discontinuing of the First Pilot program was approved by CINCPACAF on 29 September and was put into effect by the Wing. Eight Aircraft Commanders were upgraded to Flight Examiner and 26 were upgraded to Instructor Pilot. Twenty-five fully-qualified Flight Engineers were upgraded: 9 to Flight Engineer Flight Examiner and 16 to Instructor Flight Engineer.

Pilot manning figures decreased during the quarter due to the loss of one class input caused by relocation of the 4449th Combat Crew Training Squadron from Sewart Air Force Base, TN to Dyess Air Force Base, TX. At the end of the quarter, the wing was 55 pilots short of its authorized strength. Of the replacement pilots that arrived during October, November, and December, 54 percent were recent Undergraduate Pilot Training (UPT) graduates with low experience levels. Flight Engineer manning, on the other hand, remained consistently at 100 percent.

Staff assistance visits by a team composed of Wing Stan/Eval, Safety, Training, and Life Support personnel continued to be effective in measuring the performance of assigned units and aiding them in overcoming any difficulties encountered in these areas. Forty-eight spot checks were given to crews of the six airlift squadrons and numerous No-Notice evaluations were administered.

At the request of PACAF and 7AF, the 483 TAW hosted a Flight Manual Review Conference at Cam Ranh Bay from 11-14 December. The purpose of the conference was to review T.O. 1-C-7A-1 and T.O. 1-C-7A-1CL-1 in the light of experience gained in using the Caribou in SEA and to formulate and submit recommended changes and corrections to higher headquarters. The conference was attended by representatives of the 834AD, 483 TAW, each of the six TAS flying the Caribou, and a representative of de Havilland Aircraft of Canada, Ltd.

The Quarterly Standardization/Evaluation Review Panels were held at Cam Ranh Bay during December. The Flight Examiners convened on 19 December and the pilots on 22 December, each for one day sessions. The meetings were attended by Pilot and the Flight Engineer Flight Examiners from each of the airlift squadrons, the 483 TAW, and the 834AD. The minutes of both meetings were combined, published, and distributed to all aircrew members.[24]

Personnel changes in the Wing Stan/Eval Section included the arrival of Maj. Daniel P. Roberson on 25 October and the departure of Maj. Delbert D. Lockwood on 3 November and Maj. Joseph H. Stokes on 24 November when their tours in SEA ended.

Safety

In the first quarter, Lt. Col. James A. Talbot, the Wing Chief of Safety, was reassigned to MACV in Saigon and a replacement was not assigned, leaving the Safety Office manned by additional duty personnel. Maj. Richard R. Erickson and Maj. Robert E. Baltzell, both from the 458 TAS, were temporarily assigned the additional duty of Safety Officers until a qualified officer could be assigned as Chief of Safety. Sgt. Ira L. Daniels was assigned as the Safety Clerk.

On 14 January, C-7A S/N 61-2584 struck the rotor mast of a Huey helicopter while landing at the Special Forces camp at Bu Krak (also known as Bu Prang). Over six feet of the left wing were cut off. The Wing Quality Control Officer, Maj. Ernest P. Hanavan, Jr., led a team of six maintenance personnel[25] to recover the aircraft. The team brought their tool boxes, aero stands, sheet metal tools, air compressor, sheets of aluminum, and aluminum extrusions (L-shape and T-shape) and arrived at Bu Krak about 1000. All pitched in to clean up the mangled left wing tip and prepare the site for rebuilding.

Capt. William H. Poe, 5SFG commander of the camp, and his Green Beret team welcomed the recovery team at lunch. He told them that after the evening meal, each of the Air Force personnel would be assigned to a defensive position (4.2 inch mortar pit, 50 cal. machine gun tower, 60 mm mortar pit, command post) to help defend the camp in case of an attack. The team went back to work which was interrupted by the ominous "thump...thump...thump" of incoming mortar rounds as the enemy tried to destroy the C-7A before it could be repaired and flown to safety. Needless to say, the Green Berets had the full attention of the "blue suiters" for the weapons training that evening.

Maj. Hanavan was flown back to Cam Ranh Bay (CRB) on 16 January to pick up essential parts (leading edge D-duct, left outboard fore-flap, and left aileron). The piano wire hinge could not be threaded through all of its loops, so steel safety wire was used to secure the duct and the raw edges were covered over with duct tape. After installing the aileron and flap section, the team built a new skin for the underside of the wing using the aluminum extrusions and sheets of aluminum. When the field repairs were complete on 18 January, Maj. Hanavan

21

painted "Made in Bu Krak by the Good Guys" with a spray can of zinc chromate on the raw aluminum underside of the left wing.

After briefing the crew, he told the team that anyone wanting to return to Cam Ranh Bay that they should get their tool boxes and equipment and get aboard for the one-time flight to CRB. Any one else would be picked up the next day by another Caribou. Ten minutes later, all were aboard for the uphill, downwind takeoff (to avoid the mine field at the end of the 1800 foot clay/laterite runway) which went off with no problem.

When the aircraft landed at CRB and pulled onto the ramp, there were several hundred Caribou personnel on the ramp to see the recovered aircraft. They smiled and laughed when they saw the words on the underside of the left wing, because "Home of the Good Guys" adorned signs around the periphery of the Caribou maintenance hootches, with the outline of a white cowboy hat on each sign.

Col. Turk continued to emphasize the Safety program, with particular attention to flight safety[26] and aircraft accident prevention.[27] Two major accidents occurred during the quarter. The first was on 17 January at Vung Tau Army Airfield when a pilot, on his last flight in Vietnam, prematurely engaged the flight controls gust locks while in a strong crosswind. The C-7A, S/N 60-5434, was damaged beyond repair when it left the runway and crashed into the Ground Controlled Approach (GCA) unit, causing extensive damage to the unit and the aircraft.[28] Three of the crew received major injuries while the fourth member sustained minor injuries. Corrective actions resulted in emphasizing the importance of properly computing crosswind data.[29]

The second major aircraft accident occurred at Tra Bong, one of the shortest and most difficult fixed-wing strips in Southeast Asia. The aircraft touched down short of the runway and sheered the left main landing gear. The aircraft ground looped 180 degrees and came to rest in a rocky ditch, causing major damage. The three crewmen and one passenger were unhurt. There were no major aircraft accidents not resulting in aircraft damage or aircraft non-flight accidents.

On 24 January, C-7A S/N 63-9764 of the 535 TAS was reported to have sustained five .30 caliber hits while in the landing pattern at Duc Phong (V-269). The damage caused the aircraft to leave the runway shortly after touchdown. Extensive damage was sustained by all three landing gear, six feet of the fuselage nose section was crushed, all flaps and ailerons on the left wing were torn off or damaged, the left engine was broken off, and the fuselage belly was damaged. Despite sporadic enemy fire in the Duc Phong area, maintenance personnel from CRB made battlefield repairs which enabled a one-time flight to CRB. This flight enabled maintenance personnel to further repair the aircraft before a final one-time flight on 20 February to Tan Son Nhut. At TanSon Nhut, the aircraft was disassembled by an AFLC team and returned to the U.S. for complete rebuilding. See the Maintenance section of this chapter for additional information about the recovery.

Twenty-five aircraft incidents occurred during the quarter,[30] 17 resulting from in-flight engine shutdowns. Organizations of the Wing submitted 32 Operational Hazard Reports (OHRs). Twenty-one of the OHRs dealt with traffic control of fixed-wing aircraft and helicopters on and near airfields.

Of particular concern was the effective fatigue upon crew members, in general, and Flight Engineers, in particular. Previously, the Wing was visited by the Safety Survey Team of the USAF Office of the Inspector General. That team suggested a medical evaluation be made of C-7A flight engineers in relation to fatigue problems associated with flight duties. Because circumstances of crew manning would have been artificial and therefore misleading in December due to TDY augmentation, accomplishment of the evaluation was delayed until the TDY augmentees returned to their bases. The evaluation was made in January by Flight Surgeon personnel assigned to the 12th USAF Hospital at Cam Ranh Bay. The evaluation pinpointed actions which were then corrected locally.[31]

The accident rate for the first quarter was 6.3 based on 31,548 hours flown. This was slightly higher than the PACAF goal set by Mission Safety 70 (MS-70); however, the hours flown for the quarter were the highest ever in the history of Caribou operations in SEA and represented an increased exposure to the hazards of combat operations.

The Weekly Flying Safety Flashes and memos on accident/incident experience of the previous week and OHR experience were published and distributed to each squadron and mission site in the Wing.

The Wing Integrated Safety Council convened on 18 March for its quarterly meeting. The Wing Commander was Chairman and his key staff, together with the Squadron Commanders, attended. The minutes of the meeting concerned the subjects discussed and the actions taken or directed.[32] The Council stressed that Ground Safety must also be emphasized to ensure unrestricted mission accomplishment.

Three military injuries occurred during the quarter. Two USAF Motor Vehicle Accidents occurred, but no personnel injuries resulted from the accidents. Thirty-five injuries requiring First Aid treatment were reported. No private motor vehicle accidents occurred. One Vietnamese civilian was injured as a result of an aircraft accident. No explosive accidents or incidents occurred.

All Mission Safety 70 goals in the field of Ground Safety were met. Weekly Safety Flashes, emphasizing Ground Safety, were published and distributed along with the Safety Summary which outlined recent experiences.

In the second quarter, Wing aircraft received 22 hits from enemy ground fire. Aircraft damage was minor and the aircraft were capable of continuing their missions. In addition to Ben Het (V-179), numerous FAC-only and FAC/fighter missions were flown at An Hoa (V-257), Dong Ha (V-22), Duc Hoa (V-200), Katum (V-287), Quang Ngai (V-23), and Tien Phuoc (V-239). These supporting missions were flown to preclude the threat of enemy fire on C-7A aircraft and those airfields.

There were no major aircraft accidents and no minor accidents or aircraft non-flight accidents during the quarter. There was one aircraft accident not resulting in aircraft damage, when an Army enlisted man ran into the left propeller and was fatally injured at Vung Tau Air Base. The investigation established that it was an apparent suicide as the individual had reported suicidal tendencies. Sixteen aircraft incidents occurred, 14 of which resulted from in-flight engine shutdowns. Nineteen OHRs were submitted, the majority of which dealt with traffic control problems.

The accident rate for the second quarter was 3.2 per 100,000 flying hours, well below the 5.2 goal set by Mission Safety 70. The hours flown during the first six months of 1969 were the highest ever in the history of Caribou operations in SEA and represented an increased exposure to the hazards of combat operations. This reduction was accomplished even though average pilot experience level decreased about 1000 hours during the past year. Weekly Flying Safety Flashes and a summary of accident/incident experience of the past week and OHR experience were published and distributed to each squadron and mission site.

The Wing Integrated Safety Council convened on 9 June for its quarterly meeting. Col. Turk was chairman and his key staff, together with the squadron commanders, attended. Subjects discussed and actions taken were reported in the minutes.[34] Four military injuries occurred during the quarter, one being charged to the 15th Aerial Port Squadron. One USAF motor vehicle accident occurred with no injuries. One injury occurred involving an Army vehicle. The crowded conditions and apparently lower priority put on ground safety hazards by the Army at Vung Tau was a problem area. Twelve injuries requiring First Aid treatment were reported. No private motor vehicle accidents occurred. No explosive accidents/incidents occurred. Weekly Safety Flashes, emphasizing ground safety, were published and distributed along with a Safety Summary, which outlined recent experiences. Mission Safety 70 goal rate for the Wing was 21.39, above the desired rate of 20.16. The Wing Integrated Safety Council stressed that there must be an active and dynamic program throughout all supervisory levels.

Lt. Col. Robert L. Howke was assigned as Chief of Safety, Major Robert E. Baltzell as Flying Safety Officer, and Sgt. Ira L. Daniels as Safety Clerk.

In the third quarter, Lt. Col. Howke continued as Chief of Safety, Maj. Maltzell continued as Flying /Safety Officer, and Sgt. Robert V. DiGiandomenico was assigned as Safety Clerk.

Wing aircraft received 22 hits from enemy ground fire. Two of these aircraft subsequently crashed, one near Minh Long (V-102) and the other near Plei Djereng (V-285). Another aircraft made a forced landing at Song Be (V-30) as a result of engine damage and was repaired at that location. In all other cases, damage was minor and the aircraft were capable of continuing the mission.

Two aircraft losses resulted in five crew members Killed In Action (KIA). On 26 July, 537 TAS C-7A S/N 62-4186 crashed on final approach while attempting to make a single engine landing at Vung Tau as a result of loss of power on #2 engine, resulting in the death of 1/Lt. James. F. Wohrer, the copilot. There were major injuries to 3 personnel and 10 passengers had varying degrees of less serious injuries.

On 11 September, C-7A S/N 62-4187 of the 537 TAS was shot down by small arms ground fire near the Special Forces Camp at Plei Djereng, killing 1/Lt. Robert P. Weisneth, 1/Lt. Neil N. Greinke, 2/Lt. Charles B. Ross, SSgt. Frederick Wilhelm, and a U.S. Army courier.

There was one aircraft accident not resulting in aircraft damage. This accident occurred at Cherry Drop Zone (DZ) near Pleiku. On a practice jump, two Vietnamese parachutists became tangled and their chutes streamered after leaving the aircraft. One injury was fatal the other parachutist was hospitalized in critical condition. There were two aircraft losses attributed to enemy action. There were no minor aircraft accidents. Fifteen aircraft incidents occurred, 11 of which were the result of in-flight engine shutdowns. Twenty-one OHRs were submitted. There were no trends established because the OHRs covered many different areas.

The cumulative accident rate for the quarter was 3.2 per 100,000 flying hours, well below the goal of 5.2 set by the Mission Safety 70 program of PACAF.

Weekly Flying Safety Flashes and a resume of the aircraft/incident experience of the past week and OHR experience was published and distributed to each squadron and mission site. The Wing Integrated Safety Council convened on 15 September. Col. Christensen was chairman and his key staff, together with the Squadron commanders, attended.[35]

Five ground military injuries occurred. There was one government motor vehicle accident when an Airman misappropriated a van and ran into the rear of a 1½ ton truck. One private motor vehicle "hit and run" mishap took place when an Airman was struck by a Lambretta three wheeled taxi and received a concussion. The ground accident rate for the Wing was 23.17, above the Mission Safety 70 desired rate of 20.16. Weekly Safety Flashes emphasizing ground safety were published and distributed, along with a Safety Summary which outlined recent experiences. One of the major topics for ground safety was the care and operation of government motor vehicles. It was stressed that anyone caught carelessly operating a vehicle would have his driving privileges revoked. There were no explosive accidents/incidents during the quarter.

The fourth quarter, Lt. Col. Howke continued as Chief of Safety. Maj. Edwin H. Kohlhepp, Jr. was the Flying Safety Officer and Sgt. DiGiandomenico continued as the Safety Clerk.

Ten C-7A aircraft were hit by ground fire. All but one of the aircraft were flown safely to secure bases. On 26 December, C-7A 63-9723 of the 459 TAS was shot down by small arms ground fire as it approached Tien Phuoc, resulting in the loss of the aircraft and the deaths of 1/Lt. David B. Bowling and TSgt. E. J. Welch, Jr. The other crew member on the mission, 1/Lt. Richard J. Patterson, was seriously injured and was recuperating in the hospital in Japan at the end of the quarter.

One aircraft received considerable damage from mortar fragments while on the ground at Song Be (V-30), but the crew was able to fly the aircraft to Bien Hoa (V-2) for repairs. No Wing personnel were injured in this incident. No Wing personnel were declared Missing in Action.

Weekly Flying Safety Flashes and a resume of accident/incident experience and OHR experience for the past week was published and distributed to each squadron and mission site. There were no aircraft accidents during the fourth quarter. Thirteen incident reports were submitted, 12 resulting from in-flight engine shutdown and one aircraft taxi incident. Fourteen OHRs were submitted, covering many different areas. The accident rate for the fourth quarter was 2.4 per 100,000 flying hours, well below the 5.2 goal set by PACAF Mission Safety 70. The final rate for 1969 was the lowest accident rate for the 483 TAW since the Air Force took over operation of the C-7A on 1 January 1967.

Four military disabling injuries were recorded. The ground accident rate of 24.3 was above the PACAF Mission Safety 70 goal. This was an increase over the rate of 23.17 for the preceding quarter. Weekly Safety Flashes emphasizing ground safety were published and distributed with a monthly safety summary outlining recent experiences. There were no explosive accidents/incidents during the quarter.

Maintenance

On 1 January, maintenance personnel manning was 86.6 percent of authorized strength. By the end of the quarter, the maintenance function was 107 percent manned (1033 authorized and 1133 assigned), but the skill level was below par. Many 3-level personnel filled 5-level positions and many 5-level personnel filled 7-level positions.

There were many high-level managerial changes. On 15 February, Lt. Col. Ralph L. Peters, the Wing Chief of Maintenance, assumed the position of 483 Consolidated Aircraft Maintenance Squadron (CAMS) Commander and Lt. Col. William A. Ulrich was assigned as the Wing Chief of Maintenance. On 1 March, Lt. Col. Ulrich was assigned as the 483 TAW DCM and Lt. Col. Hastings became the new Deputy Commander for Material Maintenance (DCMM) and Wing Quality Control (QC) Officer, replacing Maj. Hanavan who had returned to the U.S. in the middle of February. CMSgt. Douglas B. Brower was assigned as the Maintenance Superintendent of DCMM.

The Wing gained four aircraft and lost four. The gains were aircraft returned from being rebuilt at repair facilities in the U.S. C-7A S/N 62-4178 was gained by the 535 TAS on 9 December 1968, but was not reported until January 1969. C-7A S/N 62-4170 was gained by the 458 TAS on 25 January, C-7A S/N 63-9718 was gained by the 536 TAS on 9 February, and C-7A S/N 63-9747 was gained by the 459 TAS on 19 February. A 536 TAS C-7A, S/N 60-5434, was damaged beyond repair on 17 January when it crashed into the GCA (Ground Controlled Approach) shack at Vung Tau. A 535 TAS C-7A, S/N 63-9764, was lost on 20 February due to "battle damage." A 459 TAS C-7A, S/N 63-9762, was lost on 1 March due to an accident at Tra Bong. A 458 TAS C-7A, S/N 62-4150, was lost from the inventory on 5 March when it was returned to the Warner Robins Air Materiel Area (WRAMA) at the direction of Air Force Logistics Command for Analytical Condition Inspection.

Maj. Hanavan and Maj. M. T. Smith recalled the events surrounding the recovery of C-7A S/N 9764:

> "One day, a senior officer in the chain of command entered my [Pat Hanavan] office and asked 'Where could a Caribou be hit by enemy fire during landing and end up in a ditch along the side of the runway as a result of that enemy fire?' I thought for a minute and then replied, 'Give me a few minutes to think about it and I'll bring you an answer within the hour.' Accidents, especially ones caused by pilot error, were bad news for a squadron and the Wing. As the chief test pilot for the 483rd, it was easy for me to come up with a critical part of the Caribou which could result in loss of control on landing. Any of several components in the aileron-wing flap system (e.g., wing flap attachment arm, bell crank) could prevent the pilot from holding the upwind wing down into a crosswind. A failure there, plus a narrow runway, could result in the aircraft going into a ditch.
>
> M.T. Smith [Maintenance Control Officer], faced the same question. 'I was sent to take charge of the recovery team and it was clear that the boss (Col. Turk) could not afford another pilot error accident.' The crashed aircraft was found to have a bullet hole through the aileron bell crank. The aircraft forms read, 'Right wing aileron bell crank damaged; bell crank replaced.' M.T. and Bruce Jack, the de Havilland tech rep, presented the boss with the shattered bell crank when he came to pick up the repaired aircraft ... no elaboration.
>
> His face was lit up like a beacon. He grabbed M.T. by the shoulders and said, 'I'll never forget this.' M.T. was told that he showed the damaged bell crank to the 7th Air Force Commander at one of the staff meetings ... what he said there we have no idea, we can only imagine.
>
> The AK-47 is 7.62x39 mm and the M-16 is 5.56x45 mm. It's probably a good thing that bullets expand on impact, so that it would have been difficult to determine the exact caliber of the weapon that produced the hole. We'll leave 'the rest of the story' to your imagination."[34]

The 483 TAW Maintenance Control Center was judged by the PACAF Maintenance Stan/Eval Team (MSET) as one of the best observed within PACAF.[36] SMSgt. Raymond H. Duck, replaced SMSgt. Jerome T. Kaufman, who had returned to the CONUS. Work Order

Control was found by the MSET to have an outstanding Plans and Scheduling operation. TSgt. Robert McFarland, Jr. replaced MSgt. Laurence J. Sweeney as NCOIC of the Plans and Scheduling Section. MSgt. Eugene F. Baumgartner assumed the position of NCOIC of the Work Order Control Section. MSgt. James T. Hedgecock replaced TSgt. Kenneth W. Rhodes as NCOIC of the Reports and Administration Section when TSgt. Rhodes transferred to the 483 DCM Administration Section.

Modification programs were again stressed. Three new field level Time Compliance Technical Orders (TCTOs) were received: T.O. 1C-7A-593, T.O. 1C-7A-594, and T.O. 1C-7A-595. These TCTOs were calculated to involve a total of 617 man-hours to accomplish. At the end of the quarter, 4291 man-hours of TCTO work had been completed with a backlog of only 247 man-hours. The Analytical Conditioning Program involved one aircraft, C-7A S/N 62-4150, which was flown to Warner Robins Air Material Area (WRAMA), Robins AFB, GA.

Inspection and Repair as Necessary (IRAN) continued during the second quarter. Sixty-two aircraft completed the IRAN program conducted by Philippine Airlines in Manila. At the end of the quarter, a total of 15 aircraft remained to be serviced under the existing contract. A new IRAN contract was programmed, involving the remaining aircraft of the Wing not already through IRAN. Those not through the program within two years would be recycled. The Corrosion Control program was also located in the Philippine Islands. Fifty-one out of 70 aircraft covered by the present contract received corrosion control treatment at Clark Air Base. On 14 April, Col. Turk commented at his staff meeting that he was very pleased with the IRAN facility at Clark and the work done in the last quarter. He also stated that he was pleased with services rendered at Clark Air Base.

In Materiel Control, personnel rotation created no large problems. The two ranking NCOs, TSgt. George A. McElrath and TSgt. Ray Taylor, relocated at the end of January. They were replaced by CMSgt. Bertrand A. Farrell who was reassigned from Material Control at Operating Location B (OLAB), Vung Tau, and TSgt. Lynn K. Atkins. A shortage of two warehousemen, AFSC 64730, existed throughout the quarter.

The arrival of new personnel was the beginning of a new procedure. A bi-monthly maintenance/supply conference was initiated, to be held in the office of the Chief of Supply on the first and third Thursday of each month. This conference provided a better understanding and easier solution to mutual problems. Further changes were reflected

29

in the verification procedures for Not Operationally Ready-Supply (NORS) conditions, resulting in reduction of the number of NORS cancellations. As a final change in procedure, the tail number bins, located in the receiving section of Material Control, were enclosed in a secure area to enforce supply discipline.

Other problems encountered from outside the unit, which were in the hands of others to solve, included delivery time and bench stock support. The slow response of Base Supply to supplying more parts from the warehouse to the flight line caused unnecessary cannibalization and NORS Local Delivery Delay (LDD) time. Furthermore, the percent of bins with property on hand was low throughout the quarter. Austere funding prompted Base Supply to economize on the purchase of bench stocks, resulting in a low bench stock fill rate and a high priority demand rate. Supply was made aware of both the "time" and "level" problems. The Chief of Supply attempted to correct the former and attack the latter problem by initiating a buy program.

The Quality Control (QC) Branch performed all functions required by Chapter 7 of Air Force Manual (AFM) 66-1, as supplemented. In January, 31 Functional Check Flights (FCFs) were flown, logging 20.9 hours. In February, 51 FCFs were flown, logging 31.2 hours. In March, 55 FCFs were flown, logging 31.9 hours. In January, 12 Emergency Unsatisfactory Reports (EUR) and 2 Quality Control Deficiency Report (QCDR) were filed. In February, 13 EURs, 3 QCDRs, and 1 Material Deficiency Report (MDR) were filed. In March, 7 EURs and 2 QCDRs were filed. In January, QC performed 1 Activity inspection, 6 Operational Readiness Inspections (ORIs), and 36 Phase Inspections. In February, QC performed 7 ORIs and 35 Phase Inspections. In March, QC performed 6 ORIs and 34 Phase Inspections. Quality Control gained 3 personnel in January and 3 in February, and lost 2 personnel in February and 3 in March. Routine surveillance spot inspections were performed on safety, powered and non-powered Aerospace Ground Equipment (AGE), Foreign Object Damage (FOD), pre-flights, post-flights, fuel servicing, towing, and facilities. In-process inspections were performed on required items in-shop during Phase Inspections.

TSgt. Clyde J. Sanchez replaced TSgt. McElroy in the Training Control Section when his tour was completed. One major change with which Training Control had to cope involved OJT. The Specialty Knowledge Test (SKT) was deleted as a requirement for AFSC upgrading and added as a requisite for promotion. On 29 March, Lt. Col. Alfred H. Stephens briefed key personnel in each unit on the information he obtained pertaining to the Weighted Airman's Promotion System (WAPS). TSgt. P. Houlberg from Training Control then indicated what effects WAPS would have on the Wing training program. The SKT results were not as favorable as during the last quarter of 1968. During the quarter, two personnel were tested at the 3-level and both passed, 78 were tested at the 5-level and 52 passed, and 19 were tested at the 7-level and 12 passed. The overall passing rate was 66.7 percent. This was slightly lower than the 72.4 percent pass rate in the last quarter of 1968, when 40 personnel were tested at the 3-level and 29 passed, 25 were tested at the 5-level and 18 passed, and 26 were tested at the 7-level and 21 passed.

Training Control was visited on 19 January by the MSET. The major discrepancy noted was that Proficiency Tests and Study Guides had not been prepared for nine AFSCs.[35] After the write-ups, the tests and guides were prepared and forwarded to PACAF for approval.[37] With this correction, the MSET program reached its peak. It was expected that by the end of April, all personnel rotating in October, November, and December should complete their Maintenance Standardization and Evaluation Program (MSEP) requirements.

During the quarter, 256 AFTO Forms 35 were issued. Examinations were administered to 70 Crew Chiefs, 233 Refueling/Defueling personnel, 72 Engine Run-up personnel, and 165 Supervisory personnel. A total of 340 MSEP tests, 248 Proficiency tests, and 53 Towing tests were administered.

A final Training Control problem concerned Field Training Detachment (FTD) quotas. Due to a shortage of TDY funds, FTD quotas were reduced for the second quarter of 1969.

TSgt. Billy D. Holland replaced MSgt. Leon C. Kincaid, Jr. as NCOIC of the Maintenance Analysis Branch and TSgt. Robert L. Prentice, NCOIC of the Production Analysis Section, departed for the U.S. The Deficiency Analysis Section was established in February and all three positions were filled.

On 10 February, a new building for the Engine Build-Up Shop was opened.

A 780 storage room was built at Vung Tau to allow the equipment for each aircraft to be stored in a separate, but identical, bin. The Accessories Branch moved into their new, air-conditioned building. New concrete floors for the hangar were poured. The Phase Docks constructed new cowl racks and improved their office areas. The POL building was 98 percent complete and temporary building T-130 was 10 percent complete at the end of the quarter, both with an Estimated

31

Completion Date (ECD) of 15 June.

The Operations facilities for the two squadrons were revamped by 21 March. The housing area had hot water showers and a recreation area installed and the road between the barracks was hard topped. A new dining hall was 30 percent complete at the end of the quarter and was to be opened for service on or about 15 June. A sewage system was 25 percent complete at the end of the quarter, but its ECD was unknown. A water system was contemplated, but nothing concrete was determined.

At Phu Cat, the flight line maintenance personnel moved to a new and larger building on the flight line. It was in close proximity to the aircraft and more storage space was provided. During the latter part of March, new Officer's Quarters opened, situated at the northern part of the base. New facilities such as an Officer's Club, mess hall, patios, and general landscaping were projected for future development in the complex.

In the second quarter, the manning of maintenance personnel stabilized. The overall maintenance personnel manning was 100 percent; however some specialties were overmanned and some were undermanned. Also, there was a shortage of qualified 7-level supervisory personnel.

Modification programs were again stressed. No new field-level TC-TOs were received for the C-7A. However, there were 2463 man-hours expended accomplishing TCTOs from the previous quarter. At the end of June, there were only 236 man-hours of backlog. The Wing received one depot-level TCTO, T.O 1-C-7A-589. This TCTO would be performed on all aircraft in the Wing by a depot-level team at Cam Ranh Bay. The team was due to arrive on 15 July.

The IRAN program continued. Thirteen aircraft completed the IRAN program under contract to Philippine Airlines, Manila. A new IRAN schedule was programmed to permit an input of 33 aircraft that had not received IRAN for the past two years. The Corrosion Control Program, also located at Clark Air Base in the Philippine Islands, accomplished corrosion control treatment on nine C-7A aircraft. A new corrosion control contract was scheduled to begin in July at Kadena Air Base, Okinawa and would require 24 days per aircraft.

The maintenance function experienced very few problems during the quarter; however, assistance was requested to establish an in-country engineering study of the C-7A landing gear system because of its history of frequent malfunctions. There were no major accidents or incidents and maintenance effectiveness was very high. On average there were 6.3 maintenance delays per day with an average maintenance delay time per day of 9.9 hours. This was considered to be an exceptionally fine rate considering the daily flying program of about 340 hours and 500 sorties.

The Quality Control section accomplished 65 FCFs in April, logging 39.5 hours; 43 FCFs in May, logging 27.1 hours; and 60 FCFs in June, logging 42.3 hours. In April, 8 EURs, 3 QCDRs, and 1 MDR were filed. In May, 6 EURs and 4 MDRs were filed. In June, 4 EURs, 2 QCDRs, and 1 MDR were filed. In April, QC performed 7 ORIs and 37 Phase Inspections. In May, QC performed 6 ORIs and 39 Phase Inspections. In June, QC performed 5 ORIs and 35 Phase Inspections. Routine surveillance spot inspections were performed on powered and non-powered AGE, pre-flights, post-flights, fuel servicing, towing, facilities, and safety practices.

Maintenance Training Control experienced significant changes in all programs, primarily due to considerably fewer personnel rotating and being reassigned. Training Control initiated 27 Air Force Forms 989, *Initial Evaluation*, as opposed to 150 during the previous quarter. The section issued 20 AFTO Forms 35 compared to 143 during the first quarter. The number of proficiency tests for Refuel/Defuel, Towing, Engine Run-up, etc. diminished proportionately to the number of AFTO Forms 35 issued.

The Field Training Detachment (FTD) quotas decreased slightly because of the requirement for all personnel to have six months remaining on their tour at the time of selection. This policy afforded each squadron maximum availability of personnel receiving FTD training. The number of quotas requested was expected to increase for the months of October, November, and December when a large annual turnover of personnel takes place.

The OJT program underwent a decided change. The SKT, the final evaluation of a trainee's knowledge as a requisite for upgrading, was removed from the OJT/Classification process and inserted into the WAPS. It was now the Commander's prerogative to upgrade his personnel. The number of personnel in OJT in the units at Cam Ranh Bay decreased from 133 in April to 108 in May and then to 95 in June. This decrease was due to appreciably fewer trainees being assigned during the quarter. A new 483 TAW Regulation 50-1 was written and distributed to the field. This regulation strengthened the OJT program to ensure quality training and evaluation of training accomplished.

Activity in the MSEP decreased considerably. The large backlog of personnel had been tested and their practical evaluations completed.

Current activity was restricted to incoming personnel who were evaluated and their program requirements completed within two months after arrival.

Under a Contractor Engineering and Technical Services (CETS) contract, the C-7A de Havilland Technical Representative conducted classes specifically for Crew Chiefs. These were five-day courses covering those systems where training was needed. The Technical Representative also pinpointed needed instruction in other areas for personnel assigned to the Periodic Docks and Aerospace Repair.

During the period, the Production Analysis section published the Monthly Maintenance Summary, 1-HAF-A1 (prepared by Sgt. P. Shelley), the 1-PAF-U36 (prepared by SMSgt. Raymond H. Duck), the DD INL (Q) 612 (prepared by TSgt. Maynard C. Rodell) , the 9-LOG-K75 (prepared by TSgt. Billy D. Holland), and other required monthly reports.

The Deficiency Analysis section completed special studies on engines (10 instances), augmentor tubes (16 instances), main door linkage (7 instances), and landing gear capsules (15 instances).

Twenty-four TDY trips were made to assist forward operating locations.

In the third quarter, manning of maintenance personnel was fairly stable. One field level TCTO was received, T.O. 1C-7A-596, "Inspection of Main Landing Gear Housing." Ninety-four aircraft were completed. There were 4431.2 man-hours expended in accomplishing outstanding TCTOs and, at the end of the quarter, there were only 166.4 man-hours of workable backlog. A depot level team for TCTO 1C-7A-569, "Installation of Fuel Cell Suppressant Material, C-7A Aircraft," was started in early August and, at the end of the quarter, 59 aircraft had been modified.

Thai Air, located at Bangkok, was awarded the C-7A IRAN contract for Fiscal Year 1970 (FY70). A new IRAN schedule was established with the first input on 28 September. An average of three aircraft per month were scheduled for the remaining three quarters of FY70. The last two aircraft completed IRAN at Clark Air Base, Philippine Islands, during July. Two aircraft completed corrosion control at Kadena, Okinawa. A new corrosion control schedule was received and 18 aircraft were scheduled for corrosion control during the last three quarters of FY70. It was planned that each aircraft would be at the Kadena facility for 14 days.

The overall initial launch reliability rate for the quarter was 99.5 percent and the enroute reliability was 98.6 percent. Both figures were slightly higher than the second quarter. Maintenance personnel did an outstanding job in support of the heavy flying program.

Lt. Col. Edgar N. Powell arrived in September to assume the position of Chief of Maintenance at Cam Ranh Bay. Other key personnel who arrived during the quarter were: Capt. David S. Harrigan, Maintenance Control Officer; Capt. Robert R. Jacoby, Workload Control Officer; 1/Lt. Ronald L. Cafferty, 458 TAS Maintenance Officer; 1/Lt. Robert Sides, 457 TAS Maintenance Officer; 1/Lt. George L. Mansi, CAMS Supervisor; and Capt. Robert B. Biggins, Chief of Quality Control.

The workload increased for the Maintenance Training Control section because of an increased rotation of personnel. The section initiated 60 USAF Forms 989, *Initial Evaluation*, during the quarter, compared with 27 in the second quarter. There were 35 AFTO Forms 35, *Operator Permit*, issued, compared with 20 before. A total of 98 proficiency and special qualification tests were administered in the following areas: Refueling/Defueling, Towing, Engine Run-up, Marshaling, Tower Communications, Crew Chief, and Supervision. Eighteen FTD quotas were allotted to the Wing. However, the FTD program underwent a number of changes to be reflected in future historical reports. Current plans were to conduct all FTD classes on-station, using assigned personnel as instructors.

The Quality Control section accomplished 69 FCFs in July, logging 42.4 hours; 59 FCFs in August, logging 34.4 hours; and 49 FCFs in September, logging 32.1 hours. In July, 6 EURs, 3 QCDRs, and 2 MDRs were filed. In August, 7 EURs, 2 QCDRs, and 5 MDRs were filed. In September, 2 EURs, 3 QCDRs, and 3 MDRs were filed. In July, QC performed 6 Operational Readiness Inspections (ORIs) and 34 Phase Inspections. In August, QC performed 6 ORIs and 37 Phase Inspections. In September, QC performed 6 ORIs and 33 Phase Inspections. Routine surveillance spot inspections were performed on powered and non-powered AGE, tool boxes, pre-flights, fuel servicing, towing, facilities, and safety practices. The section lost three personnel and gained three during the quarter.

The OJT in-training figures for July, August, and September were 78, 69, and 79, respectively. The program continued increasing as new personnel entered training. The OJT contact in the Consolidated Base Personnel Office (CBPO) indicated that the Wing could anticipate a large number of incoming personnel coming directly from technical training schools. An OJT class in Airframe Repair was established, consisting of two hours of instruction per day, three days per week.

Courses covering other maintenance career fields were planned as new personnel arrived and needs arose.

Task lists in the MSEP were enlarged to include a wider range of tasks. Fifty personnel took the MSEP written evaluation during the quarter. This figure was expected to quadruple in the fourth quarter when incoming personnel were tested.

Mr. Mackenzie Brown, the new de Havilland Field Service Representative, conducted familiarization classes for newly assigned maintenance personnel. The majority of the instruction was given by the over-the-shoulder method as no overhead projector was available. Transparencies and schematics would be used by Mr. Brown when a projector became available.

Capt. Paul M. Reynolds, the OIC of Material Control, rotated to the CONUS in September and no replacement arrived by the end of the quarter. The NCOIC of Material Control, CMSgt. Farrell, rotated to the CONUS in July and was replaced by MSgt. C. Torn. A total of seven other personnel rotated during the quarter. Ten new personnel were assigned. SSgt. Burley completed his OJT and was upgraded to the 7-level in September.

During the third quarter, the Production Analysis section published the 1-PAF-U36 ("Monthly Maintenance Summary" prepared by TSgt. Holland), the 1-PAF-U66 ("NORS Rate/Cannibalizations"), the 1-HAF-O41 ("PACAF Maintenance Manning Report"), and other required monthly reports. TSgt. Holland, the NCOIC of the section, made an assistance visit to Phu Cat on 3 and 4 July. He also attended a conference hosted by 7AF pertaining to data and analysis of the 1-HAF-O41 and 1-PAF-U36 reports. This conference was held at 7AF headquarters, Tan Son Nhut AB, on 29 through 31 July.

TSgt. Clyde E. Smith (AFSC 43470) was gained on 28 August and SSgt. Carl H. McDonald (AFSC 43470) was gained on 13 September. SSgt. James H. Robinson was lost on 10 September due to normal rotation.

The Deficiency Analysis Section made special studies and analyses on the following systems/components of the C-7A:

1. R-2000-7M2 engine stub pipes, to determine the reasons for excessive failures due to the pipes cracking

2. Wheel brakes, to try and isolate the reasons for excessive brake puck consumption

3. Landing gear assembly, to prevent and determine trends of excessive failure data on components of the landing gear system, in general, and additional data and statistics compiled by specific serial

number of aircraft

4. RT220B Receiver/Transmitter, to isolate the cause of excessive failures

5. Comm/Nav systems, to determine the number of component failures due to moisture, water, or corrosion

6. Tachometer generator, to determine specific trends or data contributing to the excessive failure rate

7. Re-accomplishment of labor job standards, including the specific AFSCs, special tools, and equipment required to accomplish a specific task or job

TSgt. James D. Free (AFSC 30170) was lost on 26 August due to normal rotation. The position was unfilled at the end of the quarter, leaving the section only 67 percent manned.

The Maintenance Analysis Function gained SMSgt. Norman White (AFSC 43490) on 16 July. He assumed the position of NCOIC.

In the fourth quarter, manning of maintenance personnel reached a low near the end of November, but increased with a large influx of personnel in the last week of December. Depot level TCTO 1C-7A-589 was completed. This TCTO started in the third quarter and was completed one month ahead of schedule due to the increased efficiency of the field team from the depot. Two new field level TCTOs were received. TCTO 1-C-7A-592E ("Removal of T336A Standby VHF Transmitter") was complied with on 22 aircraft by the end of the quarter. This TCTO required 30 minutes per aircraft and was scheduled to be worked when the aircraft was in the Phase Dock. Urgent Action TCTO 1-C-7A-598 ("Inspection and Rework of Elevators and Elevator Torque Tubes") was also received. This TCTO required 30.5 man-hours per aircraft. After receiving a time extension on the TCTO, it was accomplished on all aircraft during their next Phase Inspection. All aircraft affected were completed in December. There were 1025 man-hours expended on TCTOs during the quarter and there were only 8.5 man-hours of workable backlog at the end of the quarter.

Ten aircraft were delivered to the IRAN facility at Bangkok. Three were returned during the quarter and seven were still in work at the end of December. The first few aircraft through IRAN experienced some difficulties and were not delivered as scheduled. These delays were attributed to the learning curve of the contractor on the C-7A aircraft.

Six aircraft were sent through the Corrosion Control facility at Kadena AB, Okinawa. The aircraft took about 14 days of flow time through the facility and were input on a one for one basis.

Capt. Curtis A. Preston was assigned as the Electronics Officer (Comm/Nav) for the 483 CAMS and OIC of CAMS as an additional duty. CMSgt. Hila D. Conner arrived in December and was tentatively assigned to Quality Control as a replacement for CMSgt. William G. Peters. Lt. Col. Harold J. Brennen assumed duties as Assistant DCM.

The tempo picked up for Maintenance Training Control in the fourth quarter. More personnel arrived and departed than in the third quarter. Training Control initiated 124 AF Forms 989, *Initial Evaluation*, compared to 60 in the third quarter. Also issued were 105 AFTO Forms 35, *Operator Permit*, compared with 35 issued in the third quarter. The number of proficiency tests more than tripled. A total of 363 tests were administered as compared to 98 in the third quarter.

A total of 6 FTD quotas were allocated to the Wing. A shortage of funds continued to force reduction in the number of personnel going TDY for additional training. The Wing initiated training programs to eliminate training deficiencies on an as-needed basis. During October, November, and December there were 64, 51, and 53 personnel in OJT, respectively. The units assigned at Cam Ranh Bay did an outstanding job in eliminating long-term trainees, decreasing the number from 10 in October to 1 in December.

A new task list for the MSEP was completed on 21 October. It included more Type "A" tasks and was forwarded to PACAF for approval. A total of 129 personnel were administered the MSEP written evaluation. This number was expected to rise during the next quarter due to the arrival of new personnel.

The de Havilland Technical Representative conducted formal and over-the-shoulder training during December and an overhead projector was received, greatly improving the classroom instruction.

Three personnel were assigned to the Material Control Section from Base Supply on an inter-base transfer, due to the shortage of personnel in the section. A total of five personnel rotated to the CONUS in October with no replacements. In November, 1/Lt. Harris Keller was assigned as Material Control Officer. In December, he was transferred to Vung Tau to fill their Supply Officer vacancy. Weekly meetings between the Supplies Management Officer and Material Control continued to benefit both Supply and Maintenance. Requisition status and stock posture of critical C-7A items were discussed at these meetings.

Verification procedures for NORS conditions were strengthened and an improved NORS checklist was established and put in use. Bench stock fill rates continued to be low. Action was taken by Material Control and Supply to upgrade requisitions to a priority 5 to improve the bench stock fill rates in the near future. The bench stock fill rate was 88.0 percent in October, 68.4 percent in November, and 83.3 percent in December. A completely revised MOI 65-2, *Material Control Procedures*, for the Wing was submitted, approved, and awaited publication at the end of the quarter. Delivery time from Base Supply to Maintenance was still a problem and Base Supply worked on this to provide better service. Maintenance also worked to reduce the number of expedites called into Demand Processing.

Cannibalizations in the Wing increased to a total of 867 in the quarter. The high cannibalization items were: Jack Assembly, Ramp; Receiver Transmitter RT-711 (AN/APN-158 Weather Radar); Nose Gear Drag Strut; Ramp Door Actuator; Radar Inverter; Generator Control Panel; Receiver Transmitter RT-220B; Generator Tachometer; Generator, Engine Driven; and Clamp, Augmentor Tube. These items were closely monitored both in expediting repair or NRTS and close coordination was maintained with the Awaiting Parts (AWP) monitor in Base Supply on items in AWP status.

The NORS rate for the Wing increased considerably during the quarter. The rate for the third quarter was 1.7 percent compared with an average of 4.1 percent for the fourth quarter.

In October, 59 Functional Check Flights (FCF) were flown, logging 35.9 hours. In November, 38 FCFs were flown, logging 21.5 hours. In December, 55 FCFs were flown, logging 38.1 hours. In October, 16 EURs and 2 MDRs were filed. In November, 6 EURs, 1 QCDR, and 1 MDR were filed. In December, 2 EURs, 5 QCDRs, and 1 MDR were filed. In October, QC performed 6 ORIs and 34 Phase Inspections. In November, QC performed 7 ORIs and 33 Phase Inspections. In December, QC performed 4 ORIs and 34 Phase Inspections. Routine surveillance spot inspections were performed on powered and non-powered AGE, tool boxes, pre-flights, fuel servicing, towing, facilities, and safety practices.

Personnel lost in the quarter were: SMSgt. A. L. Wheeler (APG – Airplane General), TSgt. R. W. Chapman (APG), TSgt. Melvin L. Williams (APG), MSgt C. Hubbard (ENG – Engine), and TSgt. Donald E. Bertrand (ENG). TSgt. T. G. James (APG), TSgt. W. E. Brown (ENG), SSgt. D. T. Mason (APG), and MSgt. J. H. Duke (ENG) were gained.

The OIC and NCOIC visited Da Nang AB on 27-28 October for the purpose of coordinating Quality Control procedures. The NCOIC made an assistance visit to Ben Hoa on 21 October and took the site a new set of technical orders. The NCOIC also made a Maintenance staff visit to the Bangkok Mission Site and coordinated the final inspection of the first IRAN aircraft during 22-29 in November. The Blue Ribbon Landing Gear Team supervised the repair of 74 in-flight landing gear discrepancies.

The Production Analysis section published the 1-PAF-U36 ("Monthly Maintenance Summary" prepared by TSgt. C. Smith), the 1-PAF-U66 ("NORS Rate/Cannibalizations"), the 1-HAF-O41 ("PA-CAF Maintenance Manning Report"), and other required monthly reports. The section revised Part II ("Chief of Maintenance Requirements") of 1-PAF-U36 to more readily identify problem areas and/or trends. On 27 September, Sgt. Kim D. Martin (AFSC 43251) was loaned from the Reciprocating Engine Shop to work as illustrator and draftsman. On 29 October, SSgt. Ronnie D. Larsen (AFSC 22351) was assigned as draftsman and Sgt. Martin returned to the Engine Shop on 12 November. SSgt. Carl H. McDonald (AFSC 43470) was lost on 23 October due to physical problems and he was medically evacuated to Tachikawa, Japan and from there to McDill AFB. TSgt. Holland (AFSC 43470) departed on 20 October due to emergency leave while on R&R. Since he had less than 90 days remaining on his tour, he was reassigned to the CONUS. On 15 November, SSgt. Robert Wysong (AFSC 43450) was borrowed from the 483 CAMS OLAA. SSgt. Wysong returned to Phu Cat on 20 November.

The Deficiency Analysis section completed On-Equipment Job Standards on 30 December for distribution on 1 January 1970. The standards established a more effective and closer control on the documentation of cannibalization. On 18 October, SMSgt. James Sexton (AFSC 43191) transferred to Vung Tau. SSgt Elwood H. Kelley (AFSC 43171A) was gained from Quality Control in October and MSgt. Harold V. See (AFSC 30171) was gained from the Communications/Navigation branch on 6 October.

In a combined effort, the Production Analysis and Deficiency Analysis Sections physically moved from Quality Control (Building 4715) to Communications/Navigation (Building 4701). The Deficiency Analysis Section performed an extensive study of "Blue Ribbon" reports on landing gear malfunctions. This was done in an effort to determine causes, corrective actions taken, etc. to afford AFLC information on parts break-down, consumption, and maintenance effectiveness. Both sections performed a study of the RT-711 (AN/APN-158 Weather Radar) to isolate causes of excessive malfunctions.

On 21 November, the Maintenance Analysis Section was inspected by MSgt. Benson of the 7AF IG team and he found no discrepancies.

He commented on the efficiency and effectiveness of the section. In December, 7AF nominated the 483 TAW for the Daedalian Maintenance Trophy under AFR 66-36. The section provided all maintenance statistics required for this nomination.

Administration

In the first quarter, 1/Lt. Fred J. Plimpton, III continued as the Historian.

Personnel shortages in the 483 TAW were pointed out to Col. Livingston, PACAF Director of Personnel (DP), during his visit in mid-December 1968. At that time, the Wing was authorized 923 personnel, but only 821 were assigned. During September through November, there were 85 "no-shows" of personnel who were scheduled to arrive from the CONUS. Critical shortages were in Aircraft Mechanic, AFSC 431XX (30 short); Flight Engineer, AFSC 435XX (12 short), and Comm/Nav Maintenance, AFSC 301XX (11 short). Col. Turk wrote a personal letter to Maj. Gen. Burl W. McLaughlin, Commander of the 834AD, to bring the manning situation to his attention.

Manning in many areas improved and the organizational structure of the Wing was static, except for the activation of the 6483 TGP. With the Administration Section 100 percent manned, it provided more efficient service. The section monitored over 50 one-time reports from higher headquarters, in addition to the normal, recurring reports required by higher headquarters. Local reports were also established to keep the Commander informed on areas such as Personnel Manning, First Term Airmen Reenlistment Rates, and the Junior Officer Retention Program.

Flight Engineer manning was considerably improved over the last quarter of 1968. At the beginning of 1969, there were 144 Flight Engineers authorized and 116 assigned. At the end of February, there were 113 assigned, but manning improved considerably during March. The quarter ended with 128 Flight Engineers (AFSC A435X0), 4 Flight Engineer qualified Flight Mechanics (AFSC A431X0), and 9 Flight Engineer qualified Loadmasters (AFSC A607X0), for a total of 144 assigned against the authorized 144. This was the most favorable manning position the Wing had experienced during the past two years. If the Flight Engineer inputs from Sewart AFB remained at the present level, the Wing was not expected to experience any shortages in the near future.

The Flight Engineer OJT program continued to be a problem. The Career Development Course (CDC), which was to be published in

February 1969, slipped to March and then to June. Because of difficulties for each individual squadron to develop a training package for use in Flight Engineer OJT, a conference of Flight Engineer Supervisors of OJT was held at Cam Ranh Bay on 20 January. The purpose was to pool the knowledge of each squadron in the Wing to develop meaningful skill training for the Flight Engineers. It was determined that each student could receive the necessary skill training by completing CDC 43112 and supplemental information on items 22, 24, 25, 26, 28, and 29 identified in the 435X0 Specialty Training Standard (STS). In addition, the 7-level skill would require completion of CDC 0006, *Management for Air Force Supervisors*. The six squadrons pooled questions to develop a phase test for the 30 sections listed in the STS. The questions compiled by the end of the quarter were reviewed for completeness. The phase test would be reproduced and distributed to each squadron early in the second quarter.

Col. Turk instituted a Junior Officer Retention Program to enlighten the younger, undecided officers and reaffirm to the already committed officers that they were wanted and needed by the Air Force.[38] Monthly reports by the Squadron Commanders were combined with a report on their First Term Airman Reenlistment Program.[39] The section assumed responsibility for processing TDY orders for the entire Wing and 611 orders were processed in the first quarter. Numerous problems pertaining to TDY order processing arose because of the location of four of the squadrons away from Cam Ranh Bay. Most problems concerned short notice requests which had to be hand carried or ones with improper formats. A draft Wing Regulation was coordinated to standardize the administrative orders system within the Wing, thereby reducing discrepancies.

In January, the 7AF Inspector General (IG), Col. William K. Bush, inquired, through the IG at Cam Ranh Bay, about alleged travel, per diem, and leave irregularities at Vung Tau, specifically about excessive issuance and misuse of blanket travel orders and canceled leave practices.[39] The issue of blanket TDY orders involved several situations: (1) The number of personnel on blanket TDY orders appeared to be excessive in terms of mission requirements. (2) There were instances in which personnel were assigned to a parent unit and spent their entire tour on TDY status at forward operating locations, and, as a consequence, drew per diem for the entire time. (3) Some of these personnel were there under blanket travel orders, while others were there under Special Orders, often involving periodic repetitive extensions of the TDY period. (4) There were instances in which other personnel were assigned PCS to the same forward operating locations and did not draw a per diem allowance.

The Senior Air Force Officer at Vung Tau made an inquiry[41] that resulted in the 483 TAW Executive Officer reporting to the IG on 12 February that the allegations were unfounded. The issue of canceled leave practices involved personnel using an approved leave authorization to obtain space available travel on military aircraft to destinations outside the Republic of Vietnam and then having the leave canceled upon return. Some situations involved cancellation of the leave authorization after the expiration of the leave period, even though the individual had actually departed from the Republic of Vietnam base. Another situation involved using TDY orders to obtain space required travel on aircraft by personnel who should have been in a leave status. The problems being investigated by the 7AF IG were not limited to Vung Tau and the 483 TAW. They appeared to involve units in other locations within Vietnam.

During February and March, the Wing reflected 100 percent manning. However, the fact was misleading if one were not also aware that the figure was attained only because of considerable overages within the maintenance skills. Aircrew shortages were considerably improved over those of the last quarter of 1968.[42] The problem was discussed and reviewed with the host unit at Cam Ranh Bay[43] and with the 834AD.[44] The Wing took other, more positive steps to counteract inequities.[45] Reorganization within the DCO[46] resulted in a loss of seven Airman positions and one officer position. Although this did not create immediate manning problems, all of the Command and Control Technicians (AFSC 274X0) were scheduled to rotate in July. In an effort to ensure continuity of operations in the Command Post, command assistance was requested to assure that individuals who would be gained in July would report as early as possible to Cam Ranh Bay to insure proper training prior to the departure of the current personnel.

On 15 March, the 6483 Tactical Group Provisional (TGP) was activated at Vung Tau.

In January, the 555th Civil Engineering Squadron (CES) started construction of an extension to the Engine Shop. This additional structure was dedicated and opened for business on 10 February. Although not much more than a wooden lean-to affixed to the hangar, it provided approximately 500 square feet of much-needed space. On 18 January, the first shower building with hot showers and flush toilets was opened in the enlisted men's living quarters at Cam Ranh Bay. A dearth of necessary power equipment delayed indefinitely the opening of the new

Communications/Navigation building.

The opening of two lavatories with hot water showers and flush toilet facilities was a significant improvement to the housing area. These niceties, which verged on being mental, if not physical necessities, greatly increased the morale of the unit. The officers' quarters were expanded through the addition of two new hootches, housing a total of 14 men. This expansion eased the burden on the older personnel and gave all individuals concerned a bit more room to roam. Other quarters for officers were garnered through aggressive bickering for the former C-130 crew quarters. Work orders were submitted to obtain building materials to rehabilitate all ten C-130 hootches through a self-help project.

In the middle of March, construction began on the AGE Shop building, which would replace the badly deteriorating tent in which AGE was maintained. The parking apron was painted to provide several additional parking spaces. No work on a new apron was scheduled to begin until FY70. The new taxiway, begun in October 1968, was completed. It linked the East and West ramps at the North end of the airfield and greatly expedited ground traffic.

The Wing applied to 7AF for approval for a circular drive between the Headquarters building and the main road. The driveway would be utilized only by honored guests and VIPs. The Wing staff continued to utilize the front driveway, located on the side of the building away from the main road. The Wing also applied to 7AF for an addition to the Headquarters building.

Inspectors from the Base Fire Department surveyed the hootches of all Wing personnel stationed at Cam Ranh Bay (CRB). The only significant problem uncovered was generally poor electrical wiring. The Civil Engineers indicated that they were waiting for a resupply of the materials needed to do the rewiring. Lack of materials also hindered other projects, such as the pouring of concrete sidewalks throughout the Wing housing area. The same inspectors, when viewing the non-rated junior officers' quarters on "RMK hill," found and disconnected numerous light fixtures in closets. These "hot closets" were intended to keep clothing dry in the humid climate, but the disadvantages outweighed the advantages. Wiring in such a closet was the probable cause of a fire which burned a Quonset hut to the ground.

There were several items of command interest within the Wing: Civil Engineering procedures at Vung Tau,[47] water conservation at Cam Ranh Bay,[48] standardization of the hootches at Cam Ranh Bay,[49] and a Living Area Improvement Council.[50]

44

In the second quarter, 1/Lt. Karl M. Fryer was the historian. The Administration Section enjoyed 100 percent manning, enabling it to maintain efficient service. One-time reports required by higher headquarters continued to increase. The section monitored over 60 one-time reports as compared with 50 during the first quarter. A Monthly Management Analysis Summary was initiated in July. The summary presented data in chart form from all sections in the Wing. The data was used for measuring mission effectiveness and for identifying trends which might affect future operations. The summary was continued throughout the quarter.

Manning continued to improve over the first quarter. At the end of July, the Flight Engineer manning was 144 authorized and 149 assigned. At the end of May, there were 159 assigned. At the end of June, there were 152 flight engineers (AFSC A435X0), 1 Flight Engineer qualified Flight Mechanic (AFSC A431X0), and 11 Flight Engineer qualified Loadmasters (AFSC A607X0) for a total of 164 assigned. Only with continual over-manning during the third quarter and the normal inputs from Sewart AFB could the Wing hope to alleviate the large DEROS hump in the fourth quarter.

The documented history of the Wing for the first quarter of 1969 received a rating of "Excellent" from 7AF. It was named "Best in 7th Air Force" and was nominated to PACAF for the award at that level.

In the third quarter, 1/Lt. Karl M. Fryer was assigned as Chief of Administration, replacing 1/Lt. Plimpton. He also continued as the Historian. The Administrative Section enjoyed 100 percent manning for the quarter and was able to maintain efficient service. The Monthly Management Analysis Summary, initiated in July, was also published in August and September. The data was utilized for measuring mission effectiveness and for identifying trends which might affect future operations.

The 483 TAW history for the second quarter of 1969 received a rating of "Excellent" from 7AF, the second consecutive quarter that this rating was attained.

In the fourth quarter, 1/Lt. Fryer continued as Historian. The Administration Section was manned at 80 percent and had to work many hours of overtime to maintain efficient service. MSgt. Lowell C. Anderson was assigned as NCOIC of Administration, replacing MSgt. Roger B. Peacock. The Mail and Distribution Clerk was A/1C Harold D. Songy.

The Wing was manned at 95 percent, 89 percent, and 90 percent during October, November, and December, respectively. Severe manning problems were experienced in the pilot (AFSC 1055E) and aircraft maintenance (AFSC 431XX) career fields. Wing reached its lowest manning strength for the year during the fourth quarter due to the high percentage of personnel rotating upon completion of their tour and failure of replacement personnel to arrive. However, the mission did not falter, due to the special all-out effort of the assigned personnel in these career fields.

The Management Analysis Summary, which had been published on a monthly basis since it was introduced, underwent numerous changes during the quarter, in an effort to present the data in a more useful and easily understood manner.

The 483 TAW history for the third quarter of 1969 received a rating of "Excellent" from 7AF, the third consecutive quarter that this rating was attained.

Supply and Support

In January, the Deputy Commander for Materiel/Logistics (DCML) arranged for the Communications/Navigation Shop to assist the Royal Australian Air Force (RAAF) contingent at Vung Tau[51] in the repair and return of their Tactical Air Navigation (TACAN) units. The RAAF had experienced difficulty in maintaining adequate spares for this system because of slow repair at Tan Son Nhut Air Base. Future assistance would be handled on a shop-to-shop agreement, whenever the need arose.[52]

A review of supply procedures revealed that Operating Instructions for resupply of aircraft parts at six missions sites of the Wing (Can Tho, Bien Hoa, Da Nang, Pleiku, Nha Trang, and Tan Son Nhut) were inadequate. The instructions did not provide for maintenance of consumption data or Do-In-From-Maintenance (DIFM) control. New procedures were developed during March, to be distributed in July.

At the request of WRAMA, the Wing jointly reviewed the Initial Supply Support Listing (ISSSL) which itemized all spares and equipment required to initially support a C-7A squadron. The listing was purged and validated through application of the previous year's consumption experience. The updated listing was completed on schedule and then forwarded to WRAMA.

Base Supply did some purging of their own. They instituted a property disposal program in which they provided the Wing with a list of items on the 483 TAW Material Base Supply account which they identified as excess to the C-7A aircraft. These items were then screened by the 483 TAW Material Control personnel prior to disposal. The selective review prevented the loss of spares which could be anticipated as future requirements by the Wing.

The practice of joint meetings (483 TAW and Base Supply) once a month was increased to twice a month in order to combat an increase in mutual supply problems. Specifically, the areas of difficulty were slow delivery of priority call-ins and a decline in bench stock issue fill rates. The effect of the slow deliveries, especially during the period of peak aircraft recovery, was to make it more difficult for the Wing to generate operationally ready aircraft. A sample delivery time survey for one week during January showed that only 25 percent of Priority 2 demands were meeting the 30 minute time standard, while 53 percent of Priority 3 demands were meeting the 60 minute standard. The average time for a Priority 2 demand was 8 minutes and 18 seconds. The average time for a Priority 3 demand was 1 hour and 42 minutes. While some improvement was noted after the problem was brought to the attention of the Chief of Supply, future delivery time surveys were ordered to further spotlight this troublesome area.

The problem of low fill rate on aircraft bench stock at CRB was largely due to delayed funding by Base Supply. As a consequence, base stocks were gradually depleted as the pipeline was shut off. The impact was felt by the Wing late in January and reached its maximum intensity during March. By the end of March, a slight improvement was noted as the flow of bench stock procurement increased. The hardest hit activity was the Engine Build Shop which experienced a high Engine Not Operationally Ready-Supply (ENORS) rate due to a lack of bench stock items. Much effort was expended to salvage and re-condition used parts from the teardown of repairable engines. The practice was followed to an extensive degree to avoid shutdown of the build-up line.

Personnel of the DCM staff visited seven sites during the quarter. From 2-4 January, Lt. Col. Stephens and 1/Lt. Robert E. Frank, Jr. visited Da Nang and Phu Cat. From 8-10 January, Lt. Col. Noel K. Robinson and MSgt. William E. Reaves visited Vung Tau. From 14-16 January, Lt. Col. Robinson visited Tan Son Nhut and Vung Tau. From 20-21 January, Lt. Col. Stephens visited Tan Son Nhut. On 18 February, Lt. Col. Robinson visited Tan Son Nhut. On 19 February, Lt. Col. Stephens visited Vung Tau. From 8-12 March, Lt. Col. Robinson visited the Bangkok mission site. From 21-23 March, MSgt. Reeves visited Vung Tau. From 27-28 March, Lt. Col. Robinson visited Vung Tau.

The Wing NORS rate remained well below the PACAF standard of 5 percent. In January, the rate was 1.6, in February it was 1.1, and

47

in March it was 2.4.[53] NORS was experienced on 79 different items compared with 30 during the last quarter of 1968. The average number of days to clear a NORS item was 2.2. Some of the troublesome items were a Jackscrew, Actuators, Strut, Torque Tube, Tube Assembly, and Transmitter.

Cannibalizations for the quarter were 551, compared with 614 for the preceding quarter. In January there were 161 cannibalizations (1.03 per 100 sorties), in February there were 197 cannibalizations (1.36 per 100 sorties), and in March there were 193 cannibalizations (1.19 per 100 sorties).

Bench stock support dropped, primarily due to an increase in the rates at Cam Ranh Bay and Vung Tau while the rate at Phu Cat remained level. In January, the rates at Cam Ranh Bay, Vung Tau, and Phu Cat were 84.5, 86.9, and 88.9 respectively, for an overall rate for the Wing of 89.1. In February, the rates at Cam Ranh Bay, Vung Tau, and Phu Cat were 83.7, 77.1, and 90.8 respectively, for an overall rate for the Wing of 86.0. In March, the rates at Cam Ranh Bay, Vung Tau, and Phu Cat were 78.2, 80.2, and 89.6 respectively, for an overall rate for the Wing of 85.1.

The Wing equipment fill rate continued to be very satisfactory at 96.4 percent, exceeding the PACAF standard of 95.0 percent.[54] There were 999 line items authorized and 948 on hand, giving a fill rate of 94.9 percent. There were 1708 pieces authorized and 1646 on hand, giving a fill rate of 96.4 percent.

The Wing PCS Movement Plan[55] was published and distributed in March. This plan provided instructions and guidance for all types of unit movements and incorporated and updated the Wing Mobility Plan as an Annex to the basic plan.

In the second quarter, the NORS rate continued a downward trend, attesting to the reliability of the NORS verification procedures established in March. The NORS rate in the Wing dropped from 2.5 percent in March to 0.8 percent in June. Cannibalizations at Cam Ranh Bay dropped from a high of 86 to a low of 44. The bench stock fill rates improved. Units at Cam Ranh Bay attained a high of 86 percent in June. Representatives of Base Supply and Material Control closely monitored requisitions to ensure continuation of a higher fill rate.

Supply support was generally very good during the quarter, despite the inherent problems of supporting units at three different bases and maintaining mission sites in forward areas. The biggest problem continued to be that of supporting 483 TAW units at Vung Tau using the dual main support base concept. Support responsibilities were shared

48

by Cam Ranh Bay (aircraft spares) and Tan Son Nhut (equipment, vehicles, and general supplies) with limited support from the Army at Vung Tau (facilities, POL, rations, and common expendables).

During the quarter, an exhaustive study was made by the 483 TAW Logistics/Plans Division to determine the feasibility of changing from the dual main support base concept to a single main support concept, i.e., entirely supporting Vung Tau units by either Cam Ranh Bay or Tan Son Nhut. The result of this study was the decision to retain a dual concept and focus staff attention on the transportation problems between Tan Son Nhut and Vung Tau. Periodic convoys were instituted from Vung Tau to Tan Son Nhut, manned by 483 TAW personnel. This alleviated the problem of excessive delivery delays and lost or stolen property from Tan Son Nhut. The Wing considered the addition of a fragged/dedicated C-7A mission between Tan Son Nhut and Vung Tau which would further improve timeliness and effectiveness of logistics support.

The Warner Robins Air Materiel Area (WRAMA) was able to supply enough Hamilton-Standard 43D50 propellers to relieve what had been a critical shortage ever since the Air Force took over the C-7A from the Army. Production was always lagging behind the requirements for propellers until June when enough items were received to fulfill the stoppage objective.

Although the Wing was tasked with the responsibility of building up modified R2000-4 engines, several deficiencies severely hampered this operation. The primary deficiency was a lack of technical data which, in turn, impeded progress in the research and identification of stock numbers needed to requisition Quick-Engine-Change (QEC) kits and bench stock items. Although much attention was given to this problem, little progress could be realized until adequate technical data was received from the depot. Until that time, the Wing would continue to build up engines on a part for part exchange basis.

There were 178 cannibalizations in April (1.1 per 100 sorties), 158 in May (1.0 per 100 sorties), and 102 in June (0.7 per 100 sorties). The items causing the most number of cannibalizations were: Cargo Door (26), Strut (18), Augmentor Clamp (15), Ramp Door Actuator (14), RT220B Transmitter (12), Vent Door Actuator (10), TACAN Inverter (9), ARC-27 UHF Radio Transmitter (7), Antenna (6), and Rod Assembly (3).

The NORS rate was 1.8 in April, 1.0 in May, and 0.8 in June. The items causing the most NORS conditions were: Cargo Door Actuator (10), Fuel Pressure Transmitter (7), Propeller (7), Flight Actuator (6),

Strut (6), Idler Arm (4), and Integral Oil Control (4), as recorded in the reports of the Weapon Support System Logistics Officer.

Prior to the second quarter, lateral support of NORS items between Cam Ranh Bay and Phu Cat was conducted by the Material Control function in the Wing and the items were shipped on the 490 mission. While it satisfied the immediate NORS requirements, this procedure caused incorrect consumption data for C-7A aircraft spares to be recorded in the Base Supply computers. It was decided that, henceforth, all lateral support of C-7A spares, including NORS requirements, would be done through the Base Supply functions at both locations. This procedure worked very well after its institution.

Comprehensive Maintenance Operating Instructions (MOI) were published, delineating responsibilities in regard to requisitioning and delivering aircraft spares to the 483 TAW mission sites. These procedures proved extremely effective in promoting supply discipline and expediting deliveries of the required spares. The greater control of aircraft spares enabled the host Base Supply to decrease the level of spares necessary to support Wing aircraft.

The Communications/Navigation facility at CRB was modified to enable its full utilization by maintenance personnel and a new AGE maintenance building was constructed at CRB. Self-help improvements around existing living areas was slowed due to the base program to move 483 TAW personnel into newly constructed barracks.

A new dining hall was built at Vung Tau to service all Air Force personnel and a headquarters building was constructed to provide office space for the newly formed 6483 TGP.

In the third quarter, a weekly supply meeting was held between 483 Material Control and the Base Supply Management Office (SMO) established to identify and resolve mutual problems. Verification procedures for Anticipated Not Operationally Ready-Supply (ANORS)/ Anticipated Not Fully Equipped (NFE), and Not Operationally Ready-Supply (NORS)/Not Fully Equipped (NFE) were a special subject for PACAF, 7AF, and Base Supply. Therefore, all verifications were constantly monitored and methods to improve procedures were studied. A letter was forwarded to the Chief of Supply requesting issues for certain items required for an aircraft launch and recovery kit. This kit was to be located in Material Control to provide the Chief of Maintenance with a quick reaction kit to reduce aircraft maintenance delays caused by Communications/Navigation (Comm/Nav) black box outages and assist in the recovery of aircraft isolated at forward airstrips because of maintenance difficulties.

Bench stock fill rate for Vung Tau was still a problem area. A team of Base Supply Bench Stock personnel and 483 Material Control personnel visited Vung Tau during September to inventory the Vung Tau bench stock. Base Supply took management action to improve the fill rate. The Vung Tau flight line bench stock had a fill rate of 56.1 percent in August. At the same time, the average for all other bench stocks at Vung Tau was 81.6 percent. This area would continue to be monitored by all personnel concerned until a higher fill rate and overall improvement was obtained.

In August, 1/Lt. Frank was sent to Vung Tau to replace Capt. James M. Calloway who, in turn, was brought to Cam Ranh Bay. Capt. Calloway was also assigned the additional duty of Material Control Officer because of the rotation of Capt. Reynolds. During the quarter, the Wing experienced a turnover of personnel in AFSCs 431X1, 702X0, and 301X1, some skills remaining unfilled for as many as 60 days. However, this did not directly cause any significant problems.

Because of the seasonal rains, there were a number of failures in Comm/Nav equipment, especially the RT-711 (AN/APN-158 Weather Radar), RT-220B, and the radar synchronizer, SN-358. The depot experienced problems supporting demands caused by high wear and tear factors experienced during missions, the lack of parts, and the return to the U.S. of personnel highly skilled in the repair of the radar and its components. Eight of the 14 authorized Comm/Nav personnel (AFSC 301X1) made a Permanent Change of Station (PCS) move during the quarter.

The short runways from which the C-7A operated, plus the increased requirement for braking during the seasonal rains, increased the consumption of brake pucks to a critical level. To meet the demands, the depot increased quantities procured and negotiated for an early delivery date of the brake pucks.

The NORS rate was 1.2 in July, 1.7 in August, and 2.1 in September. The items causing the most NORS conditions were: O-ring (16 instances), Actuator (7), Synchronizer (4), Nut (4), Strut (4), Drag Strut (3), Jack Screw (3), Jack Screw (2), Housing (2), and RT-711 (2), as recorded in the reports of the Weapon Support System Logistics Officer.

The number of cannibalizations were 189 in July, 215 in August, and 202 in September. The items causing the most cannibalizations were: Actuator (60), RT-711 (55), Synchronizer (42), Jack Screw (37), Inverter (22), RT-220B (14), Stub Pipe (11), Indicator (11), Trim Tab (10), and Inverter (8). The Bench Stock fill rate was 84.9 in July, 87.0

in August, and 87.2 in September.

The equipment authorized versus equipment on-hand showed: 402 units authorized with 380 on-hand at Phu Cat (94.5 percent complete), 580 units authorized with 555 on-hand at Vung Tau (95.0 percent complete), and 946 authorized 921 on-hand at Cam Ranh Bay (94.3 percent complete). The overall situation for the Wing was 1958 items authorized with 1856 on-hand (94.7 percent complete). This was below the PACAF standard of 95.0 percent. Some of the items of equipment causing concern were 32 Maintenance Platforms, Type B4-A; 1 Sling, Wing; 1 Sewing Machine; 3 Test Sets, TS1414, for the APX44; 2 Test Sets; 2 Signal Generators; and 1 Test Harness.

One of the two nose docks programmed for construction was completed. Work on the other was suspended by direction of 7AF as part of the overall SEA construction moratorium. Six two-story barracks were completed to be used for housing CAMS personnel. Moving began and was expected to be completed by the end of the year.

The aircraft maintenance building at Vung Tau was accepted in early August. Lighting was installed and was operative. Water lines to the latrine were scheduled to be completed in late October, to provide a completely operational facility where, in addition to maintenance work itself, debriefings and scheduled meetings could be held.

In the fourth quarter, the equipment authorized versus equipment on-hand showed: 400 units authorized with 385 on-hand at Phu Cat (96.2 percent complete), 592 units authorized with 580 on-hand at Vung Tau (97.9 percent complete), and 886 authorized with 840 on-hand at Cam Ranh Bay (94.8 percent complete). The overall situation for the Wing was 1878 items authorized with 1805 on-hand (96.1 percent complete). This was above the PACAF standard of 95.0 percent.

With the acceptance of the completed nose dock at Cam Ranh Bay, three permanent facilities were in use. Work was restarted on the fourth dock, with an expected completion date of late in January 1970. By the end of the quarter, move of the 483 CAMS personnel into the new two-story dormitories was approximately 80 percent complete. The new orderly room and mail room were used by 1 November and buildings for a day room were in place.

At Vung Tau, a rewiring of the maintenance hangars was completed by self-help and base effort.

Awards and Decorations

In the first quarter, the Awards and Decorations (A&D) program bogged down, but the causes of the problem were ascertained and corrected. For example, when the Air Force Form 642 was utilized for Air Medal recommendations based on the print out of the Air Force Form 5, the time required to begin the completion of the 642 was six weeks from the day that an individual flew his 35th mission. Necessarily, such recommendations following the aforementioned procedure did not meet the required 7AF suspenses. In answer, the Wing formulated and published a standardized form, modeled after that of the 458 TAS, to permit daily mission count by the Operations Clerk in the squadron. On the evening after an individual's 35th mission, the clerk could advise the squadron Awards and Decorations personnel to start the Air Medal paperwork.

Another tardiness problem revolved around the placement by supervisors of last-minute recommendations for award. Hypothetically, Captain Doe rotated in January, without having been put in for an award. His supervisor, Major Lamb, when rotating in May, made sure that he, himself, would be recognized and at the same time felt remorse about his non-recognition of Captain Doe. Hence, five months after the rotation of Captain Doe, he was recommended for an award. By the time the Form 642 arrived at 7AF, it was almost six months late and stood little chance of approval. It had taken almost a month to write to Doe's CBPO for information on his previous awards, to the Military Personnel Center (MPC) for inclusive dates, and to Doe for his Social Security Number and the total missions and hours flown in SEA. To counteract such delay, all supervisors were sent a letter reminding them that award recommendations for several awards could be submitted early.[56] This reminder served to spur supervisors.

Additionally, the Wing Commander created a requirement for written explanation of all late recommendations.[57] Moreover, the Awards and Decorations personnel of the Wing became the single point of contact queries to other headquarters. Answers to Wing messages and pre-printed letters[58] invariably were more rapidly forthcoming than responses to letters from the squadron. The paperwork involved in submission of awards was further speeded up through the use of a correction key[59] of standard and easily comprehended format. Time previously spent typing laborious "instructions for correction" letters was channeled elsewhere.

To aid the squadrons in properly completing their award recommendations the first time, every time, the Awards and Decorations personnel of the Wing implemented an Awards and Decorations fact sheet to be written and distributed as needed.[60] Items of particular interest covered during the first quarter were: Block 15 of the Air Force Form

642[61], the Legion of Merit[62], a sample Air Force Form 642[63], and conversion ratios for recommendation of the Air Medal.[64]

All awards presentations to personnel of the 483 TAW stationed at Cam Ranh Bay were presented by Col. Turk. The February ceremony was held out of doors and included a change of command of the 457 TAS. Included was the award of five Vietnamese Gallantry Crosses for activity over Duc Lap. The 26 March ceremony was held indoors. During the quarter, Capt. Louis D. Drew and Capt. Karl T. Bame were awarded Silver Stars, upgraded by 7AF from Distinguished Flying Crosses, for action over Duc Lap.

The February awards ceremony with change of command of the 457 TAS was a day to remember for MSgt. Peacock, NCOIC of Administration. He recalled that day:

> "I basically took care of the mail, letters, awards and decorations, etc. I set up the audio for the National Anthem to play during the change of command ceremony on the flight line and pushed the button at the appropriate time [that day], but no sound! After fiddling with it, I got it going about halfway through. I don't think Col. Turk was too pleased about it, but he did not say anything."[65]

The morale of the men of the 483 TAW was an ever present concern of the Wing Commander. Although morale seemed generally high, Col. Turk noticed that many men were not taking an R&R (Rest and Recuperation) or a leave during their tour of duty in Vietnam. He subsequently made it clear to all that R&R were rights to be enjoyed which would not be denied.[66]

During the first quarter, the Wing continued to support the base defense program in two ways. The Wing provided Central Security Control with 12 augmentees.[67] These men were called to duty most every evening during the last week in February and much of March. However, no complaints were heard from the individual augmentees themselves, as they had joined a volunteer program.[68]

The Wing also provided a Reserve Defense Force (RDF) of approximately 50 men, organized in four flights, with an NCO and an Officer in Charge.[69] Their duty, although never called upon to actually perform it, was to defend a specific portion of the alternate base perimeter.

Maj. William A. Jordan of the 459 TAS drew several unique Caribou postcards which were printed to show, in a humorous way, the diversity of the C-7A mission in Vietnam. Three of these postcards are shown on the facing page.

GREETINGS FROM "CARIBOU" COUNTRY

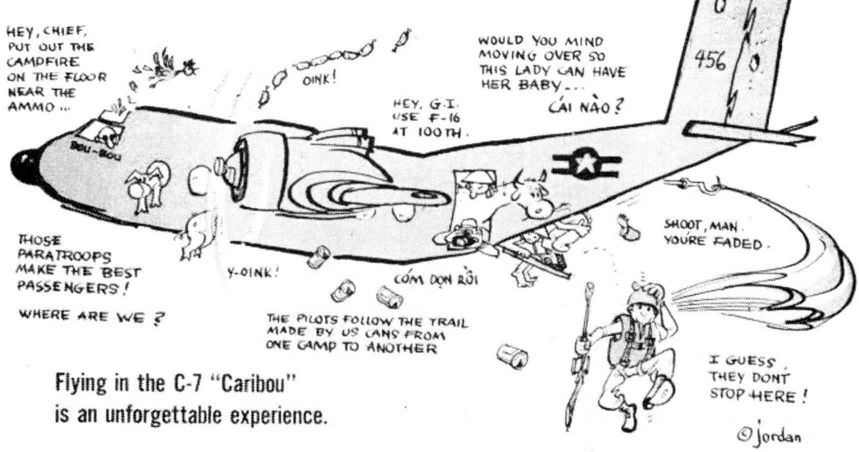

Flying in the C-7 "Caribou"
is an unforgettable experience.

GREETINGS FROM "CARIBOU" COUNTRY

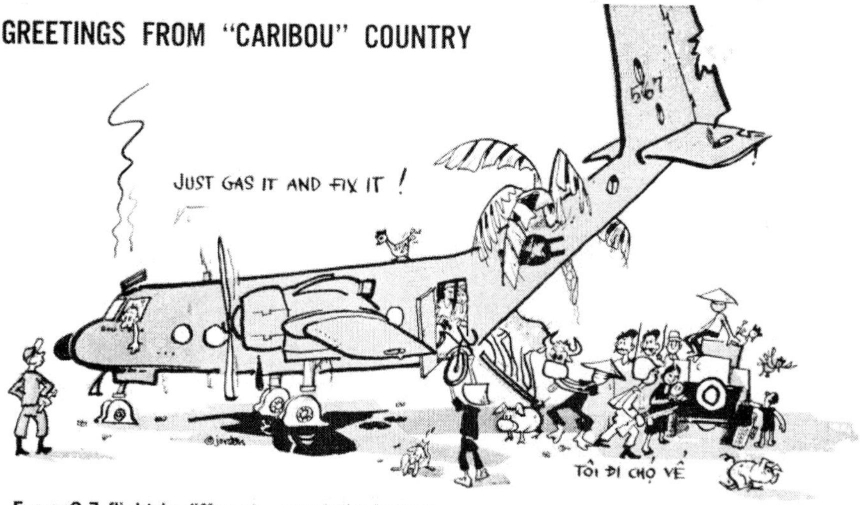

Every C-7 flight is different, except the last one...

GREETINGS FROM
"CARIBOU" COUNTRY

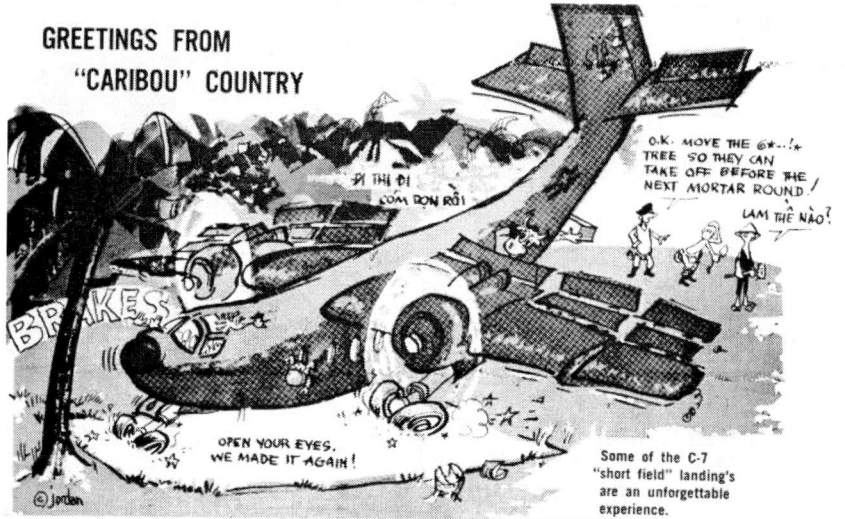

Some of the C-7
"short field" landing's
are an unforgettable
experience.

Numerous letters of appreciation were seen daily from Air Force units[70], the U.S. Army[71], Allied Forces[72], and higher headquarters.[73] Furthermore, nine Wing personnel received Category A correspondence for helping save a C-7A aircraft.[74]

In the second quarter, the Awards and Decorations program operated smoothly and almost all backlogs were eliminated. Squadron personnel became more familiar with requirements such as format, number of copies, etc. This reduced the number of recommendations which had to be returned for correction. The Wing continued to receive outstanding support from the Personal Affairs Branch of the CBPO with respect to processing of awards recommendations. Presentations of awards to personnel of the 483 TAW stationed at Cam Ranh Bay were presented by Col. Turk. Ceremonies were held on 15 April, 27 May, and 25 June.

The 483 TAW received the Air Force Outstanding Unit Award for the period 1 May 1967 to 30 July 1968.[75] The Commander of the 834AD presented the award at a ceremony held at Cam Ranh Bay on 18 June.

During the quarter, the Wing received many favorable communications. Some of the most notable were from Mr. Norman W. Hickey, Province Senior Advisor of the U.S. Aid Mission to Vietnam; General Nazzaro, Commander-in-Chief, PACAF; and Col. Harold A. Aaron, Commander, 5SFG.

In May, Lt. Gen. Julian J. Ewell, former Commander of the 9th Infantry Division, cited four C-7A squadrons (457 TAS, 458 TAS, 459 TAS, and 537 TAS) for their "enthusiastic efforts in support of his unit." In a letter to Maj. Gen. Burl W. McLaughlin, Commander of the 834th Air Division, that "Without the efforts of the Caribou units, the operations of the 9th Infantry Division would have been severely hampered." [76]

In the third quarter, many changes occurred in the Awards and Decorations program of the Wing. Among these was a new A&D Officer and new, more stringent, requirements for eligibility for award of the Distinguished Flying Cross (DFC). These included a single-event narrative for an End-of-Tour DFC and a tighter system of suspenses for all award recommendations submitted. In an effort to eliminate common problems, the Wing A&D Officer met with awards representatives of each of the seven squadrons on 4 September. Many problem areas were discussed and it was agreed that action was needed to reduce the requirements for the eligibility for End-of-Tour DFCs. Representatives from the CBPO, Personal Affairs Branch, also attended the meeting.

See Appendix VII for discussion of DFC criteria.

A ceremony was held on 29 August where 26 awards were presented by the Wing Vice Commander.

During the quarter, the Wing received many favorable communications. Some of the most notable were from General Creighton W. Abrams, Commanding General, USARV,[77] and from the Mayor and Military Commander of Cam Ranh City upon the occasion of the departure of Col. Turk.[78]

In the fourth quarter, awards ceremonies were held on 4 October and 13 November. On 9 October, Capt. Dorziack of the 7AF Awards and Decorations Section conducted a briefing to explain new policies in the upcoming AFM 900-3. Areas covered were (1) 7AF policies due to the lull in fighting, (2) DFC requirements, and (3) policy on eligibility for the Bronze Star Medal. To be eligible to be awarded the Bronze Star, an individual must have been in a position of some responsibility: (1) Management of people, (2) Management of funds, and/or (3) Management of resources.

The Wing was honored by distinguished visitors and Col. Christensen gave briefings on the mission to Gen. Nazzaro, Commander-in-Chief of PACAF, during his visit from 17-18 November; to Brig. Gen. Robert N. Ginsburgh, Commander of the Aerospace Studies Institute, during his visit on 6 December; and to the Honorable Philip N. Whitaker, Assistant Secretary of the Air Force for Installations and Logistics, during his visit from 6-7 December. All visitors commented favorably on the performance of the Wing.

Many letters of favorable communications were received. One of the more notable letters was from General Creighton W. Abrams, Commanding General, USARV, and endorsed by the 7AF Vice Commander, and the 834AD Commander in commemoration of the upcoming third anniversary of the 483 TAW.

Civic Action and Special Activities

In the first quarter, the 483 TAW set a letter to the 12th Tactical Fighter Wing (12 TFW)[79] saying that the 483 TAW would "deign to accept F-4 pilots as C-7A trainees." The 12 TFW replied that the Wing had "Only one quality pilot available – the 559th Tactical Fighter Squadron's mascot, 'Billygoat.' "[80] In a similar vein, after the 5SFG had given the 457 TAS an indigenous pig named "Porky" who found Cam Ranh Bay not at all to his liking, the Wing issued a Patient Transfer (PT-1)[81] that sent him to the 536 TAS at Vung Tau.

In the fourth quarter, all seven squadrons of the Wing participated in Project "Santa Bou" as they had done in previous years. The project was an effort by the personnel of the Wing to bring gifts and food to the Special Forces camps throughout Vietnam on the 24th and 25th of December. Six aircraft were painted with a Santa Claus face on the nose section and were flown with food, milk, ice cream, and guests to the men of the camps, both ARVN and U.S. In the two days, 83 Special Forces camps were either visited or were supplied by airdrops.

Airlift Accomplishments

During the first quarter, passengers hauled were 106,964 in January; 91,799 in February; and 107,294 in March for a total of 306,057. Cargo hauled was 8894.4 tons in January; 8543.9 tons in February; and 9340.6 tons in March for a total of 26,778.9 tons. In January, the Wing flew 15,553 sorties while logging 10,099.3 flying hours. In February, the Wing flew 14,432 sorties while logging 9487.8 flying hours. In March, the Wing flew 16,109 sorties while logging 10,781.8 flying hours. The sorties and flying hours for March were a new single month record for the Wing.

During the second quarter, passengers hauled were 102,341 in April; 94,814 in May; and 89,914 in June for a total of 287,069. Cargo hauled was 8662.8 tons in April; 8585.3 tons in May; and 7579.1 tons in June for a total of 24,827.2 tons. In April, the Wing flew 15,399 sorties while logging 10,192.0 flying hours. In May, the Wing flew 15,530 sorties while logging 10,224.0 flying hours. In June, the Wing flew 14,146 sorties while logging 9693.9 flying hours.

During the third quarter, passengers hauled were 93,025 in July; 88,170 in August; and 73,602 in September for a total of 254,797. Cargo hauled was 7326.0 tons in July; 8442.2 tons in August; and 6711.0 tons in September for a total of 22,479.2 tons. In July, the Wing flew 14,221 sorties while logging 10,083.5 flying hours. In August, the Wing flew 15,199 sorties while logging 10,396.0 flying hours. In September, the Wing flew 13,115 sorties while logging 9468.0 flying hours.

During the fourth quarter, passengers hauled were 76,300 in October; 97,649 in November; and 104,434 in December for a total of 278,383. Cargo hauled was 7441 tons in October; 7855 tons in November; and 8985 tons in December for a total of 24,281 tons.

Commander's Summary

First Quarter 1969[82]

"No problems from the previous quarter have remained unsolved and no problems during the next quarter have been contemplated. Our only prognostication for the future would be continued and greater success. Per aspera ad astra." ["Through hardships to the stars."]

Second Quarter 1969[83]

"In summary, the 483rd Tactical Airlift Wing continued to do an outstanding job in support of the USAF mission in Southeast Asia. Esprit de Corps and morale in the units remained high. We do not anticipate any problems during the next quarter which would seriously jeopardize our combat capability."

"Third Quarter 1969[84]

"In summary, the 483rd Tactical Airlift Wing continued to do an outstanding job in support of the USAF mission in Southeast Asia. Esprit de corps and morale in the units remained high. We do not anticipate any problems during the next quarter which would seriously jeopardize our combat capability."

Fourth Quarter 1969[85]

"In summary, the 483rd Tactical Airlift Wing continued to do an outstanding job in support of the USAF mission in Southeast Asia. Esprit de corps and morale in the units remained high. We do not anticipate any problems during the next quarter which would seriously jeopardize our combat capability."

End Notes – 483 TAW

[1] *19690101-19691231 483 TAW History*
[2] *483 TCW OpOrd 67-1*, 23 Dec 1966, paragraph 2
[3] Letter from Commander, 12 TFW to Col. Turk, 31 Mar 1969
[4] *19690101-19690331 483 TAW History*
[5] *Hq. PACAF SO G-326, 7 Dec 1966* and *Hq. PACAF SO G-44, 3 Mar 1969*
[6] *19690101-19690331 483 CAMS History, page vi* and *457 TAS GO-1, 19 Feb 69*
[7] *483 TAW SO G-3, 4 Sep 1969*
[8] Letter from 12TFW/OMO to Commander 483 TAW, 15 Feb 1969,

Subject: Change in Unit Manning Document

[9] Hq. PACAF letter, 8 Mar 1969, Subject: Change in Manpower Authorization

[10] *Hq. PACAF SO G-44, 3 Mar 1969*

[11] *483 TAW SO G-1, 18 Mar 1969*

[12] *Hq. PACAF SO G-1, 18 Mar 1969*

[13] *Hq. 7AF SO G-1153, 24 Mar 1969*

[14] Letter from 483 TAW/C to 834AD/C, 23 Oct 1968, Subject: Reorganization of the 483 Tactical Airlift Wing

[15] 483 TAW letter to 834AD, 28 Mar 1969 Subject: Termination of 483 Tactical Airlift Wing In-Country Mission Sites

[16] "Charts, Mission Data for January, February, and March 1969" in *19690101-19690331 483 TAW History*

[17] *7AF SO G-2429, 19 Jun 1969*

[18] *483 TAWM 51-27*

[19] 483 TAW DCO letter to All Units and Staff Agencies, 1 Apr 1969, Subject: 483 TAW Stan/Eval Review Panel Minutes

[20] Letter from 834AD/DOE, Subject: C-7A/C-123 Stan/Eval Conference Minutes, undated

[21] 483 TAW DCOS letter, dated 10 July 1969, Subject: 483 TAW Stan/Eval Review Panel Minutes

[22] 483 TAW/DCOS letter, Subject: 483 TAW Stan/Eval Review Panel Minutes, dated 10 Oct 69

[23] 483 TAW/DCOT letter, Subject: In-Country Training Program

[24] 483 TAW DCOS letter, Subject: 483 TAW Stan/Eval Review Panel Minutes

[25] MSgt. George R. Stevenson, T/Sgt. David D. Merrill, TSgt. Vincent A. Verastro, SSgt. Don R. Bednarski, A/1C William Osborne, Jr., and 1/Lt. Thomas G. Murphey, II (7AF SO G-1164, 24 Mar 1969)

[26] 483 TAW/C letter, "Flight Safety" dated 23 Jan 1969

[27] 483 TAW/C letter, "Aircraft Accident Prevention", dated 22 Feb 1969]

[28] Message 02100400Z Jan 69, Hq. 535 Tac Alft Sq to 483 TAW, "USAF Major Aircraft Accident (C-7A) Report No. 1", 2 Jan 1969

[29] Msg 02312452 [*sic*] Hq. 535 Tac Alft Sq to 483 TAW, "USAF Major Aircraft Accident (C-7A) Report No. 2", 23 Jan 1969]

[30] Message from Vice Comdr, 483 TAW, "USAF C-7A Aircraft Incident Report", 18 Jan 69

[31] Letter from SGMF to 483 TAW/C, Subject: Fatigue Evaluation, 17 Jan 1969

[32] Letter from 483 TAW/C to Council Members, Subject: Minutes of

the Quarterly Integrated Safety Council Meeting

[33] 483 TAW/C Letter to Council Members, Subject: Minutes of Quarterly Integrated Safety Council Meeting, 20 June 1969

[34] 483 TAW/C Letter to Council Members, Subject: Commander's Integrated Safety Council on 15 Sep 1969, dated 24 Sep 1969

[35] "Rules of Engagement" in C-7A Caribou Association Newsletter 19-1, pg. 7

[36] Letter from Chief MSET Det 4 of 6003 Support Squadron to 483 TAW/C, Subject: MSET Visit, pg. 9 para 5 of Attachment to letter, 25 Jan 1969

[37] Letter from Senior USAF Officer at Vung Tau to DCO 483 TAW Subject: Progress Report, 11 Mar 1969

[38] Letter from 483 TAW/C to All Staff Agencies and Units, Subject: Counseling Young Air Force Officers

[39] Letter from 483 TAW/C to All Units, 28 Mar 1969, Subject: Junior Officer Retention and First Term Airman Reenlistment Programs

[40] Letter from 7AF IG, 15 Jan 1969, Subject: Alleged Travel, Per Diem and Leave Irregularities

[41] Letter from Col. George D. Rawlings, 536 TAS Commander and Senior Air Force Officer at Vung Tau, 11 Feb 1969, Subject: Alleged Travel, Per Diem and Leave Irregularities

[42] Letter from 483 TAW/DCM to 483 TAW/C, Subject: Personnel Shortages

[43] Letter from 12 TFW/C to 483 TAW/C, 21 Dec 1968, Subject: Manning Assistance

[44] Letter from 483 TAW/C to 843AD/C, 12 Dec 1968

[45] Message from 12 CSG to 7AF CBPO, Jan 1969, Subject: C-7A Aircrew Manning

[46] PACAF letter, 15 Feb 1969, Subject: Change in Unit Manning Document

[47] Letter from 483 TAW Assistant DCO, Subject: Civil Engineering Procedures, 10 Jan 1969

[48] Letter from 483 TAW Vice Commander, Subject: Water Conservation, 3 Mar 1969

[49] Letter from Commander 483 CAMS, Subject: Standardization of Hootches, 3 Feb 1969

[50] Letter from Commander 483 CAMS, Subject: Living Area Improvement Council, 22 Jan 1969

[51] RAAF No. 35 Squadron was the first operational RAAF unit sent to Vietnam (6 Caribous at Vung Tau) and the last to leave. The "Wallabys" were presented with 128 USAF Air Medals, belatedly

awarded on 4 April 2008 to the pilots and crews who flew beside their American counterparts. The ceremony was held at the Australian War Memorial in Canberra, Australia. U.S. Ambassador Robert McCallum made the presentation, describing their efforts as "nothing short of amazing."

[52] 483 TAW/DCM letter to 483 TAW/C, Subject: Assistance to Royal Australian Air Force, 5 Feb 1969

[53] Monthly reports of the Weapon Support System Logistics Officer

[54] Equipment Status Reports prepared by MSgt. Reaves in the *Monthly Maintenance Status Reports*

[55] *483 TAW OPLAN 400-69*

[56] 483 TAW Chief of Administration letter, Subject: Awards Nomination

[57] 483 TAW/C letter, Subject: Awards Submission, 28 Mar 1969

[58] 483 TAW Chief of Administration letter, Subject: Request for Information

[59] Correction Sheet from Chief of Administration 483 TAW to Whom It May Concern

[60] 483 TAW Chief of Administration letter to All Units, Subject: Memo #1, 1 Jan 1969

[61] 483 TAW Chief of Administration letter to All Units, Subject: Memo #2, 15 Jan 1969

[62] 483 TAW Chief of Administration letter to All Units, Subject: Memo #3, 1 Feb 1969

[63] 483 TAW Chief of Administration letter to All Units, Subject: Memo #4, 15 Feb 1969

[64] 483 TAW Chief of Administration letter to All Units, Subject: Memo #5, 1 Mar 1969

[65] E-mail from CMSgt. Peacock to author on 24 May 2014

[66] 483 TAW/C letter to All Personnel, Subject: R&R and Leaves, 10 Feb 1969

[67] Letter from 483 CAMS Commander to 483 TAW/DCO and CRB based squadrons, Subject: Providing Security Police Augmentees, 22 Feb 1969

[68] Letter from 483 CAMS Commander to All Squadron Personnel, Subject: Personnel for Security Police Augmentees, 26 Mar 1969

[69] Letter from 483 CAMS Commander to All Assigned and Attached Personnel, Subject: Reserve Defense Force Personnel, 22 Feb 1969

[70] Letter from the IFFV Tactical Air Liaison Officer to 483 TAW/C, Subject: Direct Support for Ben Het Special Forces Camp, 2 Mar 1969

[71] 483 TAW/C to 535 TAS/C, Subject: Favorable Communication, 31

Jan 1969

[72] Group Captain B. Adams, RAAF letter to 483 TAW/C, 25 Jan 1969

[73] Letter from Commander, 834AD to 483 TAW/C, Subject: Letter of Appreciation, 22 Jan 1969

[74] 483 TAW/C letter to Individuals Recognized, Subject: Favorable Communication, 7 Feb 1969. Individuals recognized were: Col. Christensen, Lt. Col. Charles J. Hill (483 TAW/Operations), Lt. Col. Eugene M. Simmons (457 TAS/Instructor Pilot), Maj. Hanavan (483 TAW/QC), Maj. Richard M. Lantz (483 TAW/DCOS), Maj. Donald G. Lotermoser (483 TAW/Command Post), Capt. Frederick W. Fowler (483 TAW), Capt. John E. Haseltine (483 TAW/Safety), and SSgt. Patrick L. Hoxie (483 TAW).

[75] Department of the Air Force, SO GB-571, 1 Nov 1968

[76] *Caribou Country Clarion, Vol. 1-7*, May 1969

[77] Commander, USMACV letter to Officers and Men of 834th AD, endorsed by 834AD/C and 483 TAW/C

[78] Letter from the Mayor and Military Commander, Cam Ranh City, to Col. Wilbert Turk, 30 August 1969

[79] Letter from 483 TAW/C to 12 TFW/C, Subject: Pilot Training, 18 Mar 1969

[80] Letter from 12 TFW/C to 483 TAW/C, Subject: C-7A Pilot Training Volunteers, 27 Mar 1969

[81] Letter from Hq. 483 TAW, Subject: "PTO 1", 22 Mar 1969

[82] 483 TAW Commander's Summary, 31 March 1969, by Col. Wilbert T. Turk

[83] 483 TAW Commander's Summary, 30 June 1969, by Col. Wilbert T. Turk

[84] 483 TAW Commander's Summary, 30 September 1969, by Col. Keith L. Christensen

[85] 483 TAW Commander's Summary, 31 December 1969, by Col. Keith L. Christensen

Fini Flight of Col. Wilbert T. Turk (Copyright © 2014 Roger Peacock)

Col. Keith L. Christensen (Copyright © 2014 USAF Photo)

457th Tactical Airlift Squadron [1]

The primary mission of the 457th Tactical Airlift Squadron (457 TAS) at Cam Ranh Bay was to maintain a combat ready tactical airlift capability to perform air-land and airdrop assault missions into objective areas in direct support of counter-insurgency operations; to conduct combat logistical airlift of troops, supplies, and equipment needed to execute and support tactical or strategic missions; and to provide a mobile combat readiness capability to support contingency commitments of the Commander, U.S. Military Assistance Command Vietnam-Thailand (COMUSMACV-THAI). The squadron supported the 5th Special Forces Group (5SFG); the 1st Cavalry (1Cav); United States Army, Vietnam (USARV); First Field Force Vietnam (IFFV); Second Field Force Vietnam (IIFFV); Military Assistance Command, Thailand (MACTHAI); and Civil Operations and Rural Development Support (CORDS).

To accomplish the mission, the squadron was authorized 16 aircraft in the first quarter. The average daily availability was 14 aircraft, with one aircraft in IRAN and one in Corrosion Control. The squadron was authorized 16 aircraft during the second quarter, 16 were assigned, and no aircraft were gained or lost. The squadron was authorized 16 aircraft during the third quarter, 16 were assigned, and no aircraft were gained or lost. The squadron was authorized 16 aircraft during the fourth quarter, 16 were assigned, and no aircraft were gained or lost.

Lt. Col. Edward J. Thielen replaced Lt. Col. Donald L. Flood as Squadron Commander on 19 February.[2] On 1 March, Lt. Col. Robert L. Ruse replaced Lt. Col. Elbert L. Mott as Operations Officer and Maj. Alvin L. Walker replaced Maj. Lawrence L. Brown as Chief of Stan-Eval. On 22 September, Lt. Col. Thielen was replaced by Lt. Col. Roger E. Deyhle.

Operations

The squadron airlifted routine cargo, performed med-evac, Emergency Resupply, Tactical Emergency, Combat Essential, and airdrops of supplies equipment and personnel. The squadron was primarily dedicated to the airlift requirements of the 1Cav in III Corps, but it also performed missions for IFFV, IIFFV and 5SFG.

In the first quarter, the squadron was authorized 50 pilots and 24 flight engineers, with 47 pilots and 23 Flight Engineers assigned at the end of the quarter.

On 3 March, the 2,773rd consecutive mission, with no initial delays encountered, was launched at 0615. This represented 365 days of successful on-time launches. The completion of one year without a delay was heralded as a milestone in Southeast Asia airlift history. Coverage of the historic event was provided by the 7th Air Force News. The record was accomplished under adverse weather conditions, including typhoons, monsoon rains; and demanding combat conditions for the C-7A aircraft, crews, and maintenance personnel. The aircrews and maintenance personnel were proud of their record and continued their outstanding efforts in their drive for the next goal – two years without a delay. Increased operational effectiveness was achieved in the first quarter, with significant increases in all phases of airlift, even though fewer missions were flown than during either of the last two quarters of 1968.

One crew was maintained on alert daily at Cam Ranh Bay to perform special missions as required.

The change in bases supported during the quarter affected the average sortie length to such an extent that three Aircraft Commanders, upgraded after 15 March, flew a total of 18 missions and stood alert for three days in order to meet the scheduled daily commitment.

The squadron was authorized 50 pilots and 24 flight engineers, with 51 pilots and 23 Flight Engineers assigned at the end of the second quarter.

Lt. Col. Robert L. Ruse continued as the Operations Officer in the second quarter. On 14 June, the squadron began aerial resupply of Ben Het (V-179) by airdrops. These missions were flown to assist the 537 TAS.

The actions of 1/Lt. Curt Fischer and his crew on 20 June are reflected in his DFC citation:

> "First Lieutenant Curt Fischer distinguished himself by extraordinary achievement while participating in aerial flight as a C-7A Copilot near the Special Forces Camp at Ben Het, Republic of Vietnam, on 20 June 1969. On that date, Lieutenant Fischer volunteered to fly an Emergency Resupply airdrop mission to the besieged camp personnel who were critically low on supplies and in imminent danger of being overrun. With complete disregard for his personal safety, Lieutenant Fischer flew through extremely heavy hostile ground fire at low altitude to successfully airdrop urgently needed supplies to the camp defenders. The professional competence, aerial skill and devotion to duty displayed by Lieutenant Fischer reflect great credit upon himself and the United States Air Force." [3]

This airdrop mission over Ben Het was the last of a 3-4 plane "stick" with A-1E escorts.

Major Fischer recently recalled that day:

"My name showed up on the schedule during the middle of the week. I remember sitting around the living room of our hootch having a beer and laughing while my erstwhile roommates divided up all my worldly possessions in case I didn't return from the mission. They claimed my stereo, paintings, TV, and whatever else. I thought it quite funny at the time.

Flying out the next day, my aircraft commander was Lt. Col. Edgar Thielen. He was a good pilot who treated his copilots well. When it was time to operate the radios he would put on his reading glasses to dial in the different frequencies. Then, he would take them off and fly the airplane.

We flew to Phu Cat and briefed in one of their buildings. There were to be three or four C-7A's making the drop. We briefed the mission, then sat around waiting for the departure time. I remember the horseplay that went on as a couple of the copilots wound up wrestling on the floor. We waited while the pallets were loaded onto the planes, then we left.

The actual drop went off well enough. We orbited the area and then were called in by the ground forces. Memory is now vague. We started in on our run and an A-1E flew ahead of us trying to draw fire. There was another A-1E flying behind us. I remember noting that there were red 'flares' coming between the lead A-1E and our plane. I thought they were from the camp. I didn't learn until after we had finished our run that the flares were tracers and there were 13 or so bullets between the red tracers. I was rather naive at the time. We dropped our load, left the area without difficulty or holes in the aircraft, and flew back toward Cam Rahn to finish the day's mission.

That night, back at the hootch, we had a celebratory beer as I collected back all of my worldly possessions. The missions continued. No one from Cam Rahn was hurt and life went on. I received the DFC when I was stationed at McGuire AFB sometime in 1970. It was a nice surprise. No heroics, no outstanding feats of airmanship. We did our jobs." [4]

The actions of Maj. Charles W. Hardie and his crew on 21 June are reflected in his DFC citation:

"Major Charles W. Hardie distinguished himself by extraordinary achievement while participating in aerial flight as

Flight Examiner in a C-7A aircraft near the Special Forces Camp at Ben Het, Republic of Vietnam on 21 June 1969. On that date, Major Hardie flew an emergency resupply airdrop mission to the besieged Special Forces camp personnel who were in need of fresh supplies of food, water and ammunition. Realizing the inherent dangers involved with low altitude, slow airspeed airdrops and intense hostile ground fire, Major Hardie voluntarily completed the hazardous mission and helped to prevent the overrun of the camp. The professional competence, aerial skill, and devotion to duty displayed by Major Hardie reflect great credit upon himself and the United States Air Force." [5]

The actions of 1/Lt. John D. Mood, Jr. and his crew on 28 June are reflected in his DFC citation:

"First Lieutenant John D. Mood distinguished himself by extraordinary achievement while participating in aerial flight as Copilot of a C-7A Aircraft near the Special Forces Camp at Ben Het, Republic of Vietnam on 28 June 1969. On that date, Lieutenant Mood made an emergency resupply airdrop to the besieged Special Forces Camp personnel who were in need of fresh supplies of food, water and ammunition. Realizing the inherent danger involved with low altitude, slow airspeed airdrops and intense hostile fire, Lieutenant Mood voluntarily completed the hazardous mission and helped to prevent the overrun of the camp. The professional competence, aerial skill and devotion to duty displayed by Lieutenant Mood reflect great credit upon himself and the United States Air Force." [6]

At the end of the quarter, the squadron had expanded its total of days without an initial launch delay to a record 474.

In the third quarter, the squadron was authorized 50 pilots and 24 flight engineers, with 50 pilots (3 Flight Examiners, 8 Instructor Pilots, 11 Aircraft Commanders, 12 First Pilots, 13 Copilots, and 3 Unqualified) and 30 flight engineers (4 Flight Examiners, 4 Instructor Flight Engineers, 19 qualified Flight Engineers, 1 Instructor Loadmaster, and 2 qualified Loadmasters) assigned.

On 5 September, the squadron ended its run of 551 days of launch departures without a delay.

In the fourth quarter, Lt. Col. Robert L. Ruse continued as the Operations Officer until replaced by Lt. Col. William M. Crane on 16 November. The 7AF IG inspected the squadron from 18 to 22 November.

The squadron was authorized 50 pilots and 24 flight engineers, but the pilot strength was never equal to the number authorized. The squadron began the quarter with 43 pilots and ended the quarter with 38. Throughout the fourth quarter, 24 Flight Engineers were authorized and 25 were assigned.

The actions of Maj. Nathan T. Richardson, Jr. and his crew on 11 November, while bringing to Bu Dop a new million power searchlight on a Jeep, are reflected in his DFC citation:

> "Major Nathan T. Richardson, Jr. distinguished himself by extraordinary achievement while participating in aerial flight as a C-7A Instructor Pilot near the Special Forces Camp at Bu Dop, Republic of Vietnam, on 11 November 1969. On that date, Major Richardson flew a Combat Essential Mission into the beleaguered Special Forces Camp. With complete disregard for his personal safety, Major Richardson landed his aircraft while the landing strip was under attack and off-loaded the cargo under heavy hostile fire. His determination and superior airmanship enabled him to skillfully deliver the vitally needed cargo to the camp defenders. The professional competence, aerial skill, and devotion to duty displayed by Major Richardson reflect great credit upon himself and the United States Air Force." [7]

The actions of Lt. Col. Dawson N. White and his crew on 13 November are reflected in his DFC citation:

> "Lieutenant Colonel Dawson N. White distinguished himself by extraordinary achievement while participating in aerial flight as a C-7A Instructor Pilot at Bu Dop, Republic of Vietnam on 13 November 1969. On that date, Colonel White flew on a Combat Essential mission to deliver urgently needed supplies. Despite marginal weather conditions and the threat of hostile fire, Colonel White courageously accomplished the vital airlift mission without loss of personnel or equipment. The professional competence, aerial skill and devotion to duty displayed by Colonel White reflect great credit upon himself and the United States Air Force." [8]

Lt. Col. David Larson recalled an exciting morning flight out of Bien Hoa:

> "Cam Ranh Bay crews usually flew out in the morning and returned to CRB by evening. A few missions would remain overnight at Bien Hoa AB and then do another day's flying before returning. At CRB, we would get an intel briefing prior to departure. At Bien Hoa, we had no intel source so we usually got it from the first morning crew arriving from CRB. This morning they were delayed for some reason so we had no report on B-52 strikes.
> Our load was ammunition or fuel in rubber bladders to Bu

Dop (V-121), north of Saigon near the Cambodian border. There was hostile action close by and there was a 'FAC (Forward Air Controller) and fighter' requirement for the airstrip. We had to have contact with the local FAC and the FAC had to be in contact with nearby available fighter aircraft before we could land.

We had a TOT (Time Over Target of 9:30 AM). After a nice flight, we called the FAC at about 9:20, south of the field. He said that the fighters had not checked in and to hold off to the south for a while. We throttled back to a low power setting for holding. There was a lot of radio noise and conversation between the FAC and ground units in combat, lots of loud chaotic chatter. At 9:35, the Bou Dop ramp blew up, right where we would have been parked while unloading. The radios went really crazy with excited yelling and chatter. We held for a while and after 15 or 20 minutes the FAC called us and stated the obvious. We couldn't land.

We called for an artillery firing advisory. They read us the grid co-ordinates of an Arc Light (B-52 bomb strike) for our position from the present time and the next 15 minutes. In all the radio noise, we did not hear the alert on the Guard frequency. I went to max power and pushed the nose down to gain airspeed. Almost immediately, the plane started shaking with what we thought was engine backfiring from jamming the power from a low setting to max power. After flying several miles clear of the bombing area, we turned and looked back to see a huge cloud of smoke and debris were the bombs had impacted, about where we had been. We were feeling the shock waves from the exploding bombs.

When we got back to the Bien Hoa traffic pattern, a cloud layer pushed us about 200 feet lower on the downwind leg. About mid field, a momentary cloud break in front revealed a Vietnamese DC-3 head-on just barely above us about one second away. I thought it would take the tail off our Caribou. Seconds later, we were still flying and then made an uneventful and relieved landing at Bien Hoa. For this flight, an NCO at the aerial port had decided to ride with us as he had been in-country several months and wanted to go along on a flight. He said he was never going out again. We flew the rest of the day, happy to be alive and content with somewhat less thrilling combat bush flying."

Lt. Col. Larson was a waivered Aircraft Commander when his actions and those of his crew were reflected in his DFC citation:

"First Lieutenant David E. R. Larson distinguished himself
by extraordinary achievement while participating in aerial flight

70

as Aircraft Commander of a C-7A aircraft at Song Mao airfield, Republic of Vietnam on 27 November 1969. Lieutenant Larson flew a critically needed flight test crew from Cam Ranh Bay AB to the Song Mao airfield to effect the recovery of a damaged aircraft engine and the maintenance personnel who performed an engine change. During the night recovery operation at the small, insecure airfield, Lieutenant Larson exposed himself to hostile small arms fire and successfully completed the hazardous mission without the loss of personnel or equipment. The professional competence, aerial skill, and devotion to duty displayed by Lieutenant Larson reflect great credit upon himself and the United States Air Force." [9]

Lt. Col. David Larson recalled that challenging mission:

"I was sitting on alert at Cam Ranh Bay on November 27th. During the afternoon, my crew was one of two crews alerted to help recover a Caribou and some Air Force maintenance personnel. A C-7A had been on the ground for a couple of days at Song Mao (V-18) and maintenance men were finishing an engine change on it. Intel now thought that the airfield might be overrun by Viet Cong that evening and wanted the maintenance men and, hopefully, the aircraft, evacuated ASAP.

We landed at dusk. The maintenance men accomplished a miracle and had the grounded C-7A ready to go with the damaged engine tied down inside. We kept the engines running as the other crew ran over to the grounded Caribou while most of the maintenance men climbed into our aircraft. By now, it was dark. They got the engines started and taxied to the runway. We followed in case they had a problem and needed to abandon their aircraft. We both made lights-out takeoffs from the dark airstrip.

Once we were in the air, we saw a lot of reddish orange streaks arching towards us, some getting pretty close. The rest of the night flight back was routine with the usual terrain and weather to work around. I never heard if we had any bullet holes and we never heard anything about the planes we brought back. The aircraft I flew that evening was C-7A S/N 62-9760, which is now on display at the Air Mobility Command Museum in Dover, DE.

Overall, it was one mission of many during one of the most challenging and exciting years of my life. As a separate bit of trivia, we had a standing request to find a rainstorm to fly through on the homeward leg to help wash the day's dirt off the airplane."

An additional daily mission was acquired on 14 December and was supported through the remainder of the month. No additional aircraft or aircrew support was required. The missions were flown with existing resources. New launch and recovery procedures became effective on 15 December.

The squadron participated in a massive airlift on 31 December and assisted materially in setting new sortie, flying hour, and total tonnage records for the Wing.

Training and Stan-Eval

In the first quarter, Maj. Ralph P. Madero was Scheduling/Training Officer until relieved by Lt. Col. Lewis E. Dix on 2 February. The squadron did not use the "formed" crew system.

A significant number of qualified Aircraft Commanders, Instructor Pilots, and Flight Examiners rotated during the quarter. These included the Squadron Commander, Lt. Col. Donald L. Flood; the Operations Officer, Lt. Col. Elbert L. Mott; the Chief of Stan-Eval, Maj. Lawrence L. Brown; two Flight Examiners, Maj. Richard L. Baird and Capt. Bobbie D. Fisher; three Instructor Pilots, Maj. Madero, Capt. Victor L. Bliden, and 1/Lt. Arthur B. Mathews; and four Aircraft Commanders, 1/Lt. John D. Froelich, II; 1/Lt. Lawrence D. Lundin; 1/Lt. Ralph P. Black; and 1/Lt. Alexander Loudon. These losses, particularly of Instructor Pilots and Flight Examiners, taxed the squadron considerably. Significant flying support was received from attached Wing pilots. An aggressive training and upgrading program was initiated to ensure that the problem would be lessened in the future.

Squadron authorization was for 48 pilots and 24 Flight Engineers. Only 40 pilots (3 Flight Examiners, 7 Instructor Pilots, 10 Aircraft Commanders, 2 First Pilots, and 19 Copilots) and 22 Flight Engineers (2 Flight Examiner Flight Engineers, 2 Instructor Flight Engineers, 14 Flight Engineers, 2 Unqualified, 1 Instructor Loadmaster, and 1 Loadmaster) were assigned. Inputs from Sewart AFB included 17 pilots, with 11 pilots (Undergraduate Pilot Training graduates) having less than 400 hours total time and one pilot with no C-7A experience.

During the first quarter, all Flight Examiners and 2 Instructor Pilots were upgraded. Most of the upgrading took place in March when only one Flight Examiner and one Instructor Pilot could fly since the others had reached the maximum time allowed by AFR 60-7. On numerous occasions, two Aircraft Commanders had to fly together in order to fulfill upgrade requirements. This was a heavy burden on the Aircraft Commanders, most of whom flew their maximum time for the month as per AFR 60-7.

Upgrade actions were directed toward qualifying new arrivals for in-country operations and moving qualified individuals into higher positions. Pilots were upgraded to First Pilot or Aircraft Commander as rapidly as their experience and qualifications allowed. The Wing reduced the requirement for recent Undergraduate Pilot Training (UPT) graduates to upgrade to Aircraft Commander from 1500 total hours to 850 total hours. A total of 34 pilots were upgraded, including 3 Flight Examiners, 4 Instructor Pilots, 7 Aircraft Commanders, 10 First Pilots, and 10 Copilots. This total represented a decline from 45 upgrades during the last quarter of 1968.

At the end of the first quarter the pilot availability was 3 Flight Examiners, 3 Instructor Pilots, 12 Aircraft Commanders, 5 First Pilots, 16 Copilots, and 9 unqualified pilots. Initial qualification was accomplished by seven Flight Engineers and drop qualification by five Flight Engineers. Two Flight Engineers returned to the CONUS and one returned on a medical release.

There was also a need to upgrade personnel to the positions of Launch Officer and Supervisor of Flying (SOF). All field grade officers were required to upgrade to the position of SOF. A minimum of five periods as Launch Officer were required to upgrade to SOF.

Other requirements of the training and scheduling section were: consideration of crew rest, rest and recuperation (R&R), leave, balancing of individual flying time versus additional duties, and TDY to Bangkok and the Philippines. The goal was to provide maximum flying training commensurate with flight safety and experience. To accomplish this, records were kept for a minimum of 12 months in order to provide pertinent information to rating officials. These records also helped to ensure fair and equitable distribution of additional duties throughout the tour of each individual.

Local training flights were flown a minimum of four times per month. For pilots in an upgrade program, emergency procedures were reviewed and accomplished. For newcomers, the local mission afforded the opportunity to experience local operating procedures.

The Flight Engineers were given "no notice" check rides by the Wing. They were rated as "Outstanding." The squadron was the only one in the Wing to receive such a high rating for its Flight Engineers. This improved rating was attributed to increased effort at squadron standardization (accomplished by squadron personnel) and an increase in the average age of the Flight Engineers during the quarter by approximately 10 to 15 years per Flight Engineer. These older personnel came to the squadron with a wealth of experience and were able to affect an increased proficiency in overall performance. The quality of

Instructor Flight Engineers was extremely high, partially due to the influx of the older NCOs.

In the second quarter, Lt. Col. Louis E. Dix was Scheduling/Training Officer, replaced on 19 May by Lt. Col. Melvin K. Walker. Maj. Alvin L. Walker was Chief of Stan/Eval starting on 1 March and continuing into the fourth quarter.

Specific pilot losses were one Instructor Pilot (Lt. Col. Eugene M. Simmons) and six Aircraft Commanders (Maj. Hugh L. Filbey, Capt. James W. Wade, 1/Lt. Lee A. Phillips, 1/Lt. Fred J. Remund, 1/Lt. Robert E. Fields, 1/Lt. Larry W. Sidwell). An effective training program enabled the squadron to recover from its large personnel losses during the first quarter. Local training flights were flown a minimum of four times per month. The squadron accomplished 47 pilot upgrades: 6 Instructor Pilots, 10 Aircraft Commanders, 18 First Pilots, and 13 Copilots. This total of upgrades was an increase over the 34 and 45 upgrades during the two previous quarters. The strong upgrade program allowed the squadron to maintain a fully manned level throughout the quarter.

Pilots available were 3 Flight Examiners, 8 Instructor Pilots, 11 Aircraft Commanders, 12 First Pilots, 13 Copilots, and 3 unqualified pilots. Flight Engineers available were 4 Flight Examiners, 4 Instructors, 19 Flight Engineers, 1 Instructor Loadmaster, and 2 Loadmasters. These numbers reflected a large nucleus of qualified personnel.

Squadron aircrews were given "no notice" check rides by the Wing. The pilots were rated "Excellent" and the Flight Engineers were rated "Outstanding." Squadron leadership attributed these ratings to an increased effort at squadron standardization and the ability of the squadron to expend more effort on the training program with the increased number of instructors available.

Lt. Col. Melvin K. Walker was Scheduling/Training Officer from 1 July through 30 September. Maj. Alvin L. Walker was Chief of Stan/Eval from 1 March into the fourth quarter.

In the third quarter, an aggressive training and upgrade program was initiated in an attempt to lessen the effect of significant loss of experienced personnel. Pilot losses totaled 15: 2 Flight Examiners (Capt. Howard L. Farr, Maj. Charles W. Hardie), 2 Instructor Pilots (Maj. Harry L. French and 1/Lt. Richard L. Halsey), 10 Aircraft Commanders (Lt. Col. Edward J. Thielen; Maj. Peter G. Tuin; Capt. John W. Shoun; Capt. David J. Vivian; Capt. Spencer F. McClure; Capt. Barry W. Johnson; 1/Lt. Louis A. Anderson; 1/Lt. Charles M. Dennison; 1/Lt. Claude B. Dodson, Jr.; and 1/Lt. Philip M. Gusman); and 1 First

Pilot (1/Lt. William F. Queenan).

The squadron accomplished 35 pilot upgrades. The total included: 1 Flight Examiner, 2 Instructor Pilots, 13 Aircraft Commanders, 7 First Pilots, and 12 Copilots. Four local training flights were flown each month. Through rapid and thorough upgrading of the flying personnel and close management of crew duty and rest time, the training and scheduling sections were able to maintain a positive level of manning for each mission assigned to the squadron.

Maj. Bill Hardie recalled the *fini* flight of one of his squadron mates:

> "It seems that Howie Farr, roomie and C-7 pilot extraordinaire, wanted to do something different on his 'fini flight,' upon return to Cam Ranh-by the Bay. It seems he acquired a parachute and some smoke bombs from the Special Forces guys and on his final approach and landing was going to demonstrate how a C-7 could be operated like an F-4. So, in advance, he called the tower to advise them not to get excited if they saw some smoke coming from the back of his aircraft and received permission for a 360 overhead. Everything proceeded normally (?) until the break, at which time he had the Flight Engineer pop the smoke bombs. The tower then forgot what he had told them and thought there was more smoke than necessary and proceeded to call out the crash rescue folks. Howie continued his approach thinking everything was as briefed.
>
> Now with the desired smoke coming from the back end, Howie continued his approach. Upon landing, the Flight Engineer deployed the parachute which was secured to a tie-down ring. The parachute blossomed and pulled the tie-down ring leaving the 'chute deployed across the active runway. Needless to say, this caused greater consternation as F-4 recoveries had to be delayed until the runway was cleared. (There was a war on you know.) A call, of course, went to the Command post and 'the powers that be.' Needless to say Howie got a much bigger reception than he anticipated and truly had his FINAL FLIGHT!" [10]

Lt. Col. Melvin K. Walker was Scheduling/Training Officer until 30 November when he was replaced by Maj. Dawson N. White. Maj. Alvin L. Walker was Chief of Stan/Eval until 15 December when he was replaced by Maj. Richard W. Berggren. The aggressive training and upgrade program was maintained in an attempt to reduce the effective minimum manning and loss of experienced personnel during the fourth quarter.

Maj. Bill Hardie recalled his day with the Commander of the 834AD:

> "When I was working in the Wing Stan/Eval, the word came up from downstairs that Brig. Gen. Herring, Commander of the 834th Air Division was coming to Cam Ranh Bay to fly a C-7A mission and that he would be accompanied by one of the Stan/Eval pilots. As if by magic, Maj. Mike Nassr, Chief of Stan/Eval, had a doctor's appointment and the number two guy had something to do. I was 'volunteered' to accompany the general on his tour. The mission was set up to go from Cam Ranh to Pleiku, Plei Mei, Duc Xuyen, and back to Cam Ranh Bay. The trip to Pleiku went OK and, at the general's suggestion, he did a short field landing there for practice. After the ALCE visit for fuel and cargo, we were off again. On the trip down to Plei Mei, I opened the cockpit window on my side. The general shot another short field landing and everything went OK; however, I was asleep at the switch and allowed the general to keep the props in reverse a bit too long. Needless to say, the dust of Plei Mei came billowing in my window and covered us all with a layer of the fine red stuff. I looked over to see the general in his clean and starched fatigues (and shined shoes) covered from head to foot. What a mess! Being an old crew dog, things like that happen, but NOT when you're carrying a general.
>
> The rest of the mission went OK with a half-decent short field landing at Duc Xuyen. On the leg back to Cam Ranh, I think the general got a bit puckered when he noticed the fuel level getting below 500 pounds in each tank. We landed back at Cam Ranh with more that 200 pounds on each side and NO low-fuel warning lights. Fortunately, I did not sit in on his debriefing to the command section and nothing was said about the mission. I noted that I didn't get the 'opportunity' to escort any more high ranking officers on Caribou tours of Vietnam." [11]

Safety

In the first quarter, the squadron experienced two ground fire incidents, although tactical approaches and departures were used at strips known to be "hot spots." In addition, Forward Air Controller (FAC) aircraft and fighters were used in specific cases. No aircraft accidents or incidents occurred.

A safety opinion survey was completed by the Wing. Most crew members submitted suggestions for improvements and action was taken or considered. A Flight Engineer, TSgt. Raymond W. Miller, conducted voluntary meetings to inform pilots about reciprocating engines. His efforts were especially educational for the younger pilots. All personnel were made aware of their responsibilities with regard to safety during monthly meetings and were given frequent reminders, when appropriate. In addition to the record of initial launches without a delay, the squadron worked towards another significant event, one year accident free. At the end of the second quarter, the squadron had flown 340 consecutive days without a reportable aircraft accident. These records were accomplished in a combat environment giving proof of the spirit and dedicated professionalism of the entire squadron.

Capt. Eldon W. Zeller, the squadron Safety Officer, discussed all phases of the safety program at monthly meetings. Discussions of aircraft accidents and incidents occurring in the squadrons of the Wing helped crews foresee and prevent incidents before they occurred. With deterioration of weather expected soon, the impetus of the safety program for the next quarter was to be directed towards instrument flying.

Technical briefings were given by various support personnel and Flight Engineers to supplement information in the T.O. 1-C-7A-1. Sgt. John M. Lukens gave several personal equipment (PE) briefings to help familiarize crews once again with the survival gear available in case of an emergency.

On 25 July, the squadron completed one year without a major accident. On 26 August, the record of accident free flying was complemented by completion of one year without a combat loss. There was one incident of enemy ground fire damaging an aircraft in the third quarter.

The squadron pilots were briefed by Maj. Woodual of the base weather station on the hazards of flying during the Northeast monsoon weather period. The safety officer also impressed upon the crews the importance of checking enroute weather, especially on return to the Cam Ranh Bay area. A special briefing on explosive ordinance was given to flight crews by Sgt. John M. Lukens.

Maj. John D. Mood, Jr. (a 1/Lt. at the time) remembered his assignment to the Accident Investigation Board for the shoot-down of 459 TAS C-7A S/N 63-9723 on 26 December 1969 near Tien Phuoc:

"Christmas was spent flying 9-10 sorties out of Bien Hoa,

shuttling troops and supplies. The next day, I was goofing off, doing nothing. Sometime early that morning a call to the hooch from the squadron told me to get my young Lt.'s a** down to the Wing immediately. I could almost see the 483rd TAW HQ from our compound, so I was there ASAP. After all was said and done, within an hour a maintenance officer (maybe 2/Lt. Robert R. Sides) and myself were on board a C-130 heading north to Chu Lai. After the short flight, we thought we'd be able to get some food and drink. Wrong! A Huey was awaiting our arrival with blades turning. Bag in hand, .38 revolver on the hip, and the 2/ Lt. in tow, we jumped on the chopper and we're off to Tien Phuoc.

Where you say? We didn't know either, as us southern flyers didn't do much 'I Corps' work. On board, we were told our destination was 24 miles west of Chu Lai and an easy ride. Right! Before we could spit, the 50 cal. was off-loading empty shell casings at my feet. They are noisy! The weather wasn't cooperating either. Soon, we were ducking under the clouds and skimming across the trees. A beautiful sight, if you don't mind the fact that at any moment your blood could be splattered all over the place. We arrived unscathed and landed in a light rain amidst what seemed like a lot of 'grunts.' We found out later that Tien Phouc was a combined artillery base and Special Forces camp. The maintenance officer and I were told to hop into the Jeep and we'd be driven out to the crash site. Crash you say? Maybe I left out a few details at the onset.

As the Recorder on the 483 TAW Accident Investigation Board, I was on a short string for any accident or incident in the Wing. This was my second investigation with only nine months in-country, thus the summons to HQ, the quick plane trip, and a heart stopping 'woop-woop' ride to the camp. Back at CRB, we were told only that a Caribou from Phu Cat had crashed on landing – no other details. By the time we arrived, we had lots of questions.

Off we went to the crash site a mile or so from the aerodrome. It took about 10 minutes thru muddy streets of the local town and then a long stretch of road into another small village. We were told the plane crashed on final into a rice paddy. As we got close, we could see what looked to be the rear of the fuselage and tail thru the trees, bamboo, and betel nut palms. Another few minutes of walking a muddy trail got us close to the site. What a mess!

It eventually would take several days to figure out how the heck a Caribou could be so twisted out of shape and heading in all directions at the same time. The long Jeep ride shows you that we were not in friendly territory and a good distance from the post. Remember – one of ours just got shot down! Our friendly driver said he was not sticking around and he'd be back before dark.

Remember his words, I sure did. We were met by a guy from the camp who was in charge of the perimeter setup to keep the sheet metal from disappearing before we could get a good look and take pictures (my responsibility). One of the first soldiers at the scene of the crash explained the mess around us. I paraphrase his story. 'The aircraft was just turning on final approach to land. He never stopped his turn, but continued to the right, making a descending spiral of almost 180 degrees when the aircraft crashed into the rice field.' Fellows from the camp responded immediately and got to the crash site in a blink. As soon as the first troops arrived, they put out the fire that had started. It could have gotten out of control fast as there was lots of 115/145 Avgas everywhere. While the fire was being extinguished, others arrived, securing the perimeter and searching for survivors. Two bodies, the pilot and flight engineer, were found without much problem, but the rescuers knew there should be at least one more individual.

Luckily, the copilot was semi-conscious and making 'moaning' sounds. After a brief hunt, wreckage was pulled aside and the copilot was found still strapped in his seat, but in serious condition. A Huey was called in immediately and the survivor was flown to the Chu Lai hospital. The bodies were put in another Huey and sent along soon thereafter. We found out later, this chopper either got shot down or went down with mechanical problems, causing even more grief for the Army.

This brief verbiage was retold many times over the next days of the investigation, including lots of kudos for the guys at the camp for their rapid response. Now, [it was] our turn to study the scene to try to discern what actually happened. At that time, we didn't know that the pilot was hit by ground fire from an AK-47. There were hills on the pilot's side at nearly the same elevation as the Bou on its final turn. With the belly exposed in the right turn, it was a large target. But, we had to consider this an accident until we knew otherwise.

This was different than a previous crash scene where a senior officer pulled out his .38, spent a few rounds and declared it a combat loss, saying, 'Let's go home.' For this crash, we Lieutenants didn't have that option. One of our prime targets for inspection and salvage was the overhead throttle [assembly] from the fuselage. After some chopping of cables, we freed it. Throughout the day, we were constantly being watched by local spectators in black pajamas and cone-shaped hats. A few obviously had an unplanned holiday since a large, twisted wreckage was impairing their farm work. They didn't seem to mind, as aircraft skin brought a high price in the local market. I heard that it made great woks. Later in the day, the 'brass' showed up, including the board president, secretary [sic], etc., but like all good desk jockeys, they spent a couple hours, gave us their all-mighty directions, and retired to some late afternoon refreshments at the camp. Don't know who those guys were, but they were definitely 'eco-friendly' and had low impact on our inquiry. As the hours wore on, the sun got hot and spicy. We slogged in the paddy, photographed, drew maps, took gauge readings, noted prop positions, and tried to figure what could have gone haywire. Of course, we were not well-trained accident investigators, just a prop jockey and a wrench turner disguised as such.

As the sun was setting, our eyes were peeled for the arrival of our ride back to the camp. No one in sight, so we were getting antsy. The sun was almost set and the shadows were very long. The spectators disappeared and, to our surprise, so had the perimeter guards! Yikes, we were two ducks at the watering hole surrounded by hunters! It was time to consider the flight options. Foremost on my mind was killing the Jeep driver. With or without transport, it was time to get out of Dodge with much expediency. So, off we went, not exactly sure of our route, but adamant about getting to friendly territory.

Picture this. Two yanks in tandem, one in a flight suit and the other in fatigues, both muddy, one side arm between them, and a weird contraption with cables dangling and handles askew being carried by two fools down a dark, country road. By the way, the Vietcong owned the night in this local community. As we headed in the direction of the camp, the stares seemed hateful. We two abandoned troopers were wondering if we'd ever get to make our report. After what seemed like an eternity, but actually 30 minutes or so, by dumb luck only, we stumbled from the pitch black onto the camp gate. The guard couldn't believe two dumb Air Force types would be beyond the barbed wire after dark.

I had no comment. Thoroughly teed off at the Army Lieutenant, I barely held my rage once I found the ^#$*!, but he casually passed off our little walk as a test of courage, saying he forgot we were out there! Sleep that night was not on a par with the quiet of Cam Ranh Bay. I swear the same Army Lieutenant that forgot us decided where I was going to bunk. To his chagrin, I ended up below ground in a bunker. Not so bad except for when the 155's and 105's started their triangulation firing early that evening and continuing until dawn. My bunk was at the fire control center about 200 feet from the big guns. Talk about noise, no wonder the Army Lieutenant's brain was scrambled. Prior to this try at sleep, I got a tour of the Special Forces area which was all underground. These guys seemed to appreciate that I transported beer, beef, and ammo, so they fed and boozed me well. Heading back to the artillery side of Tien Phuoc, I asked about the gunfire down along the river which seemed out of place. 'Dogs,' my companion said. 'They are shooting stray dogs.' The next morning, on the way to the crash site, four-legged creatures were hanging in a market inside glass cases, upside down, and lacking fur. Yummy.

I don't remember much about the second day, except we continued our work. Sometime during day two or three, we were notified to wrap up our stuff. The pilot, Lt. David Bowling was killed by enemy ground fire. This crash was a combat loss. During the second day, one of the Army types gave me a roll of film he said he took as one of the first men on-site after the crash. I took these back to Cam Rahn and developed them at the photo hobby shop. Our final instructions were to destroy all our documents, notes, and findings. No one said anything about photos. I trashed the paperwork, but the photos stayed with me for some time thereafter and the negatives to this day." [13]

Maintenance

During the first quarter, Capt. Robert A. Eyrich was the squadron Maintenance Officer. Maintenance activities were concentrated on flight line maintenance: aircraft servicing and towing, brake and tire changes, engine runs, and operational checks. The crew chiefs were more familiar with the C-7A than in previous quarters, so they also performed cargo door and ramp door maintenance. Field level maintenance functions were performed by the 483rd Consolidated Aircraft Maintenance Squadron (CAMS), Operating Location B (OLAB). At the end of the first quarter there were no modification programs in effect for the assigned aircraft.

The flight line had four assigned 7-levels with an authorization for seven. This situation made the flight line critical for 7-levels during months when a requirement existed to provide supervisors for mission sites. An improvement was suggested to divide the 7-level maintenance personnel more equally within the Wing.

Maintenance provided aircraft to fly all scheduled missions. In addition, the squadron maintenance functions supported the 458 TAS on occasion by providing aircraft to meet their schedule. Engine problems continued to be the primary source of delays and aborts.

Capt. Eyrich continued as the Maintenance Officer in the second quarter. Maintenance activities continued to concentrate on flight line maintenance: aircraft servicing and towing, brake and tire changes, engine runs, and operational checks. The crew chiefs did cargo door and ramp door maintenance. Field level maintenance functions were performed by CAMS OLAB. Maintenance supported the 458 TAS on occasion by providing aircraft to meet their schedule. Maintenance enroute delays were 44 in April, 35 in May, and 25 in June. Engine problems continued to be the primary source of delays and aborts.

Flight line maintenance was authorized 54 personnel, but only 46 were assigned. The most critical shortage was in the 7-level area with seven authorized, only four assigned, and no projected inputs. The squadron provided a Functional Check Flight (FCF) crew at Cam Ranh Bay during April and June, flying FCFs for the 457 TAS and the 458 TAS.Sgt. Bruce E. Prickett was selected as Maintenance Man of the second quarter. Sgt. Ronald W. Aurand and A/1C Maurice Douglas had only one minor discrepancy on #2 engine of C-7A S/N 62-4184 which had 1065 hours since installation.

Capt. Eyrich continued as the Maintenance Officer until 25 August, when he was replaced by 1/Lt. Robert R. Sides. Maintenance activities continued to concentrate on flight line maintenance: aircraft servicing and towing, brake and tire changes, engine runs, and operational checks. The crew chiefs did cargo door and ramp door maintenance. Field level maintenance functions continued to be performed by the CAMS OLAB. The squadron experienced only four initial delays during the third quarter. Maintenance enroute delays were 37 in July, 20 in August, and 29 in September.

The squadron provided an FCF crew at Cam Ranh Bay during August, flying FCFs for the 457 TAS and the 458 TAS. As during the first two quarters, maintenance supported the 458 TAS on occasion by providing aircraft to meet their schedule. At the end of the quarter, there were no modification programs in effect for the assigned aircraft.

Sgt. Jerry W. Montero was named Wing Outstanding Maintenance

Man of the third quarter.

In the fourth quarter, 1/Lt. Sides continued as the Maintenance Officer. Maintenance activities continued to concentrate on flight line maintenance: aircraft servicing and towing, brake and tire changes, engine runs, and operational checks. The crew chiefs did cargo door and ramp door maintenance. Field level maintenance functions continued to be performed by the CAMS OLAB. The main problem affecting the maintenance section was a shortage of personnel. The Wing Chief of Maintenance was informed of the situation so that incoming personnel could be routed to the squadron. All scheduled missions were flown despite the personnel shortage. As during the first three quarters, maintenance supported the 458 TAS on occasion by providing aircraft to meet their schedule. Engine problems continued to be the primary source of delays and aborts.

A/1C William T. Hodges was named Crew Chief of the Month for November.

Administration

In the first quarter, no changes in organizational structure occurred, no changes were made in administrative procedures, no significant administrative problems occurred, and there were no proposals to increase administrative effectiveness. MSgt. Carroll M. Funk was the First Sergeant and 1/Lt. Oviel D. Thorne was the Historian.

At the end of the quarter, replacement personnel brought the pilot strength up to a total of 47 assigned, compared to 50 authorized. Flight Engineer strength increased to the point where the squadron was short only one. Programmed inputs and losses of Flight Engineers for the third quarter indicated that manning would be adequate. Flight line maintenance suffered a critical shortage of 7-level personnel, although total strength was adequate at the end of the quarter. Maintenance was authorized seven 7-levels with only four assigned and no projected inputs. Only the shortages in the maintenance area were critical enough to impair mission performance. Sufficient 5-levels were in upgrade training, but would not complete that training for another three to six months.

Eight recent UPT graduates arrived from Sewart AFB, TN during the second quarter. MSgt. Herman P. Mayo replaced MSgt. Funk as the First Sergeant on 2 September. First Lieutenant Oviel D. Thorne continued as the Historian. Administrative specialists and OJT monitors were consolidated in December into a "pool" of office and typing skills. Flight line maintenance was authorized 54 personnel and experienced a decline from 46 assigned to 38. Pilot shortages were overcome through careful scheduling and use of attached pilots. The shortage of flight line maintenance personnel was offset by scheduling and working extra hours.

The squadron was able to accomplish its assigned mission. No mission was cancelled for lack of aircraft or flight crew.

In the third quarter, 1/Lt. Oviel D. Thorne was the Historian. In the fourth quarter, Capt. John H. Bell was the Historian.

Supply and Support

All supply functions were performed by the 483 TAW Material Control.

In the first quarter, the office facilities of the squadron were adequate. However, there was no latrine or running water in the building and the nearest available facility was approximately 50 yards away. Runways and taxiways were adequate, but the parking apron continued to remain inadequate. The new spacing required all crews to maintain extra vigilance during taxi operations, particularly during the pre-dawn departures. The parking apron was repainted with new parking lines, gaining several additional parking spaces. Construction of the new parking apron was not scheduled to begin until FY 1970. The ramp facilities were maintained by the 483 TAW and they were aware of the ramp and parking conditions.

Housing consisted of one large trailer occupied by the Commander and Operations Officer, two porta-trailers for field grade officers, two large Quonset huts for squadron officers, half of a Quonset hut for Flight Engineers and Loadmasters, and 10 hootches for maintenance, administrative, and life support personnel. Only aircrew quarters were air-conditioned. Negotiations were completed for the acquisition of the former C-130 crew quarters. Through the efforts of the pilots in the squadron, the quarters were remodeled. This alleviated much of the congestion in the officer housing. An additional room was planned to be acquired for the Flight Engineers. These quarters, if and when obtained, would require extensive rehabilitation and all work would have to be done by personnel of the squadron. A work order was submitted to obtain building materials to rehabilitate the hootches on a self-help basis.

Incoming personnel left home with the knowledge that it would be many months before they saw their families again. They arrived in Vietnam filled with apprehension, fed by a pipeline of Air Force survival schools. Personnel quickly adapted to the drudgery of the

12 hour crew duty days with all weekends canceled. They achieved a tolerable relationship with their new roommate(s), even those who snored. Given all of the circumstances, morale was never better in the squadron.

The squadron was fortunate to have personnel who were aware of the realities of the situation and worked to improve existing conditions, rather than just gripe about them. The squadron offered its Junior Officers the opportunity to upgrade to Aircraft Commander as soon as minimum time requirements were met. Above all, the squadron had intelligent, dedicated leadership that was foremost in molding the squadron into a flexible, cohesive team.

Office facilities were unchanged and the problem with aircraft parking continued in the second quarter. Housing was unchanged.

Civic Action and Special Activities

The squadron Civic Action project involved the support of 11 Vietnamese school children who otherwise could not afford to go to school. Each month, scholarship money was taken to the schools personally by members of the squadron and given to the children. The project was very well received and expansion was planned to several other base organizations. During the first quarter, a total of $286 was given out in scholarship money to the 11 children. Eight children received 1050 Piasters (1050 P), approximately $9 per month. Three children in the public school received 700 P, approximately $6 per month.

In February, base reporters came to the five schools with the Civic Action officer and took pictures of the children receiving their scholarship money. A story was written for publication in a forthcoming issue of 7th Air Force News.

The squadron Civic Action project continued in the second quarter, assisting a number of Vietnamese school-age children who otherwise could not afford to go to school. Each month, scholarship money was taken to the schools personally by members of the squadron and given to the children. The majority of the efforts in the second quarter were in preparation for the coming school year.

A dinner party was planned for 26 April to bring the children, their parents, and educators on base to meet the squadron personnel. In preparation for bringing the children and their parents on base, coordination was accomplished with Food Services for the use of Dining Hall #6, Base Security, and the motor pool.

The squadron participated in the "Santa Bou" project of the Wing conducted on 24 and 25 December. Much prior planning, coordination, and effort preceded these dates. A specially painted and equipped C-7A was flown to forward Special Forces camps to bring Christmas cheer and gifts to U.S. military, advisory, and indigenous personnel and their families. The project was an unqualified success.

Squadron personnel continued to submit donations to the unit's scholarship fund used to assist needy and deserving children in the Cam Ranh Bay area. Without this money, these children would have been unable to continue their education. The scholarship recipients were in grades 7 through 12 and they accepted the scholarship money with the understanding that was to be used only for tuition, books, school supplies, or school uniforms. Sponsored students also agreed to attend school regularly and maintain above a "C" average. Squadron members delivered this money to the recipients in the presence of school officials once each month. At the time the scholarships were awarded, the squadron members and Civic Action Officer had the opportunity to talk with the students and their instructors and discuss some of the local problems in education.

On 27 December, a Christmas party was given by the squadron for the scholarship recipients. The students and their instructors were brought to the base and given a tour of the flight line. They enjoyed ice cream and candy and were given gifts of pens, pencils, paper, and small toilet articles. They also viewed "The Landing of the Eagle," a short color film which highlighted the advance efforts leading to the first manned lunar landing. The party was very successful and enjoyed by all who had the opportunity to participate.

Airlift Accomplishments [13]

During the first quarter, passengers hauled were 18,061 in January; 15,224 in February; and 18,220 in March for a total of 51,505. Cargo hauled was 1336.2 tons in January; 1185.1 tons in February; and 1374.6 tons in March for a total of 3895.9 tons. In January, the squadron flew 2518 sorties while logging 1808.8 flying hours. In February, the squadron flew 2266 sorties while logging 1661.6 flying hours. In March, the squadron flew 2624 sorties while logging 1916.8 flying hours.

During the second quarter, passengers hauled were 16,384 in April; 12,918 in May; and 12,820 in June for a total of 42,122. Cargo hauled was 1251.2 tons in April; 1317.2 tons in May; and 1076.2 tons in June for a total of 3644.6 tons. In April, the squadron flew 2459 sorties while logging 1850.8 flying hours. In May, the squadron flew 2400 sorties while logging 1784.6 flying hours. In June, the squadron flew 2146 sorties while logging 1709.1 flying hours.

From 14 June to 3 July, the squadron made airdrops of supplies to the besieged Special Forces camp at Ben Het. Nine missions were flown in support of the 537 TAS. See the chapter on the 537 TAS for details of the Ben Het effort.

During the third quarter, passengers hauled were 13,657 in July; 12,831 in August; and 10,865 in September for a total of 37,353. Cargo hauled was 1123.0 tons in July; 1228.8 tons in August; and 912.4 tons in September for a total of 3264.2 tons. In July, the squadron flew 2256 sorties while logging 1830.5 flying hours. In August, the squadron flew 2370 sorties while logging 1880.5 flying hours. In September, the squadron flew 2107 sorties while logging 1745.0 flying hours.

During the fourth quarter, passengers hauled were 13,327 in October; 14,645 in November; and 13,337 in December for a total of 41,309. Cargo hauled was 879.0 tons in October; 765.0 tons in November; and 952.0 tons in December for a total of 2596.0 tons. In October, the squadron flew 2270 sorties while logging 1785.2 flying hours. In November, the squadron flew 2296 sorties while logging 1742.4 flying hours. In December, the squadron flew 2501 sorties while logging 1828.0 flying hours.

Commander's Summary

First Quarter 1969 [14]

"The preceding pages have reviewed significant historical achievements of the 457 Tactical Airlift Squadron from 1 January 1969 to 31 March 1969. A history of this nature must be limited to a discussion of accomplishments and shortcomings of the squadron as a cohesive unit. Personalities were not mentioned, but the chemistry of individuals working together is responsible for any achievements that the 457th Tactical Airlift Squadron can claim."

Second Quarter 1969 [15]

"The preceding pages have reviewed significant historical achievements of the 457 Tactical Airlift Squadron from 1 April through 30 June 1969. A history of this nature must be limited to a discussion of accomplishments and shortcomings of the squadron as a cohesive unit. Personalities were not mentioned, but the chemistry of individuals working together is responsible for any achievements that the 457th Tactical Airlift Squadron can claim."

Third Quarter 1969 [16]

"The preceding pages have reviewed significant historical achievements of the 457 Tactical Airlift Squadron from 1 July through 30 September 1969. A history of this nature must be limited to a discussion of accomplishments and shortcomings of the squadron as a cohesive unit. Personalities were not mentioned, but the chemistry of individuals working together is responsible for any achievements that the 457th Tactical Airlift Squadron can claim."

Fourth Quarter 1969 [17]

"The preceding pages have reviewed significant historical achievements of the 457 Tactical Airlift Squadron from 1 October through 30 December 1969. A history of this nature must be limited to a discussion of accomplishments and shortcomings of the squadron as a cohesive unit. Personalities were not mentioned, but the chemistry of individuals working together is responsible for any achievements that the 457th Tactical Airlift Squadron can claim."

End Notes: 457 TAS

[1] *19690101-19691231 457 TAS History*
[2] 457 TAS GO-1, dated 19 February 1969
[3] 7AF Special Order G-2165, dated 15 May 1970
[4] Personal account of Maj. Curt Fischer told to author
[5] 7AF Special Order G-2556, dated 6 June 1970
[6] 7AF Special Order G-5284, dated 20 November 1970
[7] 7AF Special Order G-0502, dated 31 January 1970
[8] 7AF Special Order G-0617, dated 27 February 1971
[9] 7AF Special Order G-2557, dated 6 June 1970
[10] *C-7A Caribou Association Newsletter, Vol. I, No. 3, Summer 1993*
[11] *Ibid*
[12] *C-7A Caribou Association Newsletter, Vol. 20, Issue 1, April 2009*
[13] When the data in the squadron history and the Wing history differ, the Wing data is shown.
[14] 457 TAS Commander's Summary, 31 March 1969 by Lt. Col. Edward J. Thielen
[15] 457 TAS Commander's Summary, 30 June 1969 by Lt. Col. Edward J. Thielen
[16] 457 TAS Commander's Summary, 30 September 1969 by Lt. Col. Roger E. Deyhle
[17] 457 TAS Commander's Summary, 31 December 1969 by Lt. Col. Roger E. Deyhle

458th Tactical Airlift Squadron [1]

The primary mission of the 458th Tactical Airlift Squadron (458 TAS) at Cam Ranh Bay was to provide transportation of personnel and cargo for delivery by parachute or landing. The mission was to maintain a combat ready tactical airlift capability to perform air-land and air drop assault missions into objective areas in direct support of counter-insurgency operations; to conduct combat logistical airlift of troops, supplies, and equipment needed to execute and support tactical or strategic missions; and to provide a mobile combat readiness capability to support contingency commitments of the Commander, U.S. Military Assistance Command Vietnam – Thailand (COMUSMACV-THAI).

In the first and second quarters, the squadron was authorized 16 aircraft, 16 were assigned, and 14 were Combat Ready. In the third quarter, the squadron was authorized 16 aircraft, 16 were assigned, and 15 were Combat Ready. In the fourth quarter, the squadron was authorized 16 aircraft, 16 were assigned, and 12 were Combat Ready.

To accomplish the mission, the squadron was authorized 51 officers and 137 enlisted personnel in the first quarter. Of these authorizations, 38 officers and 84 enlisted personnel were assigned. The primary shortage was in aircrew personnel, of whom 50 were authorized, but only 37 were assigned. The most notable shortage in the maintenance section was in 5-level personnel with only 16 assigned of the authorized 28. The average manning rose to 89.0 percent; however, late in the quarter, several new officers were gained and the strength rose sharply toward the authorized number. On 18 January, Lt. Col. Charles E. Barnett replaced Lt. Col. John L. Thomas as Squadron Commander. Lt. Col. William C Hutchison became squadron Operations Officer.[2]

In the second quarter, the squadron was authorized 51 officers and 86 enlisted personnel. Of these authorizations, 50 officers and 89 enlisted personnel were assigned, bringing the manning up to 101 percent.

In the third quarter, the squadron was authorized 51 officers and 86 enlisted personnel. Of these authorizations, 47 officers and 89 enlisted personnel were assigned, making the manning at 100 percent.

In the fourth quarter, 51 officers and 85 enlisted personnel were authorized, but only 42 officers and 71 enlisted personnel were assigned, for a manning of 83.8 percent. On 18 October, Lt. Col. Jeff J. Piercy replaced Lt. Col. Barnett as Squadron Commander[3] and Lt. Col. Ralph V. Korhnak replaced Lt. Col. Hutchison as squadron Operations Officer.

Operations

The types of missions flown by the squadron in the first quarter included: routine cargo, support of Special Forces and other Free World forces in Vietnam, medical evacuations, Emergency Resupply, Tactical Emergencies, Combat Essential missions, radio relays, air drops of paratroopers, ammunition, building supplies, POL (Petroleum, Oil, and Lubricants), general cargo, and rations. Live cows, pigs, chickens, and fresh produce were also airdropped in support of Army of Republic of Vietnam (ARVN) troops.

In January, the squadron was assigned a mission to move a tribe of Montagnard families, some 1200 people, from the outlying Civilian Irregular Defense Group (CIDG) camp at Bu Krak to a location in the interior. Bu Krak was a red clay/laterite landing strip only 70 feet wide and 1700 feet long, with a gradual 35 foot dip. The Caribou was the largest fixed-wing aircraft allowed to land there. The strip was not level. It banked to the right for several hundred yards and then to the left. Mine fields and a six foot concertina fence ran adjacent to both runway edges. The camp commander, Capt. Lawrence M. Kerr, USA, observed that "Even light observation planes come in only in an emergency." [4]

Four C-7A's left Cam Ranh Bay before first light to fly into the camp, one after another, take on a load of passengers, make a quick takeoff and flight to the inland base, and off-load there with the engines running. Each Caribou could move about 35 people at a time, so it was expected that the movement would take two days. Lt. Col. Frederick R. Beal, movement coordinator for the 458 TAS, supervised the rapid loading of the passengers, then watched as the C-7A took off in a cloud of red dust to make way for the next Caribou to land and load. Turn-around time was in the range of 7-7.5 minutes!

Army Capt. Howard M. MacDonald, ground liaison officer for the 12th Tactical Fighter Wing, remarked: "If anyone ever doubted the capability of that airplane, they'd be convinced if they saw this operation. The C-7A is a marvelous bird – and that's an understatement."

The entire operation took about 12 hours. Each of the four Caribous flew 7 or 8 round trips from Bu Krak to the inland base and back. They flew a total of 65 sorties and transported 1207 Montagnards, while flying 42.6 hours and carrying a total of 16.8 tons. This included five tons of rice carried into Bu Krak after hauling the passengers.

The crew members for this extraordinary airlift were: Col. Keith L. Christensen, 1/Lt. Parker W. Rosenquist, Sgt. George M. Pierce, Capt. Thomas H. Mosiman, 1/Lt. Robert J. Herndon, SSgt. Donald V.

Sutterfield, Lt. Col. Edward J. Thielen, 1/lt. James A. Gray, SSgt. William T. Frye, 1/Lt. John H. Sandrock, 1/Lt. James M. Smith, and SSgt. Michael T. Murray. Bravo Zulu! It was a job well done in the Caribou tradition.

The actions on 30 March of 1/Lt. Douglas M. Boston and his crew were described in the citation for his Distinguished Flying Cross:

> "First Lieutenant Douglas M. Boston distinguished himself
> by extraordinary achievement while participating in aerial flight
> as an Aircraft Commander at Phouc Vinh, Republic of Vietnam on
> 30 March 1969. On that date, Lieutenant Boston loaded combat
> troops and took off while the airfield was under a rocket attack
> from hostile forces. Lieutenant Boston made two more trips
> into Phouc Vinh to airlift combat troops needed at Minh Thanh.
> The professional competence, aerial skill and devotion to duty
> displayed by Lieutenant Boston reflect great credit upon himself
> and the United States Air Force." [5]

Operating efficiency of the squadron remained on a high level, despite having only 89 percent of the authorized personnel. Replacement personnel, for the most part, were younger airmen with little operational experience. However, they offset this handicap with highly motivated interest in the job they were doing. Replacement flight crews were well qualified pilots and upgraded to combat ready status in a minimum of time, whether senior officers with many years of experience or junior officers just out of flying school.

The squadron maintained the mission site on the Special Forces ramp at Nha Trang. One mission per day was flown from Nha Trang in support of the 5th Special Forces Group (5SFG). The mission site at Don Muang Airport, Bangkok, Thailand continued normal operations. The mission in Bangkok was unchanged and rotation of aircraft and crews of the various squadrons in the 483 TAW operated smoothly.

There was an average of 19 "formed crews" available throughout the quarter. However, there were short periods in February and March when the Combat Ready crew availability dropped to as low as 14. Because of prior planning, the mission capability was not compromised. One qualified copilot continued to command the mission site at Nha Trang on the 5SFG ramp. The squadron maintained a backup crew at Cam Ranh Bay to handle any mission delays or maintenance breakdown. The crew was on duty all day and could be launched in minimum time.

The squadron operating efficiency increased above its normal high standards in the second quarter. The squadron operated with approximately 100 percent of the authorized personnel. Replacement personnel completed upgrading in minimum time and continued to become more efficient at their profession. The squadron was authorized 24 crews. There were 23 "formed crews" and 21 of these were available throughout the quarter. There was an average of 21 "formed crews" available throughout the quarter.

The squadron continued to maintain normal operations at the mission site at Don Muang Airport, Bangkok, Thailand. The mission was unchanged and rotation of aircraft and crews of the various squadrons in the Wing operated smoothly. The backup crew at Cam Ranh Bay continued to provide "ready to launch" support in case of mission delays or maintenance breakdown. After the mission site on the Special Forces ramp at Nha Trang was discontinued, operations were conducted through the Airlift Control Element (ALCE) at Nha Trang.

In the third quarter, the squadron was authorized 24 crews. There were 22 "formed crews" and 20 of these were available throughout the quarter. Twenty-two crews were Combat Ready. The squadron continued to maintain normal operations at the mission site at Don Muang Airport, Bangkok. The mission was unchanged and rotation of aircraft and crews of the various squadrons in the Wing operated smoothly. The backup crew at Cam Ranh Bay continued to provide "ready to launch" support in case of mission delays or maintenance breakdown.

The timely actions on 13 August of TSgt. Joseph P. Pearce and his crew were documented in the citation for his Distinguished Flying Cross:

> "Technical Sergeant Joseph P. Pearce distinguished himself
> by extraordinary achievement while participating in aerial flight
> as a Flight Engineer at Bu Dop Special Forces camp, Republic
> of Vietnam on 13 August 1969. On that date, while carrying
> munitions to Bu Dop, Sergeant Pearce's aircraft encountered a
> rocket attack while taxiing to the off-load area. Despite the hazards
> involved, Sergeant Pearce quickly rigged and speed off-loaded the
> cargo, enabling the aircraft to become airborne without extensive
> damage. The professional competence, aerial skill, and devotion to
> duty displayed by Sergeant Pearce reflect great credit upon himself
> and the United States Air Force." [6]

Later that month, the missions of 1/Lt. Steven J. Hassett and his crew on 24 August getting their load into a field with challenging M8A1 light duty steel matting were documented in the citation for his Distinguished Flying Cross:

> "First Lieutenant Steven J. Hassett distinguished himself by

extraordinary achievement while participating in aerial flight as a C-7A Aircraft Commander at Moc Hoa Special Forces Camp, Republic of Vietnam on 24 August 1969. On that date, Lieutenant Hassett flew vitally needed fuel into Moc Hoa, a landing strip that had been so badly damaged by enemy rocket attack that only one thousand feet of runway was available. Although at maximum gross weight and landing at a minimal airstrip, Lieutenant Hassett elected to fly two resupply missions into Moc Hoa, executing tactical approaches and short field landings into the insecure and damaged airstrip. The professional competence, aerial skill and devotion to duty displayed by Lieutenant Hassett reflect great credit upon himself and the United States Air Force." [7]

The actions on 18 September of 1/Lt. Richard A. Fox, Jr., noted author and researcher of the Battle of the Little Big Horn, and his crew during an Emergency Resupply mission were documented in the citation for his Distinguished Flying Cross:

"First Lieutenant Richard A. Fox is awarded the Distinguished Flying Cross for extraordinary achievement while participating in aerial flight as a C-7A Pilot at Mai Loc Special Forces Camp, Republic of Vietnam, on 18 September 1969. On that date, Lieutenant Fox airlifted quantities of whole blood to the camp on an emergency resupply mission in extremely adverse weather conditions. Excellent knowledge of flight procedures, local terrain, and superb judgment enabled Lieutenant Fox to safely reach the Camp and off-load his critically needed cargo despite hostile ground fire and weather conditions which forced low level flight at 50 feet above the ground. The professional competence, aerial skill, and devotion to duty displayed by Lieutenant Fox reflect great credit upon himself and the United States Air Force." [8, 9]

In the fourth quarter, the squadron was authorized 24 crews. There were 22 "formed crews" and 20 of these were available throughout the quarter. Twenty crews were Combat Ready. The squadron operating efficiency increased above its normal high standards even though it operated with 83.8 percent of the authorized personnel. Replacement personnel completed upgrading in minimum time and continued to become more proficient at their profession. The squadron continued to maintain normal operations at the mission site at Don Muang Airport, Bangkok. The mission was unchanged and rotation of aircraft and crews of the various squadrons in the Wing operated smoothly. The backup crew at Cam Ranh Bay continued to provide "ready to launch" support in case of any mission delays or maintenance breakdown.

In September, the tactical situation around Bu Dop (V-121), lead to some critical missions to resupply the Special Forces camp. The actions by Lt. Col. Jeff J. Piercy and his crew on 16 November were documented in the citation for his Distinguished Flying Cross:

"Lieutenant Colonel Jeff J. Piercy distinguished himself by extraordinary achievement while participating in aerial flight as a C-7A Aircraft Commander at Bu Dop Special Forces Camp, Republic of Vietnam, on 16 November 1969. On that date Colonel Piercy delivered essential supplies to the camp which was under heavy hostile attack and which required forward air controller coverage and fighter protection for all cargo missions. On the initial approach, the fighter protection was diverted requiring superior airmanship to avoid hostile ground fire to make a safe approach and landing, and to speed off-load of the critically needed cargo. The professional competence, aerial skill, and devotion to duty displayed by Colonel Piercy reflect great credit upon himself and the United States Air Force." [10]

A week later, the actions of 1/Lt. James K. Hocutt and his crew on 22 November were documented in the citation for his Distinguished Flying Cross:

"First Lieutenant James K. Hocutt distinguished himself by extraordinary achievement while participating in aerial flight as a C-7A Aircraft Commander at Bu Dop Special Forces Camp, Republic of Vietnam on 22 November 1969. On that date, Lieutenant Hocutt was carrying sorely needed rations and key replacement personnel destined for Bu Dop, which was receiving intense mortar fire at that time. Lieutenant Hocutt's skill in making tactical approaches and departures from the hostile area resulted in saving the aircraft and the lives of the crew. The professional competence, aerial skill, and devotion to duty displayed by Lieutenant Hocutt reflect great credit upon himself and the United States Air Force." [11]

A few days later, Capt. Robert L. Sonick and his crew were attacked on 27 November while on the ground at Bu Dop. Their actions are documented in the citation for his Distinguished Flying Cross:

"Captain Robert L. Sonick distinguished himself by extraordinary achievement while participating in aerial flight as a C-7A Aircraft Commander at Bu Dop Special Forces Camp, Republic of Vietnam on 27 November 1969. On that date, hostile fire had destroyed the loading ramp at Bu Dop, increasing the ground time required for off-loading. After the aircraft landed, the camp came under attack and two mortars hit within 100 yards of the aircraft. Despite the hostile fire, Captain Sonick continued off-loading the aircraft and delivered the vital cargo to the ground forces. The professional competence, aerial skill, and devotion to duty displayed by Captain Sonick reflect great credit upon himself and the United States Air Force." [12]

On the same date at Bu Dop, TSgt. James D. Myers received artillery fire on a Combat Essential mission. Their actions were documented in the citation for his Distinguished Flying Cross:

"Technical Sergeant James D. Myers distinguished himself by extraordinary achievement while participating in aerial flight as a C-7A Flight Engineer at Bu Dop Special Forces Camp, Republic of Vietnam on 27 November 1969. On that date, while off-loading Combat Essential supplies at Bu Dop, the camp came under intense hostile artillery fire causing the off-loading crew to take cover. Realizing the importance of immediate action, Sergeant Myers rigged the aircraft for a speed off-load which was accomplished successfully, enabling the aircraft to become airborne without damage. The professional competence, aerial skill, and devotion to duty displayed by Sergeant Myers reflect great credit upon himself and the United States Air Force." [13]

The battle at Bu Dop continued into December and the actions of 1/Lt. Christopher F. Nevins and his crew on 4 December were documented in the citation for his Distinguished Flying Cross:

"First Lieutenant Christopher F. Nevins distinguished himself by extraordinary achievement while participating in aerial flight as a C-7A Aircraft Commander at Bu Dop Special Forces Camp, Republic of Vietnam on 4 December 1969. On that date, Lieutenant Nevins was flying Combat Essential missions to Bu Dop which had seen extensive hostile activity for several days. Despite concentrations of unfriendly troops near the perimeter and the presence of antiaircraft weapons one-half mile off the end of the runway, Lieutenant Nevins made three shuttles to the Camp without suffering any damage to his aircraft. The professional competence, aerial skill, and devotion to duty displayed by Lieutenant Nevins reflect great credit upon himself and the United States Air Force." [14]

Song Be was a perennial hot spot in III Corps. In December, TSgt. Tom M. Owens and his crew were mortared on the ramp. Their actions on 23 December were documented in the citation for his Distinguished Flying Cross:

"Technical Sergeant Tom M. Owens distinguished himself by extraordinary achievement while participating in aerial flight as a Flight Engineer at Song Be, Republic of Vietnam on 23 December 1969. On that date, Sergeant Owens, as a C-7A crew member, had landed at Song Be, completed the cargo off-load, and was waiting for the outbound load when the field came under mortar attack. Several rounds exploded close to the aircraft and put what was later determined to be thirty-seven holes in the aircraft. Sergeant Owens made a quick external inspection, assessed the damage and recommended to the Aircraft Commander that they take off to save the aircraft from destruction. The crew took off and made an uneventful flight back to Bien Hoa Air Base, saving the crew and aircraft. The professional competence, aerial skill, and devotion to duty displayed by Sergeant Owens reflect great credit upon himself and the United States Air Force." [15]

Training and Stan-Eval

The squadron had an active upgrading program in the first quarter. At the end of the quarter, the roster showed two new Flight Examiners, two new Instructor Pilots (IPs), 11 new Aircraft Commanders, 11 up-graded First Pilots, and 6 new Copilots. Seven new enlisted personnel were upgraded to Flight Engineer. The pilots who were immediately upgraded to Aircraft Commander, though new to the combat environ-ment, had many hours of flying experience and therefore were consid-ered qualified to carry on the work of the departed Aircraft Command-ers.

Six personnel were administered the Specialty Knowledge Test (SKT) for Air Force Specialty Code (AFSC) 43121A. Four of the six personnel received a score of 95.0 percent, one received a score of 90.0 percent, and the last individual received a score of 50.0 percent. Three of these personnel were upgraded to the 5-level and the other three would be upgraded shortly. An average of 30 personnel were in training.

In the second quarter, the squadron continued its very active up-grade program. By the end of April, 1 Instructor Pilot, 10 Aircraft Commanders, 14 First Pilots, and 16 Copilots, were upgraded to their new positions. Seven new enlisted personnel qualified as Flight En-gineers. This was a significant increase over the upgrading in the first quarter, which had 39 new positions filled as opposed to 48 for the sec-ond quarter.

By the end of September, 1 Flight Examiner, 18 Aircraft Commanders, 8 First Pilots, 11 Copilots, and 9 Flight Engineers were upgraded to their new positions. By December, 2 Flight Examiners, 18 Aircraft Commanders, 11 Copilots, and 6 Flight Engineers were upgraded to their new positions.

Safety

There were no major aircraft accidents for the squadron in the first or second quarters. There were two aircraft incidents which necessitated an in-flight engine shutdown. One in-flight engine shutdown occurred in April when internal engine failure was experienced during climb out. Another in-flight shutdown in June was also caused by internal engine failure.

The Safety Office processed two Operational Hazard Reports (OHRs) in the second quarter. The reports concerned proper traffic procedures of other aircraft and the reports were forwarded to the appropriate action agency. As a result of the reports, the aircrews of several organizations were briefed concerning proper traffic procedures. All required monthly reports were forwarded to higher headquarters. These reports included squadron Safety Council minutes, monthly flying safety surveys, aircrew meeting minutes, and the ground accident summary.

The Safety Office initiated a program of fire extinguisher orientation through the unit Safety Council. All crew members of the squadron received a briefing and demonstration provided by the base fire department on the proper use of fire extinguishers found in the housing area and on the aircraft. The unit Safety Council continued to improve safety in the squadron through efforts of several branches within the squadron.

In the third quarter, C-7A's S/N 62-4144, 62-4145, 62-4154, and 62-4170 were damaged by rocket attack on 7 September at Cam Ranh Bay. C-7A S/N 62-4144 had been seriously damaged in an attack on 5 September. The squadron experienced two aircraft incidents which required precautionary landings. The first incident occurred in August when an aircraft was hit by ground fire. Although there was substantial damage to an engine, requiring replacement, it operated normally until a safe landing could be accomplished. The second incident occurred in the middle of September when a landing gear and its associated hydraulic equipment failed to operate normally and emergency procedures were required to get the gear down and locked.

The Safety Office processed six OHRs. Four of these reports involved traffic and traffic control. One report involved the use of the roller conveyors in the aircraft and one involved non-availability of radio frequencies for certain remote airfields. All were referred to the responsible agency for appropriate action.

A meeting of all squadron pilots was held during the quarter to discuss safety and the approaching bad weather. A thorough briefing was provided by the weather officer. Several of the "old heads" of the squadron added their comments and related their experience during the Northeast monsoon season last year. The safety committee worked on selecting a safety slogan to be placed on the spare wheel cover of the squadron Jeep.

In the fourth quarter, the timely actions on 7 October by 1/Lt. Maynard D. Siler, III and his crew on 7 October, when faced with an over-speeding prop, were documented in the citation for his Distinguished Flying Cross:

> "First Lieutenant Maynard D. Siler, III distinguished himself by extraordinary achievement while participating in aerial flight as an Aircraft Commander near Saigon, Republic of Vietnam, on 7 October 1969. On that date, Lieutenant Siler experienced an overspeed of his right engine which necessitated the shutdown of that engine. Because altitude and airspeed could not be maintained, Lieutenant Siler ordered the jettisoning of the load, after he had maneuvered his aircraft away from the city of Saigon to an unpopulated area. Lieutenant Siler then made a single engine landing at Ton Son Nhut Air Base. The fast and correct decisions of Lieutenant Siler enabled the safe return of the aircraft and crew. The professional competence, aerial skill, and devotion to duty displayed by Lieutenant Siler reflect great credit upon himself and the United States Air Force." [16]

C-7A S/N 62-4162 suffered extensive battle damage during a mortar attack at Song Be on 23 December. Both propellers, #1 engine cowling, and the left in-board flap section suffered extensive damage. Minor damage was sustained by the fuselage, tail section, and Copilot's windscreen.

There were no major aircraft accidents. The squadron experienced three incidents. The first was an engine that failed to go into reverse. The second was a loss of engine thrust at cruise power, necessitating a precautionary landing. The third was damage to an aircraft hit by in-coming mortars at a forward airstrip. The aircraft was flown to a major airfield for repairs.

Only one OHR was processed. It covered extensive helicopter traf-fic at a forward base and the performance of the traffic controller at that base.

A flying safety meeting was held after the pilots' meeting in the first week of each month. Topics at these meetings were: fuel requirements, flying above 5000 feet, and operating in Visual Meteorological Conditions as much as possible during Instrument Meteorological Conditions.

Maintenance

Capt. John M. Nowak continued as the squadron Maintenance Officer in the first quarter. He began these duties in July 1968 and would complete them on 3 August 1969. There were 241 enroute delays and 27 initial launch delays charged to the squadron.

From 15-18 January, C-7A S/N 61-2584 underwent extensive temporary wing repairs at the Bu Krak Special Forces camp after it contacted the rotor mast of an Army UH-1 helicopter. It was returned to Cam Ranh Bay and the entire left wing was replaced.

On 4 February, C-7A S/N 62-2584 was sent to Corrosion Control and it was returned on 21 February. On 21 February, C-7A S/N 62-4184 returned from Inspection and Repair as Necessary (IRAN). On 25 February, C-7A S/N 62-4188 was sent to IRAN. On 6 March, C-7A S/N 62-4150 departed for the CONUS for complete depot level metal analysis. On 11 March, C-7A S/N 62-4154 was sent to Corrosion Control and it was returned on 29 March. On 20 March, C-7A S/N 62-4170 was received from CONUS and added to the inventory. On 4 April, C-7A S/N 62-4188 returned from IRAN.

Maintenance manning improved to 105 percent in the quarter; however, over 25 new 3-level mechanics arrived from the CONUS. An extensive training program was put in effect to upgrade these Airmen as soon as possible.

In the second quarter, there were 187 enroute delays and 8 initial launch delays charged to the squadron. This was 71 percent fewer enroute delays and 22 percent fewer initial launch delays than in the first quarter.

On 4 April, C-7A S/N 62-4188 returned from the IRAN facility in Bangkok. On 18 April, C-7A S/N 62-4181 was sent to Corrosion Control and it returned on 6 May. On 23 May, C-7A S/N 62-4157 was sent to Corrosion Control and it returned on 15 June. No aircraft were received from CONUS and none departed for CONUS.

The OJT program was virtually completed with only two of the original 27 personnel still in training for the 5-level. SMSgt. James Sexton was reassigned to Maintenance Analysis and MSgt. James I.

Gillis, Jr. assumed the duties of Maintenance Superintendent.

TSgt. James R. Holland was selected as the Organizational Maintenance Man of the second quarter. On 23 July, C-7A S/N 63-9729 was sent to Corrosion Control and it returned on 25 August.

In August, 1/Lt. Ronald L. Cafferty assumed duties as squadron Maintenance Officer. There were 195 enroute delays and 9 initial launch delays charged to the squadron. No aircraft were received from CONUS and none departed for CONUS.

On 27 September, C-7A S/N 62-4144 was sent to IRAN. OJT status remained stable with one man upgraded to the 5-level and four men remaining in OJT. Sgt. Benedict Knaup was named Wing Outstanding Crew Chief of the third quarter.

In the fourth quarter, MSgt. Walter T. Sims assumed the duties of squadron Maintenance Superintendent. There were 140 enroute delays and 24 initial launch delays charged to the squadron. No aircraft were received from CONUS and none departed for CONUS. On 28 September, C-7A S/N 62-4144 was sent to IRAN and it returned on 11 December. On 6 November, C-7A S/N 62-4171 was sent to IRAN and it returned on 10 December. On 24 December, C-7A S/N 62-12584[17] was sent to IRAN and it did not return by the end of the quarter.

OJT status remained stable. Two men were upgraded to the 5-level. Only two personnel were in OJT at the end of the quarter.

SSgt. William D. Chaney was named Maintenance Man of the Month for December and A/1C Charles T. Hall was named Crew Chief of the Month for December.

Administration

The Administrative Section operated very smoothly in the first quarter. SMSgt. Murray L. Totty continued as squadron First Sergeant. He assumed these duties on 28 October 1968. The section was no longer required to prepare key punch cards and machine listings for the completed AF Forms 112a since the squadron was at 100 percent manning of Operations Technicians. The section continued to meet all suspense dates in a satisfactory manner. First Lieutenant Richard J. Bergholz was the Historian.

The Section continued to operate smoothly in the second quarter. SMSgt. Totty continued as squadron First Sergeant. First Lieutenant Michael W. Harris was the Historian. There were only three minor write-ups during the Staff Assistance Visit of the 834AD staff. The discrepancies were corrected. The section was commended by the Wing for having the lowest error rate in the preparation and submission of

100

OERs. All suspense dates continued to be met satisfactorily.

The Section continued to operate smoothly in the third quarter. SMSgt. Totty continued as squadron First Sergeant and 1/Lt. Michael W. Harris continued as the Historian. All suspense dates were met satisfactorily. The Pride Project nominees for Residential and Operational Facilities were selected as winners of Pride awards in September.

In the fourth quarter, SMSgt. James P. Knight assumed duties as First Sergeant and 1/Lt. Michael W. Harris continued as the Historian. The squadron administration section continued to operate smoothly. Although minor discrepancies were noted during the inspection by the 7th AF Inspector General in November, the section received a rating of "Satisfactory." The Pride Project nominees for Residential and Operational Facilities were selected as winners of Pride awards in October. The section continued to meet all suspense dates satisfactorily.

Supply and Support

The new taxiway, begun in October 1968, was completed in the first quarter, linking the East and West ramps at the North end of the airfield. As a result, ground traffic was expedited. The officers' quarters were expanded with the addition of two new hootches which could house up to 14 men. Conditions became less cramped in the old hootches and comfort was increased.

In the second quarter, the taxiway lines on the East ramp were repainted, improving ground safety. Officer and enlisted quarters were improved with the addition of some concrete sidewalks. Work began to erect a brick wall around the quarters to improve safety, convenience, and appearance.

In the third quarter, concrete sidewalks were completed around the officer and enlisted quarters. Work continued on a brick wall around the quarters to improve safety, convenience, and appearance.

In the fourth quarter, the work was completed on a brick wall around the quarters.

Civic Action and Special Activities

Squadron Civic Actions activities continued in the first quarter to provide food, clothing, and medical supplies to the people of Vietnam. Support of the Love of the Cross Orphanage continued as the primary squadron project, providing clothing, toys, food, and money to the children of the orphanage. The Civic Action organization collected and deposited $850 to be donated to the Education Scholarship Fund and many contacts were made to interest civic action minded groups in the

U.S. to participate in the programs. In the third quarter, the Civic Action organization collected and deposited $1100 to be donated to the Education Scholarship Fund and many additional contacts were made to interest civic action minded groups in the U.S. to participate in the programs. In the fourth quarter, the squadron remained very active in support of local high schools and the Love of the Cross Orphanage.

Sergeant Bruce Sasser remembered how he had more than one job while he was in Vietnam:

> "Besides the midnight shift on the flight line, I had another job while I was at Cam Ranh Bay. I was in a band called The Fugitives, of all things. There were seven of us. If you were in any of the clubs at night, you probably heard us play. Five of the guys were in the Air Force, one was in the Army, and one was a civilian.
>
> We didn't go to other bases. We played the Airmen, NCO, the Officer's club at Cam Rahn Bay and several officer squadron parties. We also played at the Navy clubs (Chief's Club and Officer's Mess) across from the flight line.
>
> We were asked to go on the USO Tour in country, but we didn't do that because they would only pay us our rank pay, whereas each independent club paid us a specified fee which was a whole lot more than rank pay. We had our own band manager, Marcus Salas, our own practice room, and vehicle to move the equipment around the base.
>
> When we needed different things for our instruments, our manager was able to get them from the Philippines through different flights there. When a person's tour in country was up, we would have an audition to replace them, and it was done mainly through word of mouth." [18]

Airlift Accomplishments [19]

During the first quarter, passengers hauled were 13,165 in January; 8924 in February; and 12,466 in March for a total of 34,555. Cargo hauled was 1439.0 tons in January; 1331.0 tons in February; and 1481.3 tons in March for a total of 4251.3 tons. In January, the squadron flew 2426 sorties while logging 1789.1 flying hours. In February, the squadron flew 2110 sorties while logging 1658.6 flying hours. In March, the squadron flew 2330 sorties while logging 1825.5 flying hours.

During the second quarter, passengers hauled were 12,951 in April; 11,897 in May; and 12,063 in June for a total of 36,911. Cargo hauled was 1287.3 tons in April; 1296.3 tons in May; and 1068.1 tons in June for a total of 3651.7 tons. In April, the squadron flew 2267 sorties while logging 1721.8 flying hours. In May, the squadron flew 2301 sorties while logging 1718.2 flying hours. In June, the squadron flew 2093 sorties while logging 1642.1 flying hours.

During the third quarter, passengers hauled were 11,929 in July; 14,505 in August; and 11,343 in September for a total of 37,777. Cargo hauled was 1140.4 tons in July; 1207.6 tons in August; and 1058.6 tons in September for a total of 3406.6 tons. In July, the squadron flew 2158 sorties while logging 1747.9 flying hours. In August, the squadron flew 2295 sorties while logging 1740.0 flying hours. In September, the squadron flew 2017 sorties while logging 1601.8 flying hours.

During the fourth quarter, passengers hauled were 13,935 in October; 10,858 in November; and 11,631 in December for a total of 36,424. Cargo hauled was 1559.2 tons in October; 1099.0 tons in November; and 1163.0 tons in December for a total of 3821.2 tons. In October, the squadron logged 1666.8 flying hours. In November, the squadron logged 1509.0 flying hours. In December, the squadron logged 1685.0 flying hours. Total of sorties flown in the fourth quarter was 6866. The squadron did not report sorties each month.

Commander's Summary

First Quarter 1969 [20]
"The 458th Tactical Airlift Squadron continued to supply its users throughout the Republic of Vietnam with excellent service. The manning improved from 85 percent to 89 percent, but it continued to cause hardships. Again, there were fewer aircraft incidents and no major or minor accidents. Squadron Operations and Administration continued the excellent work that has become common in the 458th TAS."

Second Quarter 1969 [21]
"The 458th TAS continued to supply its users throughout the Republic of Vietnam with excellent service. Again, there were few aircraft incidents and no major or minor accidents. Squadron Operations and Administration continued excellent work that has become common in the 458th TAS."

Third Quarter 1969 [22]
"The 458th TAS continued to supply its users throughout the Republic of Vietnam with excellent service. Again, there were few aircraft incidents and no major or minor accidents. Squadron Operations

and Administration continued excellent work that has become common in the 458th TAS."

Fourth Quarter 1969 [23]

"The 458th TAS continued to supply its users throughout the Republic of Vietnam with excellent service. Again, there were few aircraft incidents and no major or minor accidents. Squadron Operations and Administration continued excellent work that has become common in the 458th TAS."

End Notes: 458 TAS

[1] *19690101-19691231 458 TAS History*
[2] 458 TAS Special Order G-1, dated 18 January 1969
[3] 458 TAS Special Order G-2, dated 18 October 1969
[4] *Surfside Sentinel, Vol. 2 No. 8*, dated 28 February 1969
[5] 7AF Special Order G-2165, dated 15 May 1970
[6] 7AF Special Order G-2166, dated 15 May 1970
[7] 7AF Special Order G-2633, dated 22 August 1971
[8] 7AF Special Order G-5284, dated 20 November 1970
[9] Citation from Distinguished Flying Cross Society
[10] 7AF Special Order G-5284, dated 20 November 1970
[11] 7AF Special Order G-3182, dated 14 July 1970
[12] 7AF Special Order G-2556, dated 6 June 1970
[13] 7AF Special Order G-3183, dated 14 July 1970
[14] 7AF Special Order G-3182, dated 14 July 1970
[15] 7AF Special Order G-1941, dated 18 June 1971
[16] 7AF Special Order G-2143, dated 15 May 1970
[17] Although this S/N, 62-15284, violates the Air Force numbering system, it is the number recorded in the maintenance records of the 483 TAW and other records.
[18] *C-7A Caribou Association Newsletter, Vol. 21, Issue 1, April 2010*
[19] When the data in the squadron history and the Wing history differ, the Wing data is shown.
[20] 458 TAS Commander's Summary, 31 March 1969 by Lt. Col. Charles E. Barnett
[21] 458 TAS Commander's Summary, 30 June 1969 by Lt. Col. Charles E. Barnett
[22] 458 TAS Commander's Summary, 30 September 1969 by Lt. Col. Charles E. Barnett
[23] 458 TAS Commander's Summary, 31 December 1969 by Lt. Col. Jeff J. Piercy

459th Tactical Airlift Squadron[1]

The primary mission of the 459th Tactical Airlift Squadron (459 TAS) at Phu Cat was to provide intra-theater airlift in support of all free world military civic actions, aid forces, units engaged in combat, combat support, logistics, and civil assistance to the Republic of Vietnam. This mission was accomplished through C-7A aircraft using both conventional landings and aerial delivery of personnel and supplies. The Military Assistance Command Vietnam priorities concerning deployment of C-7A aircraft were followed. In addition, the squadron also performed other airlift missions as directed by the Commander, 483rd Tactical Airlift Wing (483 TAW).

To accomplish these missions, the squadron was authorized 54 officers and 250 enlisted personnel in the first quarter. Of these authorizations, 47 officers and 217 enlisted personnel were assigned at the beginning of the first quarter, increasing to 51 officers and 251 enlisted personnel at the end of the quarter. In the second quarter, the squadron did not include its authorized strength and number of personnel assigned in the quarterly history report. In the third quarter, the squadron was authorized 54 officers and 311 enlisted personnel. Of these authorizations, 47 officers and 277 enlisted personnel were assigned at the end of the quarter. In the fourth quarter, 54 officers and 313 enlisted personnel were authorized, but only 47 officers and 262 enlisted personnel were assigned at the end of the year. No improvement in the situation was expected in the first quarter of 1970. Many maintenance personnel at Phu Cat would be attached to the 37th Field Maintenance Squadron on 1 January 1970.

The 483 TAW mission site at Da Nang Air Base, an additional responsibility of the squadron, coordinated with the I Corps Tactical Operations Center (TOC) to support III MAF and 5 SFG in I Corps. The mission site at Da Nang was under the command of four different commanders in the first quarter. Lt. Col. Walter Glaze, Jr. commanded for the first week in January to allow Lt. Col. William C. Warrell to become Mission Site Commander of the 483 TAW mission site in Bangkok, Thailand. Capt. James R. Johnston, II became site commander during the third week in March when Lt. Col. Glaze returned to the CONUS on emergency leave. Capt. Johnston was replaced during the last week in March by Capt. Paul A. Nafziger, when Capt. Johnston went on leave.

Lt. Col. John Kozey, Jr. continued as Squadron Commander, having assumed command on 23 August 1968.[2] On 25 March, Col. Kozey began his 30 day extension leave and, in his absence, Lt. Col. Samuel A. Wareham, the Operations Officer, assumed command.[3] On 29 April, Lt. Col. Kozey returned from his leave and resumed command.

During the second week in April, Capt. Nafziger was replaced as the Da Nang mission site commander by Lt. Col. Robert D. Lipscomb. Lt. Col. Lipscomb remained in command for the remainder of the second quarter except for a two week period when Lt. Col. Arthur T. Rossing assumed command to allow Lt. Col. Lipscomb to return to Phu Cat to fulfill squadron duties.

On 17 July, Lt. Col. Wareham completed his tour and was replaced by Lt. Col. Arthur T. Rossing.

In the last week of July, Col. Lipscomb was replaced by Lt. Col. George Stalk as Da Nang mission site commander. Lt. Col. Stalk was replaced by Maj. Donald E. Henkle during the first week of September so Lt. Col. Stalk could prepare for his return to the U.S.

On 26 August, Lt. Col. Rossing replaced Lt. Col. Kozey as Squadron Commander when he completed his tour. Lt. Col. John J. Hanley became the squadron Operations Officer.[4]

On 6 November, the Tactical Operations Center changed the morning reporting time for the Officer In Charge from 0400 hours to 0500 hours.

On 11 November, Lt. Col. John D. Pennekamp, Jr. replaced Col. Hanley as Operations Officer. On 13 November, Lt. Col. Hanley was reassigned as Commander of the 536 TAS at Vung Tau. On 18 November, Maj. Charles H. Weidman, Jr. became mission site commander at Da Nang replacing Maj. Henkle, who returned to Phu Cat for other duties.

Operations

Squadron missions supported the III Marine Amphibious Force (III MAF), the Americal Division, 5th Special Forces Group (5 SFG), Army of the Republic of Vietnam (ARVN), Office of Civil Operations and Rural Development Support (CORDS), and the United States Agency for International Development (USAID) in I Corps and II Corps.

The Da Nang mission site was reduced from four to three aircraft, but the number of crews positioned there remained the same. This allowed the crews to have more days off during their temporary duty (TDY) tours there. The users at Da Nang were the 5 SFG (one aircraft) and the Americal Division (two aircraft). The professionalism of the personnel of the 459 TAS was demonstrated by the accomplishment of their mission in spite of the threat by hostile forces and the perils they presented to flying into forward outposts.

Lt. Col. Wareham continued as the squadron Operations Officer. The squadron Tactical Operation Center (TOC) was reorganized, eliminating the need for a duty officer for 24 hours a day. One duty officer opened the TOC at 0400 hours and was relieved at 1130 hours. The second duty officer then closed the TOC after all the aircraft landed and the activities of the day were completed.

The men of the squadron accomplished their mission in a professional manner during the third quarter. It is noteworthy that they did this in the face of such obstacles as the monsoon season, flying into forward airfields with no navigational aids, and enemy activity. Operations at the Da Nang mission site remained unchanged, with three aircraft working primarily for III MAF, 5 SFG, and the ARVN.

The actions of 1/Lt. David B. Bowling and his crew on 12 August were documented in the citation for his Distinguished Flying Cross:

"First Lieutenant David B. Bowling distinguished himself by extraordinary achievement while participating in aerial flight as a Pilot at Tra Bong, Republic of Vietnam on 12 August 1969. On that date, Lieutenant Bowling delivered a load of ammunition to a Special Forces camp which was under heavy attack. In spite of hazardous terrain and the constant threat of hostile ground fire, he superbly accomplished this highly intricate mission in support of free world forces combating aggression. The professional competence, aerial skill and devotion to duty displayed by Lieutenant Bowling in the dedication of his service to his country reflect great credit upon himself and the United States Air Force." [5]

On 16 August, the *Ellis* 457 mission lost a gravity airdrop load at Tra Bong Special Forces camp, five miles from the drop zone. The malfunction occurred while in straight and level flight with the six minute check completed. The failure was determined to be in the release mechanism. As a result of this incident, a new procedure was developed for securing the load prior to the release point. This involved replacement of the previously used parachute D-ring with a parachute V-ring.

The actions of SSgt. Charles H. Sitzenstock, Jr. and his crew on 25 September were documented, without identifying the actual location of the action, in the citation for his Air Medal:

"Staff Sergeant Charles H. Sitzenstock, Jr. distinguished himself by meritorious achievement while participating in aerial flight over Southeast Asia [North Vietnam] on 25 September 1969. On that date, he superbly accomplished a highly intricate mission to support Free World forces that were combating aggression. His energetic application of his knowledge and skill were significant factors that contributed greatly to furthering United States goals in Southeast Asia. His professional skill and airmanship reflect great credit upon himself and the United States Air Force." [6]

SSgt. Sitzenstock remembered that mission:

"I recall the mission into the mounds of North Vietnam at night to recover a Mike Force (five of our Special Forces guys and a special enemy KIA whom we took to Saigon). Interesting and difficult days. Many things I experienced then were so surreal that I try to remember only the good things. Try and forget the bad and the heat, dirt and stench. There were times that were absolutely funny, crazy, cruel, and some beautiful, but always dangerous. Our youth and sense of duty was the blessing that kept the fear at bay.

Every day was an adventure, a test, and a challenge. We Flight Engineers had a hand sign that we used to give to our fellow Bou comrades as we taxied out each time. Two fists together (one above the other) the top one with the thumb up and the bottom one with the thumb pointed down. I guess the interpretation is 'it could go either way today, so be careful and take care.'

You never knew what you would carry or get involved in each day. You could be hauling or dropping pallets of 105's or powder, vegetables and fruits, cases of booze/beer, wounded GIs and South Vietnamese, KIAs, cows, pigs, Montegnards; drop paratroopers (with or without their dogs); extract or rescue stranded GIs; relocate villages of scared Vietnamese civilians to a safe area; transport a missionary and his flock of school boys; move band members to play at the closing of a forward fire base; or take and pick up a damaged/repaired bird in Bangkok, then go south to Songkla, over to Phuket, north to the F-105 bases and then over Cambodia and Laos at 10,000 feet to Phu Cat.

We heard that one of our outfits got a letter from a North Vietnamese officer thanking us for transporting his troops from one place to another (you never knew who was coming onboard). I once transported a Vietnamese woman (who I initially thought was a gunshot victim) that was thrown aboard at one of our stops. Later in flight, I found out she was pregnant and I helped her deliver her baby (a girl). When we landed, she got off the plane and just walked away.

Beautiful country, but I wouldn't want to live there or die there, as so many did. I also remember the many C-141 missions into Nam, before and after my C-7A tour, transporting wounded back to the States or an entire cargo compartment full of ten pallets (4 wide, 2 high) of KIA caskets (our boys) to Dover." [7]

As in the previous quarter, the men of the squadron accomplished their mission in a professional manner. It is noteworthy that they did this in the face of such obstacles as the monsoon season, flying into forward airfields with no navigational aids, and enemy activity.

In October, Maj. Gen. Louis T. Smith (Commander, Joint United States Military Advisory Group, Thailand) recognized the C-7A airlift support accorded to USMACTHAI/JUSMAGTHAI during the period 1 August 1968 to 3 September 1969 as "outstanding in every respect." He commended the aircrews and ground personnel for their dedication and responsiveness to mission requirements and their highest degree of professional competence. His communication was endorsed by General Creighton W. Abrams (Commander, United States Military Assistance Command, Vietnam), General George S. Brown (Commander, Seventh Air Force), Brig. Gen. John H. Herring (Commander, 483AD), and Col. Christensen (Commander, 483 TAW).

The actions of 1/Lt. Gary L. Clark and his crew (1/Lt. James B. Rollins and TSgt. Roy L. Callier) on 11 October, while flying the *Ellis* 474 mission with C-7A S/N 63-9728, resulted in all of the crew members receiving the Air Medal for their exceptional flying skills. Their actions were briefly documented in the citation for his Air Medal:

"First Lieutenant Gary L. Clark distinguished himself by meritorious achievement while participating in aerial flight over Southeast Asia [Pleiku] on 11 October 1969. On that date, he superbly accomplished a highly intricate mission to support Free World forces that were combating aggression. His energetic application of his knowledge and skill were significant factors that contributed greatly to furthering United States goals in Southeast Asia. His professional skill and airmanship reflect great credit upon himself and the United States Air Force." [8]

Lieutenant Clark was presented the PACAF Order of the Able Aeronaut award by Gen. Joseph J. Nazzaro, Commander of PACAF, for the harrowing experience. He recalled the details of that mission:

"We were inbound for landing at Pleiku when we lowered the gear handle and found that the right main gear failed to extend fully to the 'down and locked' position. There was no 'green' light for the right main gear. I broke from the pattern and orbited several miles southeast of the runway to try and sort things out. We exercised the landing gear several times and we noticed that the strut inched down a bit more, but stopped short of being fully extended. At one point, I turned controls over to the copilot, 1/Lt. James B. Rollins, and went back to the cabin to take a look. The landing gear was about 12 inches away from being fully extended. The Flight Engineer, TSgt Roy L. Callier, and I decided to remove the cabin window next to the right main gear to see if we could get to the strut. The only thing we had in the cabin was a broom which we poked through the window hole. We tried to pry the strut down toward the extended position, but we couldn't get any leverage on it, so we gave that up.

Fortunately, we had enough fuel, so we had time to work through the emergency. Given that we had hydraulic pressure on the gear and since the right main wheel was extended to a point below the aircraft fuselage, I decided to try and make a cross-wind touch and go landing on just the left main tire by using a lot of left aileron cross controlled with right rudder to hold the nose straight down the runway. On landing, I planned to reduce the amount of left bank enough to allow the airplane to ease over onto the right main tire to 'bump' it on the runway just before applying full power to complete the touch and go. I configured for a no-flap approach, leaving the landing gear extended throughout. I was hoping that as the right main gear started to collapse, when I lifted back off the runway, the strut might snap back toward the down and locked position given the hydraulic pressure behind it. As we didn't have any cargo or passengers onboard, we were light when we attempted this and that really helped.

I contacted Pleiku ALCE and let them know my intentions. A few minutes later, they called me back with clearance from Wing to try it. I then declared an emergency with Pleiku tower and they rolled the fire trucks as we entered the pattern for a no-flap approach to a touch and go. On that first attempt, I landed left wing low on the left main tire, eased the wings level so the right main tire would touch the runway, then as the right main gear started to collapse I went to full power to get airborne again. I remember during the maneuver that the Flight Engineer yelled out 'it's collapsing' as I was lifting off the runway for the climb. On climb-out, the Flight Engineer reported that the right main gear had snapped back a few inches closer toward the extended position, but not enough to give us the 'green' light. That was encouraging so we left the gear handle down, climbed up into a right, closed downwind leg and set up for another no-flap approach to another touch and go.

On the second approach, I noticed ahead and to my left that a lot of guys had gathered along the taxiway to watch, so we were rapidly becoming the main attraction that day. As I made that second approach, I again landed left wing low on the left main tire and again eased the wings level so the right main tire would touch the runway, then went to full power for the go-around as the right main gear started to collapse. Again, the Flight Engineer yelled 'it's collapsing.' Fortunately, when I lifted off the runway this time, the right main gear did snap to the full 'down and locked' position with all the 'green' gear lights on, but then I encountered another problem. After I went to full power on the second touch and go, when I started to bring my power back to climb power, the right engine remained at max power. I had lost all throttle control of the right engine! The throttle linkage had failed, probably because I was too heavy handed in pushing the power up on that second touch and go.

Having just solved one issue and now working on a second issue, I was hesitant to shut the right engine down until I had the landing assured even with potential control issues with the engine operating at max power. We proceeded to pull up into a right closed downwind with the right engine at max power and the left engine at half power. While that made for some uncoordinated flying, it wasn't a major control problem. Again, I planned for a no-flap landing approach. We turned onto final at about one mile out, the gear was still showing down and locked with the gear lights all showing 'green.' On short final, I had the copilot shut the engine down and we eased the bird in for a safe landing.

It turned out that the airplane had just gone through an Inspect and Repair As Necessary (IRAN) maintenance process. During that process, the strut was machined and, apparently, some metal filings had fallen down between the strut and strut's outer case. Those filings caused the strut to bind, preventing it from fully extending. Fortunately, we were able to bring it back in one piece so it could be repaired and returned to service. Just another day in the life of a Caribou pilot!" [9]

The actions of Capt. Richard R. Lanoue and his crew on 20 November were documented in the citation for his Distinguished Flying Cross:

"Captain Richard R. Lanoue distinguished himself by extraordinary achievement while participating in aerial flight as an

Instructor Pilot at Duc Lap, Republic of Vietnam, on 20 November 1969. On that date Captain Lanoue delivered a critically needed load of rations and ammunition to the Special Forces camp which was surrounded and under attack from an unknown size hostile force. Through his personal bravery and energetic application of his knowledge and skill, he significantly furthered the goal of the United States in Southeast Asia. The professional competence, aerial skill, and devotion to duty displayed by Captain Lanoue reflect great credit upon himself and the United States Air Force."[10]

In December, action picked up at Tien Phuoc (V-239). The actions of Maj. William M. Vondersmith, Jr. and his crew on 21 December were documented in the citation for his Distinguished Flying Cross:

"Major William M. Vondersmith, Jr. distinguished himself by extraordinary achievement while participating in aerial flight as an Aircraft Commander at Tien Phuoc Special Forces camp, Republic of Vietnam on 21 December 1969. On that date, Major Vondersmith made numerous flights into an artillery outpost that was surrounded by hostile forces and was known to be an extremely high threat area. Through his personal bravery and energetic application of his knowledge and skill, he significantly furthered the goal of the United States in Southeast Asia. The professional competence, aerial skill, and devotion to duty displayed by Major Vondersmith reflect great credit upon himself and the United States Air Force." [11]

The actions of SSgt. Gilbert Nickerson and his crew on 26 December were documented in the citation for his Distinguished Flying Cross:

"Staff Sergeant Gilbert Nickerson distinguished himself by extraordinary achievement while participating in aerial flight as a C-7A Flight Engineer at Tien Phuoc, Republic of Vietnam on 26 December 1969. On that date, Sergeant Nickerson completed three sorties into Tien Phuoc in adverse weather carrying vitally needed ammunition. The base was under intense hostile fire, but off-loading was accomplished in minimum time due to the precise performance of Sergeant Nickerson. The professional competence, aerial skill, and devotion to duty displayed by Sergeant Nickerson reflect great credit upon himself and the United States Air Force." [12]

The actions of 1/Lt. Dennis A. Dokken and his crew on 26 December were documented in the citation for his Distinguished Flying Cross:

"First Lieutenant Dennis A. Dokken distinguished himself by extraordinary achievement while participating in aerial flight as copilot at Tien Phuoc, Republic of Vietnam on 26 December 1969. On that date, Lieutenant Dokken, as a C-7A crew member, flew Tactical Emergency missions into Tien Phuoc airfield, where on 26 December a C-7A crew was shot down, killing the pilot and engineer and severely injuring the copilot. With forward air controller and fighter support and under sporadic ground fire, Lieutenant Dokken and his crew continued for three days to deliver their cargo into the airfield. The professional competence, aerial skill, and devotion to duty displayed by Lieutenant Dokken reflect great credit upon himself and the United States Air Force." [13]

On 24-25 December, C-7A S/N 62-4150, flew the Operation Santa Bou mission in I Corps. Sorties were flown into Special Forces camps and artillery sites at Minh Long, Ha Thanh, Tra Bong, Tien Phuoc, and Thong Duc in I Corps. Christmas "Ditty Bags," eggnog, ice cream, and cigars were given to Army forces and candy was distributed to Vietnamese children in the area. A face of Santa Claus was painted on the nose by OLAA maintenance personnel. In a 31 December letter, Col. Christensen, Commander of the 483 TAW, thanked the squadron for the great success of the Santa Bou operation. He expressed "deep satisfaction for this uniquely interesting holiday program" and commended 1/Lt. Timothy M. Ennor for the outstanding manner in which he organized and supervised the two successful missions.

Training and Stan-Eval

Lt. Col. Tom M. Skillman was Chief of Training until his tour ended. He was replaced in the middle of March by Lt. Col. Robert D. Lipscomb. The Stan/Eval Section, led by Lt. Col. Lawrence E. Pennington, was one of the busiest components of the squadron. Thirty-three check rides and 33 emergency procedure rides were accomplished in the first quarter. In the second quarter, 28 check rides and 31 emergency procedure training flights were accomplished. In addition, the Stan/Eval section checked out 7 Aircraft Commanders at restricted Type I airfields and checked out 19 pilots for gravity and personnel air drops.

In the third quarter, when Lt. Col. Ivan R. Fry finished his tour, he was replaced by Maj. Donald K. Law as Scheduling Officer. On 7 July, Lt. Col. Lipscomb was replaced by Maj. Donald. G. Wolpert as Chief of Training. On 19 August, Lt. Col. Pennington finished his tour and he was replaced by Maj. David W. Hutchens as Chief of Stan/Eval.

The Training Section continued its vigorous upgrade program, upgrading 2 Flight Examiners, 5 Instructor Pilots, 11 Aircraft Commanders, and 12 First Pilots. All this was accomplished in spite of the fact that Minh Long, the primary Type I airfield used for Aircraft Commander upgrading, was closed for a majority of the quarter. The section prepared an instrument refresher course tailored to the operations in SEA and presented it at a series of seminars at Phu Cat and Da Nang. All squadron pilots were required to attend. The heavy training workload was predicted to continue through the fourth quarter. It would be necessary to train 9 to 10 restricted field pilots by the end of the year to replace forecasted losses. Stan/Eval remained one of the busiest sections in the squadron. They administered 35 emergency procedure flights, 36 check flights, and 26 restricted field qualification flights.

On 21 December, Maj. Wolpert completed his tour and was replaced by Maj. Richard L. Fitzpatrick as Chief of Training. Maj. Hutchens continued as Chief of Stan/Eval. The accelerated upgrading program continued to be used in providing the necessary number of Aircraft Commanders. The squadron lost two Instructor Pilots and 16 Aircraft Commanders during the quarter and gained 18 pilots, 8 of whom had prior flying assignments while the other 10 were UPT graduates.

During the quarter, a Flight Examiner, 4 Instructor Pilots, 12 Aircraft Commanders, and 16 Copilots were upgraded. Flight Engineers increased by 10 and 2 Flight Examiner Flight Engineers and 5 Instructor Flight Engineers were upgraded. A requirement to upgrade 7-8 Aircraft Commanders to Restricted Field status was anticipated for the first quarter of 1970. Stan/Eval administered 24 Emergency Procedure Flight checks, 51 Tactical Flight Checks, and 5 Restricted Field Qualification Flight Checks. Manning of Flight Engineers decreased from 25 at the beginning of the quarter to 23 at the end of the year.

Safety
In the first quarter, Maj. Roger R. Cowell was the Chief of Safety. The post-Tet Offensive resulted in the squadron reporting five ground fire hit incidents, two aircraft subjected to mortar fire at Quang Ngai, and one aircraft at Tam Ky. No damage was done to the aircraft by the hostile mortar fire and minor damage was done by the ground fire incidents. Three incidents occurred in which one nose wheel up landing was made, one wing tip was damaged, and a fuel truck backed into a rear door. No injuries resulted and only minor damage occurred in each incident.

On 7 February, a squadron aircraft landed with nose gear up at Phu Cat after all gear lowering procedures were unsuccessful. No injuries and only minor damage to the aircraft resulted. The actions of SSgt. Sitzenstock and his crew are documented in the citation for his Distinguished Flying Cross:

> "Staff Sergeant Charles H. Sitzenstock, Jr. distinguished himself by extraordinary achievement while participating in aerial flight as a Flight Engineer at Phu Cat Air Base, Republic of Vietnam on 7 February 1969. On that date, Sergeant Sitzenstock encountered gear malfunction on his aircraft. Through his personal bravery and energetic application of his knowledge and skill, a successful gear-up landing was made with little damage to his aircraft and no personal injuries to the crew or passengers. The professional competence, aerial skill and devotion to duty displayed by Sergeant Sitzenstock reflect great credit upon himself and the United States Air Force." [14]

On 21 February, the *Ellis* 432 mission escaped damage or injury from two incoming mortar rounds while on the ground at Tam Ky Special Forces camp. On 24 February, a wing tip was damaged by a tree in the parking lot at Tra Bong Special Forces camp (V-112). Minor damage resulted.

On 26 February, the squadron suffered its first aircraft loss, C-7A S/N 62-4153, in more than two years. The accident occurred at Tra Bong Special Forces camp, one of the shortest and most difficult fixed wing airfields in SEA.[15] The aircraft touched down short of the runway and sheared the left main landing gear. The aircraft ground looped 180 degrees and came to rest in a rocky ditch, causing major damage. The landing gear sheared off, the wing was damaged, a propeller broke off, and the empennage broke off. The three man crew and one passenger were unhurt, but one civilian Vietnamese was injured by flying wreckage. The aircraft was lifted by an Army CH-56 Skycrane to Da Nang, loaded on a barge, and moved to Bangkok, Thailand where it was successfully refurbished.[16]

On 24 March, the *Ellis* 431 and *Ellis* 497 missions escaped damage or injury from several incoming mortar rounds while on the ground at Quang Ngai (V-23). On 27 March, a gear door was damaged when a fuel truck backed into an aircraft at Ban Me Thout (V-12). No injuries and minor damage resulted.

In the second quarter, Maj. Cowell continued as the Chief of Safety. Two ground fire hit incidents were reported. Hits were taken at Duc Pho (V-201) and Quang Ngai; however, damage to the aircraft was minor and no injuries were inflicted by the small arms rounds. Three incidents occurred in which six men were injured. On 3 May, 1/Lt. Bernard F. Bick was seriously injured when struck by a forklift while walking across the Airlift Control Element (ALCE) parking ramp at Chu Lai (V-194). Serious internal injury necessitated hospitalization of Lt. Bick in Japan. On 12 May, 1/Lt. James W. Nelson was involved in a Jeep accident in Da Nang, resulting in a compound leg fracture. He was flown to Japan for hospitalization. On the evening of 17 June, several enemy mortar rounds landed in the enlisted men's housing area at Phu Cat. Four airmen from the squadron were injured in the attack: TSgt Donald M. Gill, TSgt James D. Wall, Sgt. Robert E. Grady, and Sgt. Michael Matiash.[17]

Mike Matiash remembered that night:

> "I was walking out of the NCO club about 2 or 3 minutes after midnight and we must have been in the area where the BX was. I recall seeing a flare go up. I believe that I heard the mortar tube go off and a buddy, Bob, said, 'It's one of ours.'
>
> Well no, it wasn't. I lost a lot of blood and was in shock. Bob wrote me while I was in the hospital that someone was killed in the hootch area, but I can't verify that. I think that up to 5 rounds landed. One or two rounds sounded as if they hit toward the flight line area. I don't recall hearing about any aircraft being hit, but I do recall that the NCO Club was hit.
>
> I was med-evac'd to Qui Nhon, so I have no knowledge of much after I was hit."

On 26 April, small arms fire was taken by the *Ellis* 432 mission while landing at Duc Pho. No injuries and only minor damage resulted. On 6 May, small arms fire was taken by the *Ellis* 433 mission while landing at Quang Ngai. No injuries and only minor damage resulted.

In the third quarter, an *Ellis* 432 mission received six small arms hits on approach to Minh Long (V-102). The right main gear collapsed on landing, but no injuries were incurred. On 12 July, the *Ellis* 475 mission, C-7A S/N 63-9728, received minor damage at Ba To (V-84) when a propeller blade tip separated and passed through the side of the fuselage. On the same day, the *Ellis* 432 mission, C-7A S/N 63-9726, had high oil temperature, low oil pressure, and loss of power on #2 engine while on the ground at Tra Bong. This was later determined to be an internal engine failure. Squadron maintenance personnel changed the engine at the forward strip in record time. On 4 August, the *Ellis* 457 mission, C-7A S/N 63-9726, received minor damage to an aileron at Ba To. The cause was determined to be an aileron bracket installed with the wrong type of rivets.

On 14 August, the *Ellis* 431 mission and the *Ellis* 432 mission, C-7A S/N 63-9728, escaped major damage or injury from incoming mortar rounds while on the ground at Tra Bong. The *Ellis* 432 mission, C-7A S/N 69-9728, received one shrapnel hit in the cargo door. Later that day, the *Ellis* 431, 432, and 457 missions were requested to fly Emergency Resupply sorties into Tra Bong. The following day, the airfield was closed and airdrops were begun. The bravery and dedication exemplified by those crews were demonstrated by other crews on other missions throughout the quarter.

On 16 August, the *Ellis* 457 mission lost a gravity airdrop load five miles short of the drop zone at Tra Bong. The cause was equipment failure. On 18 August, the *Ellis* 432 mission, C-7A S/N 62-4153, received six small arms hits on approach to Minh Long. The right main gear collapsed on landing. There were no injuries, but the aircraft was declared a combat loss. On 22 August, the *Ellis* 457 mission, C-7A S/N 63-9726, received minor damage when the hydraulic line to the left main gear broke and started a fire on the ground at Mai Loc (V-72).

On 19 August, Maj. Cowell finished his tour and he was replaced by Maj. William M. Vondersmith as Chief of Safety. On 10 September, Kenneth A. Yoder dislocated his left kneecap when he slipped on wet M8A1 matting while pushing a light cart on the flight line.

On 26 September, Lt. Col. Claire J. Reeder, Commander of Company C of the 5SFG, wrote a Letter of Appreciation to the Commander of the 459 TAS to extend his sincere appreciation to the pilots and crews of the squadron for the outstanding support given to Company C and its subordinate detachments during the previous two years. He found "particularly noteworthy" the outstanding accomplishments of the crews flying in support of troop lift movements on 18 September 1969 to Mai Loc. The six sorties flown on this date enabled the Special Forces team to rapidly react to vital intelligence information, thereby preventing an enemy attack on the camp. He noted that "prompt action by your command, together with superior flying ability in the face of strong cross winds and hazardous ground fog, allowed the mission to be completed without incident." He considered the performance of the squadron to be indicative of the support that Special Forces had come to regard as commonplace in their joint service effort.

The squadron continued its flying safety and reliability records during the third quarter. There were no reportable flying safety accidents and only one reportable ground accident. The initial launch reliability rate was 99.0 percent. This compared with the Wing initial launch reliability rate of 99.4 percent. The slight drop compared to the previous quarter was attributed to the lack of waterproofing of the C-7A, combined with the beginning of the rainy season, wet magnetos, wet radios, wet navigation equipment, etc. The enroute reliability rate was 99.4 percent for the quarter.

Maj. William M. Vondersmith continued as Chief of Safety in the fourth quarter. The actions of Capt. Spencer F. McClure and his crew on 11 November were documented in the citation for his Distinguished Flying Cross:

> "Captain Spencer F. McClure distinguished himself by extraordinary achievement while participating in aerial flight as an Instructor Pilot at Chu Lai Air Base, Republic of Vietnam on 11 November 1969. On that date, Captain McClure's plane experienced an engine failure just after takeoff, while carrying a heavy load of cargo. Through his personal bravery and energetic application of his knowledge and skill, he was able to avert a possible major aircraft accident. The professional competence, aerial skill and devotion to duty displayed by Captain McClure reflect great credit upon himself and the United States Air Force."[18]

On 11 November, *Ellis* 475, C-7A S/N 63-9730, experienced excessive hydraulic pressure (4000 psi), hydraulic fluid boiling, and bursting of hydraulic lines while on an instrument approach to Chu Lai. The Aircraft Commander, 1/Lt. Robert D. Marx, attempted to cool the fluid by cycling the landing gear. After doing this, he was unable to raise the gear, so he declared an emergency. He was sent around by the Chu Lai tower for a suspected retracted nose gear. While on a closed downwind for a second landing attempt, the hydraulic lines in the cabin burst, spraying vaporized hydraulic fluid into the cabin. The aircraft was landed without incident and the fire department was used to spray the suspected fire in the cabin. There was no significant damage to the aircraft.

On 26 December, C-7A S/N 63-9723, was shot down by ground fire at Tien Phuoc. The Aircraft Commander, 1/Lt. David B. Bowling, and Flight Engineer, TSgt. E. J. Welch, Jr., were killed and the Copilot, 1/Lt. Richard J. Patterson, was seriously injured. Lt. Patterson had arrived in Vietnam on 30 November and had not completed his checkout as a Copilot. At the end of the quarter, he remained unconscious in the hospital at Chu Lai, but was expected to be airlifted to Japan soon.

Lieutenant Patterson remembered a little about that fateful day at Tien Phuoc:

> "Dan Ahern, Tom McCloy, 'Cuffy' Kelso, and I left Travis

AFB on 30 November 1969 and felt lucky that it was the last day of the month. We could rotate home earlier in November 1970 and only spend 11 months in-country! Well, that was our thought as the first graduates from the new C-7A school at Dyess AFB.

We arrived in-country at Da Nang and spent a couple of days there before we finally got a shuttle to Phu Cat. I know it's hard to believe, but all four of us were graduates of the same class at the Air Force Academy, the same pilot training class at Vance AFB, and the first Dyess class. We arrived in Phu Cat about 14 or 15 December. Dan and I were assigned to the 459th and roomed together. Tom and 'Cuffy' were assigned to the 'other' C-7A squadron. Dan was sent back to Da Nang so he could get checked out faster and I was to get checked out at Phu Cat.

On 26 December, I took off with Dave Hutchins and flew to Chu Lai. Dave was a Flight Examiner and we were on our third or fourth training flight together. Dan flew down from Da Nang with Dave Bolling. Dan was on a check ride, but Bolling was only an IP and could not give check rides. So Dan and I changed planes. I didn't know Dave Bolling or 'Squeaky' Welch (the flight engineer), but we hit it off OK and taxied out for take-off. I remember the take-off because I had my new Pentax 35 mm camera with me and left it in the plane that Dan and Dave were flying.

The next thing I remember was being in the hospital at Tachikawa, Japan. Dave, 'Squeaky,' and I were on our way to Tien Phouc carrying 155 mm howitzer ammo. Since I cannot remember, the remainder of the story is a compilation from talks I've had over the years with people familiar with the crash. One of those people is the photographer for the accident investigation. He gave me his photos.

We were in the final turn at Tien Phouc when an AK-47 bullet, fired from over a mile away, hit Dave in the hip. Dave was the only pilot I knew who wore his flak vest. Everyone else (including me) sat on theirs to 'protect the family jewels.' But Dave didn't. The bullet passed through the space where the armor plating of the seat and plane did not overlap. He was incapacitated, so I took over. I was unable to save it – the engines were found in METO power, but the props had not been advanced.

Tien Phouc had a U.S. Army controller who was really smart. He saw that we were going to crash and dispatched a Jeep and a few soldiers to where he thought we would land. We crashed inverted about a mile from the runway. Dave and 'Squeaky' did

119

not survive the crash. The soldiers found them first. The Army flew the C-7 with a crew of two, so they thought they were done, but someone heard me. I still was strapped in under the broken airplane. Someone called the Tactical Airlift Liaison Officer and he rerouted his helicopter to the crash site. It was used to lift the aircraft off of me. I was extracted and placed in the helicopter.

They flew me to the Chu Lai hospital. I was on the operating table in less than 45 minutes from the time we crashed. That was one of the things that saved my life. Another was that the best neurosurgeon in the Army was at Chu Lai and on duty. Even though I still was wearing my helmet, my most serious injury was a right frontal skull fracture with penetration of the dura. That means that I had pieces of skull in my brain and other injuries that were not as severe. I spent a lot of time in several hospitals during my recovery and proved all the other doctors I saw wrong, except that initial neurosurgeon. He said, 'He'll either completely recover or die.'

That could be the shortest Vietnam tour." [19]

On 27 December, *Ellis* 457, C-7A S/N 62-4150, with 1/Lt. James L. Smith as Aircraft Commander, jettisoned 500 pounds of cargo over water due to a 3800 pound overload. The load was found to have been mislabeled by the aerial port personnel at Da Nang. The aircraft was landed without damage.

The squadron had no reportable ground accidents during the quarter.

Maintenance [20]

In the first quarter, Lt. Col. John E. Clegg was the Chief of Maintenance and Capt. Jack C. Gay was the Maintenance Officer in the 459th Organizational Maintenance Squadron. The Field Maintenance complex experienced significant change. It became almost fully manned and was supporting two squadrons of Caribou aircraft effectively. Several shops were relocated. When an aircraft crashed at Tra Bong, specialists from the Engine, Propeller, Repair and Reclamation, Electric, Pneudraulic, Radio, Radar, Fuel, and Structural Repair Shops participated in removing all recoverable items from the aircraft in record time. Personnel from the Metal Processing and Machine Shops designed and manufactured the braces needed to attempt a helicopter recovery of the damaged Caribou. A team from Field Maintenance Supervision, along with several specialists, rigged the downed Caribou for airlift and performed the first successful lift-out of a Caribou in

Vietnam. This action salvaged the fuselage, wings, engines, cowlings, and numerous parts of what could have been a totally lost aircraft.

The **Fabrication Branch** became 95 percent self-sufficient in items to be repaired and it repaired an average of 80 items per month. The total did not include equipment repair. Structural Repair also completed several Time Compliance Technical Orders (TCTOs). At the end of the quarter, the shop was working towards completion of TCTO 1-C-7A-593 which entailed installing the #8 cylinder drain line. The shop completed two difficult repair jobs and accomplished each with the speed and technical excellence that was the trademark of the shop.

The **Machine Shop** worked in conjunction with the 37th Field Maintenance Squadron (FMS) and accomplished 150 dispatches in support of both the C-7A aircraft and the F-100. The personnel in the Machine Shop also contributed to the overhaul and placing in-commission of all newly acquired shop equipment.

The **Welding Shop** became fully manned and self-sufficient. The shop accomplished 540 aircraft and 250 Aerospace Ground Equipment (AGE) repairs, as well as locally manufacturing many crucial aircraft parts.

The **Paint Shop** gained additional personnel and utilized them to great effect by initiating a corrosion control program. In addition to this project, the shop began painting crew chief, assistant crew chief, and new aircraft names on all assigned Caribous. These jobs were definite morale factors and contributed to the excellent overall morale of the two squadrons.

The **Fabric Shop**, aside from its regular repair and manufacturing jobs, completed the special project of manufacturing wing covers to protect the Caribou deicing boots during refueling.

The **Engine Shop** attained full manning in both the supervisor and specialist skills. The shop itself was relocated from Building 595 to Building 596. Extensive painting and carpentry work was required on a self-help basis to make the building acceptable for engine maintenance work. Special tools were inventoried and mounted on a shadowboard so that the serviceability and availability of these tools could be determined immediately. The shop was assigned the additional responsibility of accomplishing four engine Basic Post Flight (BPF) inspections each night. This resulted in more reliable engines with decreased aborts and delays. The shop changed 30 engines. Nine of these changes were accomplished at remote bases throughout Southeast Asia.

The **Propulsion Branch** obtained a new portable parts cleaner as well as special crates designed to meet the mobility requirements of the shop. The shop was called upon for much work in the field, often under adverse conditions and with short time limitations. The new mobility kits allowed them to accomplish their job effectively and quickly. The shop also designed and had manufactured four propeller hub covers to protect the hub from dust and water prior to installation on an aircraft. The shop OJT program was expanded with excellent results. Several shop personnel were upgraded to the 5-level, increasing the skill level availability within the shop.

The **Aerospace Ground Equipment (AGE) Branch** expanded its training program by sending four men to Technical Training courses at Clark Air Base, Philippines. The branch also washed, painted, and maintained both the powered and non-powered AGE assigned to the squadrons. The shop also performed required maintenance on all Caribou AGE positioned at Da Nang.

The **Radio Shop**, despite personnel losses, maintained an outstanding record, with few deviations from schedule and few enroute delays. The shop OJT program resulted in a near 100 percent self-sufficiency rate as the repairmen became more proficient. Although all radio personnel worked a minimum of 12 hours per day, 7 days a week, the morale remained extremely high and accomplishment of the mission continued to be a personal challenge to the individuals in the shop.

The **Radar Shop** attained full manning. The personnel status allowed the shop to initiate a program by which radar men were sent to each phase inspection in order to detect and eliminate minor radar discrepancies before the aircraft was inspected by Quality Control and released for flight. The shop planned to remove all navigation equipment during phase inspections for a complete shakedown. The shop enjoyed a 99 percent repair capability on all items removed for maintenance. Their efforts were integral to the continuance of the high in-commission rate of the squadron aircraft.

The **Instrument Shop** benefited from the arrival of a new shop chief who had completed the C-7A familiarization school at Sewart AFB, TN. His long hours spent training the inexperienced shop personnel resulted in the shop incurring no launch aborts and only one initial launch delay during the quarter. The effort expended by the personnel of the shop towards self-improvement led to the upgrade of all but one of the 3-levels assigned to the shop. The shop also initiated a project to lengthen the life of tachometer generators by using double-strand safety wire to secure the cannon plug to the generator, thereby allowing the generator to better withstand vibration of the aircraft. This action greatly increased the reliability of the tachometer generators on the Caribou.

The **Repair and Reclamation** (R&R) section of the Systems Branch maintained an excellent maintenance record, almost free of repeat and recurring discrepancies. The shop reached full manning, made improvements in shop layout, and added to the ability of the shop to complete its jobs more efficiently. The educational achievement of the shop was most noteworthy. The shop attained a 100 percent passing rate on the Specialty Knowledge Tests (SKTs) and achieved a 100 percent rate on the Maintenance Standardization Evaluation Team (MSET) testing program. The shop also maintained the **Wheel and Tire Shop**, where an average of 120 wheels and tires were built up and torn down per month. The shop was often called upon to go to remote and often hazardous locations to recover disabled aircraft. The personnel dispatched from the shop for these missions consistently performed in an outstanding manner, returning the aircraft to in-commission status in a minimum of time.

The **Electric Shop** increased its capability by obtaining the necessary work benches and tools for in-shop repair of items, reworking its generator test stand, and obtaining a portable ferruling tool. All of these factors expedited the work accomplished by the shop and contributed to its excellent support of the Caribou aircraft.

The **Pneudraulic** Shop repaired 107 items in support of the mission. The shop also managed a highly effective training program which saw two men upgraded to the 7-level.

The **Phase Docks** improved their working area by moving Docks #1 and #4 to new locations, by painting all dock offices and bench stock buildings, and by renovating bench stock storage bins to make them more accessible to dock personnel. The docks completed 102 phase inspections and had the lowest dock hour figure, for both the "look" and "fix" phases of the phase inspection, of all three C-7A Phase Docks in Vietnam. This excellent effort was a key factor in the 459 TAS and 537 TAS maintaining an exceptionally high in-commission rate during the quarter.

The Field Maintenance complex operated effectively only because all of the above shops worked as a team. Their very high Operationally Ready Rate, the lower number of repeat discrepancies, and initial delays, coupled with the high number of hours and sorties flown, indicated the high quality of maintenance being performed on the aircraft of the two squadrons at Phu Cat.

During the last week in April, Capt. Jerry T. Jones replaced Capt. Gay as the squadron Maintenance Officer when Capt. Gay completed his tour. Maj. Jerry J. Brown replaced Lt. Col. Clegg as CAMS (OLAA) Chief of Maintenance, on 3 May when Lt. Col. Clegg completed his tour.

The squadron contributed measurably to the safety record and reliability records set by the Wing during June. The squadron experienced a 100 percent initial launch reliability rate and a 99.3 enroute reliability rate, as well as a 100 percent safety record. This compared with a Wing initial launch reliability rate of 99.9 percent and an enroute reliability rate of 99.3 percent.

Manning in maintenance was greatly improved with all areas of the 483 CAMS OLAA fully manned except the AGE branch. The fully manned position was with respect to the number of personnel only. The problem of inadequate skill level distribution was still a serious deficiency. To maximize the available manpower, the **Propulsion Branch** dispatched a 7-level engine technician to Pleiku Air Base to support engine maintenance on transient C-7A aircraft. This action was initiated in order to reduce enroute maintenance delay time at Pleiku and was quite successful in accomplishing that goal.

Sergeant Donald W. Petrosky, crew chief of C-7A 62-4146, remembered the recovery of a Caribou from Tra Bong:

"I remember Lt. Col. Kozey flying an over-grossed C-7A out of Tra Bong after dark, with no runway lights. We had to go in there late one afternoon because one of our planes blew an engine and propeller and they wanted that plane out of there. It was not to be left over night. A group of mechanics volunteered to do the engine and prop change there with the help of an Army tank recovery vehicle with a boom and winch. Everybody survived, even the good ole Caribou.

It was over gross when we took off, because we had the broken engine, the prop, and a whole bunch of mechanics with their tool boxes. Officially, we were probably just under weight. I'm not a real religious man, but I said my prayers before that takeoff. I also remember that the Army guys there parked a jeep at the end of the runway with the lights on to let the pilot know where the end of the runway was."

The need for maximum utilization of personnel was further reflected in a change of procedure in the C-7A docks. Previously, the docks were operating with the four docks working during the day and one dock working at night. All shifts were reorganized and one of the day docks was eliminated. Three docks then operated with 12 hour shifts. These shifts had an overlap so that the night personnel could be thor-

124

oughly briefed on the daily progress of the aircraft being inspected. This departure from established procedure was still in the experimental stage at the end of the quarter; however, it appeared that this new phase inspection concept would result in faster, higher-quality phase inspection.

SSgt. Ellis V. Barker's phase dock #2 set the pace for excellence from June 27 to July 29. During this period, the dock turned out 12 phase inspections, three of which attained a zero defects rating. Quality Control found only one red cross discrepancy in all 12 inspections. The efforts of the dock crew resulted in truly superior aircraft returned to the flight line. The professionalism and technical skill of the dock crew was most commendable.

In the area of heavy unscheduled maintenance, the OLAA did not face any insurmountable obstacles. The only major problem occurred in the **Structural Repair Shop** which repaired two aircraft from the 459 TAS and three aircraft from the 537 TAS which had suffered battle damage. The shop accomplished these repairs in addition to their daily in-shop repair load in spite of being undermanned by three men at that time.

A great contribution toward more effective maintenance was made by TSgt. Mike B. Kapetanov of the **Electric Shop**. This technician designed and built a test stand for bench checking and testing generator control panels for the C-7A aircraft. Prior to the construction of this test stand, defective control panels had to be returned to the CONUS for repair. Further, there was no way of checking control panels coming out of Supply for installation on the aircraft. This had caused several maintenance delays because of new control panels that failed to operate when installed in the aircraft.

Constant inspection and careful supervisory control in all aspects of maintenance assured the fine record of the Caribou. The high number of hours and sorties flown with a low number of initial launch and enroute delays testified to the successful maintenance effort supplied by OLAA.

In the third quarter, the 459 TAS and 537 TAS continued to receive outstanding Field Maintenance support from the OLAA. The fine record set by the squadrons in regard to in-commission rate, sorties flown, hours flown, enroute reliability, and amount of cargo airlifted directly reflected the high quality of maintenance performed by the OLAA. Capt. Jones and Maj. Brown continued as squadron Maintenance Officer and CAMS (OLAA) Chief of Maintenance, respectively.

There were few changes in basic maintenance procedures during the quarter. Many personnel returned to the CONUS, causing severe shortages of skilled technicians. The **Propulsion Branch** was forced to recall its engine mechanic from Pleiku to help support the heavy workload at Phu Cat. The **Electric Shop**, also faced with a severe manpower shortage, recalled its electrician from Da Nang.

Requirements set by the 37th Tactical Fighter Wing, the host unit at Phu Cat, dictated that the C-7A Phase Docks be moved from revetments two and three on "P" row and revetments one and two on "Q" row to the new revetments built as an extension of "K" row. This move was accomplished in three days by mobilizing the entire C-7A Phase Dock work force. Using borrowed forklifts and trailers, the dock personnel moved all the heavy maintenance stands, tools, parts, and buildings that made up the C-7A Phase Docks. The docks were relocated quickly and efficiently, causing minimum disruption in the Phase Inspection schedule. Work orders were submitted for construction of a latrine facility as well as four additional offices for Dock Chiefs.

Field Maintenance was faced with several important unscheduled maintenance tasks during the quarter. The most significant job was the recovery of C-7A S/N 62-4153 which suffered battle damage and crashed at Minh Long on 19 August. A recovery crew was sent out from Field Maintenance. The downed aircraft was stripped, the wings were removed, and a recovery sling, designed and fabricated by Field Maintenance personnel, was attached to the aircraft. The Caribou was successfully evacuated from Minh Long by a U.S. Army CH-54 "Flying Crane" helicopter. The aircraft was taken to Duc Pho and then airlifted to Da Nang where it was prepared for shipment back to the CONUS where it was to be repaired. The recovery broke all established records for helicopter airlift of crash or battle damaged C-7A aircraft. This accomplishment was recognized by the 483 TAW Commander in personal letters to all members of the recovery crew.

A/1C Phillip W. Bell, crew chief on C-7A S/N 63-9730, was recognized for his outstanding work when his aircraft flew 161.3 hours in July with no initial delays or enroute delays. This was a new Wing record. TSgt. Paul C. Chamberlain was named outstanding Field Maintenance Man of the Month for August. Sgt. Nathan D. McElroy was named Outstanding Armament-Electronics Man of the Month for August. A/1C William D. Hoover was named Crew Chief of the Month for September.

The **Propulsion Branch** continued to maintain its high standards of maintenance excellence.

The **Engine Shop** changed 18 engines whose average life was 924 hours. The average engine life during the previous quarter was 645 hours. This showed an impressive improvement in engine life within a relatively short period of time. This improvement was a direct result of the high quality of maintenance and supervision in the branch. The shop improved its field maintenance capability with the receipt of an aircraft engine ignition magneto test stand. The stand provided the organization with performance testing facilities for high and low tension aircraft engine magnetos and distributors. With the installation of the stand, magneto repair capability was enhanced and the number of items returned to the depot for overhaul would be greatly reduced.

The ability of Field Maintenance to quickly recover an aircraft down with engine failure was demonstrated on many occasions. The team effort required for successful engine change was clearly demonstrated on 12 July when C-7A S/N 63-9726 was forced to land at the Tra Bong airstrip with internal failure of #2 engine. A team consisting of two engine mechanics, one propeller mechanic, an electrician, a crew chief, and a 9-level supervisor was dispatched from Phu Cat to recover the aircraft. In spite of inclement weather, lack of proper maintenance equipment, and the constant threat of enemy attack, the crew changed the old engine and checked out the new one in a mere 4.5 hours. This job normally took a minimum of eight hours.

The other branches of Field Maintenance maintained a high-performance required to support the C-7A mission at Phu Cat. TSgt. Francesco Pesce was named the Outstanding Field Maintenance Mechanic of the second quarter.

The **AGE Branch** set a high standard of excellence by maintaining a 96 percent in-commission rate throughout the quarter. The branch obtained an incredible 100 percent in-commission rate for six days in August, a feat unequalled in the Wing.

The examples of teamwork and dedication typify the work accomplished by the OLAA 483 CAMS. To meet the demanding C-7A mission in Vietnam during the third quarter, every man had produced quality maintenance. Field Maintenance met every challenge successfully and ensured the accomplishment of the C-7A mission at Phu Cat. SSgt. Terry Kinner was named Wing Outstanding Field Maintenance Man of the third quarter.

In the fourth quarter, Capt. Jones and Maj. Brown continued as squadron Maintenance Officer and CAMS (OLAA) Chief of Maintenance, respectively. The squadron aircraft had fire suppressant material added to the fuel cells by a depot modification team from Warner Robins Air Materiel Area (WRAMA). This modification, directed by

TCTO 1-C-7A-589, reduced the overall capacity of the fuel cells by five percent, but also reduced the possibility of fire in the cells if hits should be taken from hostile fire.

Several squadron aircraft experienced problems with the nose gear not extending. The problem was subsequently traced to the nose gear drag strut being corroded internally. In response to this problem, WRAMA proposed a modification to all drag struts currently in the inventory. This modification included electroplating of the internal up-lock piston and changing the retainer to a stainless steel material. The new, modified drag strut, P/N 5460-3, became available around 15 October.

The problem of water entering the cockpit area during rains was encountered again. This problem area was also reviewed by WRAMA since the operating conditions in SEA caused this to be a major maintenance problem. A complete cockpit sealing program was suggested and was being considered as a task for a WRAMA team in the near future.

For October, A/1C Stephen G. Fronce was named Crew Chief of the Month, A/1C Patrick J. Kelley was named Organizational Maintenance Man, and Sgt. Joe K. Cummings was named Field Maintenance Man. For November, Sgt. David L. Boyd was named Crew Chief of the Month and Sgt. Harold Abel-Bay was named TAS Mechanic of the Month. For December, Sgt. Samuel C. Pleasants, Jr. was named Crew Chief of the Month, Sgt. Donna E. Threatt was named Organizational Maintenance Man of the Month, Sgt. Kenneth W. Greer was named Field Maintenance Man of the Month, and Sgt. E. V. Knight was named Communications-Electronics Man of the Month.

The squadron achieved a high degree of maintenance effectiveness in the fourth quarter. Initial launch delays numbered six in October, three in November, and zero in December. Enroute launch delays numbered 23 in October, 30 in November, and zero in December. The enroute delay rate was the second lowest in the Wing with only 15 enroute deviations in December. During the quarter, there were no maintenance non-deliveries, although aircraft availability fell well below the Wing average. Initial launch reliability rate was 98.89 percent and the enroute reliability rate was 98.87 percent. The drop in reliability rates was attributed to the monsoon season, which continued to cause wet magnetos and electrical equipment.

Administration

On 22 January, Capt. Raymond E. A. Longo became the squadron

Administrative Officer. MSgt. Donald E. Gammon was First Sergeant until his tour ended and he was replaced on 28 February by SMSgt. William A. Zippel. Maj. Donald W. Frazee was the Information Officer, 1/Lt. William E. Hutton was the Intelligence Officer, 1/Lt. Robert E. Whitehouse was the Historian, and 1/Lt. Harris C. Hertel was the Security Officer.

SSgt. Sitzenstock remembered a time when he and SMSgt. Zipple were relaxing together when they were off duty:

"Bill Zipple and a bunch of us were sitting around a camp fire at Phu Cat, Vietnam in 1969 when a mortar attack by Charlie came in. We were in the middle of our evening indigenous meal (shrimp, Army steak, 6 pack) when an incoming round hit close and Bill got second and third degree burns. I told him that it's time to take him to the hospital. He said, 'They are not going to ruin our nightly meal tonight.' I said, 'Sorry, Bill, but it's not your call. It's time to get you where you need to be.'

I could feel he was hurting and he agreed. We went to the Phu Cat hospital tent. The next morning, we took off knowing our Chief was ok." [21]

Squadron manning improved during the first quarter with the addition of 11 new pilots, four of whom came from flying assignments other than Undergraduate Pilot Training (UPT). At the end of March, the squadron had 4 Flight Examiners, 6 Instructor Pilots, 13 Aircraft Commanders, 8 First Pilots, 20 Copilots, and 3 Copilot trainees. The second quarter was forecast to experience a severe Aircraft Commander shortage in the squadron, with the projected loss of six Aircraft Commanders and five Instructor Pilots. The shortage would be further accentuated by the new Wing restriction on new Aircraft Commanders. They had been allowed to land only at Type II (for C-7A aircraft) airfields and better for their first 30 days as an Aircraft Commander. The major mission area of the squadron, I Corps, had but one Type II airfield. All other airfields were Type I or an interim Type I (an extremely short, hazardous field). Since 75 percent of the squadron airlift capability was currently allocated to I Corps this restriction would place undue hardship on the squadron.

Flight Engineer manning stabilized in the first quarter. No shortage of Flight Engineers was forecast for the second quarter.

In the second quarter, Maj. Frazee (Information Officer), 1/Lt. Hutton (Intelligence Officer), 1/Lt. Robert E. Whitehouse (Historian), and 1/Lt. Hertel (Security Officer) continued in their positions. On 5 May, MSgt. Robert W. Hager replaced acting First Sergeant, SMSgt. Zippel.

On 11 June, Capt. Longo completed his tour and was replaced by Maj. Henry H. Hoopman.

The foreseen shortage of Aircraft Commanders was alleviated by an accelerated upgrading program. Fifteen new Aircraft Commanders were checked out and a total of 28 other pilots were upgraded to Flight Examiner, Instructor Pilot, First Pilot, or Copilot status. Only four new pilots arrived during the quarter, making a shortage of Aircraft Commanders in the future likely unless the accelerated upgrading program in the past were to continue.

Flight Engineer manning was enhanced with the addition of nine new Flight Engineers while losing only three. The squadron finished the quarter with 28 Flight Engineers, so no shortage was foreseen in the third quarter.

In the third quarter, Maj. Hooper and MSgt. Hager continued in their positions of Administrative Officer and First Sergeant, respectively. Maj. Charles H. Wheeler was the Information Officer, 1/Lt. Steven J. Safford was the Security Officer, and 1/Lt. John R. Oxenham was the Historian.

The forecast shortage of Aircraft Commanders was alleviated to some degree by a continuation of the accelerated upgrading program. During the quarter, the squadron lost two Flight Examiners, four Instructor Pilots, and six Aircraft Commanders. The squadron gained nine pilots, five of whom had prior flying assignments and the other four were UPT graduates.

The manning of Flight Engineers decreased from 28 at the beginning of the quarter to 25 at the end. The Flight Engineers had to share their air-conditioned quarters. Additional housing was required for Flight Engineers of the newly assigned 361st Tactical Electronic Warfare Squadron. Air-conditioned quarters at Phu Cat were distributed to Flight Engineers by rank and date of rank.

On 23-24 November, the 7AF Inspector General team inspected the squadron and the overall rating was "Satisfactory." Administrative Security, Administration, and Operations received "Outstanding" ratings.

On 15 December, Maj. Hoopman completed his tour and was replaced by Maj. John D. Diekman as Administrative Services Officer. MSgt. Hager continued as First Sergeant. First Lieutenant Timothy M. Ennor was the Historian and Information Officer, Capt. Gary L. Clark was the Intelligence Officer, and 1/Lt. James L. Smith was the Security Officer.

Supply and Support

In the first quarter, officers of the 459 TAS moved into new quarters at both Phu Cat and the Da Nang mission site. The long-awaited officers' housing at Phu Cat was completed. The squadron was given three 20-unit buildings where half of the rooms had air conditioners and were connected to the non-air conditioned rooms by an adjoining floor. However, there was some inconvenience commuting to the Dining Hall and the Officers' Club.

At the Da Nang mission site, the officers moved from the Modern Hotel in downtown Da Nang to the main compound of Phu Cat Air Base. This offered both the convenience of being close to the flight line and dining facilities and the comfort of air-conditioned rooms. The enlisted men at Da Nang also moved from their "Tent City" into air-conditioned barracks. This was a great improvement.

In the second quarter, the Flight Engineers at Phu Cat moved into air-conditioned quarters which had previously been occupied by officers. Several improvements were made to the new Bachelor Officer Quarters area. Grass was planted, a horseshoe court was constructed, barbecue pits were installed, and picnic tables were made available. Additions to base facilities included completion of a swimming pool and a steam bath-massage parlor. The Base Exchange was remodeled to provide better and faster service. Construction was also started on a new Officers' Club and a new tape center. Improvements around the squadron building included the installation of fencing and the construction of a fish pond. Plans were made for the renovation of the Da Nang mission site building in the fourth quarter.

During August, the interior of the squadron building was completely repainted and a complete renovation of the mission site at Da Nang was also accomplished. Work was begun on repairing the pierced steel planking in the "capture" revetments.

In the fourth quarter, officers TDY at Da Nang moved into new rooms in the Transient Officers' Quarters. Quarters for Flight Engineers at Phu Cat continued to be cramped, with three men to a room. The situation was not expected to improve during the next quarter with a squadron of AC-119 aircraft due to move in.

Awards and Decorations

In the second quarter, a total of 60 decorations and medals were presented to members of the squadron: 13 Distinguished Flying Crosses, 3 Bronze Stars, 4 Purple Hearts, 35 Air Medals, and 9 Air Force Commendation Medals.

On 15 July, Col. Turk, Commander of the 483 TAW, presented awards in a ceremony at Phu Cat Air Base. Twenty Air Medals and six Air Force Commendation Medals were received.

In the fourth quarter, the officers and enlisted personnel of the squadron received 6 Distinguished Flying Crosses, 2 Bronze Stars, 55 Air Medals, 34 Air Force Commendation Medals, and 4 Combat Readiness Medals. On 11 November, Col. Keith L. Christensen, Commander of the 483 TAW, presented 18 Air Medals and 14 Air Force Commendation Metals to personnel of the 459 TAS in a ceremony at the squadron.

Civic Action and Special Activities

The squadron held three parties during the first quarter. These monthly parties were used as a farewell to squadron members completing their tours and were held at the picnic grounds on Phu Cat Air Base. In the second quarter, the squadron held three parties as a farewell to departing squadron members. The parties were held out-of-doors at the new Bachelor Officers' Quarters area. In the third quarter, the squadron held two parties. These parties were used as a farewell to squadron members completing their SEA tours and were held out of doors at the Bachelor Officers' Quarters area. Squadron pictures were also taken of pilots and Flight Engineers. A copy was given to each pilot and Flight Engineer. In the fourth quarter, three parties were held in recognition of tour completion by certain squadron members. One party was held in the base picnic pavilion, while the other two were held in the Officers' Quarters area.

The Santa Bou mission had a twist of fate in 1969 for the 459 TAS. First Lieutenant Richard J. Patterson was the assigned Copilot on that mission, just a few days before he would be shot down at Tien Phuoc. He remembered the Santa Bou mission:

> "I don't remember being told about 'Santa Boo [sic].' All I remember is being told that all crew members had a mandatory formation when we returned home to Phu Cat AB after spending all day hauling 'trash' around South Vietnam. But, I better start at the beginning. In early December 1969 we arrived in South Vietnam and Da Nang AB welcomed us with open arms! We were First Lieutenants Daniel B. Ahern, James V. 'Cuffy' Kelso, Thomas M. McCloy, and me. Right out of pilot training, we were among the first graduates of the C-7A Upgrade School which recently moved to Dyess AFB, TX.
>
> Boy were we green! Everything was new – we were new

132

officers, new pilots, and, now, new war combatants. But, we were motivated and fresh! So a couple of days after arrival we started our Copilot training and Vietnam indoctrination. We were excited to be flying – we were excited about almost everything. We may have been excited, but we sure didn't know much! We fit into the squadrons, tried to learn as fast as we could, accepted a few additional duties (all First Lieutenants get 'em) and did our best.

About a week after arrival, I was told about the meeting. Not sure I remember where the meeting was, but I think it was at the O'Club. Anyway, all the experienced crew members were anticipating this meeting – for it was here that the crews of the Phu Cat 1969 Santa Bou aircraft would be selected. I do remember, though, that when the Operations Officer read '1/Lt. Patterson' everyone said, 'Who's that?' I remember saying, 'What's a Santa Boo?' So that is the story about how a brand new 1/Lt. who had been in-country less than two weeks got to fly on the premier flight of the year – it was pure luck. 'Even a blind squirrel finds an acorn once in a while!' [22]

Airlift Accomplishments [23]

During the first quarter, passengers hauled were 7285 in January; 6837 in February; and 10,306 in March for a total of 24,428. Cargo hauled was 1963.3 tons in January; 2031.4 tons in February; and 1997.5 tons in March for a total of 5993.2 tons. In January, the squadron flew 2201 sorties while logging 1597.5 flying hours. In February, the squadron flew 2231 sorties while logging 1622.2 flying hours. In March, the squadron flew 2433 sorties while logging 1863.4 flying hours.

The tonnage carried in the first quarter decreased slightly over the last quarter of 1968. This reflected, in part, the fact that the squadron had responsibility of furnishing the aircraft for the Bangkok mission site. This responsibility reduced the squadron missions in the Republic of Vietnam, taking its toll in hours flown and tonnage carried. Responsibility for the 490 mission was also a hindrance to the performance of the squadron. Previous problems with the 490 mission were eliminated in May by having it depart from Phu Cat, making one round-trip to Vung Tau with enroute stops at Cam Ranh Bay. The 490 mission rotated, on a monthly basis, between the 459 TAS and the 537 TAS.

During the second quarter, passengers hauled were 9758 in April; 6513 in May; and 6540 in June for a total of 22,811. Cargo hauled was 1790.9 tons in April; 2019.5 tons in May; and 2003.4 tons in June for a total of 5813.8 tons. In April, the squadron flew 2156 sorties while logging 1680.8 flying hours. In May, the squadron flew 2314 sorties while logging 1692.4 flying hours. In June, the squadron flew 2309 sorties while logging 1589.9 flying hours.

The decrease in tonnage carried during the second quarter was primarily the result of the Wing restriction on flying time. The restriction was a limit of seven hours logged during a crew duty day. Previously, the only limit was the 12 hour length of the crew duty day.

During the third quarter, passengers hauled were 8689 in July; 7246 in August; and 5401 in September for a total of 21,336. Cargo hauled was 1751.7 tons in July; 2393.7 tons in August; and 1485.1 tons in September for a total of 5630.5 tons. In July, the squadron flew 2303 sorties while logging 1682.1 flying hours. In August, the squadron flew 2678 sorties while logging 1792.2 flying hours. In September, the squadron flew 1926 sorties while logging 1496.5 flying hours.

The decrease in tonnage carried during the third quarter was attributed to a combination of factors: the continuation of the Wing restriction on flying time, the beginning of the monsoon season, and the temporary closing of many I Corps fields for repairs or rebuilding, e.g., Minh Long, Tra Bong, Ha Thanh, Tien Phuoc, and Ha Tan.

During the fourth quarter, passengers hauled were 6040 in October; 4641 in November; and 4165 in December for a total of 14846. Cargo hauled was 1530.7 tons in October; 1259.3 tons in November; and 1360.4 tons in December for a total of 4150.4 tons. In October, the squadron flew 1994 sorties while logging 1531.8 flying hours. In November, the squadron flew 1756 sorties while logging 1422.5 flying hours. In December, the squadron flew 1735 sorties, while logging 1445.9 flying hours.

Tonnage carried increased slightly in the fourth quarter, but the monsoon season contributed greatly to the relatively small tonnage the squadron was able to haul.

Commander's Summary

First Quarter 1969 [24]
"The 459th TAS continued to serve its assigned users in a truly professional manner. We all stood ready to perform any mission assigned to us to uphold the proud history of the 459th TAS and the 483rd TAW."

Second Quarter 1969 [25]
"The 459th TAS continued to serve its assigned users in a truly pro-

fessional manner. We all stood ready to perform any mission assigned to us to uphold the proud history of the 459th TAS and the 483rd TAW."

Third Quarter 1969 [26]
"The 459th TAS as completed another successful quarter and stands ready to provide continued professional support to its users."

Fourth Quarter 1969 [27]
"The 459th TAS as completed another successful quarter and stands ready to provide continued professional support to its users."

End Notes: 459 TAS

[1] *19690101-19691231 459 TAS History*
[2] 459 TAS Special Order G-3, dated 26 August 1969
[3] 459 TAS Special Order G-1, dated 25 March 1969
[4] 459 TAS Special Order G-3, dated 26 August 1969
[5] 7AF Special Order G-0149, dated 10 January 1970
[6] 7AF Special Order G-4923, dated 1 December 1969
[7] *C-7A Caribou Association Newsletter, Vol. 22, Issue 2*
[8] 7AF Special Order G-5139, dated 16 December 1969
[9] *C-7A Caribou Association Newsletter*, Vol. and Issue pending
[10] 7AF Special Order G-3182, dated 14 July 1970
[11] 7AF Special Order G-3182, dated 14 July 1970
[12] 7AF Special Order G-0386, dated 3 February 1971
[13] 7AF Special Order G-1950, dated 18 June 1971
[14] 7AF Special Order G-2166, dated 15 May 1970
[15] Tra Bong was described in the *Tactical Airdrome Directory* as "1000 feet, earth/gravel … do not land short … some loose gravel on surface … 5-10 foot drop-offs each side of runway, both ends … drainage ditches both sides near center portion of runway"
[16] *Caribou Roster #10*, unpublished C-7A data compiled by Wayne Buser
[17] 7AF Special Order G-2428, dated 19 June 1970
[18] 7AF Special Order G-2215, dated 19 May 1970
[19] *C-7A Caribou Association Newsletter, Vol. 19, Issue 2*
[20] The quarterly history report of the 459th TAS included the history reports of the CAMS OLAA at Phu Cat and the 459th Organizational Squadron.
[21] *C-7A Caribou Association Newsletter, Vol. 22, Issue 2*
[22] *C-7A Caribou Association Newsletter, Vol. 1, Issue 17*
[23] When the data in the squadron history and the Wing history differ,

the Wing data is shown.

[24] 459 TAS Commander's Summary, 31 March 1969 by Lt. Col. John Kozey

[25] 459 TAS Commander's Summary, 30 June 1969 by Lt. Col. John Kozey

[26] 459 TAS Commander's Summary, 30 September 1969 by Lt. Col. Arthur T. Rossing

[27] 459 TAS Commander's Summary, 31 December 1969 by Lt. Col. Arthur T. Rossing

"Sierra Hotel – Charlie Stoppers" (Copyright © 2014 Tom Finkler)

SAFE-CONDUCT PASS TO BE HONORED BY ALL VIETNAMESE GOVERNMENT AGENCIES AND ALLIED FORCES

MANG TÂM GIẤY
THÔNG HÀNH
nầy về cộng tác
với Chánh Phủ
Quốc Gia các bạn
sẽ được :

● Đón tiếp tử tế
● Bảo đảm an ninh
● Đải ngộ tương xứng

NGUYỄN VĂN THIỆU
Tổng Thống Việt Nam Cộng Hoà

TẤM GIẤY THÔNG HÀNH NẦY CÓ GIÁ TRỊ VỚI TẤT CẢ CƠ - QUAN
QUÂN CHÍNH VIỆT - NAM CỘNG - HÒA VÀ LỰC - LƯỢNG ĐỒNG - MINH.

Safe Conduct Pass (Copyright © 2014 Frank Pickart)

![Shop in Downtown Vung Tau]

Shop in Downtown Vung Tau (Copyright © 2014 Bill Craig)

Maintenance Party on Beach (Copyright © 2014 Bill Craig)

137

Home of the 535 TAS (Copyright © 2014 Bob Moore)

Engine Work in the Phase Dock (Copyright © 2014 Stan Owens)

535th Tactical Airlift Squadron [1]

The primary mission of the 535th Tactical Airlift Squadron (535 TAS) at Vung Tau was to provide intra-theater airlift in support of all free world military, civic actions, and Agency for International Development (AID) forces, and units engaged in combat; combat support, logistics and civic assistance in the Republic of Vietnam (RVN); to accomplish this through air-land and aerial delivery of personnel and supplies in conformance with established MACV priorities for employment of C-7A aircraft; and to perform other airlift missions as directed by the Commander, 483rd Tactical Airlift Wing.

The secondary mission was to provide a Liaison Officer to function as single point of contact for coordination of all C-7A airlift operations with the Army Air Transportation Coordinating Offices (ATCOs) at Tan Son Nhut (TSN). The Caribou Scheduling Officer at the 834th Air Division (834 AD) Airlift Control Element (ALCE) at Tan Son Nhut (TSN) provided him with all information on C-7A aircraft operation through TSN; to provide a Liaison Officer to function as a coordinator between all users and C-7A airlift operations out of Bien Hoa Air Base.

The organization of the 535 TAS served to support all missions, assigned directly or indirectly, in the most efficient and expedient means practical. The organization included a Support Section which supported all Air Force requirements demanded by the two Caribou squadrons stationed at Vung Tau Army Airfield.

Lt. Col. Harry F. Hunter was Squadron Commander on 1 January 1969 (until 12 April) and Lt. Col. James W. Buckley, Jr. was the Operations Officer. On 17 March, Lt. Col. Buckley assumed command of the newly activated 6483rd Tactical Group Provisional. Lt. Col. Richard D. Kimball succeeded Lt. Col. Buckley as Operations Officer who was then succeeded by Lt. Col. Andrew L. Starling.

On 12 April, Lt. Col. Kimball assumed the duties of Squadron Commander (until 1 November 1969).

On 4 July, Maj. Lawrence A. Corcoran, Jr. replaced Lt. Col. Starling as Operations Officer. On 5 September, Lt. Col. Don E. Youngmark replaced Maj. Corcoran as Operations Officer.

On 1 November Lt. Col. Clem B. Myers replaced Lt. Col. Kimball as Squadron Commander. On 13 November, Lt. Col. John J. Hanley replaced Lt. Col. Myers as Squadron Commander. On 20 December, Maj. Kenneth B. Crooks replaced Lt. Col. Youngmark as Operations Officer.

To accomplish these missions, the squadron was authorized 55 officers, 161 enlisted personnel, and 54 civilians in the first quarter. Of these authorizations, 50 officers, 169 enlisted personnel, and 51 civilians were assigned. The squadron was authorized 16 aircraft and possessed 16, but only 14 were Combat Ready. In the second quarter, the squadron was authorized 55 officers, 161 enlisted personnel, and 46 civilians. Of these authorizations, 51 officers, 154 enlisted personnel, and 43 civilians were assigned. The squadron was authorized 16 aircraft and possessed 16. In the third quarter, the squadron was authorized 50 officers and 151 enlisted personnel. Of these authorizations, 50 officers and 141 enlisted personnel were assigned. The squadron was authorized 16 aircraft and possessed 16, of which 15 were Combat Ready. In the fourth quarter, the squadron was authorized 54 officers and 151 enlisted personnel. Of these authorizations, 44 officers and 136 enlisted personnel were assigned. The squadron was authorized 16 aircraft and possessed 16, of which 15 were Combat Ready.

Operations

In the first quarter, the squadron maintained a high degree of efficiency while successfully accomplishing its mission. This was one of the most technical, yet rewarding periods, for airlift operations experienced by the squadron. The exerted efforts of all assigned personnel, regardless of rank or AFSC, contributed to the impressive Airlift Accomplishments in the quarter.

In the second quarter, Maj. Lawrence A. Corcoran was Assistant Operations Officer until assuming the duties of Operations Officer at the end of the quarter.

The squadron maintained a high degree of efficiency while successfully accomplishing its mission. The quarter was another of the most rewarding periods for airlift operations experienced by the unit. The professional efforts of all assigned personnel, regardless of rank or AFSC, contributed to Wing Outstanding Squadron Awards in April and May. These awards reflect impressive accomplishments for the two months.

Lt. Col. Michael D. Gould remembered an unusual mission:

"I arrived at Vung Tau in April 1969 as a "brown bar" (2/Lt.). A squadron mission the previous day had an in-flight emergency bad enough that it required the crew to jettison the load of .50 caliber ammunition on pallets. Knowing that this ammunition could be used against us, one objective for my mission was to see if we could spot the jettisoned load. If we could find it, then it might be possible to provide a specific location for destruction by an air or ground asset.

Our Caribou in-flight tactics were mostly designed to avoid small arms fire and/or limit our ground time to reduce the exposure to enemy mortars. We needed to reduce our altitude on this particular mission a little lower than our usual 1500 feet or more safety margin to sight the missing ammunition.

My anxiety was a little higher than normal because the bad guys could have discovered the ammunition and set up a AAA site waiting for someone to come looking for the cargo. As we were in a left-hand turn over the approximate area, with the Aircraft Commander and the Flight Engineer looking out the left side of the aircraft, my copilot seat took the opportunity to dislodge from its current height setting and bottom out.

The resounding 'thud' the seat made when it hit bottom certainly surprised us all. The A/C immediately declared that we had been hit and took action to get us to safety. Since he had been looking out the left window, he had no idea that I had dropped several inches. My reaction was two-fold, one of relief knowing we hadn't been hit and a release of nervous tension through hysterical laughter that kept me from coming on the intercom immediately to explain the 'hit.' It probably was only a few seconds before I could advise the crew of what actually happened, but it seemed longer at the time.

We never did find the missing cargo and I've never forgotten the incident only because of the unfortunate timing of my maladjusted seat. I never experienced a real 'hit' during this year which I, of course, attribute to superior airmanship (tongue firmly in cheek). At least that's the way I remember it."

On 29 May, Lt. Col. Clem B. Myers was attached to the 6483 TGP and assumed additional duty as Deputy Commander for Operations.

Captain Robert A. Ross remembered a time when it was smart to "Get out of Dodge!":

"On a pretty, routine afternoon, the Caribou saved my life at An Loc. The plan was to land on the short runway, towards the camp, turn around, off-load the cargo with engines running, and get out of there. Everything went fine until we turned around and mortars started exploding around us. A voice on the FM radio said, 'Get out!' Seemed like a good idea to me, but the cargo was still securely tied down and I had no idea if the Bou had enough performance to pick that load up on that short runway. The manual said that it was OK to occasionally over-boost the engines so off

141

we went at 100% power, plus a bit, with the cargo still on board. The race between getting enough airspeed and the end of the runway was won by the end of the runway, so I jerked the aircraft off the ground and immediately put the nose back down to stay in ground effect. After the gear was up and what seemed like hours, the bird was able to climb and we returned to Ben Hoa. Needless to say, the Army was somewhat disappointed that I brought the load back." [2]

In the third quarter, Maj. Corcoran continued as Operations Officer. The squadron maintained a high degree of efficiency while successfully accomplishing its mission. The professional efforts of all assigned personnel, regardless of rank or AFSC, contributed to impressive accomplishments for the quarter (see Airlift Accomplishments later in this chapter). On 5 July, Brig. Gen. John H. Herring, Jr., Commander of the 834 AD, visited the squadron for an orientation inspection.

The actions of Captain Hugh T. Garner, Jr. and his crew on 12 August were documented in the citation for his Distinguished Flying Cross:

"Captain Hugh T. Garner, Jr. distinguished himself by extraordinary achievement while participating in aerial flight as Aircraft Commander of a C-7A Aircraft near the Duc Hue Special Forces camp, Republic of Vietnam on 12 August 1969. On that date Captain Garner flew a Combat Essential resupply mission to the remote insecure airstrip which began to receive hostile fire while his cargo was being off-loaded. After delivering the cargo of critically needed supplies, Captain Garner completed the hazardous mission despite the fact that his aircraft was damaged by hostile fire prior to takeoff from the 1500 foot airstrip. The professional competence, aerial skill and devotion to duty displayed by Captain Garner reflect great credit upon himself and the United States Air Force." [3]

Captain Robert A. Ross remembered the challenges of hauling passengers:

"My squadron flew a lot of passenger missions, some more memorable than others. Two configurations were used, cabin 'seats down' carried about 28 GIs and their combat gear. The occasional emergency evacuation was 'seats up,' with local citizens fleeing the area sitting with their backs to the wall on either side and a cargo strap around 35 passengers on a side. The loadmaster provided our in-flight service.

One of my favorite loadmasters had an excellent technique for avoiding airsickness during emergency evacuations. He would pass out airsick bags, crack the cargo door about a third of the way up while taxiing, and indicate with body language that anyone getting airsick while airborne would be tossed out the open cargo door. It must have been the fresh air that kept everyone from getting sick.

Another loadmaster introduced what may have been the first passenger screening for explosive devices. As Vietnamese soldiers boarded, he would make them put their hand grenades in a box to be returned on off-loading. It was not unusual for him to find grenades with the pin removed and the handle held down by a rubber band, ready for action in a hot landing zone.

Medical evacuations left a lasting impression on me. Flying a plane full of wounded GIs on stretchers from where they got hurt to where they could get some serious help made me feel good about why I was in Vietnam. On the flip side, we often picked up GIs fresh off the commercial airliners as they arrived at the Saigon airport. You could see their eyes bug out of their heads as they left a shiny 707 and walked across the ramp to board the Caribou. More than once, one of these poor kids would refuse to get off upon arrival at their up-country destination.

I also remember the sad flights carrying the remains of fallen soldiers in body bags, with their escort on the first leg of their final journey home." [4]

In the fourth quarter, the squadron maintained a high degree of efficiency while successfully accomplishing its mission. This another of the most technical, yet rewarding, periods for airlift operations experienced by the squadron. Due to rotation and reassignment, the squadron had three different Squadron Commanders and two different Operations Officers during the quarter. However, the professional efforts of all personnel, regardless of rank or AFSC, contributed to impressive accomplishments for the quarter.

The actions of MSgt. Roger L. Schmidtke and his crew on 5 November were documented in the citation for his Distinguished Flying Cross:

"Master Sergeant Roger L. Schmidtke distinguished himself by extraordinary achievement while participating in aerial flight as Flight Engineer of a C-7A aircraft at Bu Dop and Bunard Special Forces camps, Republic of Vietnam on 5 November 1969. At both camps the aircraft had made a successful tactical approach, but just prior to touch down the fields came under intense hostile fire. During the ensuing go-arounds, Sergeant Schmidtke insured that the cargo was secure and surveyed the aircraft for possible damage. The professional competence, aerial skill, and devotion to duty displayed by Sergeant Schmidtke reflect great credit upon himself and the United States Air Force." [5]

The actions of 1/Lt. Walter L. Mosher and his crew on 11 November were documented in the citation for his Distinguished Flying Cross:

"First Lieutenant Walter L. Mosher distinguished himself by extraordinary achievement while participating in aerial flight as Pilot of a C-7A aircraft at Bu Dop, Republic of Vietnam, on 11 November 1969. Lieutenant Mosher, flying a combat resupply mission, was advised of hostile activity at the camp but was able to make a successful approach and landing. While off loading, however, the camp came under a heavy attack at which time Lieutenant Mosher made an immediate takeoff and tactical departure thereby evading the hostile fire. The professional competence, aerial skill and devotion to duty displayed by Lieutenant Mosher reflect great credit upon himself and the United States Air Force." [6]

The actions of 1/Lt. William C. Kassen and his crew on 20 November were documented in the citation for his Distinguished Flying Cross:

"First Lieutenant William C. Kassen distinguished himself by extraordinary achievement while participating in aerial flight as pilot of a C-7A aircraft at Thien Ngon, Republic of Vietnam, on 20 November 1969. Following a safe tactical approach and landing, hostile forces launched a ground attack against the airfield while Lieutenant Kassen's aircraft was off-loading cargo. Lieutenant Kassen coordinated the crew's actions, completed the cargo off-load and affected a safe, expeditious takeoff and tactical departure, sustaining no damage to aircraft or aircrew. The professional competence, aerial skill, and devotion to duty displayed by Lieutenant Kassen reflect great credit upon himself and the United States Air Force." [7]

From 25-28 November, the 7th Air Force Staff Assistance Team reviewed squadron activities.

The actions of 1/Lt. Michael D. Gould and his crew on 3 December were documented in the citation for his Distinguished Flying Cross:

"First Lieutenant Michael D. Gould distinguished himself by extraordinary achievement while participating in aerial flight as

144

pilot of a C-7A aircraft at Bu Dop Special Forces camp, Republic of Vietnam on 3 December 1969. The camp had been subjected to such extensive hostile fire and activity that it was necessary to provide a forward air controller and fighter coverage for the mission. However, by close crew coordination and Lieutenant Gould's skillful maneuvering of the aircraft throughout a tactical approach and departure, needed medical supplies and equipment were delivered with minimum exposure to ground fire. The professional competence, aerial skill, and devotion to duty displayed by Lieutenant Gould reflect great credit upon himself and the United States Air Force." [8]

The actions of 1/Lt. Kenneth E. Mascaro and his crew on 11 December were documented in the citation for his Distinguished Flying Cross:

"First Lieutenant Kenneth E. Mascaro distinguished himself by extraordinary achievement while participating in aerial flight as pilot of a C-7A aircraft at Duc Phong Airfield, Republic of Vietnam, on 11 December 1969. Lieutenant Mascaro briefed the crew on his intended tactical approach and landing to include evasive action in event hostile fire was encountered. Upon landing, the airfield came under an intense hostile mortar attack, at which time he quickly repositioned the aircraft for takeoff while the cargo was speed off-loaded, and continued a safe tactical departure without incident. The professional competence, aerial skill, and devotion to duty displayed by Lieutenant Mascaro reflect great credit upon himself and the United States Air Force." [9]

Ken Mascaro remembered that mission to Duc Phong:

"We landed normally at Duc Phong, northeast of Saigon and taxied to the end of the field. Due to light winds, I planned to take off in the opposite direction (runway 20), so I turned the Caribou around and the loadmaster opened the ramp, waiting for a forklift to arrive. Soon, I heard and saw a mortar round impact about 200 yards away in the direction of a mountain east of the field. Within a short time, another round impacted about half that distance away. I called to the loadmaster to prepare the load for emergency 'speed' off-load (Ground LAPES), applied power to the engines after his OK, and left the cargo to extract itself on the rollers. As soon as we were airborne, the flight engineer advised we had a few Vietnamese ramp hands who climbed on board as I was starting to roll. They may not know how lucky they were – not doing pushups under a heavy pallet. The unexpected passengers were off-loaded

145

in Saigon. Had we waited any longer, the mortar crew may have soon found our range and I would not be writing this. My crew performed excellent support and for that I am proud to salute them."

The actions of Capt. Jon E. Mickley and his crew (1/Lt. Harvin and Sergeant John R. Sator) on 15 December were documented in the citation for his Distinguished Flying Cross:

"Captain Jon E. Mickley distinguished himself by extraordinary achievement while participating in aerial flight as pilot of a C-7A aircraft at Bu Dop Special Forces camp, Republic of Vietnam, on 15 December 1969. Captain Mickley, flying a combat resupply mission, was advised of hostile activity at the camp but was able to make a successful tactical approach and landing. While off-loading, the camp came under a heavy ground attack, at which time he made an immediate tactical take off and departure thereby evading the hostile fire. The professional competence, aerial skill, and devotion to duty displayed by Captain Mickley reflect great credit upon himself and the United States Air Force." [10]

Jon Mickley remembered that day at Bu Dop:

"As we approached Bu Dop, I used the standard overhead patter to stay close to the camp perimeter as it reduced the amount of ground fire from the bad guys. We came in at 3000 feet AGL, pitched out, configured with gear and flaps, and tried to roll out on a close-in final, and low enough to touchdown on the first 'brick,' *aka* 'cloud of dirt!' As we turned final, the technique to get down in a hurry was to slip the airplane with a lot of rudder and cross-controlled aileron. I remember seeing some tracers going by, but they were well off to the left, on the outside of the turn as we were making a right turn to final. I wondered who taught those guys to shoot, as they weren't even close. Later, I learned that they were taught to just shoot in front of the airplane and let it fly into the bullets. Since we were in a big slip, the airplane was not actually flying in the direction of the nose, but to the right, hence I was not moving in the direction the guys on the ground thought we were. I have no idea if they ever figured out how an airplane can 'point one way and fly another!'

We landed and began a standard, engine running off-load in the small ramp area. I preferred the 'drop the load in the middle of the runway' technique, but there was a lot of traffic into and out of Bu Dop that day, so that wasn't possible. The folks on the

146

ground backed the duce and a half up to the ramp and we began off-loading the cargo, mostly Vietnamese food – the usual staples, live chickens and 55 gallon drums of live eels. They had to be live since there wasn't much refrigeration available for the local folks. As usual, there were a lot of local people around to help the off-load, despite the threat of getting shot at.

Shortly after the off-load started, the first mortar round hit the corner of the parking ramp, but nobody really noticed, at least not in the cockpit, since it was behind us. But, the Flight Engineer did see it and started yelling 'incoming' on the interphone, at which time the cockpit crew became involved. The Flight Engineer yelled, 'clear' and off we went. We were taught that a mortar is not really effective against a moving target, even one as big as a Bou, so we got moving. We turned onto the runway, already having set up for a quick departure (25° flaps), and off we went. We did a low speed, corkscrew climb-out over the camp, got high enough to avoid ground fire, cleaned up, and departed.

No harm, no foul, except for one minor footnote. The locals had come out to help unload and apparently one was on the airplane when the mortars came in and, well, he didn't get off. Nice enough young man, but I doubt that he had planned on taking an airplane ride when he left home that morning! Naturally, we weren't going back to Bu Dop to drop him off, so we took him to Saigon and dropped him off there. A few days later, I was talking to the crew that had flown the *Tong 452* mission the next day and they told me they took him back home. I assume that he spent the night on the ramp at Saigon. I always wondered what he told his wife when he finally got home. Perhaps it was, 'I was helping unload an airplane yesterday and ended up in Saigon, dear!' To which she replied, 'Sure honey, what was her name?' I doubt if he ever got involved in unloading another Caribou!

So, to quote Donnie Baker, 'I swear to God, it's true!' "

Training and Stan-Eval

In the first quarter, Maj. Walter F. Redpath, Jr. became the Chief of Stan/Eval when Maj. William S. Carr completed his tour. The managerial skill and professionalism of Maj. Redpath were rewarded by his nomination to the Wing as the outstanding pilot of the quarter. Lt. Col. Starling was the Training Officer until he became the Operations Officer. The squadron was authorized 24 crews, of which 22 were "formed" and Combat Ready. The squadron continued upgrading all qualified aircrew members as soon as practicable. As a result, a favorable Aircraft Commander to Copilot ratio was obtained, as was a very high degree of pilot proficiency and professionalism.

Captain Robert A. Ross remembered an early training mission during his Copilot checkout:

> "Thirty some years after the end of my flying career I only remember one flight number and when I happen across the number **452** it still brings back a vivid and slightly frightening memory. During my first night in the squadron bar, one of the experienced pilots explained the next day's schedule posting. Types of trips were by number, with 452 and 453 (*Tong* 452 and *Tong* 453) for supporting the Fifth Special Forces. I flew my first flight as Copilot the next day with an Instructor Pilot (IP). The mission was some simple passenger runs and after a while I felt I was getting the hang of it.
>
> Late in the morning, we landed at Ben Hoa and were informed that the airplane flying the *Tong* 452 sortie had broken down and we needed to pick up the flight number in order to fly an Emergency Resupply mission with ammunition for a camp under attack. Once airborne, after learning what the hot cargo ramp was all about, the IP informed me that I needed to establish radio contact with our fighter escort as soon as we were near the camp.
>
> Fighter escort! I had the feeling that I must have slept through the lesson about this type of mission in C-7A combat crew training. Contact established, the IP slowed the Caribou to stall speed over the camp while the two F-100's made strafing runs on both sides of the runway. As the Caribou started to stall, the IP dumped the nose 30 to 40 degrees and began a tight spiral down. Turning final, he horsed the nose up to bleed airspeed and called for gear and flaps.
>
> Habit patterns made it possible for me to accomplish these simple tasks just in time to land. As we rolled towards the ramp, the loadmaster cut all but one tie down strap. We pivoted at the ramp end of the runway, the last strap was cut, and we drove out from under the load on our takeoff roll skyward. My suspicion about having missed this lesson was now confirmed.
>
> Once safely airborne, I managed to say, 'Hope you didn't do all that for my benefit just because I'm new.' He replied, 'So much for the demo, the next approach and landing are yours.' " [11]

The Stan/Eval Flight Examiner and Stan/Eval Flight Engineers Review panels met at Cam Ranh Bay.

In the second quarter, Maj. Redpath continued as Chief of Stan/Eval and Maj. Daniel P. Roberson was the Flying Training Officer. The squadron was authorized 24 crews, of which 22 were "formed" and Combat Ready. On 23 June, Capt. Hugh T. Garner, Jr. was attached to the 6483 TGP and assumed additional duty as Group Training Officer.

The squadron continued a vigorous upgrade of all qualified aircrew members. Three pilots were upgraded to Instructor Pilot, 12 to Aircraft Commander, 3 to First Pilot, and 9 to Copilot. As a result, a favorable Aircraft Commander to Copilot ratio was maintained, along with a high degree of pilot proficiency and professionalism. In addition, one Flight Engineer was upgraded to Flight Examiner, 12 to Instructor, and 7 received their initial qualification.

In the third quarter, Maj. Redpath continued as Chief of Stan/Eval. The squadron was authorized 24 crews, of which 21 were "formed" and Combat Ready. The squadron continued a vigorous upgrade of all qualified aircrew members. One pilot upgraded to Flight Examiner, 4 upgraded to Instructor Pilot, 9 upgraded to Aircraft Commander, 8 upgraded to First Pilot, and 7 upgraded to Copilot. A favorable Aircraft Commander to Copilot ratio was maintained. One Flight Engineer upgraded to Flight Examiner, 4 to Instructor, and 4 received their initial qualification.

Captain Robert A. Ross remembered flying with a female Caribou pilot:

> "I was fortunate enough to spend a month as second in command (there were only two of us) of the C-7A mission site in Bangkok, so I had my wife, Helen, join me. Mostly, I did administrative stuff, but the boss and I flew once or twice a week so the crews rotating through could have a little R&R. My wife's father had an airplane so she had some stick time growing up and a high level of interest in aviation. It seemed natural to take her along as a passenger and show her what I did for a living.
>
> Most of the other passengers were Special Forces guys and their dogs. In order to impress the 'Round Eye' in the cabin, they spent the time acting tough by doing things like cleaning their fingernails with enormous knives. Since all was quiet, I had her sit in the copilot seat and take over the controls. Having the only woman on board climb into the right seat shut up the Special Forces guys for the rest of the trip and resulted in a deflation of my ego.
>
> After twenty minutes of complete control of the Caribou, my wife smiled at me, punched the microphone button, and told the

world, 'This isn't so hard.' " [12]

On 1 October, Capt. William R. Findlay replaced Maj. Redpath as Chief of Stan/Eval. The squadron was authorized 24 crews, of which 19 were "formed" and Combat Ready. The squadron continued a vigorous upgrade of all qualified aircrew members. During the quarter, 1 pilot upgraded to Flight Examiner, 2 upgraded to Instructor Pilot, 11 upgraded to Aircraft Commander, and 6 upgraded to Copilot. As a result, a favorable Aircraft Commander to Copilot ratio was maintained and a very high degree of pilot proficiency and professionalism was realized.

First Lieutenant Michael E. Harvin remembered what it was like for a C-7A Instructor Pilot to experience Caribou "Pucker Factor":

> "Pucker factor in a Caribou is ... having a recycled B-58 pilot go into reverse on you 100 feet in the air, because he couldn't get the plane to go down by diving at the runway with full flaps. It worked, since both engines went into reverse at the same time, but we had strong words on the ground!
>
> Pucker factor in a Caribou is ... having an IP go into full reverse after touchdown on a short field during an emergency landing after full electrical failure (battery fire). NOTHING went into reverse without electrics, so after a great landing we started picking up speed toward the jungle at the end of the runway. No intercom either, of course, so I am screaming at him and fighting for the throttles. A very interesting few seconds. He made me promise not to tell, in exchange for multiple beers at the bar that night." [13]

Captain Robert A. Ross remembered his experience as a new Caribou Instructor Pilot:

> "Towards the end of my tour, I was very proud to be made an instructor pilot and several students remain stuck in my mind. The first was a brand new copilot that, after climb-out over the jungle, leaned both engines to idle cutoff. I slammed the handles forward, both engines backfired, but kept on running and life was good again. The second was a very *gung ho* pilot, who was disappointed to be assigned to Caribous. He would taxi quite aggressively, seldom waiting for the loadmaster to climb into the upper hatch to clear the wing tips. The problem was solved the day our wing tip caught the great big upper antenna on a parked O-1 and tipped the aircraft over on its nose. Neither the O-1 pilot nor the camp he was supporting were happy having to wait for a return-to-service

inspection.

The third student had been flying for a great many years and certainly knew far more about propeller aircraft than I did. On one landing, he was way long so I told him to go around. His solution was to reverse both engines while we were still about fifty feet in the air and drop almost straight down to a perfect touchdown. He later told me that they used to do that all the time in the old days. I told him not to do it again, but I have no idea if he took my advice. I never had the guts to try it myself.

The final student was a Lt. Col. getting combat time after a long period of flying a desk stateside. On our first flight together, he was in the left seat. He was a pretty good pilot, but a bit hard of hearing. My habit as copilot, while dealing with the deluge of information and instructions coming over multiple radios, was to make notes on the windscreen with a marking pen. As soon as I noticed that he was not hearing what we were supposed to do next, I increased the size of my notes. His sly sidelong glances improved communication markedly.

Then, there was the nail trick that I learned from a more experienced instructor pilot. Prior to the last leg of the final flight before a check ride, he would put the head of a large roofing nail in the tread of one of the tires. He would then tell the student pilot he had found a nail in one of the tires on walk around and ask him what they should do about it. There was no right answer, but if the student's idea did not make sense, he was not ready for his check ride." [14]

Safety

Capt. James R. Gunkel (Chief of Safety until 26 May), 1/Lt. Jerry L. Dilley (Flying Safety Officer), 1/Lt. Charles S. Griffith (Ground Safety Officer), and 1/Lt. Walter V. Collins, Jr. (Explosives Safety Officer) served throughout the first quarter. The Safety Section covered all facets of flight and ground safety. Increased emphasis on the submitting of OHRs was rewarded with significant action on the problems. Helicopter traffic handling improved through analysis of the OHRs. A safer flying atmosphere resulted. Monthly flying safety meetings were held, with attendance mandatory for all pilots and Flight Engineers. Some items covered were: enroute traffic patterns, taxi accidents, crew duty time, uncontrolled airfield operations, and short field landings.

First Lieutenant Dean W. Chapman remembered his unique experiences at Quan Loi and Bien Hoa:

"Every time I went to Quan Loi, something weird happened. The first time we were landing to the north and there were several Chinooks warming up on the left side of the runway. As we approached, one of them decided it was time to take off. I never realized what a CH-47 could do when you were close and they decided to pull pitch. The runway didn't look the same for a few seconds. Instead of being straight ahead in the window, it was all over the place. After passing the Chinook, we finally settled down and were able to land and take a deep breath. Believe me, I was always aware of them after that.

Another time, we were sitting in the cockpit, backed up to the aerial port, loading passengers when I noticed two GIs walking toward the tower opposite the aerial port. They were walking from different directions and toward each other. I thought that was strange since I had never seen anyone over there before. I watched them and suddenly they just stopped and raised their M-16's. I thought they saw some enemy over there and I was a little concerned. Unfortunately, they decided to have a *High Noon* adventure and shot each other. I didn't realize the full meaning of what happened until the next day when we carried them to Saigon in body bags. Fighting the enemy is bad enough, but they decided the enemy was each other I guess.

Again, we were at the Aerial Port loading passengers for Bien Hoa when the flight engineer came into the cockpit and told me we were being hi-jacked by a young Army GI who said his Vietnamese girl friend wanted to go to Saigon because her mother was sick. Knowing Saigon and Bien Hoa were very close, I told him to tell the GI we would go to Saigon. I then got on the radio and informed the people working in the port facility what was happening. I suggested they have the Military Policeman take off the MP band on his arm, conceal his weapon, and board the aircraft like any other passenger. If he thought he could disarm the young man, he should do so, but only if he was sure no one would get hurt. If he couldn't, we would go to Saigon and the MPs could meet him there. Fortunately for us, the MP was able to disarm the young man and we went on to Bien Hoa uneventfully. I have often wondered what happened to that young GI when he discovered the price he probably paid. Surely wasn't worth the camaraderie he was receiving from the young girl." [15]

In the second quarter, Maj. David F. Edwards assumed the duties of Chief of Safety. Capt. R. William Findlay was the Flying Safety Officer and 1/Lt. Griffith and 1/Lt. Collins continued as Ground Safety Officer and Explosives Safety Officer, respectively. The Safety Section covered all facets of flight and ground safety. The monthly safety meetings examined problem areas in both flying and ground safety. Increased emphasis on the submitting of OHRs was rewarded with significant action on problems. Helicopter traffic during C-7A landings and problems associated with helicopter traffic improved through analysis of the OHRs, resulting in a safer flying atmosphere. Monthly flying safety meetings were held with attendance mandatory for all pilots and Flight Engineers. Some items covered were: weather flying during the monsoon season, water safety while taxiing on wet PSP, short field landings, and correct tie-down of speed-pallets.

Captain Robert A. Ross remembered a short field landing at Bien Hoa:

> "I never would have believed that a VNAF F-5 jet could land using less runway than a Caribou if I had not seen it with my own eyes. Taxiing out for takeoff at Ben Hoa, I was holding for an inbound emergency. The F-5, apparently out of fuel, arrived over the runway and pitched out. Roll out downwind looked OK, gear and flaps down OK, but as he turned final, the pilot started screaming in Vietnamese. The jet dropped like a stone onto the overrun, ripping off the gear and slid about 2000 feet down the runway. The canopy opened, the pilot got out and took off his helmet, walked around the jet once, and sat on the nose apparently waiting for his ride to operations. Just goes to prove the old adage, 'Any landing you walk away from is a good one.'" [16]

On 16 June, Maj. Edwin H. Kohlehepp, Jr. was attached to the 6483 TGP and assumed additional duty as Group Safety Officer.

In the third quarter, Maj. Edwards, 1/Lt. Griffith, and 1/Lt. Collins continued in their respective positions of Chief of Safety, Ground Safety Officer, and Explosives Safety Officer. All facets of flight and ground safety were covered during the quarter. Increased emphasis was placed on submitting OHRs and that resulted in significant actions on problems. Monthly flying safety meetings were held with attendance mandatory for all pilots and Flight Engineers. Some items discussed were: taxiing and taxi accidents, accidents and accidents within the command, weather during the transitions of the Southwest and Northeast monsoons, cockpit discipline, and ground safety hazards. The squadron continued its unblemished record of ground safety. The

153

squadron did not have a reportable ground accident in the first three quarters of 1969.

Major Felix R. Herrington remembered a mission into IV Corps when his crew had an opportunity to rescue the crew of another Caribou:

"On 27 August 1969, I was the Aircraft Commander and we were on short final at That Son (V-173) which had 2000 feet of PSP. This field was in IV Corps, near the Seven Sisters mountains. I saw an Aussie Caribou on the ramp being struck by a mortar attack. It lost seven feet of the wing and the crew was exiting the aircraft.

Talking to the choppers nearby on FM, I asked if they would relay to the crew to get to midfield on the airfield and I would help in their evacuation. My intention was to make a short field landing, have my flight mechanic unchain the load, turn my aircraft around after landing, and LOLEX (Low Level Extraction) the load on the runway during takeoff. Our cargo was rockets and ammo for the troops at the airfield. The chopper crew said they would evacuate the crew.

On takeoff, leaving the cargo on the runway behind us, I did a tactical departure and turned out of traffic. Tracers from a .50 caliber burst across the windshield, sounding like popcorn. After a successful departure, we returned to base and found about 40 holes in the wing.

I was within a couple months of DEROS, so I changed my strategy about flying in Vietnam. The squadron leadership was pushing for every Aircraft Commander to fly missions into I and II Corps to 'see all of Vietnam.' Most of our crews had never flown in that part of Vietnam and those fields were tricky and unknown to us. 'Seeing all of Vietnam' seemed like a 'dumb' approach to me, so I took two R&Rs and a 10 day ferry trip to Okinawa instead." [17]

In the fourth quarter, Maj. Edwards continued as Safety Officer and Capt. Smith as the Flying Safety Officer. First Lieutenant Dean W. Chapman replaced 1/Lt. Griffith as Ground Safety Officer and 1/Lt. Harry R. Bissinger, Jr. replaced 1/Lt. Collins as Explosives Safety Officer. Increased emphasis was placed on submitting OHRs and that resulted in significant actions on problems.

The actions of 1/Lt. Charles R. Erickson and his crew on 7 November were documented in the citation for his Distinguished Flying Cross:

"First Lieutenant Charles R. Erickson distinguished himself by

154

extraordinary achievement while participating in aerial flight as a Pilot of a C-7A aircraft in the Republic of Vietnam on 7 November 1969. Lieutenant Erickson was on a return mission when his plane encountered intense ground fire, inflicting numerous hits upon his aircraft which resulted in the loss of one engine and most of his fuel. With the possibility of fire due to fuel leaks, and other unknown damage to the aircraft, Lieutenant Erickson was able to navigate his aircraft and make a successful landing at home base without further incident. The professional competence, aerial skill, and devotion to duty displayed by Lieutenant Erickson reflect great credit upon himself and the United States Air Force." [18]

Monthly flying safety meetings were held with attendance mandatory for all pilots and Flight Engineers. Some items discussed were: uncontrolled traffic crossing the runway at Forward Operating Locations, taxi accidents, flying below 3000 feet, and a review of C-7A accidents.

Maintenance

In the first quarter, Organizational Maintenance continued to operate effectively, led by Capt. Jay A. Green. By 31 March, it had exceeded its authorized personnel strength by 16. All supervisory positions were filled.

A strong and comprehensive OJT program was implemented and was expected to result in upgrading of all 3-levels in AFSC 431X0 in the next quarter. Repair and maintenance of non-powered AGE continued and greatly improved the condition of the equipment. The inventory of 780 equipment reached 50 percent completion. Among the "self-help" projects was the repair and repainting of the line shack which served as a central meeting place and office for the Line Chief.

Overall improvement was made in personnel management and quality performance by establishing two flights, both having a crew chief and an assistant crew chief. This instilled personal pride in maintenance performance and developed a healthy competitive attitude which resulted in sustained, noteworthy accomplishments. This was evidenced by a 99 percent initial launch reliability rate and an average 80.6 Operationally Ready rate.

The **Vehicle Maintenance Shop** continued to operate under the very capable supervision of MSgt. Perry A. Crosier, Jr. The shop performed routine scheduled maintenance on all Air Force vehicles. Three hundred and forty-five vehicles received unscheduled maintenance and 40 received safety inspections. There were 19 Vehicles Deadlined for

Parts (VDP). Of the 10 personnel authorized, there were 11 assigned. Two personnel were lost and none were gained. Two civilian personnel were authorized and assigned.

The **Petroleum, Oils, and Lubricants** (POL) Section operated normally. The Section delivered 151,053 gallons of AVGAS and 7465 gallons of oil in January, 229,975 gallons of AVGAS and 7751 gallons of oil in February, and 284,608 gallons of AVGAS and 8945 gallons of oil in March.

In the second quarter, Capt. Green continued as Maintenance Officer and POL Officer. The Maintenance Section lost 15 personnel. This eliminated overages and stabilized manning at 100 percent with an excellent grades/skill balance. The OJT program continued to receive strong emphasis. All 3-level airmen were projected for upgrading in August. Satisfactory progress was made by the NCOs in 43171A upgrade training.

The initial launch reliability rate remained over 99 percent. Enroute delays were drastically reduced. The Operationally Ready Rate averaged 86.3 percent.

The Maintenance Section lost nine personnel during the third quarter. After a stabilized manning situation since March, no significant number of inputs were programmed into the section until November. The manning strength was 44 assigned against 49 authorized at the end of September. The OJT program continued to receive strong emphasis. All but two 3-level airmen were upgraded by the end of the quarter.

A/1C Rene E. Pothier was named Crew Chief of the Month for August and A/1C Robert G. Ingerson was named Crew Chief of the Month for September.

The Maintenance Section lost 22 personnel during the fourth quarter. Due to such a large rotation of experienced personnel, the manning was critically shorthanded. However, through the tireless efforts of all personnel, mission requirements were met with no sacrifice in the quality of maintenance. Manning at the end of the year was 49 authorized and 33 assigned. One man requested extension of his tour beyond the required 12 months, bringing to seven the number of personnel who were on extensions of their tour. This represented 21 percent of the assigned personnel. All arriving personnel were higher ranking NCOs. The OJT program continued to receive strong emphasis. All 3-level airmen were projected to upgrade during the quarter.

Administration

In the first quarter, Maj. Clinton G. Weihl was the Administrative

Services Officer, 1/Lt. Frederick A. Henderson was the Historian, and TSgt. James H. Lanier was the First Sergeant. Squadron Administration suffered two 702X0 personnel losses. On 31 March, the Unit Detail Listing (UDL) for this Air Force Specialty Code (AFSC) reflected one each vacancy in the Unit Orderly Room and in Organizational Maintenance. The Disaster Control Team (DCT) was fully manned throughout the quarter. Intensive training was conducted in preparation for the anticipated Tet offensive. This training was put to test under actual "Red Alert" conditions. On three occasions, the airfield was subjected to rocket and/or mortar attack and the DCT responded immediately and efficiently.

First Lieutenant Michael E. Harvin remembered how he got from the Philippine Islands (PI) to Vietnam:

"My first day in country was indicative of the year to come. Four of us brand new 1/Lt. pilots were inbound to C-7A slots in Vietnam and had been trapped at Snake School in the PI for about a week (getting bumped by fighter pilot in-bounds). We finally got into the course and then the school received a notice from the C-7A Wing Commander to put any C-7A inbound crew dogs on a C-7A (returning to Vietnam after maintenance) the day the class ended.

We were handed revised travel orders, got on the plane and headed out. The crew had no inkling they were going to be hauling passengers so there were no chutes, rafts, etc. for the four of us back in the back! When we landed at Cam Ranh Bay around 6 PM (after a LONG flight from the PI, remember), the crew took us to the VOQ and dropped us off. That's what they normally did when they hauled visiting pilots from other units!! We were in our tans since we hadn't processed in yet, so we stood out when we went to the O-club for dinner. Everyone else was in a flight suit or green fatigues. We couldn't buy anything since all we had were DOLLARS which didn't work in Vietnam (at least not at the O-Club). There was some consternation generated by the illegality of all of that, since it appeared that MULTIPLE laws/rules/SOPs had been busted by these four innocents.

In hindsight, it seems that everyone decided we should have waited for the inbound 'Freedom Bird' from the PI, as originally planned, so we could have been 'processed' normally! From that day on, it got more interesting." [19]

Captain Robert A. Ross remembered the Duy Tan Hotel in beautiful downtown Vung Tau:

"The quarters for the officers of the 535 TAS turned out to be

157

an old French Hotel named the Duy Tan, miles from the base with a ski boat parked inside the gate, a table in the lobby covered with paperback books to exchange, two beds to a room with a bath, air conditioner, and a bar/dining room on the roof. Now this was going to be my kind of war – fly all day, spend the evenings on the roof watching the airfield being rocketed, read a free book, sleep in relative comfort, and go water skiing on my days off. That turned out to have been mostly true, except for three things: the ski boat didn't run and the food and water had issues.

The squadron had to scrounge for food for rooftop dining and choices were limited to what the Army didn't want. Diet included non-stop rice and canned fruit cocktail, which were pretty hard to eat after months and months, even if mixed together. Water had to be supplied by truck from the airfield resulting in it always being freezing cold and frequently running out.

Cold showers were annoying, but not being able to flush the toilet was another matter. My personal solution one desperate evening was to pour four fifths of gin into the wall mounted French style toilet tank, which provided for one successful life saving flush." [20]

In the second quarter, 1/Lt. Robert P. Milazzo was the Historian and TSgt. Lanier continued as First Sergeant. Capt. Richard W. Bailey assumed the duties of Administrative Services Officer on 25 June when Maj. Weihl completed his tour. The DCT was fully manned throughout the quarter and participated in periodic practice alerts to maintain proficiency. The team chief, Capt. Patrick V. Ford, and the NCOIC, SSgt. Randal L. Sawyer, were replaced by 1/Lt. Roger L. Wells and SSgt. Thomas H. Jones.

Two Administrative Staff Assistance visits were made to the squadron. The 834 AD team was primarily concerned with security. No major discrepancies were noted. The 483 TAW team used a general approach, with particular emphasis placed on systems and classified control procedures. No unresolved malpractices were noted.

The two administrative personnel assigned to the unit Orderly Room were scheduled for rotation in early August. The Operations Clerk was relocated to the Orderly Room to assure continuity of operation and control of squadron administration.

The personnel section was authorized three slots and all were filled. One AFSC 73250 Staff Sergeant was lost and one AFSC 73270 Master Sergeant was gained. The Orderly Room of the 6483 TGP was established, consisting of one MSgt. (First Sergeant), one SSgt. (Chief

Clerk), and one SSgt. (Publications Clerk). With the forming of the Group, many functions normally handled at the squadron level were absorbed by the Group. Personnel losses were 53 and gains were 85. Due to the loss of funds, approximately 25 over-hire civilian personnel were released.

In the third quarter, 1/Lt. Milazzo continued as the Historian. Capt. Richard W. Bailey assumed the duties of Administrative Services Officer on 25 June.

Normal operation was seriously hampered by the loss of five personnel. The Chief Clerk, Operations Clerk, and Maintenance Clerk were reassigned at the end of their tours. The First Sergeant, TSgt. Lanier, retired from the Air Force and the services of the civilian secretary were discontinued due to a reduction of funds. The section gained three new clerks and a Flight Engineer, MSgt. Roger L. Schmidke, was appointed acting First Sergeant on 1 September, to fulfill those duties when not flying. A full-time First Sergeant was not programmed to arrive before 1 November.

SSgt. Robert W. See arrived on 10 August and immediately assumed the duties of Chief Clerk. On 19 August, Sgt. Mark D. Smith assumed the duties of Operations Clerk. With the arrival of A/1C Otis S. Lane on 6 September, the Administration Section was at full strength.

In the fourth quarter, Capt. Bailey continued as Administrative Services Officer and 1/Lt. Milazzo continued as the Historian. On 9 December, MSgt. Francis J. Eckert replaced MSgt. Schmidke as First Sergeant. This marked the first time since 31 August that the squadron had a full-time First Sergeant. MSgt. Schmidke returned to his full-time duties as Instructor Flight Engineer. The Administrative Services Section continued with SSgt. See as Chief Clerk, Sgt. Smith as Operations Clerk, and A/1C Lane as Maintenance Clerk.

The squadron moved into new facilities. In conjunction with the move, new administrative offices were set up and a general redecoration was accomplished. Squadron publications were consolidated in the administration area and only signed out as required by other sections. Job continuity folders for all sections were completed and a program was initiated for development of Operating Instructions for various sections and departments.

On 26 and 27 November, the 7th Air Force Staff Assistance Team inspected the Administrative Services Section. A "Satisfactory" rating was received with no major discrepancies noted. This rating was an improvement over the "Marginal" rating received the previous year.

Supply and Support

In the first quarter, Lt. Col. James C. Hilbert was Chief of the Support Division. Capt. Richard J. Weinberg was the Flight Surgeon (Flight Medical Officer). The "Green Tail Lounge," the squadron recreation hooch, underwent modification, including painting, installation of air conditioners and an exhaust system, and re-padding of the bar. A ping-pong table was installed and a pool table was anticipated in the next quarter.

After an inspection by the Inspector General, coordination with the Consolidated Base Personnel Office (CBPO) at Cam Ranh Bay resulted in the transfer of in-processing of personnel to that activity. This eliminated many problems previously encountered and offered a more expeditious and effective processing system.

Publication of mobility folders proved to be the most significant project undertaken. Coordination with and assistance from Cam Ranh Bay was expected to result in "on-file" AF Forms 711 for all officer and airman personnel assigned. This was expected to prove of great value in many areas, particularly to the Awards and Decorations program.

Approximately 66 personnel out-processed and 140 in-processed during the first quarter. Of the authorized civilian personnel, 3 were authorized in the Orderly Room, 23 in Food Service, 4 in Vehicle Operations, and 2 in the Motor Pool. Of the assigned civilian personnel, two were assigned to the Support Division, 3 were assigned to the Orderly Room, 22 were assigned to Food Service, 1 was assigned to Vehicle Operations, and 2 were assigned to the Motor Pool. Two local nationals resigned and seven were hired. Fourteen local nationals previously assigned to the now defunct 535th Civil Engineering Squadron were transferred to Detachment 1 of the 823rd Combat Engineering Squadron (Red Horse) operating at Vung Tau. The 823rd Civil Engineering Detachment #1 at Vung Tau Air Base was authorized 35 personnel, but only 25 were assigned.

The personnel picture in the Supply Section improved appreciably. Capt. Kenneth D. Matthew, II completed his tour and was replaced by Capt. James M. Calloway. SSgt. Jorge L. Pratsgoyco was gained. Aircraft bench stock responsibility was transferred to Material Control, along with two personnel slots. One Master Sergeant was programmed into the Equipment Management Section, but was diverted to fill a First Sergeant's lot for the newly activated Tactical Group Provisional. At the end of the quarter, the supply function had 18 personnel assigned against an authorized 16.

160

During the first 30 days of a recently developed transportation system for supplies, which relieved the squadron from the responsibility, the base supply transaction register reflected issues for approximately 130 items. Many of these items had not been received. Cargo being issued from Tan Son Nhut was turned over to Commercial Transportation for turnover to the Army for subsequent shipment to Vung Tau. This process caused a delay of 50 to 60 days. Notwithstanding these excessive enroute procedures, base supply at Tan Son Nhut was charging Vung Tau with receipt of property from the date of document issue. Manning problems were experienced due to lack of support from base supply at Tan Son Nhut. This was illustrated by the finding that the Not Operationally Ready-Supply (NORS) control section at Tan Son Nhut was not monitoring the problems or conducting follow-ups.

The area movie facility, the "Red Barn Theater," that was opened in the last quarter of 1968, continued to be a terrific morale booster with two and often three showings daily. A different film was shown each day.

The **Transportation Section** logged 112,343 miles and issued 168 driver permits with 9 military personnel authorized, 8 assigned, 2 slots gained, and 7 slots lost. Four civilian personnel were authorized for the section, but only one was assigned.

The **Food Service Section** supplied mess facilities four times daily to both the 535 TAS and the 536 TAS. The facilities were extremely inadequate and construction was started on a new mess hall. The new mess hall, along with equipment and utensils on order, should alleviate the major problems of providing meals in an appropriate manner, as well as adequate quality. MSgt. Wallace L. Patton, the Mess Sergeant, and TSgt Seller, his assistant, exerted every effort to deliver good service with low manpower and poor facilities.

The **Intelligence Section**, manned by 2/Lt. James N. Fujita (OIC) and MSgt. Charles A. Smith (NCOIC) began providing intelligence data for both squadrons. Maps depicting hits and incidents, Special Forces camps, friendly operations, Escape & Evasion (E & E) tips, and plant cards were displayed in the briefing rooms of both squadrons. The Aircrew Intelligence Briefing Guide, the Intelligence Library, E&E photos, and files were all brought up to date. The section had maps made of the III Corps Tactical Zone (CTZ) showing the main highways and artillery frequencies to aid new personnel in their flying.

The **Flight Medicine Section** was manned by one Flight Medical Officer and two Aeromedical Technicians who cared for approximately 750 flying and non-flying personnel of the 535 TAS and the 536 TAS, and several small detachments on TDY from other stations. In addition to handling USAF sick call, medical treatments, physical examinations, and immunizations, the section was responsible for monitoring health and safety conditions at Air Force facilities and living quarters, on and off base. This was done through monthly medical inspections and day-to-day troubleshooting. The section provided each new arrival to the area with a mimeographed medical briefing on medical facilities and area health hazards.

The Flight Medical Officer also participated in monthly flying safety meetings. In addition to caring for Air Force personnel, the Flight Medical Officer donated approximately 70 hours a month seeing Army, Navy, and U.S. civilian patients at afternoon sick call at the dispensary. The section established a Local National Health Program for the Vietnamese civilians employed by the Air Force. In addition, important contributions were made to a Medical Civic Action Program through weekly visits to an orphanage and a home for old folks. In February and March, the section was scheduled to move into a more adequate and centrally located facility in order to improve medical care for USAF personnel stationed at Vung Tau.

In the second quarter, Lt. Col. Hilbert continued as Chief of the Support Division and Capt. Calloway continued to lead the Supply Support Branch. Of the authorized civilian personnel, 3 were authorized in the Orderly Room, 1 in Flight Medicine, 18 in Food Service, 4 in Vehicle Operations, 2 in the Motor Pool, and 18 in the Security Section. Of the assigned civilian personnel, 1 was assigned to the Support Division, 3 were assigned to the Orderly Room, 1 was assigned to Flight Medicine, 22 were assigned to Food Service, 1 was assigned to Vehicle Operations, 2 were assigned to the Motor Pool, and 13 were assigned to the Security Section. Eight local nationals resigned and none were hired. Completion of construction projects by the 823rd Combat Engineering Squadron, Detachment 1 resulted in the release of 36 local nationals.

Non-powered AGE was in good mechanical condition. Receipt of four C-1 work stands reduced work stoppage during aircraft recovery operations. An inventory of 780 equipment was completed. A new flight line building was under construction with an estimated completion date of 20 August. It would provide offices for the AGE dispatchers of the 535 TAS and 536 TAS, a latrine, a large room for aircrew debriefings, and a crew chief lounge.

Two Staff Sergeants in the Supply Section were reassigned within PACAF and one Sergeant and one A/1C arrived to replace them. Two

NCOs were transferred to the Material Control Section to fill bench stock vacancies of the 536 TAS. Personnel manning status at the end of the quarter was 16 personnel authorized and 16 assigned.

During April and May, much of the equipment and furnishings for the new dining hall were received, including two prefabricated walk-in refrigerators, forks, and spoons. Also, 54 items of equipment at a cost of $20,235 was received.

On 4 April, the **Equipment/Supplies Support Section** was designated to provide its own transportation of supplies and equipment to and from Tan Son Nhut by a convoy over Highway 16. A total of 17 round trips were made, returning approximately 200,000 pounds of cargo to Tan Son Nhut and bringing approximately 270,000 pounds of cargo to Vung Tau. Most of the cargo going to Tan Son Nhut consisted of unserviceable maintenance equipment and vehicles. By providing its own transportation, loss of property between Tan Son Nuht was eliminated and in-transit time was reduced from an average of two weeks to two days.

The section furnished an NCO for a project to review all maintenance support equipment for the C-7A aircraft. This involved reviewing flight line in-shop requirements against the current Table of Allowance in compiling recommendations for additions and deletions for the three C-7A bases. The allowance conference was held at Clark Air Base, Philippine Islands, from 6-9 May. All recommended changes were approved by Headquarters AFLC and WRAMA representatives.

The equipment accounts for the 535 TAS and the 536 TAS were consolidated into one account from the Tan Son Nhut Equipment Management Office. This appreciably reduced the administrative workload required for maintaining records for the two accounts. There were 186 equipment transactions against this account during the quarter, consisting mostly of maintenance support and dining hall equipment. There were 200 expendable items received valued at $3995.28.

Vehicular Maintenance and **Material Control** experienced difficulty in obtaining parts to maintain the three R-2 Refueling Units which were received from Binh Thuy in unserviceable condition. Parts and accessories for other vehicles were received within a reasonable time. One exception was the long pipeline time required for smaller sized tires required for general-purpose vehicles.

Remodeling of the "Green Tail Lounge" was completed. This was a self-help project. The facility offered off-duty personnel a place within the squadron area for relaxation, including an air-conditioned bar with a TV set, tables, chairs, and a ping-pong table.

The **Transportation Section** logged 39,754 miles and issued 33 driver permits. Nine military personnel were authorized, 7 were assigned, and one slot was lost. There were four civilian personnel authorized, but only one assigned. On 2 May, SSgt. Willie Harris, Jr. was officially designated as NCOIC of the Mortor Pool Transportation Branch. In addition, Sgt. David J. Walker was assigned the position of Chief Dispatcher. The Motor Pool instituted a 24-hour operation; however, due to manpower shortages it was unable to provide a 24-hour taxi service. Hours of operation were 0400-2200 which proved sufficient to meet mission requirements.

On 16 May, POL, Personnel, Supply, Food Service, Civil Engineering, Transportation, Medical Flight, and 483 CAMS OLAB were attached to the 6483 Tactical Group Provisional (6483 TGP) for administrative support effective on 15 March 1969.

On 17 May, the **Food Service** branch closed and abandoned the old dining hall, Building T-119, upon completion of the breakfast meal. The new dining hall facility was officially opened at 1100 on 17 in June with ribbon-cutting ceremonies conducted by Col. Turk. In attendance were Lt. Col. Buckley (Commander, 6483 TGP), the Commanders of the 535 TAS and 536 TAS, and Col. Brinson (Chief of Maintenance, 483 CAMS OLAB). Approximately 380 officers and enlisted personnel were served a dinner comprised of grilled steak, baked beans, potatoes, assorted fruit salad, vegetables, and soft drinks.

The **Intelligence Section**, manned by 2/Lt. Fujita (OIC) and MSgt. Smith (NCOIC) provided up-to-date and timely intelligence data for both the 535 TAS and 536 TAS. In the early part of June, the Intelligence Section of the 535 TAS was attached to the 6483 TGP as a support element. Prior to this, the Intelligence Section was located in the 535 TAS Operations Building which did not allow for smooth functioning of the section due to the many other offices in the building. The intelligence function was greatly facilitated by being attached to the TGP and with an office specifically for intelligence work. The office personnel began attending the weekly Phoenix meeting, which was a gathering of various intelligence agencies throughout the Vung Tau area, to discuss the local situation and to create a more congenial atmosphere for intelligence processes among the Navy, Coast Guard, Army, and the Australian Task Force.

The 535 TAS Medical Aid Station was manned by one Flight Medical Officer, Capt. Weinberg, and two Aeromedical Technicians who cared for approximately 750 flying and non-flying personnel of the 535 TAS and the 536 TAS, and several small detachments on TDY from other stations. This facility continued to service all Air Force and attached indigenous personnel in Vung Tau in the surrounding community through the Medical Civic Action Program (MEDCAP). In addition, important contributions continued to be made through weekly visits to an orphanage and home for old folks. The new facility was expected to be available on 1 July to make it possible to more adequately do the job.

In the third quarter, an inventory of B-4 stands revealed that nine of the ten authorized stands were on-hand and in satisfactory condition. Five of the 10 authorized C-1 stands were also on-hand and in satisfactory condition. A new 780 Equipment Storage Facility was under construction and all equipment currently in CONEXes was scheduled to be moved to the new facility. The interior of the radio truck was painted as a self-help project during August. The Organizational Maintenance Office was moved from the hangar area to a newly constructed building at the end of the C-7A parking ramp. The section continued to support Vung Tau and maintain personnel TDY at Tan Son Nhut, Bien Hoa, and Bangkok.

The initial launch reliability rate was over 99 percent for the quarter. The Operational Readiness Rate averaged 82.8 percent for the quarter.

In the fourth quarter, the authorization for B-4 stands was submitted. The new 780 equipment storage facility was completed and six of the eight CONEXes were turned in. Vehicles in vehicle maintenance were a great problem. The tow tug was out of commission all during the quarter and the line vehicle was dead-lined since early November. Substitute vehicles were used until necessary parts could be obtained. Latrine facilities were completed in the Organizational Maintenance area and a bunker was under construction. Remodeling of the old dining hall was completed and on 19 November squadron operations moved into its new facilities. Everyone not involved with flying that day helped to move the squadron to its new home. For the first time, each section had separate office and filing space. The new facilities were completely air-conditioned and offered a new atmosphere under which squadron activities could be conducted.

The Organizational Maintenance section continued to support Vung Tau and maintain TDY personnel at Tan Son Nhut and Bangkok. The initial launch reliability rate was over 99 percent. A complete review of the weight and balance data for the C-7A aircraft was completed in November, resulting in a more reliable Weight and Balance Form 365F aboard each aircraft.

The 7AF Safety Team inspected the section from 18-20 December with no major malpractices noted.

Awards and Decorations

In the first quarter, the Awards and Decorations Officers were 1/Lt. Chester S. Loose and 1/Lt. Michael P. Lavelle. Numerous awards were received by squadron personnel during the last quarter of 1968. Among these were a Bronze Star, 12 Basic Air Medals, numerous Oak Leaf Clusters to the Air Medal, and three Air Force Commendation Medals. Many other awards were still pending approval.

In the second quarter, 1/Lt. Derek L. Yunkin and 1/Lt. Charles E. Erickson replaced 1/Lt. Loose and 1/Lt. Lavelle. Numerous awards were received by squadron personnel including a Bronze Star, 32 Basic Air Medals, and 16 Air Force Commendation Medals. In addition, 1 Silver Star, 17 DFCs, one Bronze Star, 55 Basic Air Medals, and 14 Air Force Commendation Medals were pending approval.

On 7 May, the squadron was presented a plaque recognizing it as the "Outstanding C-7A Caribou Unit" in the 483 TAW for March. On 4 June, the squadron was presented a plaque recognizing it as the "Outstanding C-7A Caribou Unit" in the 483 TAW for April.

First Lieutenant Robert A. Ross figured out how to handle being assigned as Awards and Decorations Officer:

> "I really hated my additional duty of Awards and Decorations Officer. The task consisted mainly of writing flowery things about bravery, courage in the line of duty, etc. so that the deserving could get Air Medals and other awards. When I asked for guidance on this job, I was informed that the most important part of the task was, 'To make sure the typewriter has clean teeth.' Several months into this assignment and bored out of my mind, I happened to fly a mission carrying live food to the Vietnamese.
>
> Fastest way to the cockpit was to climb over the top of the load. As I climbed over a wicker basket full of ducks, one reached up and bit my leg, drawing blood. Seizing the opportunity, I put myself in for the Purple Heart using my best Awards and Decorations language about my encounter with the VC duck. As soon as the paperwork hit channels, I was no longer the Awards and Decorations Officer." [21]

In the third quarter, many awards were received or were pending for squadron personnel. Among those awards were 10 Distinguished Flying Crosses, 30 Basic Air Medals, and numerous Oak Leaf Clusters to the Air Medal. On 16 August, Lt. Col. Lester P. Livesay took over the Awards and Decorations Section. First Lieutenant William C. Kassen replaced 1/Lt. Robert A. Ross as Assistant to Lt. Col. Livesay. On 12 September, Brig. Gen. Herring visited the squadron for an Awards and Decorations ceremony.

In the fourth quarter, many awards were received by squadron personnel. Among these awards were 10 Air Medals and 10 Air Force Commendation Medals. In addition, 14 Distinguished Flying Crosses, 6 Bronze Stars, 1 Airman's Medal, 14 Air Medals, and 20 Air Force Commendation Medals were pending approval. First Lieutenant Gordon E. Lewis and 1/Lt. Lawrence A. Windburn replaced 1/Lt. Erickson and 1/Lt Kassen as Awards and Decorations Officers.

Civic Action and Special Activities

No Civic Actions or Special Activities were reported in the quarterly squadron histories.

Captain Robert A. Ross remembered flying the Santa Bou mission:
> "Since holidays away from home and loved ones are a lonely time, I volunteered to fly the 'Santa Bou' on Christmas day to keep my mind busy. Lifting off from Vung Tau, my two fellow crew members and I were filled with expectation of the joy we were going to bring to all the good little boys and girls. Mostly, Christmas cheer prevailed every place we went distributing trinkets from the cargo ramp. At one camp, however, we were greeted with a message over the FM radio that went something like, 'Just push the crap off the back and get out of here, we are under attack.' I suppose Santa has the same feeling in his stomach every time he goes down a chimney and finds the fire is still burning." [22]

Airlift Accomplishments [23]

During the first quarter, passengers hauled were 32,732 in January; 29,194 in February; and 33,215 in March for a total of 95,141. Cargo hauled was 1279.6 tons in January; 1113.4 tons in February; and 1306.9 tons in March for a total of 3699.9 tons. In January, the squadron flew 3265 sorties while logging 1616.0 flying hours. In February, the squadron flew 2893 sorties while logging 1480.6 flying hours. In March, the squadron flew 3360 sorties while logging 1735.1 flying hours.

During the second quarter, passengers hauled were 31,848 in April; 30,773 in May; and 30,405 in June for a total of 93,026. Cargo hauled was 1248.5 tons in April; 1085.2 tons in May; and 967.0 tons in June for a total of 3300.7 tons. In April, the squadron flew 3213 sorties while logging 1628.5 flying hours. In May, the squadron flew 3183 sorties while logging 1675.5 flying hours. In June, the squadron flew 2989 sorties while logging 1628.5 flying hours.

During the third quarter, passengers hauled were 30,686 in July; 27,976 in August; and 24,350 in September for a total of 83,012. Cargo hauled was 1011.5 tons in July; 1093.2 tons in August; and 888.8 tons in September for a total of 2993.5 tons. In July, the squadron flew 3107 sorties while logging 1670.2 flying hours. In August, the squadron flew 3063 sorties while logging 1638.6 flying hours. In September, the squadron flew 2770 sorties while logging 1546.7 flying hours.

During the fourth quarter, passengers hauled were 77,505. Cargo hauled was 4738.2 tons. The squadron flew 5485 sorties while logging 4400.2 flying hours.

Commander's Summary

No Commander's Summaries were included in the quarterly squadron histories for 1969.

End Notes: 535 TAS

[1] *19690101-19691231 535 TAS History*
[2] *C-7A Caribou Newsletter, Vol. 20, Issue 1*
[3] 7AF Special Order G-0122, dated 14 January 1971
[4] *C-7A Caribou Newsletter, Vol. 19, Issue 2*
[5] 7AF Special Order G-4440, dated 6 October 1970
[6] 7AF Special Order G-2165, dated 15 May 1970
[7] 7AF Special Order G-4138, dated 17 September 1970
[8] 7AF Special Order G-4440, dated 6 October 1970
[9] 7AF Special Order G-5284, dated 20 November 1970
[10] 7AF Special Order G-4806, dated 26 October 1970
[11] *C-7A Caribou Newsletter, Vol. 19, Issue 1*
[12] *C-7A Caribou Newsletter, Vol. 20, Issue 1*
[13] *C-7A Caribou Newsletter, Vol. 19, Issue 1*
[14] *C-7A Caribou Newsletter, Vol. 20, Issue 1*
[15] *C-7A Caribou Newsletter, Vol. 22, Issue 2*
[16] *C-7A Caribou Newsletter, Vol. 20, Issue 1*
[17] *C-7A Caribou Newsletter, Vol. 24, Issue 2*
[18] 7AF Special Order G-3182, dated 14 July 1970
[19] *C-7A Caribou Newsletter, Vol. 19, Issue 1*
[20] *C-7A Caribou Newsletter, Vol. 19, Issue 1*
[21] *C-7A Caribou Newsletter, Vol. 19, Issue 2*
[22] *C-7A Caribou Newsletter, Vol. 20, Issue 1*

When the data in the squadron history and the Wing history differ, the Wing data is shown.

Fishing Boats at Vung Tau (Copyright © 2014 Bill Craig)

Air Conditioning for Survival (Copyright © 2014 Bill Craig)

Barracks at Vung Tau (Copyright © 2014 Bill Craig)

536TH
TACTICAL AIRLIFT SQUADRON

483RD **T AW** (PACAF)

LTC HAROLD ZWEIFEL
COMMANDER

Home of the 536 TAS (Copyright © 2014 Bill Craig)

536th Tactical Airlift Squadron[1]

The mission of the 536th Tactical Airlift Squadron (536 TAS) at Vung Tau was to provide intra-theater airlift in support of all free world military or civic actions and aid forces and units engaged in combat, combat support, logistics, and civic assistance in RVN; to accomplish this through air-land and aerial delivery of personnel and supplies in conformance with established MACV priorities for employment of C-7A aircraft; and to perform other airlift missions as directed by the Commander, 483rd Tactical Airlift Wing.

To accomplish these missions, the squadron was authorized 51 officers and 80 enlisted personnel in the first quarter. Of these authorizations, 49 officers and 91 enlisted personnel were assigned. No civilian personnel were authorized, but three were assigned. The squadron was authorized 16 aircraft and possessed 16, all of which were Combat Ready.

In the second quarter, the squadron was authorized 51 officers and 80 enlisted personnel. Of these authorizations, 43 officers and 82 enlisted personnel were assigned. No civilian personnel were authorized, but three were assigned. The squadron was authorized 16 aircraft and possessed 16, all of which were Combat Ready.

In the third quarter, the squadron was authorized 51 officers and 80 enlisted personnel. Of these authorizations, 44 officers and 73 enlisted personnel were assigned. The squadron was authorized 16 aircraft and possessed 16, all of which were Combat Ready.

In the fourth quarter, the squadron was authorized 51 officers and 80 enlisted personnel. Of these authorizations, 40 officers and 65 enlisted personnel were assigned, and 3 officers were "attached." The squadron was authorized 16 aircraft and possessed 16, all of which were Combat Ready.

On 16 January, Lt. Col. Ralph T. Ballard assumed command of the squadron, relieving Lt. Col. Miles H. Watkins.[2]

During the third quarter, the squadron witnessed an almost complete changeover in its command structure. Four field grade officers and one company grade officer left key operational positions for assignments in other commands. Lt. Col. Clifford E. Tyler, Chief of Stan/Eval, was attached to the 516th TAW, Dyess AFB.[3] Lt. Col. William E. Perry was assigned to the 6592nd Support Group, Air Force Systems Command (AFSC) at Los Angeles Air Force Station. Lt. Col. Gary E. Wiersma, Squadron Flight Examiner and Flight Commander, assumed an operations position with the 341st Combat Support Group, Malstrom

AFB, Montana. Maj. Robert S. Hamrin, Chief of Training, was assigned to Air Force Logistics Command (AFLC) at Wright-Patterson Air Force Base, OH. Capt. Robert E. Lee, Chief of Safety, was assigned to the 516th Tactical Airlift Wing (TAW), Dyess AFB, Texas. The absence of these men was felt; however, their positions were filled by officers whose capabilities, professionalism, and proficiency in their specific areas more than qualified them to fill those positions.

During the fourth quarter, the squadron experienced a large change in its command structure. Four field grade officers left key operational positions for assignments in other commands. On 4 December, Lt. Col. Ballard was replaced by Lt. Col. Buford E. Collings, Jr. as Squadron Commander.[4]

Lt. Col. Frank E. Gelsone and Maj. Daniel L. Zachary and Maj. Bobby L. Withrow also completed their tours.

Operations

In the first quarter, Lt. Col. William E. Perry continued as Operations Officer with Lt. Col. Gary E. Wiersma as his Assistant. Maj. Daniel L. Zachary was assigned as one of the scheduling officers when Capt. Michael J. Lipcsey completed his tour. Airman First Class Albert Burnett left the operations section, leaving TSgt. Edward A. Zins to man the post with assistance from SSgt. James A. Sackett, the Operations Clerk. Maj. Joseph W. Stokes, Maj. Withrow, and Maj. Zachary assumed duties as Flight Commanders. On 22 March, Maj. Stokes transferred to the Wing to be Chief of Stan/Eval.

Capt. A. Peter Rikeman experienced frustration while waiting for fighter cover so he could deliver his load to a camp:

> "Early in February of 1969, just before my return to the States, I landed in Saigon at the end of a long day to be met by a Major standing in front of a forklift with a pallet loaded with ammunition. He informed me that I had a Combat Essential mission to deliver the pallet to an airfield, almost certainly Katum, whose troops were expecting to be hit that night. I told him I needed fuel. No time, I was told, as two F-100's were in the area to cover my approach. If I delayed, they would have to leave, and I would be making the landing without air support.
>
> I took off as instructed and flew to the airfield without refueling. When I got into the area, I contacted the FAC for landing clearance. When I was told to start holding to await the F-100's, I knew I'd been had. I orbited for several minutes and asked where the fighters were. It turned out they hadn't even launched yet. Now,

172

I had to make a decision. Do I abort to get fuel, knowing that night was approaching and I would never be able to return before dark, or stick around and watch my fuel gauges plummet toward empty? When I told the FAC of my predicament, he showed a distinct lack of verbal skills, since all he would say was, 'Stand by a little longer.' I had the added distraction of having the Army guy on the ground pleading with me for the ammo.

After about a half hour, I told the FAC I had to land or leave, as fuel was now critical. Just then, the fighters reported in. They started their bombing and strafing under me and I headed for the runway. At about 1000 feet over the approach end, I dropped gear and flaps and spiraled down. I told the Flight Engineer to loosen the load so we could drop it quickly. I landed halfway down the runway, turned into the ramp area, and got rid of the load with a ground LAPES. I don't remember even slowing down, much less stopping. We turned back onto the runway and took off in the opposite direction.

Fuel was now so low that I realized Saigon was probably not feasible. Our only option was Tay Ninh. We probably landed with enough to power a Prius for a couple of minutes. Tay Ninh was not happy to see us, complaining that they had Avgas for some Bird Dogs, but not enough for a C-7A. When I told them they could scrounge it up or have a large target to interest Charlie all night, they grudgingly found enough to get us home to Vung Tau.

This was my first encounter with the famous Air Force snafu system. Had those F-100's been a little later, there might have been another picture of a downed Bou."

The squadron experienced a successful second quarter. Lt. Col. Perry continued as Operations Officer and Lt. Col. Gelsone replaced Lt. Col. Wiersma as Assistant Operations Officer. Training continued to place increased demands on time and resources, but the experience level in every phase of squadron operations remained high. Improved performance and increased stability were achieved through improved maintenance, aircraft Operationally Ready rate, and efficient use of available manpower.

Lt. Col. Gelsone, Lt. Col. Adrian E. Powell, and Maj. John H. Castles assumed duties as Flight Commanders. Other Flight Commanders were Lt. Col. Tyler, Lt. Col. Wiersma, and Maj. Withrow. Maj. Withrow was assigned as one of the scheduling officers when Maj. Zachary became Assistant Chief of Stan/Eval. When the tour of TSgt. Zins was completed, SSgt. Raymond W. Rock manned the post until he was transferred to 7AF on 15 June.

In the third quarter, Lt. Col. Gelsone assumed duties as Operations Officer, replacing Lt. Col. Perry who completed his tour. Lt. Col. Royal M. Hanning became his Assistant and a Flight Commander. Maj. Withrow was replaced as scheduling officer by Capt. Donald H. Ford. TSgt. Rene A. Roy, a Loadmaster, was temporarily assigned to Operations and made responsible for publications. SSgt. Steven Burgess and Sgt. Max C. McCright joined Operations where their help was needed to replace SSgt. Sackett who completed his tour.

In the fourth quarter, Lt. Col. Gelsone completed his tour and was replaced by Lt. Col. Paul J. Donahoe. Lt. Col. Hanning continued as Assistant Operations Officer. On 25 November, the 7AF Inspector General conducted an inspection of the squadron.

The actions of Sergeant Leonard M. Reynen and his crew on 24 December were documented in the citation for his Distinguished Flying Cross:

> "Sergeant Leonard M. Reynen distinguished himself by extraordinary achievement while participating in aerial flight as a C-7A Flight Engineer at Ca Mau, Republic of Vietnam on 24 December 1969. On that date, Sergeant Reynen flew a mission transporting critically needed fuel to the base of Cau Mau. Upon landing, the field came under hostile fire. By the time the aircraft had completed its ground roll, Sergeant Reynen had the load prepared for speed off-loading and the pilot was able to make a 180 degree turn and take off with less than two minutes of ground time accrued. The professional competence, aerial skill, and devotion to duty displayed by Sergeant Reynen reflect great credit upon himself and the United States Air Force." [5]

Training and Stan-Eval

In the first quarter, Lt. Col. Tyler continued as Chief of Stan/Eval. Maj. Hamrin became Chief of Training when Maj. William J. Lewis completed his tour. Capt. Edward A. Carlson and 1/Lt. Dennis E. Herrell continued as Assistant Training Officers. The Training Section continued a vigorous upgrade program to carry out the training objectives. Upgrade from Aircraft Commander to Instructor Pilot received heavy emphasis because of the many Instructor Pilots who had completed or would complete their tours soon. Instructor Pilots flew approximately 315 instructional flights during the quarter. Students and instructors were scheduled to fly every other day to provide rest for flying upgrade missions.

174

The squadron was authorized 24 crews, with 17 "formed" on 1 January and 20 "formed" at the end of March. The number of "formed" crews was directly related to the number of available and qualified Flight Engineers.

The section did 95 evaluations (1 semi-annual, 27 no-notice, 1 Flight Examiner, 9 Instructor, 29 Aircraft Commander, 13 First Pilot, 9 Theater Indoctrination, and 6 Airdrop). They also did 22 evaluations of Flight Engineers (3 semi-annual, 5 no-notice, 1 Flight Examiner, 4 Instructor, and 9 Theater Indoctrination). The upgrading accomplished included: 2 to Flight Examiner, 7 to Instructor Pilot, 17 to Aircraft Commander, 12 to First Pilot, and 8 to Copilot.

Maj. Stokes and Capt. James H. Tucker upgraded to Flight Examiner. Lt. Col. Wiersma, Maj. Daniel L. Zachary, Maj. Clyde E. Garrison, Capt. Lee, Capt. Terry K. Taylor, and 1/Lt. Roger L. Wisch upgraded to Instructor Pilot. Lt. Col. Ballard, Maj. Withrow, Capt. David C. Mueh, and Lieutenants Roger K. Blinn, Delbert A. Depner, Dennis E. Herrell, Peter A. McElroy, Gary L. Miller, Harry R. Mitchell, Kurt H. Mueller, [first name unknown] Stone, and Thomas W. Tiedemann upgraded to Aircraft Commander. Lt. Col. Gelsone and Lieutenants Herbert C. Davis, Joseph J. DiJanni, Harry R. Mitchell, and Thomas D. Paton upgraded to First Pilot. Lieutenants William A. Benke, Robert E. Hudson, Dennis D. Liston, Dennis R. Sandlin, and Earl L. Westergom qualified as Copilots.

The training program was greatly enlarged through the technical assistance of newly assigned NCOs. The proficiency training was about 98 percent complete with the only outstanding items being completed rapidly. The Maintenance Standardization Evaluation Testing (MSET) program progressed very well with a 100 percent qualified rate and all schedules and deadlines were met well ahead of time. The OJT program became very strong after a relatively slow start. With the change in the upgrading program, the local Career Development Course (CDC) and other training programs were expected to be of even greater value in helping all assigned personnel prepare for their promotion testing.

In the second quarter, Lt. Col. Tyler continued as Chief of Stan/Eval and Maj. Hamrin continued as Chief of Training. The squadron was authorized 24 crews, with 20 "formed" at the beginning of April and 21 "formed" at the end of June. The lower number of "formed" crews was due to a lack of pilots for the number of Flight Engineers available.

Stan/Eval did 55 evaluations of pilots (3 semi-annual, 7 no-notice,

2 Flight Examiner, 4 Instructor Pilot, 9 Aircraft Commander, 10 First Pilot, 15 Theater Indoctrination, and 5 Airdrop). They also did 21 evaluations of Flight Engineers (1 semi-annual, 1 Flight Examiner, 2 Instructor, 8 Theater Indoctrination, and 9 Airdrop).

From 4-7 June, Lt. Col. James R. Osborn and Maj. Joseph W. Stokes of the 483 TAW Stan/Eval inspected the squadron. The overall rating was "Excellent." Minor discrepancies were debriefed by Lt. Col. Osborn and Maj. Stokes in the presence of the Squadron Commander and the squadron Stan/Eval team. The squadron Stan/Eval team continued a vigorous standardization program to maintain a high degree of professionalism in the squadron.

Lieutenant Robert G. Fullenkamp became the Assistant Training Officer when Capt. Carlson completed his tour. As a result of suggestions during the visit by 834AD on 4 May, Lt. Col. Fullenkamp accomplished a thorough overhaul of all Air Force Forms 846.

Refueling Supervisor and Southeast Asia Survival Training was added to the Theater Indoctrination training for all newly assigned aircrews. All pilots upgrading to Copilot received an Initial Orientation Flight (IOF) and an "Over-the-Shoulder" flight before their first line training mission.

The upgrading accomplished during the quarter included: 2 to Flight Examiner, 4 to Instructor Pilot, 10 to Aircraft Commander, 12 to First Pilot, and 15 to Copilot. Maj. Zachary and Capt. Taylor upgraded to Aircraft Commander. Lt. Col. Gelsone, Maj. Withrow, and Lieutenants Lance Boswell and Thomas W. Tidemann upgraded to Instructor Pilot. The upgrading of 1/Lt. Boswell and 1/Lt. Tidemann to Instructor Pilot was particularly notable since they were on their first assignment after UPT. Majors John H. Castles and James R. Luntzel, Capt. Paton, and Lieutenants Davis, DiJanni, Hudson, and John D. Seines upgraded to Aircraft Commander. Captains Rudolph H. Hartog and Liston, and Lieutenants Benke, Robert E. Dias, Arturo Esquivel, John E. Heckleman, Sandlin, and Westergom upgraded to First Pilot. Lieutenants Claude E. Branscome, Robert G. Fullenkamp, Theodore Jager, George G. Kahl, Dana K. Kelly, Louis F. Landry, James A. Overton, Robert F. Palmer, Frederick J. Rowland, Ronald H. Scott, Clarence E. Uptegraph, and James K. Wansack qualified as Copilots.

In the third quarter, Maj. Zachary assumed duties as Chief of Stan/Eval when Lt. Col. Tyler completed his tour. Lt. Col. Wiersma and Capt. Taylor completed their tours. Maj. Withrow was upgraded to Flight Examiner and Capt. Rudolph H. Hartog joined the section.

The squadron was authorized 24 crews, with 21 "formed" as of beginning of July and 22 "formed" at the end of September. The lower number of "formed" crews was due to a lack of pilots for the number of Flight Engineers available.

Stan/Eval did 59 evaluations of pilots (2 Flight Examiner, 7 Instructor Pilot, 12 Aircraft Commander, 14 First Pilot, 18 Theater Indoctrination, and 6 Airdrop). They also did 21 evaluations of Flight Engineers (4 semi-annual, 2 Flight Examiner, 4 Instructor, and 11 Airdrop). A record number of seven Instructor Pilots was upgraded. One of these Instructor Pilots was 1/Lt. Seines who was on his first assignment after UPT and was selected because of his superior airmanship, excellent attitude, and Instructor Pilot potential.

Maj. Castles became Chief of Training when Maj. Hamrin completed his tour. 1/Lt. Fullenkamp continued as an Assistant Training Officer and 1/Lt. Kenneth R. Crawford was appointed as an Assistant Training Officer in charge of Air Force Forms 846. Refueling Supervisor training was deleted from the Theater Indoctrination training at the suggestion of the Wing. This training was still given informally by Instructor Pilots. An extra local flying training day was added each week to allow First Pilots and Copilots to maintain a high level of landing, instrument approach, and emergency procedures proficiency. On the two weekly training days, a total of 16 flying hours was available for local flights.

Lt. Col. Moses J. McKeithan, who had been assigned to the Wing and had not attended the C-7A school at Sewart AFB, was given the complete Phase I and II upgrading followed by Theater Indoctrination and flying training. He was a fully qualified Aircraft Commander within six weeks. The same training was given to Lt. Col. Hanning who was reassigned to the squadron from 7AF.

Maj. Withrow and Capt. Hartog were upgraded to Flight Examiner. Majors Castles and Luntzel, and Captains Ford, Liston, and Douglas M. Senter were upgraded to Instructor Pilot. Lt. Colonels Fullenkamp, Powell and Stewart, Maj. Patrick N. Kullenberg, and Lieutenants Benke, Dias, Arturo Esquivel, and John E. Heckleman were upgraded to Aircraft Commander. Lieutenants Landry, Overton, Palmer, Scott, and Uptegraph were upgraded to First Pilot. Lieutenants Michael L. Baker, Crawford, David M. Dudak, George F. Harrison, William T. Reynolds, Sidney W. Tanner, and James S. Yoder qualified as Copilots.

On 18 September, the 483 TAW Stan/Eval Team conducted a quarterly inspection of the squadron. The pilots received an "Outstanding" rating, the Flight Engineers received an "Excellent" rating, and the squadron was rated "Excellent." Minor discrepancies were debriefed by Maj. Stokes of Wing Stan/Eval in the presence of the Squadron Commander and the squadron Stan/Eval team. The team planned to continue a vigorous standardization program to maintain a high degree of professionalism found in the squadron aircrews.

In the fourth quarter, Maj. Castle upgraded to Flight Examiner and assumed the position of Chief of Stan/Eval, replacing Maj. Zachary. MSgt John W. Moll upgraded to Flight Examiner Flight Engineer and replaced TSgt. Robert L. Barker.

The squadron was authorized 24 crews, with 21 "formed" at the beginning of October and 19 "formed" at the end of December. The lower number of "formed" crews was due to a lack of pilots compared to the number of available Flight Engineers.

Stan/Eval did 52 evaluations of pilots (16 no-notice, 1 Flight Examiner, 5 Instructor Pilot, 14 Aircraft Commander, 11 Theater Indoctrination, and 5 Airdrop). They also did 21 evaluations of Flight Engineers (13 no-notice, 1 Flight Examiner, 1 Instructor, 4 Theater Indoctrination, and 2 Airdrop).

On 14 November, the 834AD Stan/Eval team inspected the squadron. From 25-29 November, the 7AF Inspector General conducted an evaluation of the squadron. The Stan/Eval Section was commended for the close liaison it maintained with the Instructor Pilots and Training Officers. This resulted in standardized procedures being included in all phases of aircrew training.

The 483 TAW Stan/Eval also evaluated the squadron during the fourth quarter. No unfavorable trends or weak areas were determined. The requirement to conduct semiannual flight evaluations was deleted. More stress on the value of no-notice evaluations for the newly qualified was recommended. The squadron Stan/Eval staff expected to continue a vigorous standardization program to maintain a high degree of professionalism found in the squadron aircrews.

Maj. Kullenberg was assigned the position of Training Officer when Maj. Castles was appointed to be the Chief of Stan/Eval. 1/Lt. Fullenkamp continued as an Assistant Training Officer and 1/Lt. Kenneth R. Crawford continued as Assistant Training Officer in charge of Air Force Forms 846. In preparation for the visit by the Inspector General, he accomplished a thorough overhaul of the Forms 846.

Five officers were upgraded to Instructor Pilot. Included in this group were 1/Lt. Esquivel and 1/Lt. Uptegraph who were on their first assignment after UPT and were selected because of their superior airmanship, excellent attitude, and Instructor Pilot potential. The upgrading accomplished during the quarter included: 1 to Flight

Examiner, 5 to Instructor Pilot, 15 to Aircraft Commander, 2 to First Pilot, and 12 to Copilot. Maj. Castles upgraded to Flight Examiner. Lt. Col. Sutter, Maj. Kullenberg, Capt. Johnson, and Lieutenants Esqivel and Uptegraph upgraded to Instructor Pilot. Col. John J. Koehler, Lt. Col. Collings, Lt. Col. Donahoe, Lt. Col. Hanning, Major William E. Branch, and Lieutenants Fullenkamp, Kahl, Landry, Overton, Palmer, Scott, and Wansack upgraded to Aircraft Commander. Lieutenant Jager upgraded to First Pilot. Capt. Hoffman and Lieutenants James E. Alexander, Richard S. Davidson, John A. Moore, Michael J. Morrison, Robert Norton, and Lee B. Robinson qualified as Copilots.

Safety

In the first quarter, the safety staff consisted of Maj. Morris C. Garrison, Chief of Safety; Capt. Lee, Assistant; Capt. Dennis E. Liston, Assistant; and TSgt. Edward L. Barnard, Assistant.

On 17 January, C-7A S/N 60-5334 was involved in a major accident making a no-flap landing at Vung Tau. The left side of the cockpit and fuselage were damaged and the Rapid Area Maintenance team evaluated the aircraft as "Destroyed." First Lieutenant William B. Morrison, III was the Aircraft Commander. First Lieutenant Robert E. Dias was the Copilot. SSgt. Richard M. Jones was the Flight Engineer and MSgt. Wilbur D. Startin was on board as a Flight Engineer in upgrade training. Army SSgt. William G. Elliott (5SFG) was a passenger. All personnel received major injuries. The Army GCA unit was destroyed.

The pilot stated that during the landing roll, at approximately 40 knots, he engaged the gust lock and, immediately after that, the aircraft went into a left swerve off the left side of runway 18, continuing in a left arc for 600 feet at which time the aircraft hit the concrete GCA bunker. After the aircraft began to swerve, the pilot applied brakes, but he did not feel the aircraft slowdown. He also applied reverse on both engines, but felt the aircraft accelerate forward after hearing a definite power change. The winds given to the aircraft by the tower upon initial entry were from 120° at 20 knots, gusting to 25 knots. On final approach, the winds were 120° at 20 knots. Normal procedure for the C-7A was to engage the gust lock when the aircraft slowed to taxi speed.

The accident investigation board was made up of: Lt. Col. Robert Stockhouse, 309 Special Operations Squadron (President), Capt. Paul R. Marlin (Investigating Officer), Capt. Jay A. Green (Maintenance Officer), Capt. Richard J. Weinberg (Flight Medical Officer), Maj. Larry A. Corcoran (Pilot Member), 1/Lt. Jerry L. Dilley (Recorder), and Maj. Charles J. Nagle (Advisor). The suspected cause factor reported by the board was that the "pilot may have exceeded the allowable crosswind complement and engaged the gust lock well above recommended speed."

Another aircraft received hits from enemy small arms fire, resulting in minor damage, i.e., bullet holes. One passenger received a minor injury.

Lt. Col. Ballard attended the 483 TAW Integrated Safety Council on 18 March at Cam Ranh Bay. The squadron Integrated Safety Council met on 29 February. The main topics were safety improvements needed in the housing area of enlisted personnel of the Red Horse squadron, aircraft First Aid tips, and pedestrian traffic, both on-base and off-base.

There were eight aircraft incidents during the quarter, consisting mainly of engine shutdowns. An incident resulting in minor aircraft damage occurred when a C-7A parked on the sloped refueling ramp at Di An Army Airfield (V-278) rolled backwards and forced the ramp extension through the ramp door.

A few OHRs were submitted by squadron aircrews and four OHRs were submitted against 536 TAS aircrews. The latter seemed to stem largely from a misunderstanding and lack of communication about standard safety operational procedures. Monthly Flying Safety meetings were held on 29 January, 25 February, and 20 March.

The squadron was charged with one ground accident. One of the Flight Engineers was engaged in preparing some meat for a steak cookout when the knife slipped and cut off the tips of his fingers. There were only seven first aid injuries. Ground Safety briefings were given at each of the Commander Calls.

In the second quarter, Maj. Garrison transferred to Headquarters 7AF. Other safety staff continuing were Capt. Lee, Assistant; Capt. Liston, Assistant; and TSgt. Barnard, Assistant.

One aircraft received hits from enemy small arms fire with minor bullet hole damage. Two passengers received minor injuries. The 834AD Safety Team conducted a staff assistance visit from 15-20 April. The result of the visit was a rating of "Very Satisfactory."

The squadron Integrated Safety Council met on 23 April, 3 May, and 28 June to discuss squadron related safety problems. Lt. Col. Ballard attended the 483 TAW Integrated Safety Council meeting on 9 June.

On 12 April, there was an aircraft ground accident at Vung Tau

Army Airfield with no aircraft damage. A U.S. Army soldier ran into the rotating propeller of #1 engine of C-7A S/N 63-9722. The accident occurred while the aircraft was parked at the 8th Aerial Port for passenger loading. There were five aircraft incidents during the quarter. All were in-flight engine shutdowns for engine failure or precautionary shutdowns. Four OHRs were submitted by squadron crews.

Monthly Flying Safety meetings were held on 22 April, 22 May, and 19 June. The minutes of each meeting were made a part of the Aircrew Information File (ACIF) to ensure 100 percent participation. Safety briefings were given at each Commander's Call. Weekly safety topics were covered by maintenance supervisors.

One reportable ground accident was charged to the squadron. A maintenance NCO cut his hand while on duty. It later became infected and required hospitalization. There were three First Aid cases, including a snakebite inflicted by a sea snake as the victim was wading along the "Back Beach."

In the third quarter, Maj. Kullenberg assumed duties as Chief of Safety, as well as being a Flight Commander when Capt. Lee completed his tour. Capt. Liston and TSgt. Barnard continued as Assistants.

Three aircraft received hits from enemy small arms fire. The aircraft were C-7A S/N 60-5431, 62-4173, and 62-4193. There was minor bullet hole damage to all of the aircraft, but no injuries to crew members or passengers.

On 10 August, the Chief of Safety for 7AF visited the squadron on an orientation trip. He was shown the squadron facilities and seemed very pleased with what he saw. The squadron Integrated Safety Council met on 27 July, 22 August, and 29 September to discuss squadron related safety problems. Lt . Col. Ballard attended the 483 TAW Integrated Safety Council meeting on 15 September at Cam Ranh Bay.

Monthly Flying Safety meetings were held on 17 July, 21 August, and 25 September. The minutes of each meeting were made a part of the Aircrew Information File (ACIF) to ensure 100 percent participation.

The ground safety record of the squadron was marred on 10 September by a ground incident at Vung Tau Army Airfield when C-7A S/N 60-5431 struck a utility pole while being towed by maintenance personnel. The resulting damage was reported as a ground incident under the provisions of AFM 127-4. There were five aircraft incidents during the quarter. Four of the incidents were in-flight engine shutdowns and one was for failure of the gear to extend. One reportable ground accident was charged to the squadron. A Flight Engineer was struck by a local Lambretta while walking on a poorly lighted street in Vung Tau. Hospitalization was required and he was subsequently evacuated by air to Clark Air Base, Republic of the Philippines. As a result of this accident, all personnel were required to carry a flashlight while walking downtown at night.

In the fourth quarter, Maj. William E. Branch, Jr. took over as Chief of Safety, replacing Maj. Kullenberg who was assigned the position of Training Officer. Maj. Branch was also appointed Flying Safety Officer. Capt. Liston, Ground Explosive Safety Officer, completed his tour. His replacement had not been appointed by the end of the quarter. 1/Lt. Reynolds was appointed Assistant Flying Safety Officer. TSgt. Barnard continued as Ground/Explosive Safety NCO and was named NCO of the Month for October.

No aircraft damage was reported from enemy ground fire and there were no reportable ground or aircraft accidents during the quarter. An aircraft incident occurred on 29 December involving an in-flight engine fire, engine shutdown, and subsequent single engine landing.

The 6483 TGP Safety Council was established during the quarter and included members from the squadron. The requirement for a separate Squadron Safety Council was eliminated. Monthly Flying Safety meetings were held on 23 October, 11 November, and 16 December. The minutes of each meeting were made available to all aircrew personnel by letter.

No discrepancies were noted during the inspection by the 7AF IG on 26 November and the Safety Staff Assistance visit by the 7AF Office of Safety on 19 December.

Maintenance

In the first quarter, there was an input of 16 new personnel and a loss of only one. There were 49 maintenance personnel authorized by the Unit Manning Document (UMD) and 64 were assigned, for a manning rate of 130 percent. The following personnel received monthly awards: SSgt. R. LeBert, Maintenance Mechanic of the Month for January (also submitted for the Wing TAS Maintenance Mechanic of the Quarter); A/1C James C. Daffin, Maintenance Mechanic of the Month for February; SSgt. Thomas P. Dirkse, Crew Chief of the Month for January; SSgt. Alfred Smith, Crew Chief of the Month for February (also submitted for the Wing Crew Chief of the Quarter); SSgt. Walter K. Kitzmiller, Crew Chief of the Month for March; SSgt. Jerry E. Briggs, Airman of the Month for February; A/1C Charles R. Davis, Airman of the Month for March; and SSgt. Reece J. Lewis, NCO of the Month for March (also submitted for Wing NCO of the Quarter).

A/1C James H. Bird was selected as the Wing Outstanding TAS Maintenance Mechanic for the last quarter of 1968. SSgt. Sanford S. Lawrence (Outstanding Crew Chief for September 1968) was selected to represent the 483 TAW for the Pacific Air Force (PACAF) Annual Outstanding Crew Chief of the Year award. Capt. Charles M. Stone, 536 TAS Maintenance Officer, was selected as the Wing Outstanding Support Officer of the quarter.

The squadron averaged 100 hours a month more flying time compared to the first quarter of 1968. In March, the squadron flew more hours than in any previous month of the squadron's history. There was a total of 70 "OK" flights, again more than any previous quarter. Aircraft S/N 62-4193 averaged 140.1 flying hours per month for the quarter. The figure would have been higher except for a five-day period lost because of a Not Operationally Ready-Grounding (NORS-G) item.

There were numerous projects completed during the quarter, but the most noteworthy ones were the 780 equipment inventory and associated construction of bins. The 780 equipment inventory was brought up to date and complete in all details. A 780 storage room was built and each aircraft had its equipment stored in a separate bin, arranged identically. The storage room was rigidly controlled to prevent losses or mixing of the contents of bins.

Several problem areas developed that affected the overall capability of the squadron. Most noteworthy was the extensive amount of corrosion found throughout aircraft. Coupling this with the various defective parts and substandard parts received through the supply system, it was very hard to maintain a good schedule in the Phase Docks, hard to prevent the overloading of aircraft in the Phase Docks, and, at the same time, hard to schedule aircraft for maintenance down days.

In the second quarter, the Maintenance Section had a net loss of 16 people, plus 4 on leave, and 80 TDY to Phan Rang Air Base. Of the 16 people lost, 11 went PCS to Thailand and the other five were normal rotations. At the end of the quarter the 536 Organizational Maintenance Squadron (OMS) was at full strength.

Many awards were received during the quarter: A/1C A. Winkle (Maintenance Mechanic of the Month for April), Sgt. C. Wolfe (Maintenance Mechanic of the Month for May), Sgt. T. Smith (Maintenance Mechanic of the Month for June), Sgt. D. Wilson (Crew Chief of the Month for May), Sgt. J. Briggs (Crew Chief of the Month for June), A/1C J. Audet (Airman of the Month for April), A/1C J. Seren (Airman of the Month for May), Sgt. C. Wolfe (Airman of the Month for

June), MSgt. G. Lewis (NCOIC of the Month for June), SSgt. R. Lewis (Wing Outstanding NCO of the quarter), and Sgt. J. Briggs (Wing Outstanding Crew Chief of the Quarter).

The overall quality of maintenance performed by the OMS personnel continued to increase. The initial launch delay and enroute delays were reduced and the number of "OK" flights continued to increase. The "OK" flights numbered 25 more than the first quarter, an increase of almost 30 percent. With the increase in quality maintenance, the overall Operationally Ready (OR) rate increased to a high of 88 percent in June and the Not-Operationally Ready Maintenance (NORM) rate correspondingly decreased. The high quality of the phase inspections also significantly help reduce the Not-Operationally Ready Supply (NORS) rate to a tolerable level.

First Lieutenant John D. Seines remembered his oversight one day departing a Special Forces camp:

> "After landing at a Special Forces camp and off-loading, I started the engines and, with a little throttle, the Bou started to move. I made a STOL takeoff and returned to the resupply point (1500 feet of hard runway) for another load. Upon landing, it became 'very' clear that I had not released the parking brake before departing the Special Forces camp. A tire/wheel/brake change resulted. My crew chief hated me!" [6]

The OJT program was very successful. Thirteen 3-levels upgraded and five more would be ready to upgrade in July. The MSET training progressed ahead of schedule and showed a 100 percent qualified rate.

Few new projects were started. More emphasis was put on maintaining stands and performing extra unscheduled maintenance on aircraft not scheduled to fly. The new flight line building was nearly completed and lacked only the hooking up of utilities. When completed, it would be a tremendous aid to morale to be able to complete all work in the ramp area, including paperwork and storage of toolboxes.

In the third quarter, Maintenance lost 10 people and gained two. Of the 10 losses, 9 were normal rotations and the other was an assignment to Quality Control. The weakest area in manning was in AFSC 43171A, with seven authorized, but only three assigned. Losses were expected to continue with few replacements forecast in the near future. At the end of the quarter, the 536 OMS was at 77 percent of UDL strength.

Many awards were received during the quarter: A/1C Richard G. Bush (Maintenance Mechanic of the Month for July); A/1C Michael P.

Lee (Maintenance Mechanic of the Month for August); Sgt. Thomas J. Crowson (Maintenance Mechanic of the Month for September); Sgt. Loren L. Cuykendall (Crew Chief of the Month for July); Sgt. David E. Whitesell (Crew Chief of the Month for August); Sgt. Herbert J. Heffer, II (Crew Chief of the Month for September); A/1C Robert R. Russo, Jr. (Airman of the Month for July); A/1C Robert V. Shular, Jr. (Airman of the Month for August); A/1C Gene P. Hawk (Airman of the Month for September); and SSgt. Robert J. Belshaw (NCO of the Month for September).

The following individuals were nominated for Quarterly Awards from Maintenance: A/1C Shular (Airman of the Quarter), A/1C Lee (Maintenance Mechanic of the Quarter), Sgt. Cuykendall (Crew Chief of the Quarter), SSgt. Belshaw (NCO of the Quarter).

The initial launch delay and enroute delays were reduced and the number of "OK" flights continued to increase. The "OK" flights numbered 32 more than the previous quarter, almost a 32 percent increase. The 536 OMS aircraft flew more hours in July than any other month in the history of the squadron.

One 3-level upgraded during the quarter and four more were forecast to be ready to upgrade to 5-level in October. The new flight line building was completed in August, adjacent to the ramp area and very convenient for the crew chiefs, as well as all flying personnel. Housekeeping on the flight line was stressed, resulting in a marked increase in the cleanliness of the ramp and a reduction in the possibility of Foreign Object Damage (FOD) to aircraft.

In the fourth quarter, there was a large turnover of personnel and a critical manning shortage existed. During one week, there were only three key supervisors available for duty and, for one month, there were only four supervisors available. There was a complete turnover of supervisory personnel except for the Maintenance Officer. The section lost a total of 24 people during the quarter and gained 19, for a net loss of five. At the end of the quarter, the section had a total of 33 men assigned and was only 67 percent manned. The weakest area was in AFSC 43131A.

The following personnel received awards for their outstanding performance: A/1C John A. Eppolito (Airman of the Month for October), A/1C Kenneth H. Brusoe (Airman of the Month for November), A/1C Richard G. Bush (Airman of the Month for December), A/1C Ralph Rutkowsky (Organizational Maintenance Mechanic of the Month for October), A/1C Richard M. McCabe (Organizational Maintenance

Mechanic of the Month for November), A/1C Brusoe (Organizational Maintenance Man of the Month for December), Sgt. Randall B. Brandon (Crew Chief of the Month for October), Sgt. Joseph B. Audet (Crew Chief of the Month for November), and Sgt. Lonnie E. Carr (Crew Chief of the Month for December). The following nominations were submitted for Wing Quarterly Awards: A/1C Bush (Airman of the Quarter), A/1C Brusoe (Organizational Maintenance Man of the Quarter), TSgt. Harold E. Ayers (NCO of the Quarter).

The OJT program was re-emphasized to accommodate incoming personnel. Four Staff Sergeants, were upgrading to the 7-level (AFSC 43171A) and three A/1C were upgrading to the 5-level (AFSC 43151A). A training session was provided five days a week to ensure the rapid progress of trainees.

Self-improvement efforts included painting the interior of the new flight line building and construction of wall charts. These efforts paid off by generating favorable comments from the IG team on the quality of maintenance housekeeping. A project was started to build a revetment around the new building. Emphasis was placed on maintaining maintenance stands to ensure safe operation.

The aircraft Operationally Ready rate remained high despite a critical shortage of personnel..

Administration

In the first quarter, Capt. Thomas D. Paton continued as Administrative Services Officer and 1/Lt. Dijanni continued as the Historian. First Lieutenant George M. Moore, III departed in January when his tour was completed and 1/Lt. Seines and 1/Lt. Sandlin assumed duties as Assistant Administrative Services Officers. This allowed Capt. Paton to concentrate on Officer Efficiency Reports (OERs).

The squadron underwent an expected, high personnel turnover. In spite of the large turnover, the experience level in every phase of the operation remained high. This could be attributed to the outstanding training program, the dedication and hard work of all squadron personnel, and the supervision offered by the new Squadron Commander and Flight Commanders. Improved maintenance, aircraft Operationally Ready rate, and efficient use of available manpower accounted for improved performance and increased productivity. The squadron showed a stabilization in the trend of its productivity, hours flown, passengers transported, and tons of cargo carried. Although the squadron seemed to be well manned in all of its functional areas, the tremendous workload being accomplished by so few enlisted individuals in the Administration Office created an expectation that a serious backlog of work would occur in the future.

SSgt. James M. Mattingly assumed duties as First Sergeant during January and Sgt. Ira L. Daniels was transferred to Cam Ranh Bay. SSgt. Antonio J. Beck assumed the duties of three individuals, as no replacements came for SSgt. Mattingly and Sgt. Daniels. The output and quality of SSgt. Beck's work were outstanding. Thirty OERs and 23 Airmen Proficiency Reports (APRs) were processed. Ten NCOs and 22 Airmen received promotions. The squadron experienced a high percentage of personnel turnover as 10 officers and 58 airmen arrived at the squadron and 12 officers and 73 airmen departed.

The greatest change in the section came as the new support unit of the Wing, the 6483 Tactical Provisional Group (TGP), assumed its duties. Administrative support for the squadron was assumed by the new organization and the Administrative Section was relieved of many duties. This enabled the section to work more efficiently and effectively.

In the second quarter, Capt. Paton continued as Administrative Services Officer, 1/Lt. Frederic J. Rowland was an Assistant Administrative Services Officer, and 1/Lt. Uptegraph was the Historian. Lieutenant Seines left his job in the Administration Section and assumed duties as Director of Administrative Services for the 6483 TGP and 1/Lt. Wansack assumed duties as Assistant Administrative Officer, with a focus on monitoring OERs.

Thirty-five OERs and 29 APRs were processed. Three NCOs and 10 Airmen received promotions. The squadron welcomed 19 officers and 40 airmen, while 12 officers and 30 airmen departed. Personnel turnover was average during the quarter.

SSgt. Beck continued to do outstanding work as Orderly Room Clerk. He did the work of three NCOs and worked 12 hour days, six days a week. The excellent productivity of the Administrative Section was due largely to his diligent efforts and conscientious work.

In the third quarter, Capt. Paton completed his tour and was replaced by 1/Lt. Wamsack. Lieutenant Uptegraph continued as Historian. The squadron experienced a high percentage of personnel turnover in the third quarter. The section processed 40 OERs and 52 APRs. 1/Lt. James S. Yoder joined the section and proved to be a great asset as his help was instrumental in achieving new records. His chief area of responsibility was to monitor OERs. SSgt. Dwight L. Fuller also joined the section and became an integral part of the system in a very short time. TSgt. Beck continued to perform in a consistently superior manner. He displayed unusual tact and diplomacy in his dealings with both officer and enlisted personnel. The excellent productivity of the section was due largely to his diligent efforts and conscientious work.

In the fourth quarter, 1/Lt. Wamsack continued as Chief Administrative Services Officer. Lieutenants Yoder and Sandlin continued as Assistant Administrative Officers. 1/Lt. Sidney W. Tanner was the Historian. TSgt. Beck completed his tour and was replaced by SSgt. Earl A. Daughtry who showed that he had all the ability and knowledge of his predecessor.

The squadron experienced a very successful and productive quarter while undergoing a high rate of personnel turnover. The section processed 38 OERs and 52 APRs. In spite of the personnel turnover, the experience level in every phase of operation remained high. This could be attributed to the outstanding training program, the dedication and hard work of all squadron personnel, and the supervision offered by the new Squadron Commander.

Sgt. Dwight L. Fuller proved to be a very diligent and dedicated administrative clerk. He had the responsibility of monitoring and typing APRs and making sure that there were completed on schedule. This, in itself, was a full-time job, but he also accomplished many other duties in an outstanding manner.

Supply and Support

In the first quarter, 1/Lt. Ronald R. Hirata completed his tour and was replaced as OIC of the Life Support Section by 1/Lt. Herrell with 1/Lt. Mitchell as his Assistant. A/1C William G. Clark was also assigned to the section. The section moved into a new building as co-tenants with the headquarters element of the 536 TAS. Other changes in the facility were a new weapons room, bins for the flight crews to store their crew gear, and a new helmet rack. Numerous survival vests were reported lost or stolen. Action was taken to report the missing items.

In the second quarter, 1/Lt. Herrell completed his tour and was replaced by 1/Lt. Milton J. Kelley. Sgt. William G. Clark became interim NCOIC of the Life Support Section when Sgt. Emery completed his tour. TSgt. Lawrence L. Bell assumed accountability for the Life Support Section account when 1/Lt. Herrell departed. The section received and signed for all weapons from supply. A monthly schedule was set up to regularly clean and inspect all weapons. The section also received 15 new water jugs for the flight crews to use on their missions. There were no equipment losses or major problems during the quarter.

In the third quarter, 1/Lt. Kelly continued as OIC of the Life Support Section. Sgt. James C. Jordan, II was named NCOIC of the section. Sgt. William G. Clark was named assistant to Sgt. Jordan. The security of Life Support Section weapons in the weapons room was improved by the installation of a steel cable and lock to secure the weapons. To enhance security, a double locking device was placed on the main door to the section. There were neither equipment losses nor major problems during the quarter.

In the fourth quarter, 1/Lt. Kelly continued as OIC of the Life Support Section and Sgt. Jordan continued as NCOIC. There were no losses or gains in personnel. As an aid to aircrew personnel, the section set up a display of the Tropical Survival Vest on the wall in the equipment room. This was done so that everyone would become more familiar with the contents and their location in the vest.

During the annual IG inspection, the section was rated "Satisfactory." The section kept and stored all weapons that had been stored previously at the Vung Tau Hotel, the living quarters for the officers. This action was directly connected with the findings of the IG inspection.

Awards and Decorations

In the first quarter, the Awards and Decorations office submitted a total of 65 decorations to 7AF for approval. These included 3 Silver Stars, 3 Distinguished Flying Crosses, 9 Bronze Stars, 25 Air Medals, and 25 Air Force Commendation Medals. It was impossible to determine the number of these awards that had been approved since consideration of these decorations by 7AF and their subsequent approval or disapproval usually involved a great amount of time. A total of 31 decorations were received for presentation.

In the second quarter, the Awards and Decorations office processed 92 recommendations for awards. These included 8 Silver Stars, 16 Distinguished Flying Crosses, 6 Bronze Stars, 54 Air Medals, and 8 Air Force Commendation Medals. It was impossible to determine how many of these awards were approved by the end of the quarter.

In the third quarter, the Awards and Decorations office processed 72 recommendations for awards. These included 17 Distinguished Flying Crosses, 2 Airman's Medals, 40 Air Medals, 5 Bronze Stars, and 8 Air Force Commendation Medals. It was impossible to determine how many of these awards were approved by the end of the quarter.

In the fourth quarter, the Awards and Decorations office processed 106 recommendations for awards. These included 1 Legion of Merit, 12 Distinguished Flying Crosses, 4 Bronze Stars, 61 Air Medals, 28 Bronze Stars, and 8 Air Force Commendation Medals.

Airlift Accomplishments [7]

During the first quarter, passengers hauled were 25,522 in January; 22,953 in February; and 22,162 in March for a total of 70,637. Cargo hauled was 1299.2 tons in January; 1255.9 tons in February; and 1415.3 tons in March for a total of 3970.4 tons. In January, the squadron flew 2856 sorties while logging 1648.6 flying hours. In February, the squadron flew 2692 sorties while logging 1534.4 flying hours. In March, the squadron flew 2930 sorties while logging 1738.2 flying hours.

During the second quarter, passengers hauled were 22,532 in April; 23,732 in May; and 21,920 in June for a total of 68,184. Cargo hauled was 1379.6 tons in April; 1271.0 tons in May; and 994.9 tons in June for a total of 3645.5 tons. In April, the squadron flew 3022 sorties while logging 1681.4 flying hours. In May, the squadron flew 3132 sorties while logging 1757.9 flying hours. In June, the squadron flew 2721 sorties while logging 1650.5 flying hours.

During the third quarter, passengers hauled were 22,306 in July; 18,069 in August; and 15,657 in September for a total of 56,032. Cargo hauled was 1088.5 tons in July; 1121.3 tons in August; and 1090.9 tons in September for a total of 3300.7 tons. In July, the squadron flew 2744 sorties while logging 1742.3 flying hours. In August, the squadron flew 2709 sorties while logging 1718.8 flying hours. In September, the squadron flew 2571 sorties while logging 1635.8 flying hours.

Although there was a decrease in passengers transported during the quarter, the squadron showed a stabilization in the trend of its productivity of hours flown and tons of cargo carried.

During the fourth quarter, passengers hauled were 12,512 in October; 11,409 in November; and 12,180 in December for a total of 36,101. Cargo hauled was 1411.5 tons in October; 1440.8 tons in November; and 1665.0 tons in December for a total of 4517.3 tons. The squadron flew 1795.5 hours in October, 1844.5 in November, and 1944.0 in December. In November the squadron aircraft logged 218.1 more hours than scheduled.

The efficient use of manpower available accounted for a record number of hours of flying time and cargo tons transported in the fourth quarter. The number of passengers transported decreased again as it had done in previous quarters. Overall, the squadron showed an increase in the trend of its productivity of hours flown and tons of cargo carried. The tonnage of cargo hauled in the quarter was greater than in any previous quarter in 1969.

Commander's Summary

First Quarter 1969 [8]

"The 536th Tactical Airlift Squadron experienced a successful and productive first quarter of 1969. Despite a large turnover of personnel and increased demand for training, the 536th Tactical Airlift Squadron maintained its performance record of the previous quarter. This performance can be attributed to the smooth transition and supervision offered by the new personnel manning the various department positions. The Squadron organization saw its biggest change during the Change of Command ceremony on 16 January 1969, when Lieutenant Colonel Ralph T. Howard, Jr. relieved Lieutenant Colonel Miles H. Watkins as Squadron Commander of the 536th Tactical Airlift Squadron.

The training program was expanded to meet the high turnover-created demand for pilots, flight engineers, and support personnel. The upgrading program from 1 January to 31 March 1969 included the upgrading of 2 Flight Examiners, 7 Instructor Pilots, 17 Aircraft Commanders, 12 First Pilots, and 8 Copilots. This accomplishment demonstrated the dedication and hard work of the Training Section.

During the period from 6 March to 9 March 1969, Major [Richard M.] Lantz of the 483rd Tactical Airlift Wing Standardization/Evaluation (Stan/Eval), conducted an evaluation of the 536th Tactical Airlift Squadron aircrews. The squadron's overall grade was 'Excellent.' Such a rating reflected the leadership, supervision, and determination of all personnel involved.

The Squadron Maintenance Officer, Captain C. Stone, was selected as the Wing Outstanding Support Officer of the Quarter. During this quarter from 1 January to 31 in March 1969, the 536th Organizational Maintenance Squadron accomplished many outstanding achievements. The 536th Tactical Airlift Squadron flew an average of 100 hours more per month in flying time during this quarter than it did in the first quarter of 1968. In March alone, the 536th Tactical Airlift Squadron reported that it flew 1855 [sic] hours. This figure was higher than any other one month period to date.

In conclusion, the 536th Tactical Airlift Squadron had a very productive first quarter in 1969 due to an excellent training and evaluation effort to work together in harmony on upgrading pilots. Thirty of the Squadron's 48 pilots were Undergraduate Pilot Training (UPT) graduates on their first flying assignment. During this quarter, 13 of these Undergraduate Pilot Training (UPT) graduates were qualified aircraft commanders and one was upgraded to instructor pilot. These young officers gave spirit and enthusiasm to the squadron by their eagerness to upgrade. Their judgment and skill was a delight to behold. I have no worry about the future of the Air Force, as these junior officers will provide tomorrow's leaders. I know they will carry on in the outstanding professional manner that is their habit today."

Second Quarter 1969 [9]

"The 536th Tactical Airlift Squadron (TAS) experienced a successful and productive second quarter of 1969. Despite an increased demand for training, the 536th Tactical Airlift Squadron (TAS) maintained its performance record of the previous quarter. This performance can be attributed to the smooth transition and supervision offered by new personnel manning the various department positions.

During the period from 4 June to 7 June 1969, Lieutenant Colonel James R. Osborn and Major Joseph W. Stokes of the 483rd Tactical Airlift Wing Standardization/Evaluation (Stan/Eval) conducted an evaluation of the 536th Tactical Airlift Squadron (TAS) aircrews. The Squadron's overall rating reflected the leadership, supervision, and determination of all personnel involved.

The training program was expanded to meet the high turnover-created demand for pilots and support personnel. The upgrading program from 1 July to 30 September 1969 included the upgrading of 2 Flight Examiners, 4 Instructor Pilots, 10 Aircraft Commanders, 12 First Pilots, and 15 Copilots. This accomplishment demonstrated the dedication and hard work of the Training Section.

The quality of maintenance performed by the Organizational Maintenance Squadron (OMS) has continued to climb with the initial launch and enroute delays reduced and the number of 'OK' flights increased. With the increased quality of maintenance, the overall Operationally Ready (OR) rate is increased to a high of 88 percent in June, while the Non-Operationally Ready Maintenance (NORM) rate has correspondingly decreased.

In conclusion, the 536th Tactical Airlift Squadron (TAS) had a very successful and productive second quarter 1969 due to an excellent training and evaluation effort to work together in harmony on upgrading pilots."

Third Quarter 1969 [10]

"The 536th Tactical Airlift Squadron (TAS) experienced a successful and productive third quarter of 1969. Despite an increased demand for training, the 536th Tactical Airlift Squadron (TAS) maintained its performance record of the previous quarter. This performance can be attributed to the smooth transition and supervision offered by new personnel manning the various department positions.

The training program was expanded to meet the high turnover-created demand for pilots and support personnel. The upgrading program from 1 April to 30 June 1969 included the upgrading of 2 Flight Examiners, 7 Instructor Pilots, 12 Aircraft Commanders, 12 First Pilots, and 13 Copilots. The Training section also upgraded two Aircraft Commanders who received no ground or flying training in the C-7A before arriving in Southeast Asia (SEA). They were given the complete Phase I and II upgrading followed by Theater Indoctrination and flying training. They were both qualified Aircraft Commanders within six weeks. This accomplishment demonstrated the dedication and hard work of the Training Section.

During the period from 18 through 21 September 1969, Major Joseph W. Stokes of the 483rd Tactical Airlift Wing Standardization/Evaluation (Stan/Eval) conducted an evaluation of the 536th Tactical Airlift Squadron (TAS) aircrews. The Squadron's overall rating reflected professionalism, leadership, supervision, and determination of all personnel involved.

The quality of maintenance performed by the Organizational Maintenance Squadron (OMS) has continued to climb with the initial launch and enroute delays reduced and the number of 'OK' flights increased.

In conclusion, the 536th Tactical Airlift Squadron (TAS) had a very successful and productive third quarter in 1969 due the outstanding training and evaluation program, and the dedication and hard work of squadron personnel."

Fourth Quarter 1969 [11]

"The 536th Tactical Airlift Squadron (TAS) experienced a successful and productive fourth quarter of 1969. Despite an increased demand for training, the 536th squadron increased its performance record over the previous quarter. This performance can be attributed to the hard work, dedication, and enthusiasm offered by personnel manning the various department positions.

The training program continued to meet the demand for pilots, flight engineers, and support personnel created by the high turnover rate. The upgrading program from 1 October through 31 in December 1969 included the upgrading of one Flight Examiner, five Instructor Pilots, fifteen Aircraft Commanders, two First Pilots, and twelve Copilots. This accomplishment demonstrated the dedication, professionalism, and hard work of the Training Section.

During the period from 25 to 29 November 1969, the Seventh Air Force Inspector General conducted an evaluation of the 536th TAS. The Stan/Eval section was commended for the close liaison it maintained with the Instructor Pilots and Training Officers, which resulted in standardized procedures being included in all phases of aircrew training. The quarterly evaluation by the 483rd TAW and evaluation by the 834th Aircraft Division Stan/Eval were conducted during this quarter. No unfavorable trend or weak areas were determined.

The quality of maintenance performed by the Organizational Maintenance Section continued to remain high even with the critical manning shortage. The squadron flew a record number of hours during the fourth quarter, surpassing the three previous quarters.

In conclusion, the 536th TAS had a very successful and productive fourth quarter in 1969 due to an excellent training and evaluation program, an outstanding maintenance effort, and the dedication and hard work of all squadron personnel."

End Notes: 536 TAS

[1] *19690101-19691231 536 TAS History*

[2] 536 TAS Special Order G-1, dated 16 January 1969

[3] The 516th Tactical Airlift Wing at Dyess AFB, TX was the new home for C-7A combat crew training which had moved from Sewart AFB, TN.

[4] 536 TAS Special Order G-2, dated 4 December 1969

[5] 7AF Special Order G-3799, dated 24 August 1970

[6] *C-7A Caribou Newsletter, Vol. 24, Issue 2*

[7] When the data in the squadron history and the Wing history differ, the Wing data is shown.

[8] 536 TAS Commander's Summary, 31 March 1969 by Lt. Col. Ralph T. Ballard

[9] 536 TAS Commander's Summary, 30 June 1969 by Lt. Col. Ralph T. Ballard

[10] 536 TAS Commander's Summary, 30 September 1969 by Lt. Col. Ralph T. Ballard

[11] 536 TAS Commander's Summary, 31 December 1969 by Lt. Col. Buford E. Collings

537th Tactical Airlift Squadron[1]

The primary mission of the 537th Tactical Airlift Squadron (537 TAS) at Phu Cat was to maintain a combat ready tactical airlift capability to perform air-land and airdrop assault missions into objective areas in direct support of counter-insurgency operations; to conduct combat logistical airlift of troops, supplies, and equipment needed to execute and support tactical or strategic missions; and to provide a mobile combat readiness capability to support contingency commitments of the Commander, U.S. Military Assistance Command Vietnam – Thailand (COMUSMACV-THAI).

To accomplish these missions, the squadron was authorized 51 officers and 80 enlisted personnel in the first quarter. Of these authorizations, 49 officers and 91 enlisted personnel were assigned. No civilian personnel were authorized, but three were assigned. The squadron was authorized 16 aircraft, 15 were operational, and one was in Inspection and Repair as Necessary (IRAN) at the end of the quarter.

In the second quarter, the squadron was authorized 51 officers and 82 enlisted personnel. Of these authorizations, 49 officers and 75 enlisted personnel were assigned. The squadron was authorized 16 aircraft, 15 were operational and one was in the Phase Inspection Dock.

In the third quarter, the squadron was authorized 51 officers and 81 enlisted personnel. Of these authorizations, 41 officers and 64 enlisted personnel were assigned. The squadron was authorized 16 aircraft, 15 were possessed, and 14 were Combat Ready and one was in the Phase Inspection Dock.

In the fourth quarter, the number of authorized and assigned officers and enlisted personnel was not included in the fourth quarter squadron history. The squadron was authorized 16 aircraft, 15 were possessed, and 14 were Combat Ready, on the average.

Hallmarks of the squadron for the fourth quarter were increased morale as evidenced in the squadron and, particularly, the effect this higher morale had on mission accomplishment. In most cases, the squadron exceeded the mark set in the third quarter and took great pride in doing so. The work accomplished was of such a caliber that it would be much easier for the squadron to produce even better totals in the future quarters.

On 1 February, Lt. Col. Gayle C. Wolf attended the second Caribou Anniversary celebration.

On 18 February, Lt. Col. George C. Marvin, who arrived at Phu Cat in December, assumed the position of Squadron Commander,[2] replacing Lt. Col. Wolf. Also in February, Lt. Col. Irwin K. Holdener replaced Lt. Col. Rupert S. Richardson as Operations Officer. Like Lt. Col. Marvin, Lt. Col. Richardson had two months in country to become qualified while learning the operation of the squadron and the Wing.

On 14 November, Lt. Col. Donald J. MacFarren assumed duties as Squadron Commander.

Operations

In the first quarter, the type of missions flown by the C-7A included routine cargo, support of Special Forces and all other Free World forces in Vietnam, medical evacuations, Emergency Resupply, Tactical Emergencies, Combat Essential missions, airdrops of paratroopers, ammunition, building supplies, POL, general cargo, rations, and such oddities as live cows, pigs, chickens, and fresh produce. The livestock and produce were airlifted in support of ARVN troops, due to the lack of refrigeration in the field.

During part of the quarter, the aircrews were restricted by the Wing to seven flying hours during a crew duty day. Consequently, some loads were turned down and crews returned early to remain within this restriction.

Flight commanders were Lt. Col. MacFarren, Lt. Col. Lyle B. Marshall, Lt. Col. Robert H. Taylor, and Maj. Robert H. Dugan.

During February, Maj. Kent M. Monroe, Aircraft Commander of *Soul 454*, and Maj. Delbert D. Lockwood, Aircraft Commander of *Soul 455*, flew an Emergency Resupply to Ben Het (V-179). A total of four sorties were flown directly from Pleiku (V-12). All airdrops were successful and on target.

Lt. Col. Henry L. Jones, Tactical Air Liaison Officer of IFFV, sent a Letter of Appreciation to Col. Turk on 2 March to recognize the direct combat support for the Ben Het Special Forces camp:

"1. The Special Forces camp at Ben Het, under direct hostile attack for two days, required ammunition resupply by airdrop on the afternoon and evening of 24 February 1969.

2. Mission number 454 and mission number 455 voluntarily responded to meet the urgent ammunition requirements of the beleaguered camp. Three airdrops were completed with unbelievable accuracy as all the loads impacted inside the camp perimeter located on top of a very small hill.

3. The calm professionalism and extreme accuracy displayed by these crews is singularly responsible for providing the friendly

unit with the capability to continue resisting the hostile siege. Please, extend to both crews the appreciation and gratitude of this entire headquarters for such an outstanding accomplishment under the most hazardous conditions."

On 27 March, Lt. Col. MacFarren flew a Combat Essential mission from An Khe (V-13). The *Soul 407* mission successfully airlifted 24 Vietnamese troops.

In the second quarter, the squadron continued to support the Bangkok mission site, supplying aircraft, maintenance personnel, and briefings. On April 15, the squadron was directed by Col. Leslie J. Greenwood, the Wing Deputy Commander for Operations (DCO), to relinquish control of the Pleiku mission site, "Blite Control," to the ALCE. Maj. Octavio Jordan led the shut-down task and reported to Lt. Col. Marvin, by letter dated 15 April, the actions he took to relocate or dispose of equipment. This released one crew for flying duties which had previously manned the mission site for TDY periods of one month.

Some aircrews participated in personnel drops in the vicinity of Pleiku. Novice indigenous personnel and seasoned troops were dropped in sticks of approximately 26 per run for a total of 485 troops on 8 April, 10 May, and 11 May. There was one malfunction reported which led to an aircraft configuration change for personnel airdrops. The parachute of an indigenous novice became entangled on an aircraft tie-down ring located on the empennage of the aircraft. After a number of anxious moments, he was persuaded to release his reserve chute which freed him from the aircraft. Resulting injuries were minor due to the ability and quick thinking of Maj. John W. Black, the Aircraft Commander, who averted a potentially fatal situation. Because of this incident, all aircraft empennage tie-down rings were to be removed prior to paratroop drops.

Capt. Jon E. Drury remembered when caution was called for instead of eagerness to deliver a load:

"During the last part of my year based in Vietnam, we had a small outpost on the flight line at Pleiku to more closely coordinate the loads from Pleiku to Special Forces and Army camps. Some of those loads were food or live animals, and on some occasions they were airdropped. Once we had our outpost on the flight line, we protected it with sandbags because Pleiku periodically took rocket or mortar fire. On one occasion, I loaded at Pleiku for a mission to Ben Het. The Major commanding the outpost directed me, 'If Ben Het is taking incoming, do not land.'

I had a load of eight inch (155 mm) artillery ammunition, a

type the base used for some of their guns. I flew down the road to Ben Het, past Kontum. When I arrived opposite the base, I could see a mortar or rocket round land in the marsh beside the base. The enemy might have fired a test round to zero in their weapon, or they might have fired it to scare me off, indicating they would fire on me if I attempted a landing.

The situation brought up an interesting question. How badly do they need this ammunition? If they say they need or desperately need this ammunition, then I have to decide whether I am going to go in, despite the Major's orders, and try to dump it at the end of the runway. How much had they zeroed in the ends of the runway? I did not know. I radioed the camp on the FM frequency we used to coordinate our work with them and asked 'I am carrying eight inch artillery ammunition, how badly do you need this stuff?'

The troop on the other end of the radio just hollered 'We're taking incoming. I'm going to the bunker.' Repeated calls got no response. I returned to Pleiku with my load." [3]

On 25 April, Lt. Col. Marvin flew an Emergency Resupply mission from Pleiku to Nhon Co (V-21). This was one of the few missions of this priority flown by the 483 TAW in the quarter and was accomplished successfully and without incident. The actions of Lt. Col. Marvin and his crew were documented in the citation of his Copilot's Distinguished Flying Cross:

"First Lieutenant Robert P. Wiesneth distinguished himself by *heroism* while participating in aerial flight as the Copilot of a C-7A aircraft near the Special Forces camp at Nhon Co, Republic of Vietnam on 25 April 1969. On that date he flew an Emergency Resupply mission in direct support of the besieged camp. With complete disregard for his personal safety, he flew through extremely heavy hostile automatic weapons fire to successfully air drop vitally needed supplies without which the camp may have been overrun. The outstanding heroism and selfless devotion to duty displayed by Lieutenant Wiesneth reflect great credit upon himself and the United States Air Force."

On 3 June, crew skill and professionalism of the squadron were called upon to airdrop supplies on various Emergency Resupply and Combat Essential missions into the besieged CIDG Special Forces camp at Ben Het. New airdrop procedures were evolved and established ones were refined (see Appendix XI). Hostile artillery, mortar attacks, ground fire, and enemy proximity to the perimeter discounted further landings for resupply. Combat conditions, terrain features, enemy positions, and enemy capabilities necessitated the modifications in airdrop techniques. Debriefings held after each airdrop served to make each successive airdrop more effective.

The actions of SSgt. John D. Mellert and his *Soul 455* crew (Maj. Delbert D. Lockwood and Capt. Edward L. Furchak) on 10 June were documented in the citation for his Distinguished Flying Cross: [4]

> "Staff Sergeant John D. Mellert distinguished himself by extraordinary achievement while participating in aerial flight as a Flight Engineer of a C-7A Aircraft near the Special Forces camp at Ben Het, Republic of Vietnam on 10 June 1969. On that date, Sergeant Mellert elected to fly an Emergency Resupply mission in direct support of the besieged camp. With complete disregard for his personal safety he flew through hostile fire to successfully air drop vitally needed supplies without which the camp may have been overrun. The professional competence, aerial skill, and devotion to duty displayed by Sergeant Mellert reflect great credit upon himself and the United States Air Force."

The actions of SSgt. Frederick Wilhelm and his crew on 12 June were documented in the citation for his Distinguished Flying Cross: [5]

> "Staff Sergeant Frederick Wilhelm distinguished himself by **heroism** while participating in aerial flight as a Flight Engineer of a C-7A aircraft near the Special Forces camp at Ben Het, Republic of Vietnam on 12 June 1969. On that date Sergeant Wilhelm flew an Emergency Resupply mission in direct support of the besieged camp. With complete disregard for his personal safety, he flew through extremely heavy hostile automatic weapons fire to successfully air drop vitally needed supplies without which the camp may have been overrun. The outstanding heroism and selfless devotion to duty displayed by Sergeant Wilhelm reflect great credit upon himself and the United States Air Force."

The actions of Capt. Max L. Allison and his *Soul 454* crew (1/Lt. Michael T. Riess and TSgt. Kenneth L. Davenhall) on 13 June were documented in the citation for his Air Medal: [6]

> "Captain Max L. Allison distinguished himself by meritorious achievement while participating in aerial flight over Southeast Asia [Special Forces camp at Ben Het] on 13 JUne 1969. On that date, he superbly accomplished a highly intricate mission to support Free World forces that were combating aggression. His energetic application of his knowledge and skill were significant factors that contributed greatly to furthering United States goals in Southeast

Asia. His professional skill and airmanship reflect great credit upon himself and the United States Air Force."

First Lieutenant William F. Quinn, Jr. remembered his *Soul 416* mission to Ben Het on 13 June with Maj. William A, Evalenko as Aircraft Commander and TSgt. Emile P. Broussard as Flight Engineer: [7]

"On 13 June of 1969, Bill Evalenko was in the left seat and we were making drops at Ben Het. We took a couple of fifty cal. hits on the way down. One of them came up between my legs and could have made life a lot less dramatic during my earlier years. The shell casing lodged in my boot, stopped by the steel plate or I'd be toeless. It was quite a deal.

Ev took over ... cool, calm, and collected, assessing the situation and making all the necessary cockpit decisions with his mike on hot mike. When I got out of the airplane back at Papa Kilo [Pleiku], some of the guys were there to see us in. They looked at my flight suit that was shredded a bit below the knee and, in fact, was actually kind of bloody from some shrapnel damage of a minor nature.

We all laughed and kidded that I might get a Purple Heart out of the deal. Darned if I didn't! It was the third drop of the day. The first two with A-1E Spads flying cover were uneventful as far as effective ground fire was concerned, not that they weren't shooting the s**t out of us. They just weren't leading enough or something.

On the last flight, there was a mix up with the Spads and we had Army Hueys flying cover. They were great, but just not quite as potent and effective as the Spads and that's when it happened." [8]

The actions of Maj. Michael Murphy and his *Soul 454* crew (Capt. Edward L. Furchak and TSgt. Ralph E. Chasteen) on 14 June were documented in the citation for his Air Medal: [9]

"Major Michael Murphy distinguished himself by meritorious achievement while participating in aerial flight over Southeast Asia [Ben Het] on 14 June 1969. On that date, he superbly accomplished a highly intricate mission to support Free World forces that were combating aggression. His energetic application of his knowledge and skill were significant factors that contributed greatly to furthering United States goals in Southeast Asia. His professional skill and airmanship reflect great credit upon himself and the United States Air Force."

The actions of 1/Lt. Neil N. Greinke and his crew on 17 June were documented in the citation for his Distinguished Flying Cross: [10]

"First Lieutenant Neil N. Greinke distinguished himself

200

by *heroism* while participating in aerial flight as a Copilot of a C-7A Aircraft near the Special Forces camp at Ben Het, Republic of Vietnam on 17 June 1969. On that date Lieutenant Greinke flew an Emergency Resupply mission in direct support of the besieged camp. With complete disregard for his personal safety he flew through extremely heavy hostile automatic weapons fire to successfully air drop vitally needed supplies without which the camp may have been overrun. The outstanding heroism and selfless devotion to duty displayed by Lieutenant Greinke reflect great credit upon himself and the United States Air Force."

The actions of Capt. Richard L. Brethouwer and his *Soul 413* crew (Capt. Edward L. Furchak and TSgt. Kenneth L. Davenhall) on 21 June were documented in the citation for his Distinguished Flying Cross: [11]

"Captain Richard L. Brethouwer distinguished himself by extraordinary achievement while participating in aerial flight as a Copilot of a C-7A Aircraft near the Special Forces camp at Ben Het, Republic of Vietnam on 21 June 1969. On that date Captain Brethouwer flew an Emergency Resupply Mission in direct support of the besieged camp. With complete disregard for his personal safety he flew through extremely heavy hostile fire to successfully air drop vitally needed supplies without which the camp may have been overrun. The professional competence, aerial skill, and devotion to duty displayed by Captain Brethouwer reflect great credit upon himself and the United States Air Force."

The actions of TSgt. Billy P. Owen and his *Soul 454* crew (Maj. Kent M. Monroe, 1/Lt. Robert F. Poland, and SSgt. Larry O. Overcash) on 22 June were documented in the citation for his Distinguished Flying Cross: [12]

"Technical Sergeant Billy P. Owen distinguished himself by extraordinary achievement while participating in aerial flight as flight engineer of a C-7A Aircraft near the Special Forces camp of Ben Het, Republic of Vietnam on 22 June 1969. On that date Sergeant Owen elected to fly an Emergency Resupply mission in direct support of the besieged camp. With complete disregard for his personal safety, he flew through hostile fire to successfully air drop badly needed supplies without which the camp may have been overrun. The professional competence, aerial skill and devotion to duty displayed by Sergeant Owen reflect great credit upon himself and the United States Air Force."

The actions of TSgt. John W. Quarles and his *Soul 454* crew (Maj.

John H. Wigington and Capt. Dale Grigg) on 26 June were documented in the citation for his Distinguished Flying Cross: [13]

"Technical Sergeant John W. Quarles distinguished himself by extraordinary achievement while participating in aerial flight as a Flight Engineer of a C-7A aircraft near the Special Forces camp at Ben Het, Republic of Vietnam on 26 June 1969. On that date, Sergeant Quarles elected to fly an Emergency Resupply mission in direct support of the besieged camp. With complete disregard for his personal safety he flew through extremely heavy hostile automatic weapons fire to successfully air drop the vitally needed supplies without which the camp may have been overrun. The professional competence, aerial skill, and devotion to duty displayed by Sergeant Quarles reflect great credit upon himself and the United States Air Force."

The actions of 1/Lt. William L. Witzig and his *Soul 455* crew on 26 June were documented in the citation for his Distinguished Flying Cross: [14]

"First Lieutenant William L. Witzig distinguished himself by extraordinary achievement while participating in aerial flight as a Copilot of a C-7A Aircraft near the Special Forces camp of Ben Het, Republic of Vietnam on 26 June 1969. On that date, his mission, *Soul 455*, was shuttling as required from Pleiku Air Base. The camp at Ben Het in the Central Highlands had been under siege for several weeks and was in danger of being overrun. Lieutenant Witzig, with deep concern for his fellow man and with great risk to his own life, volunteered to fly an Emergency Resupply mission to the camp, and was able to successfully complete the low airspeed, low altitude airdrop in the face of heavy hostile fire. The professional competence, aerial skill and devotion to duty displayed by Lieutenant Witzig reflect great credit upon himself and the United States Air Force."

First Lieutenant Clyde M. Wilson remembered what missions to Ben Het were like:

"During the run-up to the air drop missions, the first flight of the day to arrive at Pleiku would be sent to Ben Het. When you landed and taxied to the ramp, the next step was the off-load, then the mortars would start to land around you,. You would leave as fast as you could, call *Hilda* to report the shelling and the base would be closed for rest of the day. Each morning, the first crew would land at Ben Het knowing that they would receive incoming and they always went." [15]

He received the Distinguished Flying Cross[16] for the *Soul 424* mission on 26 June with Lt. Col. MacFarren and SSgt. Donald H. Houghtling.

The actions of TSgt. John L. Thomas, Jr. and his *Soul 416* crew (Lt. Col. George C. Marvin and 1/Lt. William C. Berta) on 27 June were documented in the citation for his Distinguished Flying Cross: [17]

> "Technical Sergeant John L. Thomas, Jr. distinguished himself by extraordinary achievement while participating in aerial flight as a Loadmaster of a C-7A Aircraft near the Special Forces camp at Ben Het, Republic of Vietnam on 27 June 1969. On that date, Sergeant Thomas elected to fly an Emergency Resupply mission in direct support of the besieged camp. With complete disregard for his personal safety, he flew through hostile fire to successfully air drop vitally needed supplies without which the camp may have been overrun. The professional competence, aerial skill and devotion to duty displayed by Sergeant Thomas reflect great credit upon himself and the United States Air Force."

A total of 77 airdrops of food, water, ammunition, medical supplies, and other essentials were accomplished by the squadron into the camp during June. In all, C-7A crews from Phu Cat and Cam Ranh Bay dropped more than 215 tons of supplies (food, ammunition, water, and medical supplies) in 178 sorties from 10 June to the end of the month, when it was considered hazardous for aircraft to land on the airstrip. Aircraft received intense ground fire with subsequent battle damage. Seven incidents were reported with 10 hits, causing various degrees of damage.

Three 537 TAS aircrew members were awarded the Purple Heart for injuries received on 13 June from bullet fragments or shrapnel. Maj. Delbert D. Lockwood received facial wounds from bullet fragments. 1/Lt. William F. Quinn, Jr. received fragments in his right leg. TSgt. John E. White was wounded in the right arm by shrapnel. A total of 2 Silver Stars, 25 DFCs, 3 Purple Hearts, and 7 Air Medals were awarded to C-7A crews for their heroic actions in supporting Ben Het. See Appendix XII for the report of the Mission Commander.

All crews functioned professionally and meritoriously under adverse combat conditions to successfully accomplish the mission. Maximum utilization of both aircrews and Caribou capabilities was achieved in a combat environment. The Caribous and the crews were a decisive factor which served to maintain the only lifeline to the camp during the major portion of the siege. The effectiveness of the resupply became manifest in the successful defense of the camp and the consequent lifting of the siege and dispersal of the enemy.

The majority of these C-7A sorties received excellent FAC and fighter coverage while in the target area. More intense enemy ground fire was suppressed by escort A-1E Skyraiders ("Spads") and FACs to make it less hazardous. The Skyraiders also laid a screen of smoke to blind the view of the enemy. In addition to tactical fighter support, B-52 crews supported the camp by making strikes against NVA weapons positions and base camps nearby. Two AC-119G gunships provided overnight illumination and fire support. Maj. James P. McCarthy, an F-100 pilot making air strikes against enemy bunkers, observed: "The Ben Het area was the busiest beehive I've seen since I've been here."

On 16 July, Seventh Air Force News described the close air support for Ben Het:

"Among the favorite sounds of the Ben Het defenders was the rolling, earth-shattering thunder of the B-52 Stratofortress raids. During a B-52 attack, all activity in the camp stopped; the men came out of their bunkers to watch the columns of flaming debris left in the wake of exploding bombs marching across the jungle hillsides occupied by NVA troops.

F-4 Phantoms from Cam Ranh Bay, Da Nang, and Phu Cat Air Bases; F-100 Supersabres from Tuy Hoa and Phan Rang; and A-1 Skyraiders and Vietnamese Air Force A-37's from Pleiku and Nha Trang Air Bases provided a close air support punch.

To the men on the ground, the arrival of the tactical fighters meant a respite from enemy mortar and artillery fire. When the Air Force planes appeared overhead, the enemy gunners were reluctant to fire. The muzzle flashes and smoke from their weapons revealed their location to sharp-eyed Forward Air Controllers and fighter pilots.

'We were always glad to see those fighters come in,' commented Army SFC Carl A. Mayse, a Special Forces advisor at the camp. 'The Spads (A-1 Skyraiders) were particularly good, because they carried a lot of ordnance and put it right where we wanted.'

Daily, lumbering C-7A Caribou transports dropped tons of food, ammunition, and other supplies to the men at Ben Het. Because of intense enemy activity along the road from nearby Dak To to Ben Het, airdrops were often the only source of resupply for the embattled camp.

Before the Caribou crews arrived, Skyraider pilots flew low between the camp and the NVA positions outside the perimeter, dropping clusters of bomblets which exploded in the air, releasing billowing clouds of dense white smoke. Then, hidden from enemy gunners behind the smokescreen, the C-7A's roared in. Over the camp, Loadmasters pushed out the cargo-laden pallets, their parachutes bloomed, and Ben Het was again resupplied."

Tribute must be paid to the individuals who, with dedication and a high degree of professionalism, flew missions supporting the airlift to the Ben Het CIDG camp. Air cover and air support were rendered by the following units: 12th Tactical Fighter Wing (TFW), Cam Ranh Bay; 31st TFW, Tuy Hoa; 35th TFW, Phan Rang; 37th TFW, Phu Cat; 633rd Special Operations Wing (SOW), Pleiku; and 3rd TFW, Bien Hoa. Without the aid and assistance of these units, air resupply missions may not have been successfully accomplished, the enemy would have been able to inflict greater battle damage and casualties, and the defenders of Ben Het might have fallen.

Colonel James H. Davis (1/Lt. at the time) remembered the challenging days into Ben Het:

"The primary mission of the 537 TAS was to support the Army's 1st Cav in the Central Highlands region. We had some close calls, even tragedies during my year. The flight crews, maintainers, and aircraft got a workout when the NVA surrounded and put a significant siege on the Special Forces camp at Ben Het in June of 1969. I remember that everything that could fly close air support (including B-52's) for our twenty-second in-trail re-supply airdrops did so. I remember the heroic efforts of everyone involved with the Caribou mission busting their buns to get the aircrews, payloads, and aircraft ready to perform the mission that only the Bou could perform. Ben Het would be saved! I learned lessons about pilotage, teamwork, sacrifice, professionalism, and 'higher headquarters support' that I would carry with me for the rest of my flying career! Yes, the Caribou community took some hits, but thankfully no loses at Ben Het." [18]

In the third quarter, the squadron continued to support the Bangkok mission site, supplying aircraft, maintenance personnel, briefings, and accommodations for personnel from Vung Tau and Cam Ranh Bay. The southwest monsoon season continued to exert an influence on mission accomplishment. Bad weather, which either completely obscured or adversely affected field conditions as in the case of the partially inundated runway at Tieu Atar, caused various loads to be returned. Missions working out of Pleiku also experienced a number of weather holds.

The Ben Het resupply was successfully completed at the beginning of July. The last Combat Essential missions by the Caribou crews were flown into Ben Het on 2 and 3 July. Normal procedures were modified in accordance with the special conditions under which the Ben Het resupply was conducted.

A steady decline in crew strength occurred. At the end of the quarter, there was a shortage of 10 pilots and the minimal strength of Flight Engineers was apparent. Due to combat and accident losses, five pilots and two Flight Engineers were not expected to be replaced within the normal, pre-planned input flow. Manning, however, was adequate for accomplishment of the mission. Sufficient individuals were available continuously for formation of the necessary combat ready crews.

In the fourth quarter, the squadron continued to support the Bangkok mission site, supplying aircraft, maintenance personnel, briefings, and accommodations for personnel from Vung Tau and Cam Ranh Bay. There was no change in the normal missions of the squadron. Flight Commanders were Lt. Col. Otto F. Schwanke, Lt. Col. Taylor, Maj. Thomas B. McHugh, and Maj. Harold B. Lee.

The northeast monsoon season exerted an influence on mission accomplishment. The monsoon brought seasonally bad coastal weather which extended sortie time because of time added to the flight by instrument approaches at coastal bases. The weather at Pleiku and surrounding areas improved greatly and increased the number of sorties successfully flown in this area. Although the weather at Phu Cat was bad much of the time, there were no departure holds because of the weather.

The actions of Capt. Josh M. Smith, Jr. and his crew on 20 October were documented in the citation for his Distinguished Flying Cross:

"Captain Josh M. Smith, Jr. distinguished himself by extraordinary achievement while participating in aerial flight as an Aircraft Commander of a C-7A aircraft near the Special Forces Camp at Bu Krak, Republic of Vietnam, on 20 October 1969. On that date Captain Smith volunteered to qualify two student pilots and deliver combat necessary ammunition to the camp which had been under siege for several days. Contact was made with the camp and it was learned that the area around the camp was saturated with hostile forces. Captain Smith was able to successfully complete two missions to the camp under the cover of air strikes and bombing raids without sustaining aircraft damage or aircrew injury. The professional competence aerial skill and devotion to duty displayed by Captain Smith reflect great credit upon himself and the United States Air Force." [19]

The actions of Maj. Charles R. Vanness and his crew on 17 November were documented in the citation for his Distinguished Flying Cross:

> "Major Charles R. Vanness distinguished himself by extraordinary achievement while participating in aerial flight as an Aircraft Commander of a C-7A aircraft at Bu Krak Special Forces Camp on 17 November 1969. On that date Major Vanness elected to fly a Combat Essential resupply mission in direct support of the besieged camp. In an extremely hostile environment and under very marginal weather conditions Major Vanness was able to complete two on-target air drops into the camp. The professional competence, aerial skill, and devotion to duty displayed by Major Vanness reflect great credit upon himself and the United States Air Force." [20]

Airdrops were flown to qualify all personnel in the airdrop category. At the end of the quarter, 21 airdrop sorties had been flown, delivering a total of 36.2 tons of men and material.

Training and Stan-Eval

In the first quarter, the Training Section, headed by Maj. Daniel C. Yost, experienced very heavy and active training, as evidenced by the number of pilots upgraded. By establishing new parameters for upgrading to Aircraft Commander, the upgrading program accelerated its pace. Aircraft Commanders in the upgrade program had sufficient flying time and did not require special waivers. The acquisition of additional Aircraft Commanders helped to alleviate the flying burden caused by the rotation of a large number of Aircraft Commanders.

A letter from the Wing established the requirement of qualifying all pilots and Flight engineers as Refueling Supervisors upon completion of a standardized refueling test. This served to make pilots and Flight Engineers more conscious of fuel contamination possibilities and the importance of proper grounding procedures. A standardization of procedures was also maintained with a series of 38 spot checks. The Wing Stan/Eval gave the squadron a rating of "Excellent" after various spot checks.

In the second quarter, the Training Section continued a vigorous training program led by Lt. Col. Taylor, who relieved Maj. Yost. The new change in upgrading personnel, initiated at the end of the first quarter, became manifest. In general, upgrading accelerated, increasing five-fold above the previous quarter. Under the new system, more continuous study became necessary for the individual. An overall view of performance became the criteria for upgrading. More responsibility for upgrading individuals was placed upon the Commander.

A general balance of personnel in the positions of Flight Examiner, Instructor Pilot, Aircraft Commander, First Pilot, and Copilot was maintained. The only deficiencies noted were in Instructor Flight Engineers. Maximum effort in upgrading and maintaining a high degree of proficiency through close coordination with the Stan/Eval Section were the goals. Three Flight Examiners were upgraded: Maj. Lockwood, Maj. Monroe, and Capt. Alan L. Girod. The squadron upgraded two wavered Aircraft Commanders: 1/Lt. Dennis A. Maki and 1/Lt. Robert P. Wiesneth.

The squadron Stan/Eval conducted 63 flight evaluations in the quarter: 3 Flight Examiner upgrades, 2 Instructor Pilot upgrades, 11 Aircraft Commander upgrades, 8 Aircraft Commander semi-annual, 17 First Pilot upgrades, 9 Copilot qualifications, 5 Airdrop Qualifications, and 8 Spot Checks.

Capt. Jon E. Drury remembered the time when there was "Silence Over Cheo Reo":

> "We took off from An Khe on a sunny day in the Spring of 1969 on one of my new missions as an Aircraft Commander. We took off to the north, on runway 03, then turned crosswind to climb around Monkey Mountain, scarred by aircraft crashes because it rose so abruptly from the high plain. We headed south, climbing over jungle, then leveling at 4,000 feet, going south over Cheo Reo, a V-shaped airstrip that we serviced periodically. Getting to altitude was always one of the nicest parts of the flight.
>
> Details of loading in the daytime heat, preparations for takeoff in a hot airplane, and the takeoff were past. 'Whoosh!' All of a sudden, both engines quit and it was like we hit a wall of air as we decelerated quickly with neither engine pulling. 'What in the fat!' We both jerked into action, reaching for controls, trying to solve a double engine failure. Looking over at my copilot, I realized that he had pulled back both mixtures to shutoff. That is exactly what the engines did!
>
> When we got to altitude, we always ran the cruise checklist in which we moved the overhead mixture levers to auto lean. My first mistake was doing the checklist silently. My copilot, thinking that we had not done the cruise checklist, quietly did it himself. Then, wanting to move the mixtures to auto-lean, instead of moving them one at a time per the checklist, he pulled both back at once to the next stop – idle cutoff! Both engines dutifully did what he

208

commanded.

All I could think to do was say 'Put them back in,' then moved the mixtures back to auto-lean myself and the engines were running again. At the time, I did not remember that I needed to retard the propeller levers, to be sure we did not get an over-speed. Thankfully, we did not, and again we were flying.

As the old saying goes. 'What's flying like?' 'Answer: Hours of boredom, interspersed with moments of stark terror!' Sometimes the moments come suddenly." [21]

The Wing conducted a series of spot checks during May. The results were "Outstanding." The 834AD conducted check rides and emergency procedure testing during June. The results were also "Outstanding."

No unsatisfactory trends were noted. Continuing emphasis was placed on restricted air field qualification during upgrade.

First Lieutenant William F. Quinn, Jr. remembered flying with the Chief of Stan/Eval:

"Al Girod was always convivial and welcomed at any beer drinker's table, socially, but, I recall that if you were riding with him as a Copilot or taking a check ride as an A/C, you'd better have your book knowledge ready, and set to go. I was getting pretty senior as a Copilot when I got Al's right seat for the *Soul 454* or the *455*. We all loved those missions because almost all of the sporty C-7A flying, usually staged out of Pleiku.

One of our sorties took us to the normally routine strip of Duc Lap. Duc Lap was not really a challenge with at least 1500 feet and a lot of PSP[22] at both ends. It was a typical backwoods fly-in. It was cloudy, but not quite overcast, gray, but not wet. It was the time of year when there was activity on the ground. The siege at Ben Het wasn't too far into the future. It was a VC [Viet Cong] time of year in the Central Highlands.

Following procedures, we'd call into the base on Fox Mike [FM radio] using the names given like Whisky Treetop. They'd answer, tell us everything was all right and we'd roll in, unload, and off we'd go. When we got hold of them, for some reason, there was a combination of discernible anxiety of some kind coming from their end, but nevertheless, an 'A-OK' on making the landing.

When we got to the off-load end of the runway, the guys rushed over and told us to unstrap our load, put the pedal to the medal, slide out from under, and just keep on going out of the valley. Being good cadets, we did as we were told. We were there at one end of the runway, engines winding up, the Bou starting to move when down at the other end of the runway an explosion went off. The bad guys were mortaring.

We moved down the runway, gathering speed, when at about 200 yards or so, poof another one, this one equally close. Al was flying the heck out of the plane, looking for enough airspeed to get it off the ground and out of range. It was taking a long time. We were getting ready for the next one which might be a lot closer when the C-7A lumbered its way into the air as only a Caribou can do.

Al had the flying hands of a surgeon. As we broke ground and lifted into the air, we were not the usual C-7A lift machine that we were used to. Al tried to bank into a climbing turn to get completely above and off-line. Then he noticed that, in the excitement, the flaps were still up. Down they came and off we went none the worse for wear. I've always told that on Al, in my mind, but actually it's on me. I was the Copilot and should have run the Before Takeoff checklist, mortars or no." [23]

In the third quarter, the appointment of Lt. Col. Lyle B. Marshall as OJT Training Officer, made during the second quarter, was approved on 3 July. The Training NCO, SSgt. Larry D. Mitchell, departed with an exemplary record of accomplishment. SSgt. Jack L. Newton was appointed to fill his position on an interim basis. Training operated quite smoothly.

There was an unusual exodus of Flight Examiners, Instructor Pilots, Aircraft Commanders, and Flight Engineers. An average of three Flight Examiners and 6-7 Instructor Pilots was maintained through an active upgrade program. A total of three waivered Aircraft Commanders were upgraded. There were eight pilots in the three phases of training at the end of the quarter. Two new Flight Examiners were upgraded: Lt. Col. Charles E. Ketring and Maj. Charles R. Vanness. Lt. Col. Ketring became Chief of Stan/Eval when Maj. Murphy ended his tour in August.

All training records were reviewed, reworked, and updated in accordance with *834AD Manual 60-1, dated 27 January 1969* and *483 TAW Supplement 1, dated 15 September 1969*. The few minor discrepancies were acted upon. October was the target date for completion of corrective actions.

A new policy concerning takeoffs and landings was initiated by *PACAF Regulation 55-25, dated 1 August 1969* as supplemented by *483 TAW Supplement 1, dated 9 September 1969*. This necessitated implementation of special Proficiency Training rides to keep First Pilots and Copilots current in the right and left seats. Stan/Eval performed 13 evaluations (6 Aircraft Commander, 6 First Pilot, and 1 Copilot) in July, 16 evaluations (1 Flight Examiner, 5 Instructor Pilot, 3 Aircraft Commander, 2 First Pilot, and 5 Copilot) in August, and 10 evaluations (1 Flight Examiner, 3 Aircraft Commander, 1 First Pilot, and 5 Copilot) in September. Continued emphasis was placed on maintaining airdrop qualification of all Aircraft Commanders as soon as possible. A series of spot checks was given and no unsatisfactory trends were noted.

In the fourth quarter, SSgt. Newton continued as Training NCO. The OJT program received the added responsibility for requisitioning materials for the Weighted Airman Promotion System (WAPS) and the testing program. Most of the materials were on hand and others were ordered through the Extension Course Institute. There were 10 personnel in the upgrade training program and all progressed normally. At the end of the quarter, two individuals were awaiting final results for upgrade to their new levels. Under the guidance of SSgt. Newton, the program continued to upgrade personnel at a steady rate.

Upgrading new arrivals as expeditiously as possible was the focus of the Training Section in order to maintain the level of manning necessary to fly the designated number of sorties. The task was further complicated by new personnel arriving in groups as large as 10, making it impossible to upgrade all personnel concurrently.

The Section prepared 84 personnel for check rides given by Stan/Eval. The Training Section had six Instructor Pilots and Stan/Eval had three Flight Examiners. One Instructor Pilot and two Copilots were in the upgrade program at the end of the year.

Maj. Charles R. Vanness replaced Lt. Col. Ketring as Chief of Stan/Eval on 7 November. No new Flight Examiners were upgraded because the current Flight Examiners had at least five months left on their tour. TSgt. Edward G. Hardy replaced MSgt. Hugh M. Overcash as Chief of NCO Stan/Eval for Flight Engineers. TSgt. Henry F. Bell and TSgt. Dale E. Christensen upgraded to NCO Flight Examiner.

In October, Stan/Eval evaluated six Aircraft Commanders, seven Copilots, and five Flight Engineers. In November, Stan/Eval evaluated nine Aircraft Commanders, three Copilots, and seven Flight Engineers. In December, Stan/Eval evaluated 2 Instructor Pilots, 17 Aircraft Commanders, 5 Copilots, and 5 Flight Engineers.

Continued emphasis was placed on maintaining all Aircraft Commanders qualified in all of the restricted fields in II Corps, as well as airdrops. A series of spot checks was given and no unsatisfactory trends were noted. Initial Orientation Flights and Emergency Procedure Flights totaled 27, with 18 no-notice checks.

Safety

In the first quarter, six ground fire reports were submitted. On 26 February, Maj. Michael Murphy encountered one hit of .30 caliber fire at 3500 feet on the 200 radial of TACAN Channel 107 (Pleiku) at 10 nautical miles on the *Soul 455* mission. On 3 March, Lt. Col. Holdener encountered 11-25 rounds (no hits) over Ben Het at 2900 feet on the *Soul 415* mission. On 8 March, Lt. Col. Marvin encountered 1-10 rounds (one hit) at an unknown location on the *Soul 414* mission. On 10 March, Maj. Yost encountered 11-25 rounds (no hits) five nautical miles south of Channel 107 at 1700 feet on the *Soul 454* mission. On 11 March, Lt. Col. James C. Swarts took 6 hits of .30 caliber fire at ¼ nautical mile on final approach to Dak Pek (V-42) on the *Soul 454* mission. On 18 March, Maj. Monroe received one hit enroute from Phu Cat to Pleiku on the *Soul 455* mission.

During January, the squadron Office of Safety was inspected by a survey team from 7AF. All phases of activity which influenced flying safety were observed and found to be among the best noted in South Vietnam.

The 483 TAW Supplement to the *834AD Accident Prevention Plan* was received and implemented. The Safety Officer, Maj. Jordan, held three meetings at the squadron, once each third Tuesday of the month. One comment brought out was about the effective results of OHRs. One example was the fence being built around English Airfield (V-232) after three OHRs were submitted for people being on the runway.

In the second quarter, the majority of battle damage was received during the airdrops at Ben Het. On 12 May, the *Soul 416* mission, with Maj. William A. Evalenko as Aircraft Commander, received three hits in the empennage from exploding mortar or rocket rounds on the ground at Ben Het. Flight controls were slightly damaged. On 26 May, the *Soul 454* mission, with Maj. Murphy as Aircraft Commander, received one hole in the empennage from small arms fire 4 nautical miles southwest of Pleiku. Total incidents for the quarter were nine with a resultant 14 hits.

The squadron experienced no flying accidents or incidents. The OHR program continued to obtain satisfactory results and was emphasized at all Flying Safety meetings. Monthly Flying Safety meetings were held with a broad range of subjects presented to the aircrew

212

members. A Flying Safety Opinion Survey was conducted and the results were presented to all crew members.

Safety visits by the 483 TCW and the 834AD were made during June. The squadron Flying Safety program was found to be "Excellent" by both inspection/assistance teams. Monthly Safety Surveys were conducted in the 537 TAS and the 537 OMS. The results were forwarded to the Wing Safety Office.

In the third quarter, Capt. Josh M. Smith, Jr. replaced Maj. Monroe as Chief of Safety when he completed his tour. On 21 July, the 483 TAW Safety Office sent a message to all squadrons with information for all aircrew members, quoting a message from PACAF:

"1. Despite repeated publication of warning articles, concerning flying in or near severe weather areas, in safety and operational periodicals, incidents and accidents continue to occur. In a recent 48 hour period, USAF lost four aircraft, one pilot sustaining fatal injuries. All of these aircraft were operating in areas of either forecast or existing severe weather. Additionally, nine incidents involving similar situations in severe weather were recorded. These incidents could have become major accidents and aircrew fatality statistics had luck not prevailed.

2. Preliminary investigation indicates that in some cases mission requirements were not of sufficient priority to dictate flying in or near the type of weather encountered. Commanders and supervisors of flying should reemphasize to all aircrews the necessity of critically evaluating enroute and terminal weather forecasts, especially during the seasons when thunderstorms and severe winds can generate rapidly.

3. The Air Force cannot afford loss of life and equipment due to deficiencies in supervision or aircrew professionalism on flights that can be canceled or delayed without degrading the mission."

On 26 July, an accident occurred at Vung Tau Army Air Base, resulting in the loss of C-7A S/N 62-4186 and crew member 1/Lt. James F. Wohrer (awarded a DFC for action at Ben Het). On takeoff, the *Soul 490* mission experienced difficulties and a subsequent loss of power on #2 engine. Upon attempting to land, aircraft control was lost. Other crew members and passengers sustained various, though not fatal, injuries. An Aircraft Accident Board was convened and their findings and recommendations were reported on 19 August 1969.

Battle damage was light due to the decrease in enemy activity. No operation comparable to the Ben Het resupply, which exposed aircraft and crews to intense enemy ground fire, occurred. In August, a hole, apparently caused by small arms fire, was noticed during post-flight of C-7A S/N 63-9727. Two hits from small arms fire were received north of Pleiku by C-7A S/N 62-4155. Although operation of the fuel system and flight controls was affected, the aircraft was returned safely and without incident to Pleiku.

On 30 August, Capt. Edward E. Furchak, as Aircraft Commander, made a series of troop drops at DZ Cherry, three nautical miles south-west of Pleiku. During the fourth drop, a chute apparently malfunctioned and two CIDG jumpers became entangled and streamered to the ground. An Accident Investigation Board was convened and their findings were reported on 17 September 1969.

On 11 September, the squadron suffered a combat loss west of Pleiku, near Plei Djereng. The aircraft, C-7A S/N 62-4187, was destroyed upon impact. The crew members were 1/Lt. Robert P. Wienseth, 1/Lt. Greinke, 2/Lt. Charles B. Ross, and SSgt. Frederick Wilhelm. All crew members lost their lives and received the Purple Heart.[25] After considerable delay due to weather and the dense, nearly impassable jungle terrain, the crash site was reached by an Army search team. The aircraft wreckage manifested various degrees of enemy inflicted battle damage. Enemy movement and activity in the area were found to be considerable.

Monthly Flying Safety meetings were held on 14 July, 12 August, and 19 September. Topics presented included emphasis on checking for contaminated fuel, the psychological aspects of an individual's tour in SEA, and review of the Flying Safety and Ground Safety problems accompanying the northeast monsoon season.

The fourth quarter battle damage was very light, with only one hit reported. The one hit occurred on 6 October approaching Dak Pek (V-42). The round struck and pierced the top edge of the rudder. A continued lull in enemy activity was considered responsible for this record as well as continued emphasis by the squadron Safety Officer on minimum safe altitudes.

Monthly Flying Safety meetings, led by Capt. Smith, were held on 23 October, 19 November, and 23 December. Topics covered in the meetings included: continued emphasis on checking for contaminated fuel, crosschecking with navigational aids on instructions relayed to aircraft from ground control sites, detailed discussions of propeller and engine oil leaks, summary and report on nine OHRs turned in during the quarter, and many other Flying Safety items.

There were no aircraft accidents involving the squadron during the quarter.

Maintenance

In the first quarter, there was a drastic improvement in manning of the Maintenance Section. The squadron was authorized 47 personnel and 46 were assigned. New personnel quickly gained the needed experience while working on the C-7A. This was supported by the fact that the squadron experienced only nine percent of the total maintenance delays recorded by the Wing. Other factors for the commendable record were evening engine run-ups, communication-navigation preflights, and a more conscientious effort on the part of all personnel.

A major change was initiated in training and upgrading enlisted maintenance personnel. Specialty Knowledge Tests (SKT) were eliminated effective 1 April. Completion of Career Development Courses with proficiency tests became the determinants for upgrading to higher skill levels.[24] Immediate supervisors and the Squadron Commander then approved the recommendations. This less complex method of training and testing elevated the squadron's effective proficiency level. The pre-SKT PACAF examinations since February were used as factors for promotions. There were no problems or deficiencies concerning maintenance personnel.

In the second quarter, maintenance reliability remained the same with Phu Cat accounting for 25 percent of the maintenance deviations in the Wing. Corrosion Control was moved from Clark Air Base, Philippines to Kadena Air Base, Okinawa beginning 1 July. The maintenance function moved to its new organizational maintenance building. A work order was submitted for air conditioners for the new building. Fourteen maintenance personnel were sent PCS to Nakhon Phanom (NPK) Air Base, Thailand. Line maintenance was somewhat undermanned, causing all personnel to be divided into two shifts, each working 12 hours a day with one day off each week. No immediate solution to this problem was foreseen. In April, six individuals were upgraded to the 5-level and two to the 7-level. In May, seven individuals were upgraded to the 7-level.

Sergeant Darrold R. Paulson remembered interesting times when he was an avionics technician at Phu Cat:

> "I was on what we called the Blue Ribbon team as the avionics tech and we went out and recovered any Bou that broke down at a forward fire base (the Army didn't like them hanging around). One time, we off-loaded the cargo at a base before heading to fix a Bou. As we taxied down the short runway for takeoff, mortar shells started falling on the runway behind us. Needless to say, we were all lifting, trying to help the bird off the ground before we got

215

clobbered.

One time, a crew was delivering a steer in a crate via a parachute drop. The bottom of the crate was not too sturdy and the steer went through it when the chute opened. He bellowed on the way down, but it was instant hamburger. Not sure who was supposed to get the steer.

Another time we did a drop at night and took out the perimeter fence instead of putting the drop on the runway. Always a fun time for the Army guys on the ground!" [26]

In the third quarter, maintenance facilities experienced various changes which were to greatly enhance and ease operation. The Periodic Dock revetments Q-1, Q-2, P-1, and P-2 were relocated from the south to the north end of the field. The main revetment area was also enlarged further with the addition of revetments L-7, L-8, and L-9. A new wash rack was under construction on the north end of the revetment area. When completed, the wash rack would decrease towing time and effect an overall enhancement of aircraft internal and external appearance.

C-7A S/N 62-4183 was flown to Bangkok for IRAN. The move of IRAN from the Philippines to Bangkok eliminated the necessity to install the ferry fuel system. The systems, however, were installed on C-7A S/N 62-4180 and 61-2591 which were treated at the Corrosion Control facility at Kadena AB, Okinawa. The engine shop initiated a program to cover the engine "P" leads with waterproof "spaghetti." This was done in anticipation of the northeast monsoon season and the subsequent problems encountered.

Sgt. Robert Fritch was named Crew Chief of the Month for August and A/1C Moffat J. Nelson was named Crew Chief of the Month for September.

As of 3 October, 2/Lt. Theodore N. Witt replaced 1/Lt. Woodbury as Maintenance Officer. TSgt. Leonard N. Webster departed for the CONUS on emergency leave and was reassigned for humanitarian reasons. No new personnel were received during the quarter.

Trends worked toward better maintenance and cleaner aircraft. A prime reason for this trend was the upgrading of all 3-levels to 5-levels and their increased proficiency as Crew Chiefs due to OJT and study of Technical Orders.

In the fourth quarter, the organizational maintenance statistics did not reflect any significant improvement over the third quarter. The enroute delays numbered 63 in October, 34 in November, and 54 in December. These totals, as well as the initial delays, corresponded to the average in the Wing: seven in October, two in November, and five in December.

November figures reflected a vast improvement over October, but returned to the average in December. A contributing factor to the low in-commission rate was the inclement weather associated with the monsoon season. Many times the weather prohibited flying of FCFs. Except for three days in December, two aircraft were at the IRAN and Corrosion Control facilities.

There were eight engine failures in the quarter. Seven of the engines were changed because of internal failure, while only one was replaced for time. There were no common causes attributed to the engine failures. C-7A S/N 62-4138 went through IRAN from 7 October through 18 December and S/N 63-9755 from 15 November through 31 December. C-7A S/N 63-9757 left for Corrosion Control on 21 December and was expected to return on 9 January 1970.

On 26 November, a message arrived stating that TCTO 1C-7A-598, "Inspection of Elevators and Elevator Torque Tubes" should be complied with as the aircraft went through the Periodic Docks. The last aircraft was completed on 25 December. The work performed on 30 October on C-7A S/N 61-2406 completed TCTO 1C-7A-589, "Installation of Fuel-cell Suppressant Material."

Radio equipment was constantly failing because of wet weather. A cover was locally manufactured to keep water off of the radios. The idea proved so effective that the covers were installed on all assigned aircraft. After the installation of the covers, there was a marked decrease in the number of radio communications and navigation failures.

Annually, between the months of November and January, an almost complete changeover of maintenance personnel occurred. By the end of the quarter, no great problem was seen because the replacements were arriving steadily. The new personnel were outstanding in that they came more fully qualified and at a higher level than in the past. At the beginning of the quarter, the maintenance squadron was manned with only one SMSgt., one MSgt., no TSgts., and three SSgts. At the end of the quarter, the figures were one SMSgt., two MSgts., five TSgts., and eight SSgts. The number of Sergeants and Airmen remained approximately the same.

The 7AF Inspector General team inspected the squadron in late November. The inspection was good and maintenance received a "Satisfactory" rating. Phu Cat Air Base started a new Foreign Object Damage program. In the past months, the revetment area received "Fair" and "Satisfactory" ratings.

Sgt. Tino Cristina was named Crew Chief of the Month for November and A/1C Pedro Rodriguez was named Crew Chief of the Month for December.

Administration

In the first quarter, Capt. Richard D. Brethouwer assumed duties as Administrative Services Officer. The position had been vacant since September 1968. He helped the new administration complete much back work. 1/Lt. Theodore L. Hanchette was the Historian.

The squadron began the year with a slight shortage of pilots and Flight Engineers. By the end of the quarter, however, the squadron was one pilot over authorization and two Flight Engineers under authorization. This manning was quite adequate to carry out the mission. The squadron was elevated to that manning level by the extra effort of the Training Section and by the arrival of new personnel. There were no noteworthy deficiencies in manning at the end of the quarter. No recommendations were submitted to change any unit manning documents, nor were any deficiencies foreseeable for the next quarter.

In the second quarter, 1/Lt. Jerome P. Smolinski was the Historian. The squadron was sufficiently manned. Strength was high at the beginning, but diminished somewhat near the end of the quarter due to departing personnel and insufficient replacements. A balance of arriving and departing personnel was maintained to a degree, although a slight shortage of three Flight Engineers and two pilots was experienced at the end of the quarter. This, however, had no effect on mission accomplishment. New arrivals were expected and an accelerated upgrading program would readily fill these positions. Prospects for the next quarter appeared promising for a greater influx of personnel.

The primary change during the quarter involved NCOs in the Administration Section. Three personnel departed and were replaced by two arrivals. The vacancy was expected to increase the workload on the remaining personnel.

The squadron began the quarter with a slight overage of pilots and Flight Engineers. At the end of the quarter there was a shortage of two pilots and three Flight Engineers. This manning was adequate for accomplishing the mission.

In the third quarter, 1/Lt. Thomas M. Mullen assumed duties as Administrative Services Officer. TSgt. Luther L. McCray replaced MSgt. Marshall R. Headle as First Sergeant and Assistant Administrative Officer. 1/Lt. Smolinski continued as Historian. In the quarterly squadron history report, he summarized the impact of the operations.

"Two events, which claimed the lives of five outstanding individuals, befell the 537th TAS during the past quarter. To these dedicated and selfless men who, in the course of duty to their country and self convictions, sacrificed their lives is the present history of the 537th dedicated. For their bravery, power, and devotion to duty and professionalism may they always be remembered. Their names, deeds, and individual personalities will not be forgotten in the hearts and minds of the men of the 537th Tactical Airlift Squadron."

A number of deficiencies were noted in various AFSCs at the end of the quarter. Departing personnel exceeded incoming personnel. Subsequently, a comparative decrease in manning strength over the second quarter was experienced. A decrease in the number of pilots and Flight Engineers restricted scheduling latitude to a certain degree. The burden was also experienced in the Maintenance Section.

The OJT program continued to upgrade personnel at a steady rate. During July, four individuals were upgraded to the 5-level. In September, four were upgraded to the 5-level and one to the 7-level, leaving three in training at the end of the quarter.

In the fourth quarter, 1/Lt. Mullen continued as Squadron Administrative Officer and TSgt. McCray continued as First Sergeant and Assistant Administrative Officer. 1/Lt. Robert E. Croach, II continued as the Historian. Incoming personnel exceeded outgoing, so manning in most areas was far ahead compared to the third quarter. An increase in the number of Copilots resulted in more time for work on additional duties and an increase in squadron morale. Manning throughout the quarter was adequate for mission accomplishment. Sufficient individuals were available for formation of the necessary Combat Ready crews. Some deficiencies existed in various AFSCs at the end of the quarter, but the squadron was nearly at its authorized manning level.

Supply and Support

In the first quarter, the tour of duty was made more bearable with the occupancy of new air-conditioned officers' quarters.

The 780 equipment, such as rollers, roller clamps, and tie-down straps, finally arrived. This ended one of the major problems previously encountered during morning launch. Transporting this equipment from an unscheduled aircraft to a scheduled aircraft was no longer necessary.

Since a reactivation of the anti-ice, oxygen, and heating systems was directed, it was necessary to order all the missing components.

This equipment was not in the aircraft upon receipt from the Army. The parts were issued slowly. The major work of activating these systems was delayed until all parts arrived.

During the latter part of March, the squadron relocated to new officers' quarters situated at the northern part of Phu Cat Air Base. New facilities such as an Officer's Club, Mess Hall, patios, and general landscaping were projected for future development in the complex. Flight line maintenance personnel moved to a new and larger building on the flight line. More storage space was provided while maintaining a close proximity to the aircraft.

In the second quarter, the activation of the heating, oxygen, anti-icing, and de-icing systems on the C-7A was carried over from the preceding quarter and remained the major implementation program. All TCTOs were complied with as parts arrived on station. Receipt of supplies was good with the exception of parts for the heating, oxygen, anti-icing, and de-icing systems. This inhibited implementation of the pertinent TCTOs.

An effort by the entire squadron succeeded in completing an 18 foot by 18 foot patio adjacent to the BOQs assigned to the squadron. The first part of this work was bringing materials in by truck and pouring concrete, while nearly the entire last half was mixing and pouring by hand. Many future facilities and beautification projects remained in the planning phase at the end of the quarter.

The Flight Engineers moved into new quarters, which had previously been vacated by the officers. Air-conditioners were provided and installed by the support group.

Capt. Jon E. Drury remembered a unique decoration in Maj. Delbert D. Lockwood's room:

> "Delbert kept a broken R-2000 cylinder in his room. On a mission he flew out of An Khe, a cylinder failed completely and the engine steamed fire out of the top of the engine. Delbert feathered the prop and shot the fire bottle to the engine with no effect. An engine fire is one of the most critical emergencies an aviator faces. He returned to An Khe, shut down, and discovered that the failed cylinder had separated from the engine and jammed in the cowling. The cylinder became a display in his room.
>
> Missions into Ben Het in June of 1969 were seldom routine. He flew one of the dangerous airdrop missions and received the Purple Heart for a wound to his face received on 13 June when an enemy round hit part of the aircraft and debris sprayed his cheek. He was flying the *Soul 455* mission with Capt. Edward L. Furchak

and SSgt. John D. Mellert." [27]

The squadron held various functions with specific activities planned for each month. These activities served to boost morale. Lieutenant Quinn organized a most enjoyable Hawaiian luau in April. Roast pig, poi, fish, pineapple, coconut, and many other island delicacies were enjoyed at the well attended function. The first outdoor cookout at the new BOQ was hosted by Lt. Col. Marvin in May. The "chef" offered barbecued chicken, barbecued steak, salad, and other appealing items. In June, the officers made use of the Bamboo Room of the Phu Cat Officer's Open Mess for a party. An open bar was available along with a variety of food, including chicken and pizza.

An exchange program to promote inter-service cooperation and understanding was initiated by the Army Ground Liaison Officer, Maj. Phil R. Norman. Lt. Quinn was the first officer to utilize the program by taking a Swift Boat ride and learning about its various functions and operations. Future plans were projected for more Swift Boat rides, visits to various fire bases, and reciprocal visits from Army and Navy units to observe the Caribou operation.

In the third quarter, thirteen aircraft had TCTO 1C-7A-589 complied with at Cam Ranh Bay. This entailed the installation of explosion suppressant in the fuel tanks. The problems encountered, primarily fuel leaks upon reinstallation of the tanks, were soon corrected.

Work continued on the new Officer's Club in the BOQ area and sidewalks were installed connecting the various buildings. No new squadron facilities were planned for the near future.

In the fourth quarter, Base Supply gave excellent support to the squadron. Most items were received in as short a time as possible, usually within a half hour. The only major difficulty was in obtaining heater, anti-icing, de-icing, and oxygen system reactivation items. These items were upgraded to "NFE" status and were slated to arrive in January.

Work continued toward completion of the new Phu Cat Officer's Club with a forecast date of mid-February for the opening. Two professional quality tennis courts were completed and added to the physical conditioning facilities of the base.

Awards and Decorations

In the second quarter, Air Medals were awarded to Maj. Kent M. Monroe, 1/Lt. William C. Berta, 1/Lt. Dennis A. Maki, 1/Lt. William K. Ryland, 1/Lt. Robert P. Wiesneth, TSgt. Hugh M. Overcash, and SSgt. John D. Mellert. Air Force Commendation Medals were awarded to Lt. Col. Robert H. Taylor and TSgt. Stuart B. Crafton.

In the third quarter, Purple Hearts were awarded to Maj. Delbert D. Lockwood and TSgt. John E. White.

Civic Action and Special Activities

In the second quarter, 1/Lt. Charles C. Taylor accepted responsibility for Civic Actions when 1/Lt. Jon E. Drury completed his tour. The squadron continued to supply a daily ambulance driver for the off-base dispensary.

In the third quarter, the squadron was unable to supply an ambulance driver each day for the off-base dispensary, due to the tight scheduling of personnel. No new programs were initiated during the quarter.

In August, a party hosted by the departing Majors was held in the Bamboo Room of the Officer's Club. In September the "brown bars" of the squadron organized a function in honor of their promotion to First Lieutenant. The program initiated by the Army Ground Liaison Officer, Maj. Norman, was continued. A Swift Boat ride was experienced by 1/Lt. George L. Harmon and operation of the firebase at LZ English was experienced by 1/Lt. Taylor and 1/Lt. Quinn.

The squadron held a festive holiday gathering in the Bamboo Room of the Phu Cat Officer's Club and a good time was had by all 41 officers in attendance.

No new Civic Action programs were undertaken due to the influx, training, and upgrading of new personnel.

Probably the most noted and most rewarding endeavor undertaken by the squadron in the fourth quarter was the Santa Bou program. C-7A Caribou aircraft, with their nose section painted to resemble Santa Claus, visited various Special Forces camps throughout Vietnam. The aircraft delivered candy, presents, and other gifts and "goodies" to the men in the field, helping to boost the morale of the fighting men in Vietnam.

In a letter to the 483 TAW on 14 December, Gen. Creighton W. Abrams took special note of this program, remarking that, ". . . your project 'Santa Bou' during the Christmas season has earned both the respect and gratitude of Americans and Vietnamese alike." In a similar letter of appreciation on 31 December, Col. Keith L. Christensen, Commander of the 483 TAW, wrote, "I especially wish to commend your ' Santa Bou' project officers, 1/Lt. Robert B. Strang and 1/Lt. Stephen B. Smaby, for the outstanding manner in which they organized and supervised the 537th TAS 'Santa Bou' effort." From the Army, Lt.

Col. Donald M. Wood, Infantry Commanding, wrote on 30 December, "The quality of the unique decorations showed that numerous extra hours had been used in decorating the Santa Bous. We appreciate all the thoughtfulness your unit expressed to make this Christmas a most enjoyable and memorable one."

Airlift Accomplishments [28]

During the first quarter, passengers hauled were 14,286 in January; 17,350 in February; and 23,358 in March for a total of 54,994. Cargo hauled was 1240.3 tons in January; 1629.1 tons in February; and 1808.6 tons in March for a total of 4678.0 tons. In January, the squadron flew 2108 sorties while logging 1247.1 flying hours. In February, the squadron flew 2415 sorties while logging 1526.9 flying hours. In March, the squadron flew 2974 sorties while logging 1643.9 flying hours. There was a definite increase in hours flown and cargo hauled nearly doubled from last quarter of 1968. This was attributed to the acquisition of the Pleiku Mission Site and conversion from a dedicated user of the 1Cav to a common carrier.

During the second quarter, passengers hauled were 21,890 in April; 27,724 in May; and 27,737 in June for a total of 77,351. Cargo hauled was 2033.6 tons in April; 1830.7 tons in May; and 1792.1 tons in June for a total of 5656.4 tons. In April, the squadron flew 2290 sorties while logging 1623.5 flying hours. In May, the squadron flew 3197 sorties while logging 1671.0 flying hours. In June, the squadron flew 3084 sorties while logging 1541.5 flying hours. Weather, in particular the southwest monsoon season, was a primary factor in decreasing both sorties flown and tonnage hauled. Adverse weather conditions prevailed over much of the Central Highlands. Numerous airfields were obscured by cloud cover and there were various down days spent at Pleiku Air Base waiting for the weather to break. Aircraft were forced to either terminate early or remain on a weather hold at Pleiku. Instrument and weather procedures were given greater emphasis.

During the third quarter, passengers hauled were 31,822 in July; 27,685 in August; and 28,998 in September for a total of 88,505. Cargo hauled was 1929.6 tons in July; 1729.9 tons in August; and 1574.9 tons in September for a total of 5234.4 tons. In July, the squadron flew 3362 sorties while logging 1684.8 flying hours. In August, the squadron flew 3131 sorties while logging 1628.8 flying hours. In September, the squadron flew 2992 sorties while logging 1612.1 flying hours.

During the fourth quarter, passengers hauled were 27,211 in October; 25,069 in November; and 25,225 in December for a total of

77,505. Cargo hauled was 1489.9 tons in October; 1459.4 tons in November; and 1788.9 tons in December for a total of 4738.2 tons. In October, the squadron flew 2933 sorties while logging 1503.1 flying hours. In November, the squadron flew 2810 sorties while logging 1453.2 flying hours. In December, the squadron flew 3042 sorties, while logging 1520.8 flying hours.

Commander's Summary

First Quarter 1969 [29]

"The 537th TAS produced a good record of work accomplished during the quarter from 1 January-31 March 1969. This was commendable since several factors would normally have disrupted the mission. A new administration, faced with new problems and even a few leftover ones, adjusted with little problem. New restrictions were always being initiated for the sake of safe flying, while it was seldom that old ones were removed. Also during the quarter, some missions had to terminate early, simply due to the lack of loads to move. It was the combined effort and esprit de corps that made a squadron such as the 537th function."

Second Quarter 1969 [30]

"Despite numerous adverse conditions, the 537th TAS compiled an admirable record for the quarter 1 April-30 June 1969. Weather, the Southwest Monsoon Season in particular, and a crew flying hours restriction were the principal deterrents to greater achievements.

Particularly outstanding during this quarter was the aerial resupply of the CIDG Camp Ben Het. All crews exerted maximum effort through a high degree of crew coordination, skill, and professionalism to successfully accomplish their mission. The Caribou aircraft and the crews of the 537th TAS proved to be a crucial link in the successful defense of the besieged camp."

Third Quarter 1969 [31]

"Much was learned as a result of the various losses experienced during the last quarter. The ever present danger of the enemy on the ground and the perpetual hazards of adverse weather were instilled in the minds of all. Everyone received stark reminders of the skill and professionalism needed to successfully accomplish the mission in SEA.

The 537th can, however, look in retrospect upon an admirable record. Results of the Ben Het resupply are self-explanatory. Future aspirations will remain high and greater accomplishments will be indicative of the spirit of the 537th TAS."

Fourth Quarter 1969 [32]

"As can be seen for the individual reports and supporting statistics, the 537th TAS effectively carried out their assigned mission in an environment of professionalism despite numerous hardships which had to be overcome.

And with increased manpower experience, the squadron can be expected to improve on this quarter's performance in the first three months of 1970. Adding to the squadron's reliability were additional pilots and Flight Engineers, improved maintenance techniques and personnel, and an efficient Standardization/Evaluation program.

The role of accomplishments of the 537th TAS truly demonstrated their ability to materially assist the armed forces and civil population in the Republic of Vietnam, as well as to emphasize the extreme flexibility of United States air power around the world."

End Notes: 537 TAS

[1] *19690101-19691231 537 TAS History*
[2] 537 TAS Special Order G-1, dated 18 February 1969
[3] *C-7A Caribou Association Newsletter, Vol. 3, Issue 2*
[4] 7AF Special Order G-2166, dated 15 May 1970
[5] 7AF Special Order G-3912, dated 27 September 1969
[6] 7AF Special Order G-0786, dated 20 February 1970
[7] 7AF Special Order G-4698, dated 15 November 1969
[8] *C-7A Caribou Association Newsletter, Vol. 21, Issue 2*
[9] 7AF Special Order G-0992, dated 6 March 1970
[10] 7AF Special Order G-3909, dated 27 September 1969
[11] 7AF Special Order G-2137, dated 15 May 1970
[12] 7AF Special Order G-2166, dated 15 May 1970
[13] 7AF Special Oder G-5224, dated 22 Dec 1969
[14] 7AF Special Order G-5285, dated 20 November 1970
[15] Personal note from Clyde M. Wilson to the author
[16] 7AF Special Order G-2166, dated 15 May 1970
[17] 7AF Special Order G-2166, dated 15 May 1970
[18] *C-7A Caribou Association Newsletter, Vol. 1, Issue 21*
[19] 7AF Special Order G-5284, dated 20 November 1970
[20] 7AF Special Order G-2556, dated 6 June 1970
[21] *C-7A Caribou Association Newsletter, Vol. 24, Issue 2*

[22] Steel matting for runways and ramp areas was developed during WW II and was referred to as Pierced Steel Planking (PSP).
[23] *C-7A Caribou Association Newsletter, Vol. 22, Issue 2*
[24] Training was in accordance with *AFM 35-1* and *AFM 50-23*.
[25] Department of the Air Force Special Order GB-702, dated 29 September 1969
[26] *C-7A Caribou Association Newsletter, Vol. 18, Issue 2*
[27] *C-7A Caribou Association Newsletter, Vol. 24, Issue 1*
[28] When the data in the squadron history and the Wing history differ, the Wing data is shown.
[29] 537 TAS Commander's Summary, 31 March 1969 by Lt. Col. George C. Marvin
[30] 537 TAS Commander's Summary, 30 June 1969 by Lt. Col. George C. Marvin
[31] 537 TAS Commander's Summary, 30 September 1969 by Lt. Col. George C. Marvin
[32] 537 TAS Commander's Summary, 31 December 1969 by Lt. Col. Donald J. MacFarren

Special Forces Camp at Ben Het (Copyright © 2014 Denny Dillon)

483rd Consolidated Aircraft Maintenance Squadron [1]

The primary mission was to accomplish the functions of field maintenance squadron, communications/navigation activity, and phase inspection activity in the 483 TAW and to accomplish the heavy shop maintenance and specialist maintenance required on the C-7A aircraft assigned to the Wing and maintain the Wing Aerospace Ground Equipment. The squadron also assisted in the base defense by providing 12 Security Police augmentees and a Reserve Defense Force of 50 men.

To accomplish this mission, in the first quarter the squadron was authorized 8 officers and 297 airmen, but fewer personnel were actually assigned. The number of personnel assigned was 278 at the end of January, 288 at the end of February, and 291 at the end of March. In addition, 26 officers and 30 airmen were attached. In the second quarter, the squadron was authorized 8 officers and 297 airmen, but fewer personnel were actually assigned. The number of personnel assigned was 300 at the end of April, 302 at the end of May, and 299 at the end of June. In addition, 28 officers and 20 airmen were attached. In the third quarter, the squadron was authorized 7 officers and 302 airmen. The number of personnel assigned was 304 at the end of July, 306 at the end of August, and 331 at the end of September. In addition, 26 officers and 25 airmen were attached. In the fourth quarter, the squadron was authorized 8 officers and 315 airmen. The number of personnel assigned was 380 at the end of October, 344 at the end of November, and 346 at the end of December.

In the first quarter, Lt. Col. Edgar A. Hastings continued as Commander. On 15 January, Lt. Col. Ralph L. Peters assumed command of the squadron,[2] which continued in the second quarter.

On 10 July, a Letter of Commendation was received from the 7AF Deputy for Maintenance on improvement in engine maintenance. On 30 August, Lt. Col. James W. Thompson assumed command of the squadron,[3] which continued in the fourth quarter.

On 30 December, the entire 483 CAMS supported a successful "max effort" attempt of the Wing to establish one-day operational records for the C-7A aircraft.

Maintenance Shops

In the first quarter, the workload in each shop was normal when compared with previous quarters in 1968. No failure to meet scheduled maintenance was recorded. Every shop continued to achieve a high level of maintenance effectiveness.

AGE Shop: In the first quarter, TSgt. Carl M. Taylor was the Branch Chief. The shop had four of its 11 equipment repair men constantly used as drivers for the Material Control shop and initiated a request that vehicle operators be authorized on the Wing Unit Detail Listing (UDL). The squadron Orderly Room operated with just two of the three administrative specialists it was authorized. To help this office, a series of maintenance personnel who were either excess to their shops or physically disqualified from flight line duty temporarily worked as Unit Mail Clerks.

Forty-five scheduled inspections of AGE were completed. Five engines, four compressors, and seven components of AGE were repaired and returned to the Reparable Processing Center (RPC) as serviceable. Twelve other items processed were returned to the RPC as Not Repairable This Station (NRTS) Code 1.[4] NRTS Code 2 was the reason for turning in three more items. One repairable item awaited parts. The AGE in-commission rate was 98 percent. Two men were in training for the 5-level and one was in training for the 7-level. One man was newly assigned.

In the second quarter, TSgt. Taylor continued as the Branch Chief. The shop completed 43 scheduled inspections of AGE. The RPC items processed included 10 compressors, 5 engines, 4 regulators, and 2 generators. Four of these items were returned to service and 12 others were turned in to the RPC as NRTS Code 1. The five remaining items were turned in as NRTS Code 2. Two airmen were in training for the 5-level and one for the 7-level. One airman was upgraded to the 5-level.

In the third quarter, TSgt. Estil Whitehead was the Branch Chief. The shop completed 33 Periodic Inspections on powered AGE. It processed 14 RPC items, of which four were returned to service, four were turned in as NRTS Code 1, four were turned in as NRTS Code 2, and two were turned in as NRTS Code 9. TCTO 441-87-505, "Replacement of Sliding Wave Compressor with Reciprocating Compressor," was completed. Two airmen were in OJT, one for the 7-level and one for the 5-level. Manning and shop facilities were adequate.

In the fourth quarter, TSgt. Whitehead continued as the Branch Chief. The branch completed 65 periodic inspections on powered AGE and processed 14 RPC items, of which 11 were NRTS Code 1 and the remaining 3 were NRTS Code 2. TCTO 34Y1-87-505, "Replacement of Sliding Wave Compressor with Reciprocating Compressor," was completed on one unit. Two airmen were in OJT for the 7-level and one to the 5-level. No personnel were upgraded. During the quarter,

228

seven personnel departed and two replacements were received.

Aircraft Repair Shop: In the first quarter, SMSgt. Earl P. Stoneking was the Branch Chief. Shop personnel completed 682 scheduled flight line work orders on the C-7A aircraft. They also processed 151 RPC items. One hundred and three of these items were repaired. Twenty-nine items were NRTS Code 1, 12 were NRTS Code 2, and 5 were NRTS Code 9. Thirteen items awaited parts. Of the three men in training for the 5-level, one was upgraded. Two men were newly assigned.

In the second quarter, the shop completed 635 scheduled and unscheduled flight line work orders. Fifty-nine of these items were repaired, 12 items were NRTS Code 4, and four items were NRTS Code 9. Twenty-seven items awaited parts. The one man in training to the 3-level was upgraded and two of the three men in training for the 5-level were upgraded. One man was reassigned to the Phase Maintenance Section.

In the third quarter, the shop completed 587 scheduled and unscheduled flight line work orders. In addition, 95 RPC items were processed. Fifty-eight items were returned to service, nine items were NRTS Code 2, eight items were NRTS Code 4, and one item was NRTS Code 9. Seventeen items awaited parts. TCTO 1C-7A-596, "Inspection of Main Landing Gear Housing," was completed on seven aircraft. Training accomplishments included the upgrading of one man to the 7-level and two men to the 5-level. No manning or shop facility problems were experienced.

In the fourth quarter, the shop completed 603 scheduled and unscheduled flight line work orders. It processed 233 RPC items, of which 221 were returned to service and 32 were turned in to the RPC in a NRTS status. Forty items were awaiting parts. TCTO 1C-7A-596, "Inspection of Main Landing Gear Housing," was completed on one aircraft. TCTO 1C-7A-583 was completed on one aircraft. TCTO 1C-7A-598, "Inspection and Rework of Elevators and Elevator Torque Tubes," was completed on 31 aircraft. One man was in OJT for the 7-level. Seven personnel departed and five replacements were received.

Communications/Navigation Shop: In the first quarter, TSgt. Robert E. Espinoza was the Shop Chief. The shop processed 795 Communications and Navigation electronic units. Of these, 688 repaired units were returned to service, 9 units were NRTS Code 1, and parts were not on hand for the remaining 98. The shop also completed 2038 scheduled and unscheduled flight line work orders. TCTO 1C-7A-592, "Removal of T-66A Standby Very High Frequency (VHF) Transmitter," was complied with on 33 aircraft. In the OJT program, one man attained the 7-level and two others attained the 5-level. Three personnel rotated and six were gained.

In the second quarter, MSgt. Philip E. McKinley was the Branch Chief. The shop processed 546 Communications and Navigation electronic units. Five hundred repaired units were returned to service. Three items were NRTS Code 1, two units were NRTS Code 6, and parts were not on hand for the remaining 41. The section also completed 1365 scheduled and unscheduled flight line work orders. In addition, 46 aircraft phase inspections were accomplished. In the OJT program, two Staff Sergeants were in training for the 7-level. One of the two airmen in training for the 5-level was upgraded. One shop member was transferred to the Wing Maintenance Analysis Shop and three personnel were gained.

In the third quarter, MSgt. McKinley continued as the Shop Chief. The shop processed 676 RPC items. Six hundred thirteen of these were repaired and returned to service. Four items were NRTS Code 1, 10 items were NRTS Code 2, three items were NRTS Code 4, and six items were NRTS Code 9. Parts were not on hand for 116 units. The shop completed 1728 scheduled and unscheduled flight line work orders and participated in 64 aircraft Phase Inspections. A Class I modification,[5] "Removal of APX-44 and Installation of APX-46," was performed on C-7A S/N 62-4181. Water and moisture became a problem when the windy season arrived. Water penetrated equipment and connections, causing short-circuits and corrosion, and, in general, reduced equipment capability.

In the fourth quarter, Capt. Curtis A. Preston was assigned as OIC of the shop on 17 October and MSgt. Richard A. Todd replaced MSgt. McKinley as Shop Chief on 7 December. The shop processed 755 RPC items, of which 691 were returned to service and 101 items were in the shop awaiting parts. Seven items were turned in NRTS Code 1, 36 NRTS Code 2, 78 NRTS Code 4, 2 NRTS Code 6, and 6 NRTS Code 9. The shop completed 1515 scheduled and unscheduled flight line work orders and participated in 54 aircraft phase inspections. TCTO 1C-7A-592, "Removal of T366A Standby VHF Transmitter, C-7A Aircraft," was completed on one aircraft. A Class I modification, "Removal of APX-44 and Installation of APX-46," was performed on C-7A S/N 62-4145. Water and moisture continued to cause problems through October and into November by penetrating equipment and connections and causing short-circuits and corrosion. Several times during the quarter, the shop was forced to terminate operation due to the safety hazard of water on the floor caused by the leaking building. Three men were in OJT for the 7-level and two for the 5-level. One man was upgraded to the 7-level and two to the 5-level. Seven personnel departed and five replacements were received.

Corrosion Control and Paint Shop: In the first quarter, 172 scheduled and unscheduled work orders were completed. All of the 195 RPC items processed through the shop were repaired. Eighty-four phase inspections were performed. One man left on a Permanent Change of Station (PCS).

In the second quarter, the shop completed 133 scheduled and unscheduled work orders. All 71 RPC items processed through the shop were repaired. Seventy-six phase inspections were performed. There were three trainees for the 7-level and one for the 5-level. Two men left on PCS.

In the third quarter, the shop processed 269 RPC items and 266 of these were returned to service. Sixty-one scheduled and unscheduled work orders were completed and 91 Phase Inspections were performed. The shop was moved from the area in front of the docks because of the large amount of sand surrounding the area. The structure was damaged in the process of moving and had to be torn down and completely rebuilt by five shop personnel.

On 1 July, the Paint Shop was discontinued and personnel cross-trained as Corrosion Control Specialists. Two airmen took the by-pass specialist test for the AFSC 535X0 career field. Both men successfully completed the 3-level by-pass and were awarded the three-level. They then entered OJT for the 5-level. One other man was upgraded to the 5-level.

In the fourth quarter, all of the 232 RPC items processed were returned to service. The shop completed 45 scheduled and unscheduled work orders and participated in 3 phase inspections. One man was in OJT for the 5-level and one man was upgraded to the 5-level. One man departed and five new men were received.

Electric Shop: In the first quarter, the shop completed 1336 work orders and 112 phase inspections. The shop repaired 191 of the 576 repairable components that it processed, returned 337 to the depot as NRTS, retained 81 in an Awaiting Parts (AWP) status, and condemned 4 as beyond economical repair. Shop personnel also accomplished TCTO 1C-7A-590, "Switching Air Delivery System Panel with Deicer Panel," on 27 aircraft.

In the second quarter, the shop completed 1175 work orders on the C-7A electrical equipment and 104 phase inspections. The shop

231

repaired 165 of the 505 repairable components that it processed and retained 123 in an AWP status. The shop returned 174 components to the depot as NRTS Code 1, 62 as NRTS Code 4, 15 as NRTS Code 6, and 6 as NRTS Code 9. Shop personnel accomplished TCTO 1-C-7A-595, "Installation of Emergency Toggle Switch, Nose Steering," on 23 aircraft.

In the third quarter, the shop completed 1180 work orders on the C-7A electrical equipment and 103 Phase Inspections. The shop returned to service 184 of the 557 RPC items processed and retained 170 in an AWP status. Returned to the depot were 106 components as NRTS Code 1, 1 as NRTS Code 2, 13 as NRTS Code 6, and 28 as NRTS Code 9. Shop personnel accomplished TCTO 1C-7A-595, "Emergency Toggle Switch, Nose Steering," on three aircraft.

In the fourth quarter, the shop completed 1093 work orders on the C-7A electrical equipment and 110 phase inspections. Four hundred and ninety-one RPC items were processed, of which 161 were returned to service and 64 were AWP. One hundred twenty-two units were turned in as NRTS Code 1, 49 as NRTS Code 2, 11 as NRTS Code 6, and 34 as NRTS Code 9. Shop personnel assisted in the accomplishment of TCTO 1C-7A-592E, "Removal of T366A Standby VHF Transmitter," on 15 aircraft. Three men were in OJT for the 5-level and one man was upgraded to the 7-level. Eight men departed and six replacements were received.

Engine Build-Up Shop: In the first quarter, the shop built up 81 engines and shipped 94 more engines back to the depot after disassembling them. Of 195 items processed through the shop, 101 were turned in as NRTS Code 1 and 94 as NRTS Code 6. TCTO 1C-7A-577, "Rerouting of Electrical Cables for Propeller Reversing," was completed on 81 engines. The section had two personnel losses and nine gains. On 10 February, a new building for the Engine Build-Up Shop was opened.

In the second quarter, the shop built up 90 engines and shipped 77 more engines back to the depot after disassembling them. Of 181 RPC items processed, 100 were turned in as NRTS Code 1, 74 as NRTS Code 6, and 7 as NRTS Code 9. The shop completed TCTO 1C-7A-577, "Rerouting of Electrical Cables for Propeller Reversing," on 70 engines and TCTO 1C-7A-593, "Installation of Number Eight Intake Manifold Drain," on 42 engines. Two trainees were upgraded to the 5-level, while six more continued in training for the 7-level. One man left on PCS.

In the third quarter, the shop built up 18 engines. Of 140 RPC items processed, 71 were turned in as NRTS Code 1 and 69 as NRTS Code 6. Shop personnel completed TCTO 1C-7A-593, "Installation of Number Eight Intake Manifold Drain," on 65 engines. Two trainees were upgraded to the 7-level and three more continued in training for the 7-level.

In the fourth quarter, the shop built up 32 engines and processed 203 RPC items, of which 67 were returned to service and 136 were turned in as NRTS. Shop personnel completed TCTO 1C-7A-593 on 32 engines and TCTO 1C-7A-577. Two men were in OJT for the 7-level and five for the 5-level. Nine personnel departed and seven replacements were received.

Engine Conditioning Shop: In the first quarter, the shop completed 1332 scheduled and unscheduled flight line work orders. It also conducted 157 phase inspections. One airman was upgraded to the 3-level. Two men departed and four were newly assigned.

In the second quarter, the shop completed 1242 scheduled and unscheduled flight line work orders. It also conducted 54 inspections on the engine test stand and 230 engine phase inspections. Six personnel were in training for the 7-level.

In the third quarter, the shop completed 1048 scheduled and unscheduled flight line work orders and 222 engine phase inspections. Additional inspection requirements on the engine exhaust system were initiated and added to the inspection work cards. The shop received a Letter of Commendation from the 7AF DCM concerning improvement in engine maintenance at Cam Ranh Bay. Two men in OJT were upgraded to the 7-level.

In the fourth quarter, 1105 scheduled and unscheduled flight line work orders were completed and 134 engine phase inspections. Two men were in OJT for the 7-level and four for the 5-level. Ten personnel departed and six replacements were received.

Hydraulic Shop: In the first quarter, the shop accomplished 921 scheduled and unscheduled work orders and 43 phase inspections. It repaired 213 of the 432 items processed, returned 176 to the RPC as NRTS Code 1, and returned 12 as NRTS Code 9. Thirty items awaited parts. Three personnel in training were upgraded to the 5-level. One airman joined the shop.

In the second quarter, the shop accomplished 784 scheduled and unscheduled work orders and 48 phase inspections. It repaired 233 of the 424 RPC items processed, returned 172 to the RPC as NRTS Code 1 and returned 3 as NRTS Code 9. Sixteen items awaited parts. Five airmen in training were upgraded to the 5-level, two airmen continued in training for the 5-level, and one continued for the 7-level. The shop lost five personnel and gained two.

In the third quarter, the shop accomplished 620 scheduled and unscheduled work orders and 54 phase inspections. It repaired 159 of the 407 RPC items processed, returned 124 as NRTS Code 1, 63 as NRTS Code 2, and 5 as NRTS Code 9. Forty-six items awaited parts.

In the fourth quarter, shop personnel accomplished 723 scheduled and unscheduled work orders and 44 phase inspections. It processed 461 RPC items, returning 142 to service and turning in 174 as NRTS. Fourteen items awaited parts. One man was in OJT for the 7-level. Five personnel departed and four replacements were received.

Instrument Shop: In the first quarter, the bench check and repair section processed 296 aircraft instrument components. Of these, 127 components were repaired and returned to the supply stocks. Seven of the remaining components were turned in as NRTS Code 2 and the other 162 were turned in as NRTS Code 1. The shop also corrected 1087 malfunctions on the C-7A aircraft. The personnel accomplished 2 standardizations of the pilot's and copilot's instrument panels, 10 ground compass wings, 50 torque wrench calibrations, and 12 in-flight calibrations of the stall warning system. Two airmen rotated and one was newly assigned.

In the second quarter, the shop completed 983 scheduled and unscheduled work orders. Of the 331 instrument components processed, 142 were repaired and returned to the supply stocks and the other 189 were turned in as NRTS Code 1. The shop also accomplished 14 phase inspections, 16 in-flight calibrations of the stall warning system, 11 in-flight compass swings, and 84 torque wrench calibrations. There were two airmen in training for the 7-level.

In the third quarter, the shop completed 1181 scheduled and unscheduled work orders. It processed 411 RPC items. Of these, 137 were returned to service, 157 were NRTS Code 1, 2 were NRTS Code 2, and 93 were NRTS Code 9. Twenty phase inspections were completed. A J-2 Compass mockup was completed, increasing the effectiveness of training and troubleshooting. At the end of the quarter, no 7-level personnel were assigned. One man was in OJT for the 7-level and two men were in OJT for the 5-level.

In the fourth quarter, the shop completed 664 scheduled and unscheduled work orders. It repaired 71 of the 325 RPC items processed, returned 106 as NRTS Code 1, 26 as NRTS Code 2, and 86 as NRTS Code 9. Eleven phase inspections were completed. Two men were in OJT for the 7-level and one for the 5-level. The shop received eight personnel and lost three.

Machine Shop: In the first quarter, the shop completed 318 unscheduled flight line work orders and repaired all 38 RPC items that it processed.

In the second quarter, the shop completed 334 unscheduled flight line work orders and repaired all 47 RPC items that it processed. One airman attained his 5-level.

In the third quarter, the shop completed 155 unscheduled flight line work orders and repaired all 18 RPC items processed. The 12th Field Maintenance Squadron (12 FMS) was preparing to take over the 483 CAMS machine shop functions due to departure of all CAMS machinists in early October.

In the fourth quarter, shop support was provided by the 12 FMS with the 483 CAMS providing a 3-level machinist.

Phase Maintenance Section: In the first quarter, SMSgt. Oscar G. Garringer was the Branch Chief. The section completed 114 phase inspections. The bench stock was made more useful with the incorporation of items required by engine and structural repair specialists. One trainee was awarded the 5-level. Six airmen departed PCS and 14 were newly assigned.

In the second quarter, SMSgt. Garringer continued as the Branch Chief. The section completed 115 phase inspections. Ten trainees were upgraded to the 5-level. At the end of the quarter, seven personnel were in training for the 5-level and two for the 7-level. One man left PCS and two were newly assigned, one being transferred from the Aircraft Repair Shop.

In the third quarter, SMSgt. Garringer continued as the Branch Chief. The section completed 115 phase inspections of the C-7A. Dock #3 construction was completed. Dock #4 construction was halted in the middle of construction for lack of funds.

In the fourth quarter, SMSgt. Garringer continued as the Branch Chief. The section completed 104 phase inspections. Two men were in OJT for the 7-level and three for the 3-level. Four men upgraded to the 5-level. The section lost 22 men and received only 10 replacements. Increased commitments and personnel shortages resulted in reduced production.

Propeller Shop: In the first quarter, the shop accomplished 946 scheduled and unscheduled work orders, 110 phase inspections, and 4 special propeller inspections. It also processed 105 units for repair, but had to turn all the units in as NRTS Code 1. Three personnel were upgraded to the 5-level. Two men were newly assigned.

In the second quarter, the shop accomplished 873 scheduled and unscheduled work orders, 117 phase inspections, and 5 special propeller inspections. It also processed 74 RPC units, but had to turn all the units in as NRTS, 69 as NRTS Code 1 and 5 as NRTS Code 9. One airman was awarded the 5-level. Two personnel continued in training for the 5-level and one for the 7-level. Four men departed PCS.

In the third quarter, the shop accomplished 716 scheduled and unscheduled work orders, 96 phase inspections, and 70 special propeller inspections. All RPC items processed were turned in, 48 as NRTS Code 1 and 4 as NRTS Code 9. Three men were in OJT for AFSC 42151A.

In the fourth quarter, the shop completed 444 scheduled and unscheduled work orders and 149 phase inspections. It processed 100 RPC items, of which 51 were returned to service. Forty-three were turned in as NRTS Code 1, 5 as NRTS Code 2, and 1 as NRTS Code 4. Three men were in OJT for the 5-level and two men were upgraded to the 5-level. Five replacements were received and five men departed.

Propulsion Branch: SMSgt. Tommy L. Quintier was Branch Chief in the first, second, and third quarters. The Branch included the Engine Build-Up Shop, the Engine Conditioning Shop, and the Propeller Shop. In the fourth quarter, SMSgt. Alvin A. Jahnke was Branch Chief.

Sgt. Gary A. Miller recalled a difficult engine change:

> "I was in Cambodia doing an engine change. Had to do two changes because the first engine from the depot was missing rings in the bottom jug. What a memory. I also experienced a B-52 *Rolling Thunder* strike one mile away. What Power!" [6]

Structural Repair Shop: In the first quarter, the shop completed 556 scheduled and unscheduled work orders and 109 phase inspections. Of 735 RPC items processed, 629 were repaired, 16 awaited parts, and 90 were returned to the RPC as NRTS. Of the 90 NRTS items, 82 were NRTS Code 1, 3 were NRTS Code 6, and 5 were NRTS Code 9. TCTO 1-C-7A-591, "Installation of External Grounding Receptacle," was complied with on 16 aircraft. Two men in OJT were upgraded to the 5-level. One man departed PCS. MSgt. William A. Epps was Branch Chief of the Fabrication Branch.

In the second quarter, the shop completed 834 scheduled and unscheduled work orders and 83 phase inspections. Of the 434 RPC items processed, 349 were repaired, 54 awaited parts, and 31 were returned to the RPC as NRTS. Twenty-two irreparable items were NRTS Code 1, one was NRTS Code 6, four were NRTS Code 8, and four were NRTS Code 9. MSgt. Epps continued as Branch Chief of the Fabrication Branch.

In the third quarter, the shop completed 632 scheduled and unscheduled work orders and 103 phase inspections. It processed 541 RPC items. Of these, 186 were returned to service, 37 were AWP, 41 were NRTS Code 8, and 37 were NRTS Code 9.

On 6 September, nine aircraft received battle damage caused by shrapnel from an incoming rocket that hit in the parking ramp area. Eight of the aircraft were repaired and ready for missions the following day.

At the end of the quarter, the shop was overmanned. However, the workload was considered above normal. Nine assigned men were in OJT for the 5-level. TSgt. Verastro was Branch Chief of the Fabrication Branch.

In the fourth quarter, the shop completed 561 scheduled and unscheduled work orders and 96 phase inspections. It processed 680 RPC items and returned 594 to service. Twenty-six RPC items were AWP and 86 were turned in as NRTS. The shop assisted in completion of TCTO 1C-7A-598, "Inspection and Rework of Elevators and Elevator Torque Tubes," on two aircraft. Seven men were in OJT for the 5-level. Two men departed and five replacements were received.

Survival Equipment Shop: In the first quarter, the three men in the section completed 80 scheduled and unscheduled work orders. They also processed 220 articles of survival equipment.

In the second quarter, the three man section completed 70 scheduled and unscheduled work orders and processed and made serviceable 671 items of survival equipment.

In the third quarter, the shop was consolidated in a facility with the 12 FMS. The shop repaired 746 of the 747 RPC items that were processed and turned in 1 item as NRTS Code 8. One man continued in training for the 7-level. On 16 September, all shop equipment was turned in and the function was moved to operate with and from the 12 FMS Parachute Shop in Building 3237. Sixty scheduled and unscheduled work orders and 515 items of survival equipment were processed.

In the fourth quarter, the shop, co-located with the 12 FMS, accomplished 87 scheduled and unscheduled work orders and processed 235 items of survival equipment. One man was in OJT for the 5-level and one upgraded to the 7-level. One man departed and two arrived.

Welding Shop: In the second quarter, the shop repaired 574 of the 781 RPC items that it processed and turned the remaining 207 in as NRTS Code 9. One man was in training for the 7-level. In the fourth quarter, the shop, consolidated with the 12 FMS, returned 245 items to service of the 305 RPC items processed. The remainder was turned in as NRTS. Two men were in OJT for the 5-level. One man departed and three men were received.

Wheel and Tire Shop: In the first quarter, the shop processed and repaired 480 tires. It also made serviceable 26 main wheels and turned in 12 others as NRTS Code 9. In the second quarter, the shop processed and repaired 444 tires. It also made serviceable 50 wheels and turned in 8 as NRTS Code 9. One man was in training for the 7-level. In the third quarter, the shop processed 287 RPC items, of which 25 were returned to service and 200 were turned in as NRTS Code 9. In the fourth quarter, the shop processed 354 RPC items, of which 12 were turned in as NRTS Code 9. One hundred and fifty-three nose wheels and 189 main wheels were built up. One man departed and one replacement arrived.

Sgt. Laverne W. Waldron was named the Outstanding Field Maintenance Man of August for the CAMS.

Training and the Maintenance Standardization and Evaluation Program

In the first quarter, 76 squadron personnel were in upgrade training. Of 12 trainees who took their Specialty Knowledge Test, five passed and were upgraded. Four failed their test and the remaining three had not received their scores at the end of the quarter. In all, 2 Airmen were upgraded to the 3-level, 10 to the 5-level, and 2 to the 7-level. The Training Section received 73 points out of a possible 100 on the quarterly report for OJT effectiveness. Based on the formulas in *Cam Ranh Bay Regulation 50-1*, the training effectiveness for the different skill levels was rated as 100 percent for the 3-level, 83 percent for the 5-level, and 50 percent for the 7-level.

In the second quarter, 80 personnel participated in the squadron OJT program. Thirty-six of these trainees were upgraded, 28 to the 5-level and 8 to the 7-level. In AFSC 431X1A alone, 12 of 23 airmen in training were awarded the 5-level.

In the third quarter, 62 personnel participated in the OJT program. Sixteen of these were upgraded. In AFSC 432X1 alone, five airmen were awarded the 7-level and in AFSC 431X1 four airmen were awarded the 5-level. The number of personnel in OJT at the end of the quarter was 62.

In the fourth quarter, the OJT program involved 144 trainees. Nineteen of these trainees were upgraded, 4 to the 7-level and 15 to the

5-level. At the end of the quarter there were 44 men in the OJT program.

Administration

In the first quarter, 1/Lt. Robert A. O'Brien continued as Historian. He was also the Squadron Section Commander. SMSgt. Elton P. Strom was the First Sergeant, Capt. Norman D. Bautsch was the Maintenance Supervisor, and CMSgt. Curtis L. Singleton was the Maintenance Superintendent.

Both in quantity and quality, the manning of the squadron was adequate to perform the mission. The personnel turnover was comparatively light. Becoming highly proficient in their various tasks, the personnel who joined the squadron in the last months of 1968 found that they could do more work in less time. Several senior NCOs who reported in during the quarter brought much-needed experience to certain superintendent and supervisory positions. Lt. O'Brien observed that: "The leisure time that they would ordinarily receive as a reward for this achievement developed instead into time spent filling a massive levy of details imposed by echelons as high up as 7AF."

On 10 March, the squadron Orderly Room was selected for the Wing monthly Project PRIDE award for February. On 28 March, the Engine Shop was selected for the Wing Project PRIDE award for March.

In the second quarter, 1/Lt. O'Brien continued as Historian and Squadron Section Commander. MSgt. Johnye R. Parks was the First Sergeant. Capt. Bautsch continued as the Maintenance Supervisor and CMSgt. Singleton continued as the Maintenance Superintendent.

The squadron had an adequate number of personnel. Personnel turnover was light and a much desired stability existed throughout the squadron. In skill levels of experience, the picture was also good. The squadron was able to continue to perform its primary mission of aircraft maintenance. In June, more manpower became available to the squadron shops when the kitchen police detail in the base dining halls was decreased from 4 to 3 airmen a day. Hampered by the continuous use of four equipment repairmen as drivers of the Material Control shop, in the first quarter the AGE shop requested that vehicle operators be added to the Wing UDL. This request was disapproved in April due to the manpower ceilings existing in Vietnam.

Sgt. Jerry C. Presley, an engine mechanic in the Phase Docks, remembered his time on Kitchen Police (K.P.) duty:

"Every enlisted man (E-4 and below) that served in the Air

Force during the 1960's got the privilege of participating in a little dog-and-pony show called K.P. It was one of those little aggravations that you just put up with and went on about your business. I put it in the category of getting a root canal. Cam Ranh Bay was no exception to the rule. At the 483 CAMS, every E-4 and below was a candidate for K.P. If my memory serves me right, K.P. came along about every three or four months, depending on the number of warm bodies in the squadron. It amounted to being assigned to some Mess Sgt. for three or four days to help out in the kitchen doing all the flunky work. My roommate used to refer to it as 'an opportunity to hone your culinary skills.'

The job you were assigned was determined by the order in which you reported for duty at the mess hall, the best job being 'outside man' and 'pots and pans' the worst. The first to report got 'outside man' duty and the last to report got 'pots and pans' duty. The ones who reported in-between these two parameters got the in-between stuff like clipper, dining room orderly (DRO), serving line, salad maker and so on down the line. As you can see, it was in your best interest to get there pronto in order to get a decent job.

One day, after breakfast, we were assigned to our respective jobs. Each group had a regular cook that they were assigned to. I would liken him to a boss who kept an eye on us to keep us from running amuck and blowing up the kitchen or scalding each other. You might call him a disaster control guy. The cook who was in charge of the DROs was a nice guy, but he was a real clean freak. My wife is a clean freak, but she doesn't compare to that guy. He made sure we swept and mopped the floor and wiped and scrubbed the tables after each meal, kept the serving line and milk dispensers immaculate, filled and cleaned the salt and pepper containers, and mopped the kitchen from one end to the other whenever he thought it necessary. If it didn't move, you wiped, scrubbed, or mopped it. Anyone who ate there during this guy's tour ate in a clean mess hall. We immediately dubbed him 'Mr. Clean.'

When the breakfast rush was about over and everything was spotless, Mr. Clean let us take breaks in shifts. I guess he wanted to give us a rest before the next phase. Some of us were sitting in the back of the chow hall shooting the breeze and drinking coffee when a Colonel and his entourage came in. We continued our break and didn't think much of it. The next thing we knew, the Colonel sent a Major over to tell us to remove our caps. We were all smart enough to realize that when a Bird Colonel sent word to do

240

something, you did it. The last thing we needed was to rile up some Colonel before he had his morning coffee and SOS.

About that time, the Mess Sgt. sends Mr. Clean over to tell us to put our caps on (the hair-in-the-food thing again I suppose). We put our caps back on. The Major comes back with a note pad wanting to know our names, squadron, and our First Sergeant. He told us that we weren't showing proper respect by not uncovering while in the mess. This was turning into a bad game of Simon Sez. We had a Bird Colonel on one side of the place saying take it off and a Mess Sgt. on the other side saying put it on. We were in a no-win situation here and these two guys were unaware of the other's orders. Finally, I mustered all the military courtesy I could and told the Major; 'Sir, we're on K.P. and the Mess Sgt. told us to leave our caps on.'

The Major reported back to the Colonel, who in turn walked over and talked to the Mess Sgt. The Colonel then walked over to our table, told us to be at ease and apologized for the misunderstanding.

I can't recall who the Colonel was, but I think he was a hell of a man to apologize to a group of E-3 and E-4 Airmen. He made an impression on me by showing us some real character." [7]

In the third quarter, 1/Lt. O'Brien continued as Historian and Squadron Section Commander. MSgt. Parks continued as First Sergeant. First Lieutenant George L. Mansi was the Maintenance Supervisor and CMSgt. Singleton continued as the Maintenance Superintendent.

The Squadron was adequately manned to perform the primary mission of aircraft maintenance. Manning remained fairly constant for the first portion of the quarter with relatively little turnover. However, beginning in September, personnel arrivals outnumbered departures. This was a prelude to the heavy rotation of the fourth quarter.

On 30 September, Hootch A-13 and the Propeller Shop were selected to receive Wing Project PRIDE awards for September.

In the fourth quarter, 1/Lt. James N. Parsons was Squadron Section Commander and Capt. Curtis A. Preston was the Historian. SMSgt. James P. Knight was the First Sergeant. First Lieutenant Mansi continued as the Maintenance Supervisor and CMSgt. Singleton continued as the Maintenance Superintendent.

The manning position of the squadron deteriorated, showing a net loss at the end of the quarter. Beginning in October, departures outnumbered arrivals. This trend continued throughout most of the quarter. Only in the last few days of December was there any indication that the manning situation would be rectified. The Phase Docks alone showed a net loss of 10 men. The primary mission of aircraft maintenance was adequately performed only through the tireless effort, devotion to duty, and personal pride in every individual assigned to the squadron.

Supply and Support

On 18 January, a significant change in the enlisted men's living quarters was made with the opening of two buildings with hot water showers and flush toilet facilities. This greatly increased the squadron morale. In March, inspectors from the base Fire Department surveyed the hootches. Most significant hazard discovered was that poor electrical wiring was still in many hootches. The Civil Engineers indicated that they were only awaiting a supply of the needed materials to do the rewiring. This lack of supplies existed in other projects also, e.g., in the building of sidewalks throughout the area.

The 555th Civil Engineering Squadron started building an extension to the Engine Shop in January. On 10 February, the structure was dedicated and opened for use. Although not much more than a wooden lean-to affixed to the hangar, it provided approximately 500 square feet of much-needed space. The lack of necessary power equipment delayed the opening of the new Communications/Navigation building indefinitely. Construction began in the middle of March on the AGE shop building to replace the deteriorating tent in which all AGE was being maintained. All in all, good progress was made in improving the squadron's facilities.

In the second quarter, the squadron was informed that its enlisted personnel would move from their hootches into two-story, 56-man barracks under construction in April. Pressured by the Military Assistance Command, Vietnam (MACV) to justify constructing these barracks, the Base Civil Engineer declared that the squadron would begin moving on 5 June. However, on that date no building was ready for occupancy. A firm schedule was then developed. New personnel who joined the squadron in the third quarter, the time of heavy personnel turnover, would move into the barracks and, as the present occupants of the hootches rotated and gradually vacated the hootches, those buildings would be destroyed. In the meantime, deficiencies noted in the hootches, such as substandard electrical wiring, went uncorrected.

Two construction projects begun much earlier were completed. A new building was dedicated and opened for the AGE Shop on 10 May.

On 12 June, a new building was opened to house the Communications/ Navigation Shop, the Instrument Shop, and the Survival Equipment Shop. This building was selected for the Wing Project PRIDE award for June. Also in June, work was begun on the nose docks to replace the ones presently used for Docks #3 and #4. Through self-help labor, the Hydraulic Shop repaired the room which was to be its Test and Repair Room. This facility waited only the installation of electrical power and air conditioning before it could be put to use. Significant improvements occurred in the squadron work areas.

On 23 September, Dock #3 was completed. The Base Civil Engineers accepted the new 56-man dormitories on 8 September. Buildings 4055, 4056, 4057, 4058, 4059, and 4060 were assigned to the 483 CAMS on 11 September. All squadron personnel who arrived on base during June, July, August, and early September were moved into the new dormitories. At the end of the quarter, 140 men were living in the new facilities. These new dormitories were considered adequate. However, open bay style dormitories allowed little personal privacy and the latrine facilities were insufficient in number to properly accommodate 56 men. In addition, heavy rains revealed several leaky roofs. Efforts to correct the deficiency continued until the end of the quarter. On 30 September, approximately 160 personnel were still living in the old and rapidly deteriorating hootch area. It was anticipated that normal rotation would completely empty the hootch area by the end of the year.

On 8 November, a self-help work order for the orderly room complex was approved by the Base Civil Engineers. In December, work was restarted on Phase Dock #4 which had been terminated earlier due to lack of funds. Completion was anticipated by the end of the quarter, but minor problems remained to be solved. Existing facilities were adequate to perform the mission. On 15 December, relocation of CAMS personnel to the new "super hootches" was completed. This marked the first time since 5 September that any enlisted personnel were located in a single dormitory area. Numerous self-help projects in the area of beautification were completed. The squadron orderly room and mail room were relocated adjacent to the barracks area. Work was started to convert discarded hootches to a squadron day-room, also adjacent to the living area. Work was also started to convert a discarded cold water shower to a unit gun room. The relocation of hootches was accomplished by Navy Seabees. Work on these activities continued after the end of the quarter.

Awards and Decorations

On 19 February, MSgt. Richard J. L. Keller was awarded the Air Force Commendation Medal. On 3 March, SSgt. Edgar A. McGinnis was chosen as the Maintenance Man of the Month for February. On 29 March, MSgt. Gordon E. Carpenter was awarded the Air Force Commendation Medal.

On 30 April, Sgt. Antone R. Coelho of the Communications/Navigation Branch was chosen as the squadron Maintenance Man of the Month for April. On 31 May, SSgt. Haron Ryals was chosen as the squadron Maintenance Man of the Month for May.

On 28 June, the following personnel were awarded the Bronze Star Medal: Maj. Monroe T. Smith (for recovering a C-7A in the field); TSgt. Vincent A. Verastro (for the recovery of C-7A S/N 61-2584 from Bu Krak); SSgt. Ralph M. Hanna; Sgt. Frank W. Kluthe, II; SSgt. William Osborne, Jr. (for the recovery of C-7A S/N 61-2584 from Bu Krak); and Sgt. Thomas C. Troiani. On 30 June, A/1C Kim D. Martin of the Engine Shop was chosen as the squadron Maintenance Man of the Month for June. Sgt. George A. Oliver was selected as A&E Mechanic of the second quarter.

On 29 July, SSgt. Ralph M. Hanna of the Engine Shop and SSgt. Frank M. Blas of the Hydraulic Shop received the Bronze Star Medal for maintenance support at Duc Phong.

On 1 August, A/1C William R. Steed of the Structural Repair Shop was chosen as the squadron Maintenance Man of the Month.

On 13 November, MSgt. Philip A. McKinley was presented the Air Force Commendation Medal by Brig. Gen. Herring, Commander of the 843AD.

Civic Action and Special Activities

In February, the squadron Security Police augmentees responded nightly to a base security alert. Their intensive training in the methods to use at their frequent exercises showed good results. Their sustained superior performance during the period won praise from the Base Commander.

In March, squadron personnel organized a team to contend in the base inter-squadron softball league. Interest in the team was high and large numbers of squadron personnel participated in the practice sessions. As the start of playing season approached, expectations to win the league championship grew.

At the end of June, the squadron team in the National League of the base softball league won seven games and lost seven. The team ranked fifth in a league of ten teams. Expectations to win the league championship dimmed, but interest in the team continued strong. Squadron personnel enjoyed the opportunity each game presented and teamwork formed in the shops.

On 21 December, two aircraft were decorated by the Corrosion Control Shop for Project "Santa Bou." By 31 December, the squadron basketball team had won one game and lost five. Squadron personnel enjoyed the opportunity to further the teamwork and cooperative spirit found on the job.

Commander's Summary

First Quarter, 1969 [8]

"From January through March of 1969, the 483rd Consolidated Aircraft Maintenance Squadron continued to perform its mission in an outstanding manner. The squadron enjoyed good manning during this period. Although many of its airmen were without prior experience on the C-7A, they quickly gained at least an elementary knowledge of the plane. Their highly professional effort of their jobs, and the efforts of all squadron personnel, contributed significantly to the records set by the Wing in effective tactical airlift."

Second Quarter, 1969 [9]

"From April through June of 1969, the 483rd Consolidated Aircraft Maintenance Squadron continued to perform its mission in an outstanding manner. The manning of the squadron was the best it had been in three quarters, not only in numbers but also in the important factor of experience. The improved maintenance facilities made a noticeable impact on successful mission performance. In the squadron, men and equipment joined to enable the 483rd Tactical Airlift Wing to constantly provide reliable support to the Free World Military Forces fighting in defense of Vietnam."

Third Quarter, 1969 [10]

"From July through September of 1969, the 483rd Consolidated Aircraft Maintenance Squadron continued to perform its mission in an outstanding manner. The manning of the squadron continued to be good, both in quality and quantity. The efforts of all squadron personnel contributed significantly to the accomplishment of the 483rd Tactical Airlift Wing mission."

Fourth Quarter, 1969 [11]

"From 1 October through 31 December 1969, the 483rd Consolidated Aircraft Maintenance Squadron continued to provide quality maintenance in an outstanding manner. The efforts of all squadron personnel contributed significantly to accomplishment of the 483rd Tactical Airlift Wing mission. The 483rd CAMS 'Good Guys' kept them flying."

End Notes: 483 CAMS

[1] *19690101-19691231 483 CAMS History*
[2] *483 CAMS Special Order G-1, dated 15 February 1969*
[3] *483 CAMS Special Order G-3, 30 August 1969*
[4] See the List of Acronyms (Appendix X) for the meaning of the codes.
[5] In the Air Force, a Class I modification is a change in the form, fit, or function of a system or component. A Class I change requires the approval of the System Manager or Item Manager. The System Manager for the C-7A was at Warner-Robins Air Material Area (WRAMA) at Robins AFB, GA
[6] *C-7A Caribou Association Newsletter, Vol. 20, Issue 1*
[7] *C-7A Caribou Association Newsletter, Vol. 1, Issue 14*
[8] *483 CAMS Commander's Summary, 31 Mar 1969* by Lt. Col. Ralph L. Peters
[9] *483 CAMS Commander's Summary, 30 June 1969* by Lt. Col. Ralph L. Peters
[10] *483 CAMS Commander's Summary, 30 September 1969* by Lt. Col. James W. Thompson
[11] *483 CAMS Commander's Summary, 31 December 1969* by Lt. Col. James W. Thompson

CAMS Hootches at CRB (Copyright © 2014 Jerry Presley)

6483rd TGP [1]

Mission

The 6483 Tactical Group Provisional (6483 TGP) was activated at Vung Tau Army Airfield effective 15 March 1969 under the following authorities:

a. Para 1, Special Order G-44, Headquarters (Hq.) Pacific Air Forces (PACAF), dated 3 March 1969 was the activation order.

b. Para 1, Special Order G-1, Hq 483rd Tactical Airlift Wing, dated 18 March 1969, appointed Lt. Col. James W. Buckley, Jr. as the first commander of the 6483 TGP.

c. Para 1 and 2, Special Order G-1153, Hq. Seventh Air Force, dated 24 March 1969, attached the 535 TAS, the 536 TAS, and the 483 CAMS OLAB to the TGP for command-and-control. In addition, this order attached the TGP to the 483 TAW for command-and-control.

"The primary mission of the 6483 Tactical Group Provisional is to command, maintain operational control, and be responsible for logistical and administrative functions for the two tactical squadrons at Vung Tau." This responsibility included maintenance, supply, and administration of the Inter-service Support Agreement. Additionally, the Commander, as the senior Air Force representative at Vung Tau Army Airfield, was responsible for all actions and functions at the base.

One officer was authorized and assigned. Ten officers, 68 airmen, and one civilian were attached.

On 1 August, Lt. Col. Clem B. Myers assumed command of the 6483 TGP[2] and he was subsequently replaced by Col. John J. Koehler on 5 September 1969.[3]

In the fourth quarter, one officer was authorized and assigned. Thirteen officers, 75 airmen, and two civilians were attached.

Safety

In the third quarter, Maj. Edwin H. Kohlhepp was Chief of Safety, but was reassigned to the 483 TAW as Flying Safety Officer. There was no immediate replacement, but an inbound Lt. Col. for the 535 TAS was slated to fill the position.

In the fourth quarter, Lt. Col. Wilson M. Petefish was assigned additional duty as the Chief of Safety. He established an Integrated Safety Council comprised of members from all organizations in the Group. The Council met in November and December. On 19-20 December, the 7AF Office of Safety made a safety staff assistance visit to the TGP and its subordinate units.

Flight Medicine

In the third quarter, Capt. Richard Weinberg was the Flight Medical Officer. In June, the Medical Aid Station (MAS) was authorized an interpreter/translator and the Local National Health program was subsequently expanded because of the improved communication between the medical unit and the local nationals employed by the USAF.

On 1 July, the MAS moved into its long awaited new facility in the USAF cantonment area. Besides providing more working space in a more sanitary facility, the new location proved to be much more convenient for those in need of medical services. Shortly thereafter, a small pharmacy and laboratory were added. One of the AFSC 901xx personnel was placed on OJT to do basic, routine laboratory procedures at the 36th Evacuation Hospital.

The MAS conducted on/off-base health inspections and prepared a new mimeograph health handout for incoming personnel. Important contributions were made to the Medical Civic Action Program (MEDCAP) and an additional MEDCAP at a local orphanage was undertaken. There were many improvements made during the quarter which Capt. Weinberg hoped would continue to set the pace for the future.

TSgt. (David) James Winters and Sgt. Craig M. Hoffman arrived in August and September, respectively, to replace TSgt. Albert E. Teasley and Sgt. Frederick D. Bynum.

Capt. Weinberg was replaced by Capt. Gary K. Borrell in October when Capt. Weinberg returned to the CONUS. A Rudmose audiometer was installed in the MAS, allowing the initiation of a hearing conservation program. The equipment needed to conduct a noise hazards survey was not available in Vietnam, but individuals at risk were identified by AFSC and carefully followed. In December, with the aid of a previously authorized interpreter, the office re-emphasized the need for basic laboratory data and immunizations for Vietnamese employees. Subsequently, those items were proceeding at a satisfactory rate.

Throughout the quarter, the MAS conducted on/off-base health inspections and continued MEDCAP visits to a local orphanage.

Administration

In the third quarter, the organization of the 6483 TGP served to support the 535 TAS, the 536 TAS, and the 483 OLAB and all support matters, either directly or indirectly, in the most efficient and expedient means practical. The Unit Detailed Listing (UDL) for the TGP authorized only the position of commander. All other personnel manning Group functions appeared on the UDL of the 535 TAS and those personnel were attached to the Group for duty by Special Orders.

The Administrative Services Officer was 1/Lt. John D. Seines, MSgt. John M. Cody was the First Sergeant, and 1/Lt. James N. Fujita was the Historian. Lt. Col. Adrian E. Powell was Chief of Plans with 1/Lt. Clifford E. Smith and 1/Lt. David M. Dudak as his assistants. The Administration Section suffered two AFSC 702X0 losses, but welcomed replacements Sgt. Robert M. Young and Sgt. Gregory K. Currier. The Disaster Control Team (DCT), under the leadership of MSgt. Cody, was fully manned throughout the quarter. Intensive training during practice and actual "Yellow Alert" conditions kept the DCT poised for action.

On 21 July, the mail distribution system for all Air Force personnel was consolidated and centrally located. As a result, hours of operation were extended to satisfy personnel for parcel pick-up.

TSgt. S. C. Peck was NCOIC of the Personnel Office. Sgt. Randolph L. Hay became NCOIC of the Finance Office, replacing SSgt. Michael H. Fletcher who returned to the CONUS. MSgt. Darrel C. Post was reassigned to the host CBPO at Cam Ranh Bay. During the quarter, 116 personnel out-processed and 95 were gained.

In the fourth quarter, 1/Lt. Ronald M. Scott was the Administrative Services Officer, replacing Lt. Seines and Lt. Col. Gould performed the duties of Historian. Lt. Col. Powell continued as Chief of Plans. Lieutenants Smith and Dudak were relieved of their duties in Plans on 1 December. TSgt. Roy F. Williams replaced MSgt. Cody as First Sergeant. Sgt. Young and Sgt. Currier continued as Administrative Clerks. A/1C Ron Holifield joined the section as Unit Mail Clerk, helping to alleviate some of the administrative workload carried by the two clerks. The 7AF IG inspection found only one discrepancy, attesting to the fine job performed by TSgt. Peck and Sgt. Hay.

On 2 December, Lt. Col. Powell was appointed Disaster Control Officer with TSgt. Clair C. Wolfgang, Jr. as Disaster Control NCO. Capt. Delivan B. Oswood (CAMS OLAB) was appointed Assistant Wing Mobility Officer and 1/Lt. Harris Keller was appointed Mobility Logistics Officer.

A Disaster Control Plan was drafted and prepared for publication at the end of the quarter. TSgt. Wolfgang conducted a series of Disaster Control briefings in conjunction with Commander's Call. Subjects covered were survival, use of protective equipment, and use of bunkered and revetted areas. A new Recall Plan (*OPLAN 301-70*) was published.

Personnel losses in the 535 TAS, 536 TAS, and CAMS OLAB totaled 193 personnel, while inputs totaled only 157.

Intelligence

In the third quarter, 1/Lt. James N. Fujita was the Intelligence Officer and MSgt. Charles A. Smith, Jr. was the Intelligence Technician. They demonstrated their excellent work, managerial ability, resourcefulness, and initiative in supporting the 535 TAS and 536 TAS. All incoming aircrew members were briefed on Escape and Evasion techniques, were issued appropriate Escape and Evasion aids, and were given current situation briefs on the Republic of Vietnam.

In July, an Intelligence Unit Assistance Team from 7AF visited the intelligence section to provide assistance and iron out any problems. One recurring problem mentioned was that of the requirement for aircrew photos and slides. Through the coordination of 7AF, the 483 TAW, and the 600th Photo Squadron, all aircrew members, upon arrival at Cam Ranh Bay for in-processing, would fulfill the requirements.

Lt. Fujita was able to visit the intelligence offices on the 483 TAW, the 834AD, and 7AF. He was impressed with higher-level operations and recommended that each airman, NCO, and officer in the intelligence field have the opportunity to tour and visit with other intelligence agencies in Vietnam after being in-country for a few months.

MSgt. Smith's knowledge in the field of intelligence and security would be sorely missed when he rotated at the end of the quarter. There was no information about his replacement.

In the fourth quarter, TSgt. Luis. L. Regalado was in charge of the Group Intelligence Office after the departure of 1/Lt. Fujita. Up to date and timely intelligence data was continually provided to both the 535 TAS and 536 TAS. All incoming aircrew members were provided briefings on Escape and Evasion techniques, issued appropriate E&E aids, and given current situation briefs on the Republic of Vietnam.

Supply and Support

In the latter part of August, Lt. Col. Jack K. Gould replaced Lt. Col. James C. Hilbert as the Deputy for Support, attached to the 6483 TGP. Lt. Col. Gould continued in the position of Deputy for Support through the end of the year. The Deputy for Support function controlled the majority of personnel attached to the Group for duty. Support functions included: a Supply Branch, a Food Service Branch, a Transportation Branch, a Fuels Management Branch, a Security Branch, a Civil Engineering Branch, and a Civilian Personnel Office.

Supply Branch: 1/Lt. Robert E. Frank, Jr. was transferred from the staff of the 483 TAW Deputy Commander for Materiel (DCM) to the 535 TAS and was attached to the Group as OIC of the Supply Branch, replacing Capt. James M. Calloway. SMSgt. Paul A. Lunday arrived and replaced SMSgt. James R. Lovin as NCOIC of the Supply Branch. The branch experienced a 60 percent turnover of personnel during the third quarter.

Supply support from the host Base Supply at Tan Son Nhut Air Base was generally good in spite of the inherent problems associated with the location and distance to the forward operating location (Vung Tau). The Supply Branch depended entirely on the "Red Ball Express" convoy system to haul in supplies and ensure that no property was lost in shipment. Twelve round trips were made with 133,000 pounds of cargo transported to Tan Son Nhut (primarily excess property) and 100,000 pounds were transported to Vung Tau.

Vehicle spares support was good, but the poor condition of the fleet increased the burden of keeping them operational. The biggest problem encountered was the inability to get parts for two 4000 pound warehouse tugs and having to cannibalize parts from them to keep a third one operating. Aggressive follow-up did not get satisfactory assistance.

A program was started in September to turn in all excess Equipment Authorization Inventory Data (EAID) equipment to Tan Son Nhut. All ASC-000 (excess not authorized) items were turned in, along with some items which were not authorized and were on hand in excess of needs. The goal of the program was to simplify equipment accounting records and to make needed storage space available for essential equipment and supplies. During September, the Tool Issued Center crib within the Supply Branch was completely inventoried, all bins were relabeled, and new levels of on-hand tools were established to match the number of toolboxes authorized in the maintenance complex. All excess tools were turned in to Tan Son Nhut.

Food Service Branch: The mess hall was officially dedicated and opened in June and continued to provide excellent meals. During the quarter, there were 24,040 breakfasts served; 24,626 dinners served; and 23,677 suppers served. The average daily ration was 262. Several innovations were made to improve conditions in the mess hall. A can sanitizer was installed in the trash storage area for use in steam cleaning cans after garbage pickup. A swinging door was installed between the kitchen and dining room to facilitate the restocking of milk and juice dispensers. Two new gas ranges were installed in the kitchen to expedite preparation of meals for Air Force patrons. In early August, the food service personnel participated in a self-help beautification project on the grounds of the mess hall. A rock garden was arranged, giving the area a very pleasant atmosphere.

Transportation Branch: CMSgt. Paul E. Vied arrived in July and was assigned as NCOIC of the Transportation Branch. During the quarter, there were 95,876 miles driven with no reportable accidents. The Vehicle Maintenance Section performed 17 scheduled Safety Inspections and 341 scheduled maintenance tasks. At the beginning of the quarter, there were 11 Vehicles Down for Parts (VDP), declining to 5 at the end of the quarter. The Vehicles Down for Maintenance (VDM) rate was 1.7 for the quarter.

Numerous innovations were introduced to improve operations. Six-passenger pickup trucks were equipped with box covers and seats and used as buses during certain low passenger times, saving wear and tear on the two 29 passenger buses. The potable water delivery schedules to the three hotels occupied by USAF personnel (Blue Villa, Vung Tau, and Duy Tan) were changed from morning to evening. As a result, water was immediately available at the airfield with no waiting in line to fill the delivery tanker at the fill stands. In addition, vehicle maintenance personnel accompanied each of the 12 "Red Ball Express" supply convoys from Vung Tau to Tan Son Nhut and back. Their mission was threefold: to act as armed guards enroute, to provide a maintenance repair capability in the event of a breakdown of any of the vehicles, and to provide the experience necessary to find and acquire suitable substitutes from Base Supply for vehicle spares requisitions.

Fuels Management Branch: The Fuels Management Branch provided refueling service of 115/145 aviation gas (AVGAS) and oil to all branches of service possessing reciprocating engine aircraft at Vung Tau Army Airfield. Service was provided to: USAF aircraft (two C-7A squadrons, O-1C, and O-2A Forward Air Controller aircraft), U.S. Army aircraft (U-6A, U-1A, O-1G, O-1D, and U-1U), Royal Australian Air Force (one C-7A squadron), Pacific Architecture & Engineering (PA&E) aircraft (two C-7A aircraft), and transient aircraft (USAF C-47D and C-123K; USN C-117 and UH-34; USA O-1E, U-10B, and OH-23). The branch issued 281,042 gallons 115/145 AVGAS in July; 265,871 gallons in August; and 225,271 gallons in September. During July, 7595 gallons of aviation oil were issued; 7957 gallons in August, and 7642 gallons in September. Aviation gas service was provided for 1587 aircraft in July, 1472 aircraft in August, and 1043 aircraft in September. Aviation oil service was provided for 684 aircraft in July, 780 aircraft in August, and 670 aircraft in September. An average of 82 transient aircraft per month were provided with service, for a quarterly total of 247.

Maintenance support of the refueling vehicles was excellent. A rate of 94 percent of vehicles in commission was maintained. One R-2 refueling vehicle was VDP for an engine at the end of the quarter.

The POL dispatch facility and refueling fleet were equipped with radios during the quarter, eliminating runs back and forth to the dispatch shack for fueling instructions. Therefore, the dispatcher was able to direct refueling trucks to the next customer in accordance with call-in priorities and provide better and faster service.

A project to provide electrical power and water to the POL maintenance and dispatch facility was approved and funded by 7AF. Installation date of 15 October was sent. Upon completion of the work, the dispatch function would be moved into the new building. Another project, laying a hard surface around the POL maintenance building was sent to 7AF, but had not been approved by the end of the quarter. The lack of hard surfacing will not preclude the movement into or operation from the facility.

In the fourth quarter, upon completion of the installation of electrical power and water, the POL branch moved into its new facility by the dispatch office, driver's lounge, and latrine with a three stall, covered, drive-through POL vehicle maintenance facility. No word had been received by the end of the quarter from 7AF relative to approval of the project to hard surface a POL vehicle parking area adjacent to the new POL facility.

The branch continued to provide 115/145 aviation gas and oil servicing to all units based at Vung Tau Army Airfield plus transient aircraft of all services. In October, 244,615 gallons of AVGAS were issued; 226,846 gallons in November; and 251,369 gallons in December. In October, 500 gallons of aviation oil were issued; 574 gallons in November; and 676 gallons in December. Two hundred eighty-seven aircraft received service during the quarter, averaging 95 per month.

Supply shortages of parts for the antiquated POL vehicle fleet contributed to the high VDP rate for the quarter. Command interest was created and word was received that at least one depot-overhauled R-2 refueler would be redistributed from Da Nang to Vung Tau for use by the branch.

Civil Engineering Branch: TSgt. Leonard Sheppard was NCOIC of the branch. A number of self-help projects were completed in the third quarter, contributing greatly to the health and welfare of the Air Force personnel stationed at Vung Tau. The projects included:

1. Construction of a metal roof over the walk-in refrigerators at the rear of the mess hall to provide protection for the "reefers" to improve overall efficiency by an estimated 40 percent.

2. A small screened-in building with running potable water was constructed at the rear of the mess hall for use by the kitchen personnel in the preparation and cleaning of fresh vegetables.

3. An enclosed patio was constructed adjacent to the mess hall, complete with two stone-faced barbecue pits, picnic tables, and benches. It was available to all assigned and attached Air Force personnel.

4. Laundry facilities, consisting of a concrete slab with a lean-to roof and several water faucets, were constructed adjacent to latrines in two quarters areas for use by *mama sans* doing laundry for enlisted personnel.

5. An outdoor recreation area adjacent to the "Red Horse" quarters area was under construction. An outdoor theater was completed and, upon receipt of projection equipment from Special Services, nightly movies would be shown. Under construction were horseshoe pitching pits and a combination volleyball/basketball court.

6. To promote taxiing safety on the C-7A parking ramp, a method was devised for painting wide yellow stripes on the two main taxiways. Parts of the area which were very stable were painted using parallel boards and a roller. The less stable portions, which had reverted to gravel, were drip painted.

7. Materials and labor were provided for the installation of eight double screen doors at the An Phong Orphanage in Vung Tau to protect the children from flies and mosquitoes. This was part of a community relations effort and was done in conjunction with the MEDCAP activities of the Flight Medical Officer.

In the fourth quarter, TSgt. Wolfgang replaced TSgt. Sheppard as NCOIC of the Civil Engineering Branch when TSgt. Sheppard rotated. The more significant projects completed during the quarter were:

1. The West wing of Building T-124, formally the 535 TAS mess hall, was completely renovated to house the 535 TAS Operations and Orderly Room. Salvaged material was used to construct partitions and to provide semi-private office spaces. A new operations counter and storage counter were constructed. The building was painted throughout, all windows were secured, and air conditioning was installed. This project improved the operational efficiency and morale of personnel in the 535 TAS.

2. Air conditioning was installed in Building T-240, the USAF dining hall, alleviating the problem of sand and dust blowing through

the screened areas and creating an unsanitary condition. The interior paneling was painted white and created a very attractive dining area. This work contributed greatly to the comfort, health, and morale of the people using and working in the facility.

3. Due to the termination of the lease contract for the Blue Villa, which housed the senior NCOs living off base, Building T-249 was chosen to house these personnel on base. Room interiors were painted to improve the appearance.

4. Bunkers, constructed several years ago, were found to be deteriorating and were repaired to maintain them in a safe condition to protect personnel from enemy attack. Six additional dive-in revetments were constructed to provide protection for auxiliary guards during increased security conditions.

5. A weapon storage room was constructed in the Duy Tan Hotel which houses the officers of the 535 TAS. The storage room replaced the half CONEX adjacent to the building which had been used to store weapons and ammunition in case of enemy attack.

6. Three large clothesline poles were constructed from steel pipe and installed adjacent to the *mama-san* wash rack area. Previously, clothes were hung on barbed wire fences and were being torn. Many clothes were strung up in a haphazard manner which could result in serious injury to personnel during hours of darkness.

Security Branch: Detachment 1 of the 377th Security Police Squadron continued to provide internal security for the C-7A parking area. MSgt. Robert L. Landis, Detachment Commander, did an outstanding job in providing the required security coverage with a reduced force of guard personnel. The manning authorization was reduced from 34 to 20 personnel. The men were assigned to Vung Tau for six month tours. The personnel turnover was approximately four or five men per month. The Detachment provided an additional, valuable service to the 6483 TGP in that they posted the USAF military augmentee guards at night at the hotels and villas in Vung Tau City. They also provided supervisory assistance to the Local National gate guards on duty at the hotels, villas, and the 1876 Communication Squadron Operating Location facility at Back Beach.

From 14-18 September, the 6483 TGP helped sponsor a Security Police Conference held at Vung Tau by providing them with a place to meet, equipment for briefings, and refreshments.

In the fourth quarter, MSgt. Landis and his 20 man guard force continued to provide round-the-clock protection of the C-7A parking ramp and maintenance hangar areas. Guard personnel were replaced by the parent unit at the rate of 4 or 5 a month.

MSgt. Landis performed a real service for the 19th TASS Detachment ("Jade" FAC) on Christmas Eve when one of their O-2A aircraft crashed near the southeast end of the main runway at Vung Tau. He proceeded to the accident scene on his own initiative and provided security for the crash site, using flares to light the area for the crash rescue team, and then assisting in the recovery of the classified radio equipment in the downed aircraft.

Civilian Personnel Office: The Annual Classification Survey of the Local National Civilian positions was conducted on 17-18 September. Results of the survey indicated that 17 of the 44 authorized civilian positions needed reclassification based on new job descriptions as listed in the Job Description Manual. There were six paydays for the Local Civilians during the quarter. On each occasion, an officer from one of the assigned squadrons at Vung Tau was designated as the Class "A" Agent Finance Officer and sent to Tan Son Nhut Air Base to pick up the Vietnamese Piasters to pay the civilian employees at the Group. Miss Vu Thi Cap from the Civilian Personnel Office assisted in the actual paying of civilians by providing recognition and interpretive assistance.

In the fourth quarter, civilian personnel manning was reduced by three spaces by a directed reduction in force (RIF) of Local National food service personnel. There were seven civilian personnel paydays during the quarter. For the last three paydays, the Finance Office at Tan Son Nhut sent enlisted paymasters to Vung Tau to perform the service in lieu of utilizing Air Force officers detailed to perform the task.

Supply Branch: When 1/Lt. Harris Keller was transferred from the 483 TAW and assigned as Supply Officer, he replaced 1/Lt. Frank who returned to the CONUS. SMSgt. Lunday continued as NCOIC of the Supply Branch and signed for the accounts. He was acting Supply Officer for the interim time from the departure of Lt. Frank and the arrival of Lt. Keller.

Normal rotations, directed transfer of supply personnel to Base Supply of the 12th Combat Support Group, and the input of new personnel resulted in the Branch never reaching authorized strength. The quarter ended with 16 authorized and 14 assigned. An additional building, adjacent to the supply compound, was obtained in November and converted to a warehouse for storage of bulk supplies. Utilization of this facility eliminated much congestion in other facilities and provided protection for property formerly stored outside. Inventory of 30 of the 53 EAID accounts was performed by the custodians and inventory personnel. The total value was $812,676 in use and $934,466 authorized.

Supply support from the host Base Supply of the 377th Combat Support Group at Tan Son Nhut was generally good except in the areas of local purchase items and vehicle spares. A number of vehicles were carried on the "Hangar Queen" report (VDP over 60 days) including a crew bus and several tugs critical to the OLAB Maintenance Section.

A marked decrease was recorded in the weight of cargo transported by supply convoy between Vung Tau and Tan Son Nhut. Thirty-six thousand pounds were delivered to Tan Son Nhut and 35,000 pounds of serviceable items were brought to Vung Tau in 12 round trips. Reductions were a result of budget limitations and heavy elimination of excess property during the quarter.

The Vehicle Parts Store and its related Material Control were completely reorganized and re-warehoused in an effort to give better control of parts and better availability and responsiveness to needs. A bench stock parts list was identified and submitted to the host base for approval.

Food Service Branch: A slight reduction was experienced in the total number of meals served in the fourth quarter, compared to the third quarter. There were 18,967 breakfasts served; 27,210 dinners served; and 23,370 suppers served. The average daily ration was 257. The breakfast meal showed the greatest reduction and overshadowed an increase in new dinners. Outstanding holiday meals were served on both Thanksgiving and Christmas. The dining hall was appropriately decorated for both occasions. Many favorable comments were received for the quality of the meals and the pleasant atmosphere created for these traditional holidays.

A new coffee maker was received and installed in November and the milk dispenser and one stove and one grill were replaced with new equipment. The dining hall was equipped with air-conditioning in December which not only added to the comfort of the patrons, but eliminated dust entering through formerly louvered and screened areas.

TSgt. Arlus Hensley assumed the duties of NCOIC when MSgt. Albert H. Patton rotated. The branch suffered a reduction in authorization of Local National kitchen help and three personnel were terminated. Food Service personnel participated in a spruce-up self-help project and painted the structure over the patio and the fence around the dining hall.

Transportation Branch: CMSgt. Vied continued as the NCOIC; however, he was out of country on a 30 day emergency leave from

16 October to 15 November. In his absence, TSgt. Virgil Townsend acted as NCOIC. CMSgt. Vied took his 30 day tour extension leave commencing 18 December and SSgt. Charles E. Cornish carried on as NCOIC. During the quarter, there were 112,195 miles driven, 138 driving permits processed, and no reportable accidents. The Vehicle Maintenance Section performed 16 scheduled Safety Inspections and 348 scheduled maintenance tasks. During the quarter, there were 20 Vehicles Down for Parts (VDP), ending the quarter at 12. The Vehicles Down for Maintenance (VDM) rate was 1.3.

With the move of the POL branch into its new facility, adjacent to the flight line, there was sufficient covered POL vehicle maintenance space to do all refueling equipment repair and overhaul. This eliminated a safety hazard from the congested area of the general-purpose vehicle maintenance area. One mechanic was assigned on a full-time basis to perform the required refueling and vehicle maintenance at the new POL facility. Facilities improvements included painting the interior of the tire shop and reorganizing the storage of tires.

Civic Action and Special Activities

On 5 July, Brig. Gen. John H. Herring Jr., the new 834th Air Division commander, visited the Air Force units on an orientation tour. On 20 September, Brig. Gen. Herring visited Vung Tau to participate in an Awards and Decorations ceremony and to visit other VIPs.

On 25-29 in November, the 7AF Inspector General team conducted its annual inspection of the TGP and its subordinate units. The Group and its units received an overall rating of "Satisfactory."

On 24-25 December, the annual "Santa Bou" missions were flown in conjunction with other 483 TAW squadrons. Each squadron decorated a C-7A aircraft with a comical likeness of Santa Claus on its nose. Thousands of pounds of gifts furnished by the USO, Red Cross, and squadron donations were delivered. Brig. Gen. Herring, 834AD Commander, visited the Vung Tau Army Airfield on 24 December to observe the "Santa Bou" operation.

Commander's Summary

No summary by the Commander was included in the histories.

End Notes: 6483 TGP

[1] *19690701-19691231 483 CAMS OLAB History*
[2] 6483 TGP Special Order M-14, dated 1 August 69
[3] 6483 TGP Special Order M-20, dated 5 September 69

483rd CAMS OLAB [1]

Mission

The primary mission was to "accomplish the functions of Field Maintenance, Communications/Navigation, and phase inspections for the 535 and 536 Tactical Airlift Squadrons (TAS) at Vung Tau." With the exception of engine buildup, which was accomplished/performed by the 483 CAMS at Cam Ranh Bay, all heavy shop maintenance and specialist maintenance required on the C-7A aircraft assigned at Vung Tau was accomplished by OLAB. Furthermore, OLAB maintains all AGE.

To accomplish this mission, the squadron was authorized 189 personnel in the third quarter. The number of personnel assigned was 189 at the end of July, 188 at the end of August, and 184 at the end of September. In the fourth quarter, the squadron was authorized 189 personnel. The number of personnel assigned was 168 at the end of October, 166 at the end of September, and 188 at the end of December.

Maintenance

In the third quarter, Maj. Wallace H. Little, Maintenance Control Officer, departed PCS and was replaced by Capt. John T. Woods. When Lt. Col. Pat D. Brinson departed PCS, Capt. Woods assumed the duties of Chief of Maintenance. Capt. Delivan B. Oswood was OIC of Field Maintenance. SMSgt. Samuel A. Hines was Maintenance Superintendent and SSgt. Dwight Walker was NCOIC of Maintenance Administration. TSgt. Howard A. Beck was NCOIC of the Aerospace Systems Branch and TSgt. George S. Moteki was NCOIC of the Accessories Branch.

Plans and Scheduling operated a centralized debriefing in the new flight line maintenance building. SSgt. Bobby R. Marion was loaned to Job Control from the Analysis Section. A MSgt. Maintenance Controller departed PCS. Offices were under construction which would enable Maintenance Control to be located on the ground floor. These offices were expected to be occupied during the fourth quarter.

In Material Control, MSgt. Joseph Hatton was the NCOIC. The bench stock fill rate held between 80 percent and 85 percent. However, the critical items were still obtainable only by ANORS/GNORS. Brake pucks, ramp jackscrews, ramp door actuators, small augmentor tube clamps, cowling latches, pins, and springs caused the most NORS conditions. The section had nine personnel rotate and it received nine replacements, leaving the section fully manned.

259

In the fourth quarter, Maj. Richard H. Lewis was the Chief of Maintenance and CMSgt. Shifflett continued as NCOIC, Chief of Maintenance. Capt. Oswood continued as OIC of Field Maintenance and SMSgt. Hines as Maintenance Superintendent. SMSgt. Clarence Bauer was the Field Maintenance Superintendent. All excess property in the shops was turned in, approximately 800 items valued at $10,000. Maintenance Control was relocated to the main floor of Hangar S-1 and completely revetted.

In December, MSgt. Bobbie J. Spears was NCOIC of Material Control. MSgt. William Holman was NCOIC of the Aerospace Systems Branch.

Three aircraft were extensively decorated with Christmas paintings for missions to Special Forces camps. The aircraft were marked with "Santa Bou" and red noses (radomes). The propellers were painted with a candy stripe pattern and the fuselage with "Merry Christmas" and snowflakes. Christmas cheer packages were delivered throughout the Special Forces area of operation.

AGE Shop: In the third quarter, TSgt. Donald MacDonald was NCOIC of the shop. SSgt. Peter G. Leith and A/1C Ray O. Mulholland repaired an MB-8 air compressor and rewired the unit to operate in a cycling manner, prolonging its life. Six of seven MC-2A air compressors were converted to the new reciprocating compressor, ensuring better support for both shops and the flight line. While on an intra-country R&R, A/1C Joseph A. Ryan was responsible for the return of a MC-2A air compressor which had been taken by an Army unit. Upon spotting this unit, even though it had been painted, Airman Ryan reported it and returned with the unit. He was named Outstanding Field Maintenance Man of the Month for August. The shop lost four men and gained eight.

In the fourth quarter, TSgt. Donald MacDonald continued as NCOIC of the shop. The office was painted, including the floor and walls. The old, open wooden bins that gathered dust and cobwebs were replaced by metal cabinets with drawers. In addition to the bench stock items, the cabinets had ample space for parts ordered for specific units. Although the squadron was without a qualified painter for approximately one month and a half, the shop was able to repaint 12 units. This was almost 25 percent of the assigned units.

Aero Repair Shop: In the fourth quarter, the Repair and Reclamation shop assisted in 99 phase inspections involving some major and minor repairs. In November, TSgt. Gerald W. Spelde was NCOIC of the shop. During November and December, TCTO 1C-7A-598, "Inspection of Elevators and Elevator Torque Tubes," was accomplished. The torque tubes were found to be unserviceable and were reworked for the shop by the Army depot ship, *Corpus Christi*. Two control column torque tubes were also removed and replaced. The shop was involved in the activation of the wing and tail deicer system, propeller deicer, heater, and oxygen systems.

The fuel cell work during the quarter consisted primarily of fuel stains and leaks on aircraft during phase inspection. The largest number of hours expended for any one job was the installation and removal of ferry tanks. Having only one man assigned to fuel cell repair caused long hours to be expended at times. During December, SSgt. Lester L. Dates was sent TDY to an airfield where the C-7A was down due to contaminated fuel. The situation involved flushing out the system three times and then refueling with serviceable fuel for the return trip.

The shop lost three people and gained eight. The remainder of the more experienced personnel were scheduled to depart in January 1970.

Communications/Navigation Shop: In the third quarter, SMSgt. Oliver D. McElroy was NCOIC of the shop. He was named the Outstanding Armament-Electronics Man of the Month for August. In the fourth quarter, MSgt. L. D. Frost was NCOIC of the shop. The shop lost one SMSgt. (AFSC 30195), three AFSC 30151's, two AFSC 30130's, three AFSC 30131's, and one AFSC 30150. One AFSC 30130 was upgraded to the 5-level. The frequency counter was awaiting parts at PMEL for 73 days. The in-shop backlog of repairable equipment increased over 200 man-hours during the last weeks of December due to shortage of skilled personnel and the increase of unscheduled maintenance on the flight line. Two AFSC 30151's on TDY from Cam Ranh Bay helped out for four days to relieve the backlog.

Corrosion Control and Paint Shop: In the third quarter, the Corrosion Control shop performed 35 inspections. Some extensive corrosion problems were found, but most were of a minor variety. The Paint Shop was terminated and the two personnel were assigned to Corrosion Control. In the fourth quarter, the shop lost three men and gained three. The shop was completely rearranged and painted. Three C-7A aircraft were painted for the yearly Santa Bou project. Two were painted with water colors and one with lacquer. After adequate drying time, the water colors held up well.

Electric Shop: In the third quarter, the shop had 11 TDYs for maintenance at forward bases. The shop assisted with the completion of TCTO 1C-7A-596, "Inspection of C-7A Main Landing Gear Housings for Cracks," on all assigned aircraft. Nine radar inverters were repaired that otherwise would have been ordered ANORS. The shop lost four personnel and received two replacements.

In the fourth quarter, TSgt. Lester R. Gerber was NCOIC of the shop. Shop personnel participated in a total of eight recoveries of C-7A aircraft. A small building was moved to a location near the electric shop and was remodeled for use as a battery shop. An emergency shower was installed near this building. The B-8 rectifier, used to run all the equipment in the shop, was out of commission for parts throughout the quarter. Eighteen reverse current relays on the C-7A were replaced because of burned contacts and resistors. The shop lost three people and gained four.

Engine Shop: In the third quarter, the shop accomplished 18 engine changes. Eight were accomplished at forward locations. Due to high quality maintenance, the average engine life was 932 hours. A total of 37 cylinder changes were accomplished. The reasons for changing the cylinders were: 13 for low compression, 11 for valve malfunctions, 6 for leaking intake bosses, 5 for not repairable integral studs and bearings, and 2 for cracked cylinder heads. The shop completed 551 unscheduled work orders, 190 in July, 185 in August, and 176 in September. Repeat write-ups were negligible, with only eight for the entire quarter.

One hundred and twenty-four phase inspections were completed with an average of one Quality Control discrepancy per inspection. Three special tools were devised and put in use. One was a special plate to cover the carburetor opening mounting pad on the impeller section of the engine when not in use or during maintenance. Another was a tool to tighten the front standpipe on the engine for the sump assembly. The last was a special plate to cover the magneto drive padding gear when not in use or during maintenance.

Ten personnel were upgraded, six to the 7-level and four to the 5-level. Three personnel were lost and three were gained. One man was on loan for fuel cell work and one was transferred from the shop for a physical disability.

In the fourth quarter, the shop lost nine personnel and gained nine. It participated in 14 recovery missions and changed a total of 22 R-2000 engines. Average engine life at Vung Tau was better than 1100 hours compared to a Wing average of 900 hours and a life expectancy of 750 hours. A building was prepared to store and secure serviceable engines. In December, MSgt. Robert W. Lowdermilk was NCOIC of the shop.

Fabrication Branch: MSgt. Roy R. Wright was branch chief in
262

the third quarter. The six Vietnamese on the wash rack were terminated by the Air Force. This increased the workload of flight line personnel. MSgt. Wright continued as branch chief in the fourth quarter.

Fabric Shop: The shop received a new sewing machine during the third quarter, greatly increasing the repair capability. The shop inspected 210 life preservers and 120 life rafts. Numerous repairs were made on the life preservers and nine were condemned. In September, SSgt. Larry O. Overcash was assigned to the shop. In the fourth quarter, shop personnel inspected and repacked 120 LRU 3/P life rafts and 450 LPU 2/P life preservers. They manufactured 30 water jug holder straps.

Hydraulic Shop: In the third quarter, the shop had 26 TDYs, mostly for landing gear malfunctions. The most significant was C-7A S/N 63-9742. The left main landing gear and all its components had to be replaced due to the aircraft landing at Ben Hoa with a gear up. The shop assisted with the completion of TCTO 1C-7A-596, "Inspection of C-7A Main Landing Gear Housings for Cracks," on all assigned aircraft.

In the fourth quarter, the shop lost three men and gained two. Three men were sent TDY pending PCS, but one of these returned to Cam Ranh Bay. Eight TDYs were supported to forward operating locations. During most of October, the shop had only three men assigned and many hours of overtime were put in. At the beginning of the quarter, the availability of brake linings caused work stoppage on brakes. At the end of the quarter, a work stoppage was caused by a shortage of grips.

Instrument Shop: In the third quarter, the shop set up the new torque testers and the PMEL calibrated them. Quality Control performed an activity inspection on the shop, making only two write-ups, both of which were on technical orders. There were no TDYs during the quarter. Three new men arrived and one man departed.

In the fourth quarter, the shop lost one man on emergency leave. The gains were one SSgt., one Sgt., and two A/1C. SSgt. Chappell was upgraded to the 7-level. The shop experienced a rash of fuel quantity malfunctions caused by inoperative fuel quantity indicators. No cause of the indicator failure was found.

Machine Shop: In the third quarter, the shop continued its excellent support of aircraft and AGE. The appearance of the shop was improved by the rework of termite-infested portions of the walls. The shop saved approximately 27 engine changes during the quarter and manufactured and installed numerous bushings.

In the fourth quarter, the assigned machinist rearranged all cabinets and work tables. He manufactured precision bushings for AGE equipment that had to be within .0005 of an inch and modified a hydraulic press so that the bushings in the nose gear and main gear torque arms could be replaced easier and quicker. The shop replaced more than 100 exhaust studs on the 32 C-7A aircraft. The shop received a new milling machine. All equipment was painted and all drawers were rearranged and labeled. One man was lost and one was gained.

Phase Maintenance Section: In the third quarter, the docks performed 104 phase inspections. Results of Quality Control inspections showed a slight increase in write-ups due to added emphasis on the landing gear system. Write-ups by Quality Control increased from an average of two per aircraft in July to an average of four per aircraft in August and remained stable during September.

In August, SMSgt. Lee E. Wettstein was assigned as Phase Dock Superintendent. Significant losses were TSgt. Charles L. Heick, Dock #1 Chief, who transferred to Quality Control; SSgt. Richard L. Smith, Dock #3 Chief, and Sgt. Donald R. Privett, Dock #2 Chief, who completed their tours. At the end of the quarter, all Dock Chief positions were filled with 5-levels who were performing satisfactory inspections. Manning at the end of the quarter became critical and was expected to become acute during October and November due to projected losses. All eligible 3-level personnel were upgraded to the 5-level. Training continued and greater emphasis was placed on safety, technical data, and MSEP.

In the fourth quarter, SMSgt. Wettstein continued as Phase Dock Superintendent. The section completed 99 phase inspections with a slight increase in overall discrepancies due to added emphasis on phase time standards and operations. All personnel previously in OJT completed training requirements and upgraded in their AFSC. Manning was critical during the entire period, but became acute in November and December. Three men arrived TDY to assist with the manning shortage. Replacements were slow in arriving, causing 12 to 14 hour days, 7 days a week.

Dock Chiefs were lost in September and October and they were not replaced until the latter part of December. A parts shortage occurred during the same period, resulting in increased cannibalization and dock time. Although the dock offices and areas were repainted and standardized, the overall quality of production was satisfactory.

The 7AF IG team inspection in December rated the phase dock as "Satisfactory." The outlook for 1970 looked good, with new personnel scheduled to arrive. Some existing supply problems were expected to improve with assistance from the 483 TAW and 7AF. Emphasis in the future would be placed on OJT of newly assigned personnel and continued focus on safety, technical data, and MSEP.

Propeller Shop: In the third quarter, the shop supported 92 phase inspections. The shop sent personnel TDY 19 times to support aircraft at forward locations. Eighty propeller and/or Integral Oil Controls were removed and replaced or reinstalled. Some were for time change and some were to facilitate other maintenance on the engine. One new man was assigned to the shop and one departed.

In October, MSgt. David O'Melia was NCOIC of the shop. The shop had a 70 percent turnover in personnel in the fourth quarter. At the end of the quarter, there were 10 people assigned. An extensive OJT program for both the 5- and 7-level AFSCs was active. The program plan was to continue throughout 1970. Personnel in the shop accomplished seven aircraft recoveries from various airfields. The number of changes of the drive brackets increased. This item caused approximately 60 propellers to be removed and reinstalled during phase inspections. The following items were removed and replaced during the quarter: 29 control and brush pad assemblies, 10 propeller assemblies, 2 slip ring assemblies, and 2 auxiliary pump motors.

Propulsion Branch: In the third quarter, MSgt. William C. Cornish was NCOIC of the branch. In the fourth quarter, SMSgt. W. D. Wheeler was NCOIC of the branch.

Repair and Reclamation Shop: In the third quarter, the shop assisted on approximately 105 phase inspections. In compliance with TCTO 1C-7A-596, sixty-seven landing gears were removed and reinstalled. Ten nose landing gears were changed as a result of failures and several flight control surfaces were removed and replaced. Shop personnel assisted on numerous landing gear retraction tests. Shop personnel were sent TDY on numerous occasions to recover aircraft at forward operating locations. One significant recovery was that of C-7A S/N 63-9742 which had a gear up landing. The shop lost four personnel due to completion of tours and received no replacements.

Sheet Metal Shop: In the fourth quarter, the shop lost seven men and gained seven. All shop equipment was painted and attached to the floor or benches. The shop manufactured 32 water jug holders.

Structural Repair Shop: In the third quarter, the shop received a pneumatic cherry rivet gun. This gun increased the repair capability and efficiency. The most significant repair was performed on C-7A S/N 63-9742, which had a gear up landing. The shop received two SSgts.

and one A/1C during the quarter.

Welding Shop: In the third quarter, the shop was manned with only one SSgt. during most of the quarter. One Sergeant was assigned late in the quarter. Many man-hours were expended in repair of augmentor tubes and short stacks. In the fourth quarter, the shop lost one man and gained one. The assigned welder completely repainted the shop. He welded 42 maintenance stands and all toolbox hinges for the flight line, docks, and field maintenance. He also welded 25 chains for the Air Force dining hall.

Wheel and Tire Shop: In the third quarter, the shop built up over 500 tires and remodeled the shop. The degreaser was hooked up, but was still inoperative due to lack of a degreasing solution. A light was received for inspection of cracked wheels; however, the light was of no use because no bulb was received.

In the fourth quarter, the shop built up 117 main wheels and 81 nose wheels. There was a shortage of nose wheels and the shop was working with only five extras. Several wheels were returned to the depot with cracks. An addition was made to the tire shop to house the degreaser acquired last quarter. Two personnel reported in to replace two men scheduled to depart in January 1970.

A/1C Thomas D. Orwick was named Outstanding Armament-Electronics Man in August and A/1C Adrian Vuletic was named Outstanding Tactical Squadron Mechanic of the Month for August. SSgt. John F. McLeod was named Wing Outstanding A&E Mechanic of the third quarter. For November, A/1C Walter T. Lambert was named Field Maintenance Man of the Month, A/1C Dennis L. Forer was named Communication-Navigation Maintenance Man of the Month, and A/1C James Tabares was named TAS Maintenance Man of the Month. SSgt. Richard P. Bernsen was named Field Maintenance Man of the Month for December and TSgt. Oran E. DeRemer was named Communications-Electronics Man of the Month for December.

Training and MSEP

In the third quarter, TSgt. Christopher L. Hartley was NCOIC of Training Control in the third and fourth quarters. Thirty-one personnel were upgraded, leaving 85 personnel in OJT at the end of the quarter. In the fourth quarter, The annual IG inspection by 7AF was conducted and the training programs were rated as "Excellent." Training Control received no write-ups. During the fourth quarter, 17 personnel were upgraded and 71 remained in OJT at the end of the year. The MSEP written evaluations were administered to 186 personnel and 145 men completed task and flight line evaluations.

Administration

In the third quarter, three replacements arrived. In September, Capt. John T. Woods was assigned as Acting Chief of Maintenance, CMSgt. Samuel R. Shifflett was assigned as NCOIC, Chief of Maintenance, and SSgt. Gerald F. Colfer was assigned as NCOIC, Maintenance Administration.

A large number of squadron personnel completed their tours in Vietnam during the third quarter, the beginning of the annual temporary crisis caused by the simultaneous rotation of a large number of personnel. The departure of so many in such a short time caused hardships on many shops for short periods of time. Phase Maintenance lost all 7-level Dock Chiefs and had to use 5-levels as Dock Chiefs. Two of these 5-level Dock Chiefs were A/1C promoted to Sergeant during the quarter. Material Control had a 90 percent turnover of personnel and it received mostly 3-level replacements. The AGE Shop had a 50 percent turnover of personnel. Quality Control had a 65 percent turnover.

The experienced personnel remaining worked longer hours every day to train the inexperienced replacements and to complete all required maintenance. By the end of the quarter, many of the new men were well on their way toward mastering their jobs.

In the fourth quarter, Capt. Woods continued as Maintenance Control Officer. A large number of squadron personnel completed their tours. The experienced personnel remaining worked longer hours every day to train the inexperienced replacements and to complete all required maintenance.

Despite the loss of personnel, the ability of the squadron to perform its mission did not diminish.

Supply and Support

In the third quarter, many major projects were completed. New offices were under construction for Maintenance Control and Plans and Scheduling. The lower shop areas of Hangar S-2 were reworked, removing and repairing termite-infested areas. Phase inspection docks were remodeled and painted.

Considerable progress was made in improving the squadron living area. Grass was planted to hold the sand in place, enabling airmen to keep their rooms much cleaner. A system of policing the area, using Vietnamese workers, was implemented. This greatly improved the appearance of the area.

Awards and Decorations

In September, TSgt. Charles L. Heick was named Outstanding NCO of the Quarter and A/1C Jack W. Morrow was named Outstanding Airman of the Quarter. SSgt. L. G. Gothrup was named Field Maintenance Man for October. A/1C Robert A. Ward was named Communications-Electronics Maintenance Man for October and Sgt. Larry Goines was named TAS Maintenance Man for October.

Civic Action and Special Activities

Capt. John T. Woods reported that "During the third quarter of 1969, the OLAB organization has continued to perform its mission in an outstanding manner. This can be attributed in part to the increase of knowledge by assigned personnel in all phases of duty."

Commander's Summary

No summary by the Commander was included in the quarterly history reports for the third and fourth quarters.

End Notes: 483 CAMS OLAB

[1] *19690701-19691231 483 CAMS OLAB History*

Phase Dock Work in Progress (Copyright © 2014 Earl Gilbert)

4449th Combat Crew Training Squadron [1]

The mission of the 4442nd Combat Crew Training Wing (4442 CCTW) at Sewart AFB, TN was to operate the USAF Combat Crew Training School (Tactical Airlift) (USAF CCTS). The mission of the USAF CCTS was to train entry-qualified pilots and Flight Engineers in the C-7A aircraft for the USAF.[2]

Col. Richard J. Gibney commanded the 4442 CCTW. Lt. Col. William R. Elmer was the Acting Deputy Commander for Operations until 7 February 1969 when Lt. Col. Mike Kasarda stepped in to fill the position. Col. Don M. Grimwood was Deputy Commander for Materiel.

On 1 March, the organization was placed under the organizational concepts of TACM 65-2 which established the directorate system rather than the dual Deputy concept under which the wing had previously operated. Lt. Col. Kasarda became the Director of Operations and Col. Grimwood became the Director of Materiel. The Safety Division, Executive Office, Management Analysis Office, and Administrative Service Section were staff elements directly responsible to the Wing Commander. The Director of Operations (DO) and Director of Materiel (DM) reported to the Commander. The DO staff included the Operations and Plans Division, Training Division, School Secretary, and Standardization/Evaluation Division. All operating under the dual deputy concept, the 4449th Combat Crew Training Squadron (4449 CCTS) was under the Deputy Commander for Operations (DCO) in the chain of command.[3] When the Wing went under the concept of TACM 65-2, the 4449 CCTS was directly responsible to the Wing Commander. The 4449 CCTS was responsible for C-7A combat air crew training.

The Logistics Plans Office, Chief of Maintenance, 4442 Field Maintenance Squadron (FMS) , and the 4442 Organizational Maintenance Squadron (OMS) were under the Deputy Commander for Materiel (DCM) prior to the reorganization on 1 March. Under the directorate concept, the 4442 OMS was de-activated since the organizational-level maintenance was accomplished by the squadron and the 4442 FMS was made directly responsible to the Wing Commander. The Director of Materiel was directly responsible for the Supply Division, Logistics Plans Division, Maintenance Division, and Quality Assurance Division.

Lt. Col. Fred W. Schaumburg was assigned as Commander of the 4449 CCTS on 31 October 1968 and continued in that position in 1969.

On 29 April, a survey of facilities was conducted at Dyess AFB. The areas surveyed were Life Support, Tactical Training, Aerial Port, and Flight Records Section. No major problems were encountered in any of these areas. In July, a survey team from Sewart AFB visited the Abilene area, surveying several outlying fields for possible use by the 4449 CCTS to avoid over-congestion of the parent base. Letters of Agreement between the 4442 CCTW and Sweetwater Municipal Airport, Mathis Municipal Airport, Goodfellow AFB, Abilene Municipal Airport, Brownwood Municipal Airport, Olney Municipal Airport, and Dyess AFB were initiated to avoid delay in the C-7A Combat Crew Training Program.

On 8 August, Maj. Gen. William A. Moore, Director of Operational Requirements and Development Plans, Deputy Chief of Staff, Headquarters USAF, was the guest speaker at a dining-out held by members of the 4442 CCTW in honor of the departing 4449 CCTS.

On 26 August, Class 70C-1 completed C-7A training at Sewart Air Force Base. It was the last class of graduates from Sewart AFB. On 27 August, the 4449 CCTS moved to Dyess AFB, TX with its 18 C-7A's and approximately 33 officers and 225 enlisted personnel, in accordance with direction from Headquarters TAC.[4, 5] Operations continued at Sewart AFB until 4 September when the squadron was transferred to the 516th Tactical Airlift Wing at Dyess AFB.

Operations

The Operations and Plans Division of the 4442 CCTW assisted the DO with his functions and directed the Programming and Scheduling Branch. The Programming and Scheduling Branch accumulated data necessary for developing C-7A training requirements directed by Headquarters USAF. That branch also had the responsibility to plan and supervise flying schedules and to compile necessary statistics and facts for several pertinent reports.

The squadron was allocated 5450 hours of flying time for the first six months of 1969 and flew all of the assigned hours, for a utilization rate of 1.79.

On 4 March, Maj. Harold H. Davies replaced Maj. James M. Dillard, Jr. as Operations Officer of the 4449 CCTS.

Prior to Class 69C-10, the training program included Low Altitude Parachute Extraction System (LAPES) drops at Landing Zone Four in the Fort Campbell restricted area. Two pallets were loaded aboard each aircraft at Sewart AFB and delivered to the extraction zone near Fort Campbell. The 483 TAW in Vietnam developed a new procedure using a release device on each load. The device was 24 inches long and required 40 inches between loads on the aircraft. The new procedure prevented two loads from being carried on the C-7A at the same time, because the forward center of gravity of the aircraft was out of limits when the aft load was dropped. In order to ensure that each student received equal training in LAPES, the drop zone at Sewart AFB was used. This made it possible for new loads to be secured in minimum turn-around time at Sewart AFB.

Training and Stan-Eval

The Standardization/Evaluation Division administered required written examinations and flight checks to student Instructor Pilots and Flight Engineers. The division monitored the technical publications and flight manuals used in flying and other training programs, and worked closely with the Training Division to assist the DO in assuring quality training. The Division reviewed and checked classroom, simulator, and flying training lessons and presentations. Other activities included responsibilities for issuing operator's permits to assigned Instructor Flight Engineers and continuous work on C-7A manuals and technical orders, other manuals, and tests.

The Training Division performed the functions of writing and revising C-7A curriculum outlines, instructor lesson guides, student study guides, regulations pertaining to training, training records, and other instructional materials for the flying phases. Close coordination with the 304S Field Training Detachment (FTD) and review of FTD course charts were also tasks of the Training Division. Members of the division also worked closely with all squadrons in supervising training, monitoring student progress, training aids, and all phases of the training program. General military and other required training for assigned personnel was also monitored by the Training Division. The most important function of the Training Division was that of training analysis and development.

The 304S Field Training Detachment operated the technical training portions of the C-7A courses. Operational control of the detachment belonged to Air Training Command, but close coordination and cooperation were easily effected with all units of the wing, especially the Wing Training Division.

The C-7A pilot students received 36 hours of classroom technical training; 12 hours of classroom tactical training, presented in 2 six-hour blocks after completion of FTD; and 60 hours of flight time, including a check ride. Flying training lessons remained at four hours in length.

Flight Engineers received 53 hours of classroom technical training and 45 hours of classroom tactical training in the first six months of 1969. This was an increase of 23 hours in classroom technical training due to increasing weight and balance computations from 6 hours to 15 hours and adding 14 hours of rigging to their curriculum. The students received 40 hours of flying training, which included 8 ground hours and 32 flight hours, including a check ride. In the third quarter, the flying training for Flight Engineers was 45 hours. In addition, the Flight Engineers received 10 hours of flight line maintenance training.

There were 28 pilots in course 69C-6, 28 in course 69C-7, 28 in course 69C-8, 24 in course 69C-9, and 26 in course 69C-10. There were 16 Flight Engineers in course 69C-6, 16 in course 69C-7, 11 in course 69C-8, 12 in course 69C-9, and 14 in course 69C-10. C-7A graduates for the first six months totaled 133 pilots and 69 Flight Engineers. All pilot graduates were assigned to PACAF. Fifty-nine Flight Engineers were assigned to PACAF, 6 to the Military Airlift Command, and 4 to the Tactical Air Command. One Flight Engineer and one student pilot were medically eliminated. Twenty Instructor Pilots and 20 Instructor Flight Engineers were authorized for FY69-3, decreasing to 19 Instructor Pilots and 19 Instructor Flight Engineers for FY69-4.

In January, there were 15 C-7A Instructor Pilots and 14 Instructor Flight Engineers available for duty. At the end of June there were 11 C-7A Instructor Pilots and 19 Instructor Flight Engineers available for duty.

In the third quarter, class 69C-11 had 22 student pilots and 15 Flight Engineer students. Class 69C-12 had 24 student pilots and 18 Flight Engineer students. Class 69C-13 had 24 student pilots and 14 Flight Engineer students. There were 70 pilot graduates and 47 Flight Engineer graduates. PACAF received 68 pilot graduates and HQ-COMD received two. PACAF received 24 Flight Engineer graduates, MAC received 19, AFLC received one, and TAC received three.

In July and August, 17 Instructor Pilots were authorized, but only 10 were assigned in July and 13 in August. Authorization for Instructor Flight Engineers was 26 in July and 20 in August, but only 19 and 16 were assigned, respectively.

During the first six months of 1969, a training movie (TF-6269) was filmed at Sewart AFB.[6] The film depicted C-7A operational procedures for short field landings, personnel drops, heavy equipment drops, Low Altitude Parachute Extraction System drops (LAPES), etc. It was used to train students who were unfamiliar with tactical airlift operations. A request to produce the film was submitted in the fall of 1967 and approved in late summer of 1968. The project was assigned to the 4449 CCTS in September 1968 and the script was researched and completed in October 1968. Filming was accomplished by the 1365th Photographic Squadron. Most of the scenes were shot at Sewart AFB with the heavy equipment and personnel drops completed at Fort Campbell, KY. In May 1969, the finished product (23 minutes long) received final approval from TAC for printing and distribution. It was expected to be in the field by early fall 1969 as a valuable tool which embraced the indoctrination and training of newly assigned Caribou students.

Safety

The Flying Safety Office promoted and supervised programs and policies concerning flight safety. The office prepared and coordinated accident prevention and investigation plans, established investigation boards, assured an effective OHR system, monitored operational and maintenance practices and policies, conducted quarterly safety surveys, distributed safety printed materials to squadron safety offices, conducted monthly safety analysis and evaluation meetings with unit safety officers, monitored surveillance of local and nearby auxiliary airfield facilities, and continued other motivational activities encouraging safety.

Maintenance

The Director of Materiel was responsible to the Wing Commander for planning, problem solving, guidance, and staff level surveillance of all materiel functions within the wing. To assist the DM in these functions, a Logistic Plans Division, a Supply Division, a Maintenance Division, and a Quality Assurance Division functioned under his control. The wing reorganization on 1 March changed this function from Deputy Commander for Materiel to Director of Materiel.

The Maintenance Division controlled the assignment of aircraft within the wing and selected aircraft for depot maintenance. The division participated in quarterly, monthly, and weekly flying maintenance planning. It was also responsible for ensuring that an effective materiel training program was conducted throughout the entire maintenance complex. The review of incoming deficiency reports for applicability to assigned weapons systems or equipment and determination of action required were also among the responsibilities of the division. It was also charged with ensuring the equitable distribution of materiel

273

resources which were jointly utilized by wing organizations and with performing maintenance analysis for the wing.

The Quality Assurance Division provided the "eyes and ears" for the Wing Commander. The division was responsible for assuring that the procurement, manufacture, maintenance, and storage of all materiel used in direct support of assigned weapons systems and their supporting AGE within the wing conformed to quality and reliability requirements of AFR 66-44. It assured that the actions of all wing materiel functions reflected proven materiel practices, sound discipline, good housekeeping, and were dedicated to mission accomplishment. Quality Assurance conducted detailed activity inspections of the Quality Control Function of each unit, inspections of selected activities within each unit, and conducted no-notice spot checks of all material activities.

Until 1 March, the 4442 CCTW functioned under a centralized maintenance concept in accordance with AFM 66-1 and the TAC supplements thereto. TACM 65-2 (Draft) decentralized concepts were also applicable within the wing. These concepts generated confusion, higher operating costs, and a lack of standardization within units of the wing. After considerable planning, research, and compiling of factual information, a proposal for reorganization was compiled for submission to higher headquarters. The proposal to the Wing Commander was that the wing either operate under the provisions of AFM 66-1 or convert to TACM 65-2 (Draft) to eliminate confusing conditions created by both centralized and decentralized operations. The proposal was evaluated by the Wing Commander, who personally presented it to commanders at higher headquarters (9AF and TAC). Concurrence with the proposed reorganization plan under TACM 65-2 (Draft) decentralized concepts was received and reorganization plans were made with an effective date of 1 March.

Through effective planning, the wing experienced no significant loss of efficiency in accomplishing its mission during the ten day reorganization. The old title of Deputy Commander for Materiel was disposed of and the new title of Wing Director of Materiel was assumed by Col. Don M. Grimwood who directed and exercised control of materiel operations from 28 July 1968 to 1 in March 1969.

From 1 March through 30 June, results of operations under the Director of Materiel proved that decentralization was justified as evidenced by reports on savings of manpower and overall cost reduction in support of the assigned mission of the wing: i.e., savings in authorized manpower slots were $9,919 per month with FY70 average savings of approximately $89,271 to be achieved.

During the first six months of 1969, the Logistics Plans Division was tasked with the coordination and compilation of plans and programs to precede the closing of Sewart AFB by June 1970. This planning and programming included the movement of all aerospace vehicles, equipment, and personnel of the 4442 CCTW to Dyess AFB, TX. The first element of the wing selected for movement was the 4449 CCTS. Programming and plans for the movement were scheduled for completion by 13 June. The plan was completed on the target date and the initial advance parties were programmed for movement in August. Orders were issued and all specified actions were carried out on schedule with the squadron to be in place and operational on 17 September, at which time the 4449 CCTS would be placed under the command of the 516th Tactical Airlift Wing (516 TAW).

In January, the C-7A aircraft utilization average was 53.1 percent, the NORS rate was 1.1 percent, the NORM rate was 10.6 percent, and there were 21 cannibalizations. In February, the C-7A aircraft utilization average was 54.6 percent, the NORS rate was 2.0 percent, the NORM rate was 5.6 percent, and there were 31 cannibalizations. In March, the C-7A aircraft utilization average was 54.6 percent, the NORS rate was 1.2 percent, the NORM rate was 9.1 percent, and there were 12 cannibalizations.

In April, the C-7A aircraft utilization average was 55.9 percent, the NORS rate was 32.5 percent, the NORM rate was 11.7 percent, and there were 24 cannibalizations. In May, the C-7A aircraft utilization average was 50.5 percent, the NORS rate was 36.6 percent, the NORM rate was 14.3 percent, and there were 35 cannibalizations. In June, the C-7A aircraft utilization average was 44.2 percent, the NORS rate was 16.7 percent, the NORM rate was 14.0 percent, and there were 14 cannibalizations. See the **Supply and Support** section of this chapter for an explanation of this drastic change in NORS and NORM performance.

In July, the C-7A aircraft utilization average was 47.6 percent, the NORS rate was 9.0 percent, the NORM rate was 10.6 percent, and there were 13 cannibalizations. In August, the C-7A aircraft utilization average was 68.2 percent, the NORS rate was 7.5 percent, the NORM rate was 10.5 percent, and there were 21 cannibalizations.

Administration

The Administrative Services Section was responsible for directing and supervising administrative functions of the headquarters, including records management, correspondence, publications and forms, control of classified material, publications and distribution of orders, the wing locator file, allocation of details, manning strength data, and Airmen of the Month and NCO of the Quarter programs. Capt. Wade C. Humphries was the Historian of the 4442 CCTW for the first and second quarters and Maj. Chester R. Golka was historian for the 4449 CCTS.

The 4449 CCTS continued to experience serious C-7A aircraft Instructor Pilot manning problems. In a letter of the squadron commander to the Wing Commander, the problem that had existed since the activation of the 4449 CCTS in December 1966 was explained in detail:

> "... the apparent Instructor Pilot selection process includes assignment to the 4449 CCTS of pilots from Vietnam who have established retirement or separation dates. As an example, of the last 20 SEA returnees, one was Duty Not Involved Flying (DNIF) upon arrival and remained DNIF until he left the squadron; one was medically retired shortly after arrival; and 10 had established retirement or separation dates. The average availability of replacements was 10 months where 24 months for continuity, quality, and safety would be considered as an absolute minimum."

In a telephone conversation with TAC Headquarters, the Wing Commander requested C-7A Instructor Pilot manning assistance, a more stabilized Instructor Pilot program, and a reduction in the student load to match present Instructor Pilot manning until the first two requests were met. Replying to this request, TAC asked USAF Manpower Control to allocate four C-7A Instructor Pilots to TAC for assignment to the 4449 CCTS. TAC succeeded in diverting three Instructor Pilots within the next four months, but not soon enough to completely alleviate the problem.

To quickly correct the problem areas, the Wing Commander requested that Classes 69C-10, 69C-11, 69C-12, and 70C-1 be reduced from a full 14 aircrews to 13, 12, 13, and 13, respectively. The Commander also requested that the pilot manning entitlement be increased to 100 percent to ensure adequate future manning. TAC responded by decreasing the size of the suggested classes. All other requests to increase the manning were disapproved. Manning problems and stability were corrected by assignment criteria focused on retainability.

There were no problems with C-7A Flight Engineer manning during the first two quarters of 1969.

A shortage of C-7A technical instructor personnel was encountered in September 1968. The Wing Commander recommended that the

304S FTD get authorization for one Flight Engineer (AFSC 43570), one aircraft Loadmaster (AFSC 60770), and one aircraft maintenance technician (AFSC 43171A) and add them to the FTD instructor group. The request was not favorably considered by Air Training Command.[7]

Correspondence with the 483 TAW showed that the recommended additions to the FTD were desperately needed due to the unique role of the C-7A in Vietnam, especially in supporting the Special Forces in combat; i.e., daily landings on short narrow dirt strips and cargo varying considerably in weight, size, and shape, to be delivered and picked up by the Caribou. With only one airplane general (APG) instructor assigned to the FTD, and with one class session from 0600-1200, another from 1200-1800, and still another from 0730-1430, APG could not be scheduled on the first day of training for each group. Headquarters, Air Training Command did not favorably consider the suggestion, because of the projected deletion of the C-7A phase of 304S FTD at Sewart AFB. Time would not be available to authorize, qualify, and effectively utilize instructors in a PCS status; however, the training requirements were met by using temporary duty instructors.[8]

Officer manning of the 4449 CCTS averaged 83 percent during the first two quarters of 1969. Enlisted manning averaged 81 percent during the same period. On 1 January, the squadron was authorized 28 officers and 217 enlisted personnel, but only 22 officers and 158 enlisted personnel were assigned. On 1 July, there were 29 officers and 195 enlisted personnel authorized, but only 24 officers and 187 enlisted personnel were assigned.

In January, there were 20 Instructor Pilots and 20 Flight Engineers authorized, and 18 Instructor Pilots and 24 Flight Engineers were assigned. At the end of June, there were 17 Instructor Pilots and 26 Flight Engineers assigned. At the end of July, there were 20 Instructor Pilots and 20 Instructor Flight Engineers authorized, but only 17 Instructor Pilots and 25 Instructor Flight Engineers were assigned. At the end of August, 19 Instructor Pilots and 24 Instructor Flight Engineers were assigned.

Many Graduate Evaluation Forms (AF Forms 241) were returned from C-7A graduates with valuable comments and recommendations. Several often-mention discrepancies were: unfamiliarity with radio procedures and associated equipment, checklist procedures, power-off approaches, too little time in the right seat, and lack of a Copilot checkout program. Unfamiliarity with radio procedures was the most mentioned discrepancy and all were about recent UPT graduates. In view of the complex facilities and large number of radio calls necessary for each mission in Vietnam, it was difficult for the school to simulate combat conditions and still complete the curriculum. However, increased emphasis was directed at this problem area with all Instructor Pilots providing additional instruction on the radio console. A tape recording of radio calls on a typical mission was requested from the 483 TAW for student orientation.

In the first quarter, the 4442 CCTW trained 98 copilots in a program which consisted of the complete school course, but with crews of three student pilots rather than two. This was the best program possible at the time, even though problem areas were discovered in the copilot training. The main problem areas were in descent and landing, communicating IFF/SIF, and formation flying. Specific landing problems were: erratic power control, landing in a crab, poor crosswind techniques, and a general lack of round-out on landing. Communication problems centered around unfamiliar frequencies and call signs, hesitations, and making calls without prompting. Formation write-ups centered around erratic power changes and flying too far back and low.

In the third quarter, personnel reporting to Sewart AFB for crew training continued to report in without mandatory clothing and equipment as prescribed in AFM 50-5. The wing budgeted for the shortage of equipment for personnel reporting for training; however, until the individual actually reported in there was no way of knowing what shortages would exist. Therefore, a problem was generated in budgeting and maintaining an adequate stock level of flying clothing and equipment. Headquarters TAC tried to eliminate the situation by soliciting the assistance of other major commands to ensure that personnel reporting for crew training had adequate equipment in their possession upon arrival.

Supply and Support

The Supply Division was responsible for managing the equipment and supply funds for all wing staff agencies; acting as cost reduction monitor for supplies and equipment; conducting inspections of all supply activities assigned to the wing; reviewing daily, monthly, and quarterly supply listings; and keeping the DM apprised of the overall supply situation.

On 1 March, Maj. Edward H. Darcey assumed the position of Materiel Officer of the 4449 CCTS, who was replaced by Maj. Emory E. Smith on 26 May.

Until 1 March, the wing did not operate unit supply functions. Under concepts of AFM 66-1, supply support was rendered to the wing by the host base; however, there was a Maintenance Support Unit (MSU) operated by the wing headquarters, which provided supply support for all assigned aircraft and AGE. Support provided by the host base was satisfactory. On 1 March, the wing was reorganized to a decentralized concept, thereby establishing unit supply sections for the squadrons, including the 4449 CCTS.

Squadron supply officers acted as property custodians for all Equipment Authorization Inventory Data (EAID) property within the squadron. The change made one person, the squadron supply officer, accountable for squadron EAID equipment. As of 1 March, the squadron MSU assumed the responsibility of requisitioning, receiving, storing, issuing, delivering, turning-in, and accounting of aircraft components and spares. Items were delivered by Base Supply to the MSU, unloaded, then reloaded and delivered to the aircraft. Squadron supply sections were responsible for storing all 780 equipment not installed on an aircraft and for maintaining records and files on 780 equipment.

On 1 May, management of AF Forms 538, *Personal Clothing and Equipment Record*, previously maintained by the host base was assumed by the squadron supply section. Individual toolkits, also previously issued and maintained by the host base, were taken over by the squadron supply section. Centralized tool cribs were established to supply squadron maintenance personnel with specialized tools. With the decentralized supply concept of the wing, bench stocks remained stable and were operated in a satisfactory manner.

Due to the reporting instructions in TACR 55-83, the NORS rate as of 1 April increased tremendously. All systems listed in TACR 55-83 were required to be fully operational or reported as NORS. This reporting method caused an unrealistic picture of the Operationally Ready Rate. Aircraft were reported NORS when the aircraft was actually performing a mission. For example, the APN-158 Weather/Radar Systems were removed during 1967 and shipped to Vietnam. Upon implementation of TACR 55-83, C-7A's assigned to the 4449 CCTS were short the system. Consequently, the NORS rate soared.

The quarters provided for officer students were considered to be outstanding. Enlisted students complained about the appearance, size of rooms, lack of air conditioning, and noise in their quarters. It was not possible to make any improvements in this area due to the projected base closure in 1970. Classroom technical training and tactical training on the C-7A were held in Building 412. Building 425 house the 304 S FTD. Classroom facilities were adequate.

In the third quarter, the Operationally Ready Rate, with reference to the AN/APN-158 Weather Radar System, improved. Through the support of AFLC and TAC, all aircraft had the AN/APN-158 installed. Sufficient stock of spare parts was provided to enable the 4442 FMS to repair and maintain the system.

Between 4 August and 2 September, the orderly transfer of the squadron to Dyess AFB was accomplished. An advance party of three enlisted men and one officer proceeded to Dyess AFB to establish the necessary support for receiving the equipment and AGE at Dyess. Equipment used at Sewart AFB was inventoried, tagged, and prepared for shipment. Necessary documents were prepared and processed through the Base Equipment Management Office (BEMO) prior to the shipment. After completion of the move, base auditors from Sewart AFB perform a complete audit of documents to ensure accountability of equipment terminated at Sewart AFB and that accountability was assumed by Dyess AFB. No discrepancies were noted.

In the third quarter, the quarters provided for officer students continued to be praised by those occupying them. Enlisted students continued to complain about the appearance, size, and noise in their quarters. Due to the projected base closure in 1970, very little was done to improve facilities on Sewart AFB.

Awards and Decorations

During the first two quarters of 1969, Maj. Franklin K. Busse, SSgt. Leroy Hill, and SSgt. Jack B. St. Pierre were awarded the Distinguished Flying Cross for their service in Vietnam and SSgt. David R. Eggen was awarded the Purple Heart for his service in Vietnam.

On 23 May, the 4449 CCTS received the TAC Unit Achievement Award for accident free operation during the period 7 April 1968 through 6 April 1969.

C-7A Crew Chief of the Month was TSgt. Charles M. Dobson for January and February, A/1C David L. Brown for March, Sgt. Edward G. Eckert for April, Sgt. Ronald D. Beasley for May, Sgt. Frank A. Vallone for June, and SSgt. Dennis R. Shoemaker for July.

SSgt. James A. Norris was named Maintenance Man of the Month for May.

A/1C Byrd D. Patterson, Jr. was named Airman of the Month for February.

TSgt. James L. Buckner, NCOIC of the Aircraft Repair/Reclamation Section, through his own initiative and inventive abilities saved TAC and the USAF approximately $141,000 per year with a suggestion to interchange two gears on the C-7A. He was awarded a check for $1000 for his suggestion, with possible additional monetary benefits to follow.

Commander's Appraisal

January through June, 1969 [9]

"Changes and planning for changes and movements dominated our activities during this historical reporting period. Conversion of the wing from the centralized maintenance concept of AFM 66-1 to the decentralized concept of TACM 65-2 (Draft) was completed on 1 March 1969, and represented our major change. This was perhaps a most fortunate change, since shortly after the conversion was completed it was announced that during the forthcoming relocation the 4449 CCTS would be separated from the parent wing for about nine months. With their maintenance complex already separate, planning for their movement was made somewhat easier and the plan was completed in June.

Shortages of personnel, particularly C-7A Instructor Pilots, were a major problem. By shifting personnel throughout the wing as the tasks dictated, and by utilizing all staff officers as instructors, we were able to complete our mission. All students were graduated as scheduled and are serving with distinction throughout the world."

July through December, 1969 [10]

"Planning for changes in movements continued to dominate our activities during this historical period. The relocation of the 4449th Combat Crew Training Squadron to Dyess Air Force Base, Texas was successfully accomplished during this period and plans to move the remainder of the wing were being developed."

End Notes: 4449 CCTS

[1] *19690101-19690930 4442nd Combat Crew Training Wing* history
[2] *839 Air Division Regulation 23-2*, dated 9 February 1967
[3] 4442 CCTW Organization Chart
[4] Headquarters TAC Movement Order 13, dated 19 [*sic*] May 1969
[5] 4442 CCTW/DO Letter to 3560 Pilot Training Wing/DCOOO, Subject: Unit Move, Transfer of 4449 CCTS, Sewart AFB, TN to Dyess AFB, TX, dated 17 July 1969.
[6] This film can be seen on YouTube by searching for "C-7A training film."

[7] Letter from Headquarters 3750th Technical School (ATC) to the Commander of the 4442 CCTW

[8] *Ibid*

[9] 4449 CCTS Commander's Appraisal, 30 June 1969 by Col. Richard J. Gibney

[10] 4449 CCTS Commander's Appraisal, 30 September 1969 by Col. Richard J. Gibney

483 CAMS Engine Shop (Copyright © 2014 Stan Owens)

Engine Change at Bearcat (Copyright © 2014 Lloyd Boyd)

18th Tactical Airlift Training Squadron [1, 2]

On 27 August, the 4449 CCTS moved to Dyess AFB, TX. Operations continued at Sewart AFB until 4 September when the squadron was transferred to the 516th Tactical Airlift Wing (516 TAW) at Dyess AFB, TX. The 4449 CCTS was redesignated as the 18th Tactical Airlift Training Squadron (18 TATS) effective 15 October 1969.[3] Effective on 24 December, the 516 TAW was assigned directly to Twelfth Air Force (12AF).[4]

Lt. Col. Fred W. Schaumburg continued as Commander of the 4449 CCTS until the squadron moved to Dyess Air Force Base, where he continued to command the squadron under its new designation of the 18 TATS.

This was the first time that the versatile Caribou had been stationed in TX and the first time it had been stationed on a Strategic Air Command base. In August, an advance team was sent from Sewart AFB to Dyess AFB to coordinate and make advance preparations for the unit moved. Some of these preparations included setting up operations, standardization, training, maintenance, supply, and related support activities. The advance team was also responsible for briefing the new wing commander and his staff on the training requirements of the squadron because the 516 TAW had no previous knowledge of the C-7A.

The move did not change the unit mission in any respect. However, the change in physical facilities made slight changes in unit organization necessary.

Operations

In the third quarter, Maj. Harold H. Davies continued as the Operations Officer of the 4449 CCTS.

Fourteen Caribous departed Sewart AFB at 15 minute intervals on 27 August, bound for Dyess AFB with a refueling stop at Barksdale AFB, TX. The crews were made up of squadron Instructor Pilots, student pilots who graduated in Class 70C-1, and squadron Flight Engineers. When all of the aircraft arrived at Dyess, the crews boarded support C-130's and returned to Sewart AFB on the same day.

Squadron personnel were released to depart from Sewart AFB on 28 August and proceed to Dyess AFB to start training Class 70C-2 on 4 September.

Many significant changes were made and problems were encountered in the areas of operations and training. Prior to the move, the

4442 TAW Command Post was responsible for maintaining takeoff and landing times and monitoring maintenance activities on delayed departures and aborts. At Dyess, the squadron operations section operated an FM radio to give the commander a greater degree of flexibility and control over his aircraft. Additionally, it provided the commander with the ability to give immediate assistance to in-flight emergencies.[5] The squadron also adopted a Supervisor of Flying system employed by many organizations in the Air Force.

The aluminum Tri-Service landing strip west of the main runway was made available for C-7A operations. The Army Corps of Engineers constructed a 1500 foot dirt practice landing strip to the west of the landing complex at Dyess. The dirt strip provided for realistic assault landing practice, simulating conditions encountered in Vietnam.

There was a shortage of VFR transition runways available at Dyess for C-7A training. Even with four parallel runways, only a maximum of two were available for simultaneous use. When drops or LAPES runs were conducted, only one runway was available. There was also a problem with the gusty crosswinds which are quite often present in west Texas. The problem was expected to be alleviated when a transition field could be made available with several runways such as the runway complex at Sweetwater, TX. Despite all efforts, the problem of not having auxiliary airfields for the C-7A existed at the end of the fourth quarter.

The move also resulted in discontinuing actual personnel drops, formation training, and corridor training due to the non-availability of jumpers. Ground training was still conducted in these aspects of C-7A operation, which was considered adequate.

One C-7A was flown to Miami, FL for engine certification and then flown to Edwards AFB, CA to reevaluate the single engine performance data section of T.O. 1-C-7A-1.

Training and Stan-Eval

Responsibility for training C-7A pilots and Flight Engineers was relinquished by the 4442 CCTW when the 4449 CCTS transferred to Dyess AFB under control of the 516 TAW.

Prior to Class 70C-1, all student Flight Engineers received nine instructional flights during their training. Starting with Class 70C-1, all 7-level student Flight Engineers with over 100 hours total time received only five instructional flights and a check ride. As a result of the move, the squadron had the additional requirement of providing 18 hours of Flight Engineer ground training in aircraft loading and rigging. At Sewart AFB, the Aerial Port Squadron provided this training, but Aerial Port personnel were not available at Dyess.

A modification of the flying training program was also required in the area of pilot instrument training. At Sewart AFB, the tower gave traffic advisories to VFR practice instrument approaches. At Dyess, all practice approaches were conducted while on an IFR clearance. This procedure decreased the number of practice approaches, but was necessary due to the volume of diversified aircraft operating in the local area.

The general military training (GMT) program of the squadron lagged due to the unit move. New personnel had to be tested because a sizable portion of the squadron personnel remained at Sewart AFB. This area was given top priority and the training and testing progressed rapidly.

The first class of students for the C-7A maintenance course arrived in the middle of August. The FTD was well prepared for the arrival of the class and ground training was completed without difficulty. however, the practical maintenance portion of the course, which included shop training and flight line training, was not completed. This was caused by the lack of C-7A aircraft and shop facilities and was rectified only with the arrival of the squadron. An interim measure was the use of one C-7A sent to Dyess as a training aid, but this did not prove to be a successful substitute for actual training on the flight line. As a result, the first two classes of maintenance students were graduated early with the concurrence of TAC headquarters.

A conference was held at Goodfellow AFB to determine the feasibility of using that base for C-7A training. However, Air Training Command (ATC) took the position that combined use of Goodfellow AFB constituted a safety hazard and refused to open the field to C-7A's. This was in spite of the fact that ATC was using Mathis Field, TX with civilian traffic only 6 miles away.

In the fourth quarter, the lack of auxiliary airfields for use by the C-7A resulted in less qualified Caribou pilots being graduated from the course. It was expected to be an even larger problem in the first months of 1970 with the winter weather in west Texas.

In early October, the training film, titled "C-7A Operations," arrived and was immediately introduced into the training program. The film proved to be a valuable tool in indoctrinating and training new pilots as they entered the flying phase of C-7A training.

Recent correspondence from PACAF indicated a need for increased training in Flight Engineer loading procedures. A staff study was initiated and the conclusions were forwarded to TAC/DOAL for their approval. The study concluded that a new program was needed. This program was divided into three phases:

1. In the FTD phase, a two hour block of academic instruction in aircraft loading and related subjects was initiated.

2. A practical course in tie-down and loading procedures was developed by squadron personnel and presented between the academic and flying phases. The phase was 20 hours in duration and consisted of use of the load adjuster, working with the DD Form 365F (*Aircraft Weight and Balance*), tie-down devices, loading, rigging, airdrop procedures, litter kit installation and loading, and familiarization with the PACAF forms.

3. Various pallets, weighing between 500 and 1500 pounds, were included in the flying phase. The loads were varied and included railroad ties, weighted fuel drums, sand bags, Jeep trailers, and miscellaneous bundles.

By exposing the student Flight Engineers to different types of loads, their proficiency in correct load positioning and tie-down procedures was greatly enhanced. The new procedures were introduced into the course in November and continued to be used with each class.

A study was made on the feasibility of dropping LAPES training from the curriculum. PACAF indicated, with consideration based on operational requirements, that LAPES training was not required for tactically qualified personnel in Vietnam. The decision to eliminate or continue the LAPES training was being considered by TAC/DOAL at the end of the year.

Safety

On 19 November, all of the C-7A's of the squadron were grounded for defective elevators. Maintenance had enough aircraft ready for Functional Check Flights by 23 November and the squadron started flying student sorties on 24 November. Having the aircraft grounded for five days required extra effort by all squadron personnel in order to graduate Class 70C-4 on schedule.

Maintenance

In the third and fourth quarters, the Maintenance Officer was Capt. William S. Thompson.

The 4449 CCTS was authorized the following maintenance personnel: seven officers, fourteen 9-levels, eighty-three 7-levels, two hundred and nineteen 5-levels, and eighty-two 3-levels. The assigned personnel for these authorizations were: nine officers, seventeen 9-levels, seventy-five 7-levels, one hundred and forty-six 5-levels, and one hundred and four 3-levels. These authorizations were dropped from the manning of the 4442 CCTW on 28 August when the 4449 CCTS relocated to Dyess AFB.

At Dyess, the squadron maintenance function incurred an increased workload. In spite of the difficulties associated with preparing for the move, the in-commission rate of the C-7A aircraft steadily increased during July, August, and September.

The actual unit move started on 4 August with the deployment of the first of three advance parties. Team I arrived in the last week of July and consisted of one officer and three NCOs with Maj. Erickson as OIC and CMSgt. Hughes as NCOIC. The team was responsible for receipt of all equipment arriving at Dyess for the squadron, establishing supply accounts, and accomplishing initial furnishing of offices. The first task was establishing an orderly room and a supply receiving area. Vacant areas of hangar 5020 were used with the very able assistance of CMSgt. Hughes. Inspection of the squadron operations area in building 4302 revealed that the entire building was badly in need of painting, the floor was buckling in several areas, and the general condition of the building was very poor. However, funds were not available for refurbishing the new operations area. The squadron Flight Engineers initiated a self-help project and the building was ready for general use on 12 September.

Team II arrived at Dyess on 20 August and consisted of two officers and three NCOs. The second team supplemented Team I and was responsible for establishing processing procedures for the remainder of the squadron. Team II was commanded by Lt. Col. Edmond P. Gaudin who was assigned to the 516 TAW as OIC of the C-7A Stan/Eval Section. He immediately began an in-depth study of all local regulations and directives pertaining to flying activities in the Dyess area. This led to several conferences with base representatives, revisions of TACM 55-17, and local regulations. The Army Corps of Engineers started preliminary studies on the construction of a 1500 foot dirt assault strip to be completed in September. This construction was not completed on schedule due to adverse weather, but was expected to be finished by 1 January 1970.

Team III consisted of one officer and 35 enlisted personnel who arrived at Dyess on 26 August. This final team of advance parties was responsible for receipt of the C-7A aircraft at Dyess and the maintenance necessary to return the aircraft to operational status.

The first C-7A to be ferried to Dyess arrived on 9 August. This aircraft was used to support the FTD maintenance school. The remaining aircraft were ferried to Dyess on 27 August. These aircraft were serviced by an enroute maintenance team at Barksdale AFB and then proceeded to Dyess. No major maintenance difficulties were experienced by any of the C-7A aircraft and they all arrived at Dyess as scheduled. One C-7A remained at Smyrna, TN for shipment to Wright Air Materiel Area (WRAMA). Another C-7A was already at WRAMA and the last one was in Florida, enroute to Edwards AFB for performance testing.

On 15 and 16 September, maintenance supported pilot proficiency and local area orientation flights. On 18 September, student training flights resumed when Class 70C-2 entered the flying phase.

Two C-7A aircraft were scheduled into IRAN and both were completed. The Maintenance Division developing a new parking plan to accommodate the 17 C-7A aircraft transferred from Sewart AFB.

There were four air aborts and two ground aborts in September.

The three-month maintenance statistics were: Operationally Ready Rate of 89.9 percent, NORM rate of 6.7 percent, and Abort Rate of 2.2 percent. Maintenance expended 442 man-hours in September on C-7A TCTOs. This represented 92 percent of the outstanding TCTO man-hours at the beginning of the month.

Twelve delays were charged to maintenance. Maintenance effectiveness was rated at 97.5 percent and maintenance reliability was rated at 93.3 percent, based on the current TAC standards. Maintenance man-hours per flying hour were 13.7 for the 7939.7 maintenance man-hours expended. Two R-2000 engines were removed, one for time and the other for broken blower case studs.

Powered AGE in-commission rate was 98.8 percent.

In the fourth quarter, the maintenance challenges were particularly demanding and were met only by highly efficient and congenially professional efforts of the materiel complex. The squadron flew 1167 sorties, logged 2351.9 flying hours and 10,096 landings, with an average of 4.3 landings per flying hour. In spite of this heavy flying commitment, the squadron experienced only 18 maintenance aborts, establishing an abort rate of 1.4 percent for the quarter, well below the TAC standard of 3.0 percent.

However, the most significant challenge to the materiel complex occurred in the latter part of November. On 19 November, maintenance personnel discovered, on C-7A S/N 61-2398, that the right elevator had separated from the elevator torque tube assembly at the

288

elevator attaching bracket. Further investigation revealed that the left elevator attaching bracket had several elongated bolt holes and cracks in the weld bead of the elevator torque tube assembly. Discovery of these discrepancies was followed by an immediate inspection of the elevator attaching brackets and torque tube assemblies of all C-7A aircraft assigned. On 20 November, the inspection was completed and all 15 aircraft were grounded due to either elongated bolt holes in the elevator attaching brackets or cracked elevator torque tube assemblies.

An Emergency Unsatisfactory Report (EUR) was immediately submitted to WRAMA, the system manager of the C-7A weapon system. The EUR resulted in an Urgent Action Time Compliance Technical Order (TCTO) for all C-7A aircraft in the USAF inventory. After submitting the EUR, the squadron materiel branch immediately undertook the monumental task of returning its assigned Caribous to an Operationally Ready status. By working around the clock into 12-hour shifts, the maintenance section was able to repair eight aircraft by 23 November. These eight aircraft flew four sorties daily to meet the operational requirements of the squadron.

By continuing to work two 12-hour shifts per day, the maintenance section not only supported these eight aircraft, but also repaired six more by 28 November. The final C-7A at Dyess was repaired on 10 December. Due to the efficient and professional efforts of the materiel branch, the operational requirements were only briefly interrupted as a result of this major malfunction of the elevator system. It was particularly noteworthy that during this trying period, all students are graduated on time without any reduction in flying training.

There were three personnel in OJT for the 3-level, 22 for the 5-level, and nine for the 7-level. All maintenance personnel, who took their skill level test in the fourth quarter, passed the test. Two individuals were upgraded to the 5-level and two to the 7-level.

In the fourth quarter, maintenance expended 13.5 man-hours per flying hour in October, 18.5 in November, and 18.0 in December. Maintenance was charged with 19 delays in October, 14 in November, and 6 in December. Maintenance reliability was 92.4 percent in October, 81.6 percent in November, and 95.4 percent in December.

Administration

On 1 July, the 4449 CCTS was authorized 29 officers and 195 enlisted personnel, but only 24 officers and 187 enlisted personnel were assigned. There were 20 pilots and 20 Flight Engineers authorized. In July, there were 17 pilots and 25 Flight Engineers assigned. In August, there were 19 pilots and 24 Flight Engineers assigned.

Capt. Wade C. Humphries was the Historian of the 4442 CCTW and SSgt. Kenneth R. Fuhrman was Historian for the 18 TATS.

As a result of prior planning and coordination, the squadron did not encounter any problems in administration during the move to Dyess AFB.

In early July, a final determination was made of the personnel to be transferred to Dyess. Eighteen officers and 168 enlisted personnel were scheduled for transfer. Processing, both in-processing at Dyess and out-processing at Sewart, was consolidated to obtain the greatest possible efficiency. Many actions were accomplished well in advance of the actual move. These actions include early completion of many in-processing details for Dyess as the normal out-processing paperwork at Sewart. Outstanding cooperation and coordination with both the 314 Combat Support Group (CSG) and the 96 CSG enabled the move to be completed with a minimum of problems.

Upon arrival of the squadron at Dyess, two authorizations were added to the UDL in AFSC 473X0, so that the squadron could adapt to the vehicle control system at Dyess.

The personnel transferred to Dyess included 18 officers, one Chief Master Sergeant, two Senior Master Sergeants, 7 Master Sergeants, 30 Technical Sergeants, 38 Staff Sergeants, 45 Sergeants, and 45 Airmen First Class.

In August, 223 personnel were authorized, but only 57 were assigned. In September, the number of assigned personnel increased to 189. There were 20 Instructor Pilots and 20 Instructor Flight Engineers authorized, but only 16 Instructor Pilots and 19 Instructor Flight Engineers were assigned.

AGE personnel at Sewart AFB did not transfer to Dyess due to a shortage of AGE personnel at Sewart. The resulting vacancies were to be filled by AGE personnel from Dyess. However, when the squadron arrived at Dyess, adequate numbers of personnel were not available to fill the vacant positions. This caused a delay in the preparation of AGE which was temporarily solved by TDY specialists from the 347 TAS and the 348 TAS at Dyess.

In the fourth quarter, with the movement to Dyess completed in September, personnel problems associated with the move began to be rectified during October. No personnel in the AFSC 421X2 career field (AGE) were transferred from Sewart AFB. Eight airmen were immediately made available from 516 TAW resources, with three more being made available later in the quarter, bringing the squadron to a fully manned status in this career field. Base transportation was unable to support the requirements for crew transportation. Since there were no authorizations for vehicle operators in the squadron, two Airmen from the supply section were assigned to full-time duty as crew bus drivers.

The overall manning of the squadron improved substantially during the quarter. Officer strength at the end of 1969 was 29 authorized, but only 27 were assigned. Enlisted strength was 194 authorized and 195 assigned. The most significant improvement was in the AFSC 1055E (Instructor Pilot) area,which showed that the squadron would be 100% manned in the near future. Another area of improvement was in the AFSC 702X0 (Administrative) field. A continuing problem was the rapid turnover of AFSC 431X1A (Maintenance) personnel due to requirements in Southeast Asia. Many 3-level personnel were receiving Southeast Asian notifications within a few weeks of their arrival at Dyess. This rapid turnover resulted in a shortage of middle supervisors (SSgts. and TSgts.) in this career field.

In the fourth quarter, 223 personnel were authorized, but only 192 were assigned in October. In November, 200 personnel were assigned. In December, 208 personnel were assigned. At the end of 1969, the squadron was short one officer and 14 enlisted personnel. In December, two enlisted personnel completed their enlistments and one officer left the Air Force when he reached his Date of Separation. In the second half of 1969, 25 percent of the squadron's eligible first-term Airmen re-enlisted, and 100 percent of the eligible career Airmen re-enlisted.

Throughout the quarter, 20 Instructor Pilots and 20 Instructor Flight Engineers were authorized, but only 16 Instructor Pilots and 19 instructor Flight Engineers were assigned.

Supply and Support

The Materiel Officer was Lt. Col. Bert G. Means. After the move to Dyess, funds were requested to construct a shelter for fire fighting equipment at Sweetwater, but it had not been approved by the end of September.

Crew transportation was another problem area after arrival at Dyess. At Sewart AFB, crew transportation was radio controlled with a dispatcher located in the Base Operations building and there was very seldom a delay of more than 5 minutes. At Dyess, a driver and vehicle were available from the motor pool to take crews to base operations and then to the aircraft for the morning flights and pick up the crews from the afternoon flights. An additional driver and vehicle were available for the noon turnaround. This arrangement was not as effective as previously experienced at Sewart. After the first class graduated, a vehicle was assigned to the squadron with the driver provided from squadron resources. Two drivers were taken from the squadron supply section and assigned to work in two shifts to provide crew transportation. One vehicle did not provide enough transportation during the midday turnaround, so it was necessary for most of the afternoon crews to provide their own transportation to base operations and the aircraft in order to make their takeoff times.

All office equipment belonging to the squadron was transferred to Dyess as it became available for shipment. AGE and shop equipment was transferred into groups. The first group, required to support the inbound C-7A's, arrived on 26 August. The remaining AGE and shop equipment arrived on 2 September.

A problem area arose in the number of maintenance supply items. The number of peculiar and common C-7A spares shipped to Dyess, based on four or more demands in the 365 days preceding the move from Sewart, proved to be restrictive and resulted in a shortage of necessary parts for effective C-7A maintenance.

The billeting of students was a problem area. The quarters were barely adequate, but the problem was quickly rectified through the efforts of the Base Housing Office. As the base became geared to the large number of students, a favorable change of facilities and services in all areas was soon evident. A School Secretariat was organized and in operation by 15 August. The OIC was Capt. Gary Lashley and the NCOIC was Sgt. Updike. They often worked 12 to 14 hours per day to accomplish their many and varied tasks in preparation for the influx of students.

During the last two weeks of August, personnel arrived in rapidly increasing numbers and the orderly room and squadron operations were moved to building 4302 and the shop and maintenance facilities were near completion in hanger 5020.

A major problem area was encountered at this time. The ramp tie-downs were not being completed on schedule and would not be ready to accommodate all the squadron aircraft when they arrived. An alternate solution using tie-down chains proved successful until the permanent tie-downs were secured. As the squadron personnel arrived during the latter part of August and early September, housing proved to be a problem only in the lower enlisted ranks and it was only slowly resolved.

When the first student pilot class arrived in September, no difficulties were noted except for the billeting, which was less than desirable, but these problems were soon rectified. All agencies at base level directly associated with the C-7A, such as the Fire Department, RAP-CON, and Base Operations were briefed on the mission of the unit and many were given a tour of the aircraft.

All logistic action programs to support the 4449 CCTS were transferred from Sewart AFB to Dyess AFB in August and were completed by 30 September. Complete supply support was established, general and special purpose vehicles were obtained, non-TAC radios were leased, building and dormitory space was allocated, C-7A tie-downs were installed, communications were activated, and a new C-7A landing zone was constructed.

The C-7A landing zone was constructed in record time by the 63rd Engineer Battalion, Fort Hood, TX, under the command of Lt. Col. O. Kirk Ehlers. This organization was tasked by CINCARSTRIKE to do the job at the request of TAC because of the short deadline imposed, i.e., 21 September, and inability to contract the work on a timely basis. The quick response of Lt. Col. Elhers and his staff in moving personnel and equipment to Dyess and in completing the project under frequently adverse weather conditions was most commendable. The project was started on 2 September and was completed on 29 September. Except for weather delays, it would have been completed ahead of schedule.

The NORS rate in July and August was 14.8 percent and 4.1 percent, respectively (for C-7A aircraft possessed by Sewart AFB). The NORS rate for September was 3.9 percent, well within the command objective of 5 percent. The NORS rate was based on possession of aircraft only during the month of September and was not truly representative. All known management techniques were used in achieving a low NORS rate, including self-sufficiency, local purchase, and lateral support. The NORM rate in September was 7.7 percent and the Operationally Ready Rate (ORR) was 88.4 percent. The USAF standards were: 71 percent for ORR, 24 percent for NORM, and 5 percent for NORS. There were only 2 cannibalizations in September. Aircraft utilization was 36.2 percent for the 16 aircraft possessed, with 17 aircraft assigned.

In the fourth quarter, the supply section went from a manning of 68 percent to 57 percent, based on assigned versus authorized positions. This situation was below the minimum acceptable level specified in the Manpower Personnel Authorization Document. Due to inadequate manning, a complete revision of mission objectives and operational standards within the section was necessary. Standards of performance in most areas were lowered and numerous responsibilities and tasks were either deleted or consolidated. Consolidation of tasks was mainly in the operational support function. All tasks and responsibilities in this area were assigned to one individual, where previously one NCO and two Airmen had been assigned.

As a consequence, looser controls of property resulted in a delayed reaction to requirements for expendable supplies being built into the system. Responsibilities and tasks deleted in the area of administration, records maintenance, management reviews, and the responsibility for maintaining a reference library made up the bulk of the changes. Complete review in this area was accomplished and, wherever possible, the task was completely deleted. Where deletion was not possible, the task and responsibilities were assumed by the squadron Maintenance Administrative Section.

The shortage of personnel also created a situation where the assigned branch chiefs and experienced supervisors were required to assume menial supply tasks. When this occurred, numerous management reviews of operational data, normally accomplished by the first line supervisors, were not accomplished.

Efforts were directed toward upgrading the standards of operations in the maintenance support function of squadron supply, regardless of all other operational commitments. This alone was the major factor in the directed decrease of management interest in other areas of supply.

In support of the 17 C-7A aircraft assigned, the maintenance support function of squadron supply management recorded 4 GNORS conditions, 22 ANORS conditions, and 79 maintenance-directed cannibalization actions.

The section committed $100,000 for supplies during the fourth quarter, with actual expenditures of $83,000. The difference was money committed to purchase items which were back-ordered and not issued during the period. The maintenance support function processed 3228 individual demands to Base Supply. They processed 1535 non-expendable, recoverable items into base maintenance for repair and return to the supply system. This function was manned by an operator during all periods when aircraft maintenance was being performed. Normal operation was 16 hours per day. Generally, the function remained manned from 18 to 22 hours per day. This was considered necessary to adequately support maintenance, regardless of the extreme shortage of assigned personnel.

During this period, the maintenance support personnel completely rebuilt the 780 equipment storage area. The storage area housed approximately 1200 individual items required at different times to accomplish the mission. The items in storage must be separated and binned by aircraft tail number so that immediate action could be taken to issue a complete set of equipment to any given aircraft, day or night.

In the operational support area, supply personnel managed 1698 items in use within the squadron. The total cost of these "in-use" items was $314,361. There were 134 additional items required, which were on back-order pending availability at the depot, funding, receipt of command authorization, etc. Constant follow-up and management review was required to ensure that these requirements were being furnished as expeditiously as possible. The cost of these 134 items was $43,000.

The unavailability of spares to repair RT 711/711A units resulted in nine NORS incidents for a total of 2103 NORS hours. The problem was alleviated upon receipt of spares and authority from WRAMA to repair the units at Dyess. The NORS rate increased 4.7 percent from the previous three months. The increase was due, in part, to 15 items being first-time demand items and the change in NORS/NFE reporting by TAC through the implementation of TACR 55-83. The NORS rate was 6.8 percent in October, 12.4 percent in November, and 6.6 percent in December, for a quarterly NORS rate of 8.5 percent.

Cannibalizations were 11 in October, 42 in November, and 31 in December. The high number of cannibalizations was attributed, in part, to six instances for elevators which caused the grounding of all C-7A aircraft. A total of 12 items were first-time demand items. Inadequate supply support by the depots on priority 17 requisitions (stock replenishment) for engine cowling latches and radio inverters was also a cause factor. The majority of items cannibalized during the period did not have sufficient consumption to warrant a demand level, mostly due to the fact that the Caribous were assigned to Dyess AFB in September. All cannibalizations were reviewed by the host Base Supply Stock Control monitor to justify special levels as necessary.

A semiannual activity inspection was accomplished in the squadron and no major deficiencies were noticed, resulting in a rating of "Satisfactory."

For the fourth quarter, the Operationally Ready Rate was 74.6 percent in October, 56.2 percent in November, and 79.5 percent in December. The NORM rate was 18.6 percent in October, 31.4 percent in November, and 13.9 percent in December. The NORS rate was 6.8 percent in October, 12.4 percent in November, and 6.6 percent in December. The Abort Rate was 1.5 percent for the quarter, with five air aborts and three ground aborts in October, three air aborts and four ground aborts in November, and one air abort and two ground aborts in December. Utilization rate was 62.1 percent in October, 52.2 percent in November, and 42.1 percent in December.

Plans were formulated by Capt. Jerry A. McLean, the base optometrist, to survey the C-7A to determine the instrumentation distances for personnel flying the aircraft who require corrective glasses for defective vision. Upon completion of the survey, the clinic added the distances, for the different C-7A crew positions, to the previously determined distances taken by a special survey.

Training Accomplishments

In September, the squadron flew 271 training sorties of the 285 scheduled, logging 578.8 hours and 2572 landings.

In the fourth quarter, the squadron was allocated 933 flying hours per month. The squadron logged 930 hours in October and 438 sorties, 797 hours and 407 sorties in November, and 649 hours and 323 sorties in December.

Commander's Appraisal

January through June, 1969 [6]
"Changes and planning for changes and movements dominated our activities during this historical reporting period. Conversion of the wing from the centralized maintenance concept of AFM 66-1 to the decentralized concept of TACM 65-2 (Draft) was completed on 1 March 1969 and represented our major change. This was perhaps a most fortunate change, since shortly after the conversion was completed, it was announced that during the forthcoming relocation, the 4449 CCTSq would be separated from the parent wing for about nine months. With their maintenance complex already separate, planning for their movement was made somewhat easier and the plan was completed in June."

July through September, 1969 [7]
"Planning for changes and movements continued to dominate our activities during this historical period. The relocation of the 4449th Combat Crew Training Squadron to Dyes Air Force Base, Texas was successfully accomplished during this period and plans to move the remainder of the wing were being developed."

July through September, 1969 [8]

"The move was accomplished on schedule. All unit personnel involved in the move received all possible assistance. During the entire operation, the squadron experienced a perfect safety record with no ground accidents and no aircraft accidents or incidents.

The first student pilot class started flying and graduated on schedule. There were a few problems noted. It is noteworthy that the 4449 CCTS is the only squadron of Caribous operating in the CONUS. Their assignment to Dyess has expedited the role of the 516 TAW and offered both a challenge and an opportunity to expand our horizons in the field of airlift."

July through September, 1969 [9]

" We were able to assimilate a new training mission within the wing with the arrival of the 4449th Combat Crew Training Squadron and their C-7A Caribous."

October through December, 1969 [10]

"I am pleased to note the achievements of the 18th Tactical Airlift Training Squadron which completed its move to Dyess and began the demanding task of training our future combat ready aircrews in the C-7A."

End Notes: 18 TATS

[1] *19690101-19690930 4442nd Combat Crew Training Wing* history
[2] *19690701-19691231 516th Tactical Airlift Wing history*
3 Headquarters, Tactical Air Command Special Order G-161, dated 27 August 1969
[4] Headquarters, 12th Air Force letter, dated 20 December 1969
[5] The Strategic Air Command philosophy can be seen in this approach to operational control during a mission.
[6] 4442nd CCTW Commander's Appraisal, 30 June 1969 by Col. Richard J. Gibney
[7] 4442nd CCTW Commander's Appraisal, 30 September 1969 by Col. Richard J. Gibney
[8] 516 TAW Commander's Summary [re: 18 TATS, pg. 37], 30 September 1969 by Col. Charles W. Borders
[9] 516 TAW Commander's Appraisal, 30 September 1969 by Col. Charles W. Borders
[10] 516 TAW Commander's Appraisal, 31 December 1969 by Col. Joel C. Stevenson for Col. Charles W. Borders

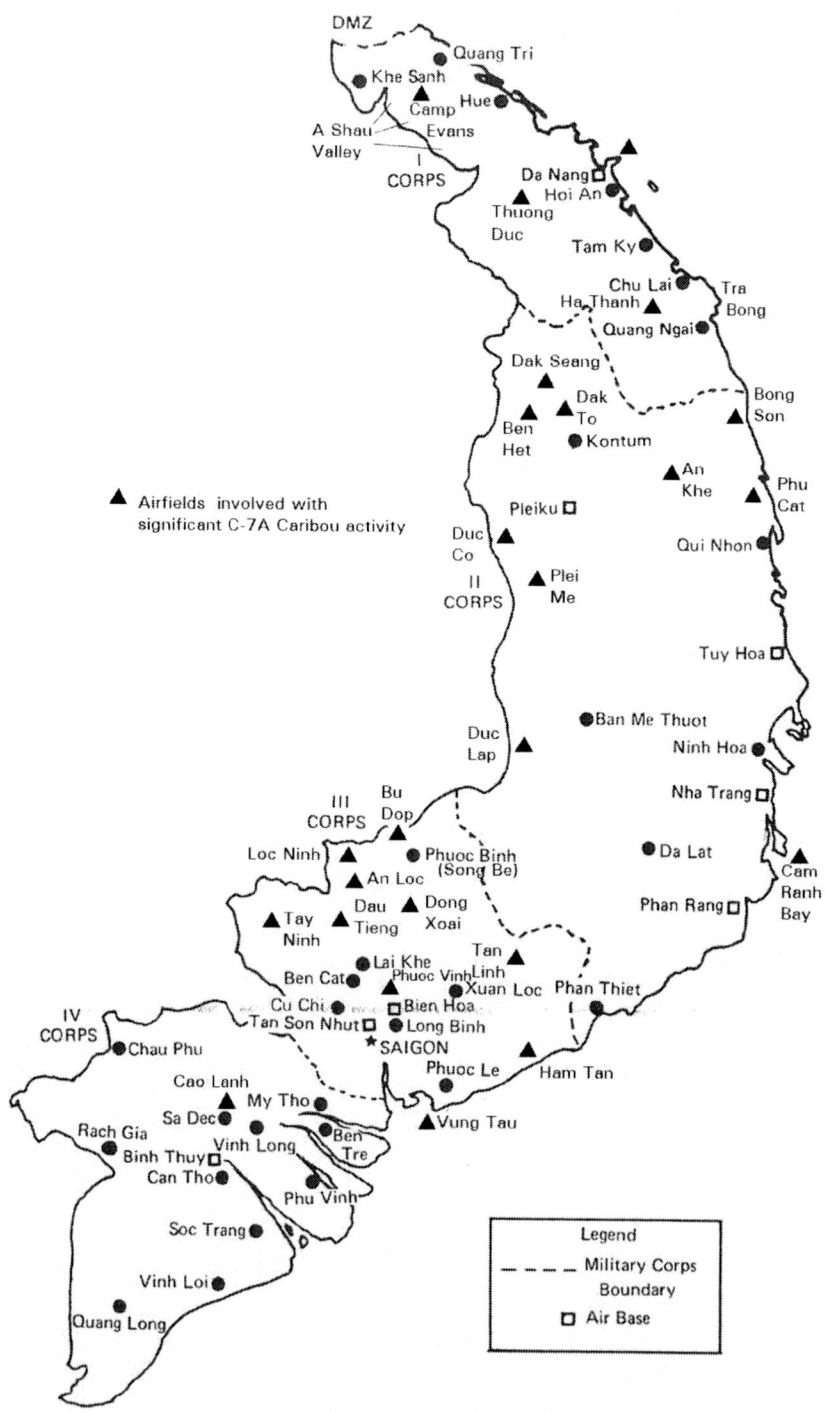

DMZ

Quang Tri

Khe Sanh

Hue

A Shau
Valley

Camp
Evans

I
CORPS

Da Nang

Hoi An

Thuong
Duc

Tam Ky

Chu Lai

Ha Thanh

Tra
Bong

Quang Ngai

Dak Seang

Dak
To

Bong
Son

Ben
Het

Kontum

An
Khe

Phu
Cat

▲ Airfields involved with
significant C-7A Caribou activity

Pleiku

Qui Nhon

Duc
Co

Plei
Me

II
CORPS

Tuy Hoa

Ban Me Thuot

Duc
Lap

Ninh Hoa

Nha Trang

Bu
Dop

III
CORPS

Loc Ninh

Phuoc Binh
(Song Be)

Da Lat

Cam
Ranh
Bay

An Loc

Dau
Tieng

Dong
Xoai

Phan Rang

Tay
Ninh

Tan

Lai Khe

Linh

Ben Cat

Phuoc Vinh

Xuan Loc

Cu Chi

Bien Hoa

Phan Thiet

IV
CORPS

Tan Son Nhut

Long Binh

Chau Phu

★ SAIGON

Phuoc Le

Ham Tan

Cao Lanh

My Tho

Sa Dec

Rach Gia

Vinh Long

Ben
Tre

Vung Tau

Binh Thuy

Can Tho

Phu Vinh

Soc Trang

Legend

Vinh Loi

Military Corps
Boundary

Quang Long

□ Air Base

298

Picture History of Bous in Vietnam

Ben Het C-7A crews (Copyright © 2014 George Harmon)

Goodies for the children (Copyright © 2014 Frank Godek)

C-7A Caribous on Ramp at CRB (Copyright © 2014 TomKoza)

Cow for Special Forces Camp (Copyright © 2014 Tom Finkler)

Softball on the Beach at Vung Tau (Copyright © 2014 Jay Baker)

Pet Snake at Vung Tau (Copyright © 2014 Jay Baker)

Inspecting the Prop (Copyright © 2014 Bill Craig)

Supply Area at Vung Tau (Copyright © 2014 Bill Craig)

Sights on the Way to Work (Copyright © 2014 Jay Baker)

Pleiku Junk Yard (Copyright © 2014 Frank Godek)

Pre-dock of C-7A S/N 62-4160 "Pamela Ferne"
(Copyright © 2014 Stoney Faubus)

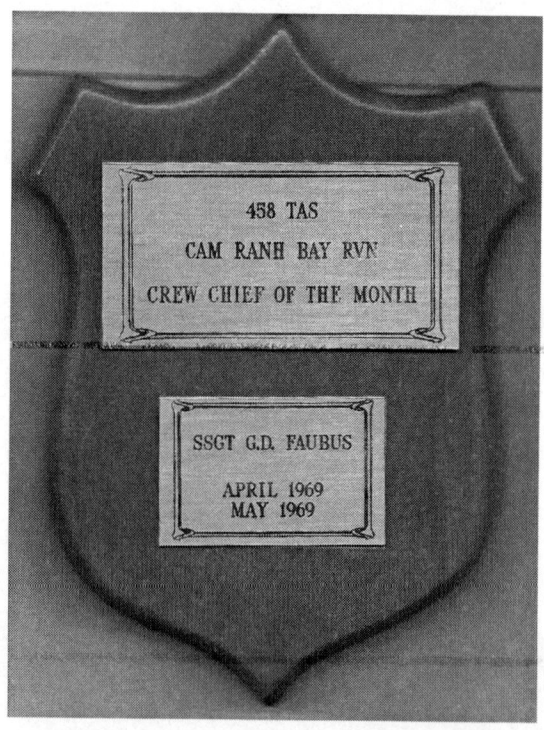

458 TAS
CAM RANH BAY RVN
CREW CHIEF OF THE MONTH

SSGT G.D. FAUBUS

APRIL 1969
MAY 1969

Crew Chief of the Month (Copyright © 2014 Stoney Faubus)

"Home of the Good Guys" Protected by Sandbags
(Copyright © 2014 Stan Owens)

C-7A S/N 63-9723 from the Air (Copyright © 2014 John Mood)

C-7A S/N 63-9723 at Tien Phuoc (Copyright © 2014 John Mood)

Counter-battery Fire at Tien Phuoc (Copyright © 2014 Frank Godek)

Dak Pek – C-7A Type I (Restricted) (Copyright © 2014 Frank Godek)

"Baby Bou" on Flagpole in Front of 483 TAW Headquarters
(Copyright © 2014 Dana Kelly)

C-7A in Phase Dock (Copyright © 2000 Roy Bell)

Refueling Caribou at Da Nang (Copyright © 2014 Tom Finkler)

Speed Off-load at SF Camp (Copyright © 2014 Tom Finkler)

Touchdown markers at Duc Phong (Copyright © 2014 Billy Hamlin)

Dunking Lt. Col. Charles E. Barnett After *Fini* Flight
(Copyright © 2014 Roger Peacock)

Loading Cow for Air Drop (Copyright © 2014 Al Cunliffe)

Santa Bou Team (Copyright © 2014 Rick Patterson)
(Left to Right) 1/Lt. Henry E. Wilborn, unidentified USAF pilot,
two unidentified ladies, TALO from Chu Lai, 1/Lt. Timothy M. Ennor,
two unidentified USAF personnel, 1/Lt. Richard Patterson)

535 TAS Logo (Copyright © 2014 Bill Craig)

Appendix I: Blue vs. Green

In the early 1960's, there was a battle between the Air Force and the Army over helicopters and the size of fixed wing aircraft that the Army should have in its inventory. On 15 September 1965, Deputy Secretary of Defense Cyrus R. Vance approved Air Force use of CH-3C helicopters ("Jolly Green Giants"), noting that the stated mission appeared to be an Army function, and he qualified his decision as contingent on further clarification of the matter of transfer of the CH-3C unit to the Army. A week later the Chief of Staff USAF (CSAF), General John P. McConnell, replied on behalf of the Joint Chiefs. He advised that the CH-3C unit would be used to support Air Force activities and to supply remote sites in Laos, and he omitted any reference to conventional ground force support. McConnell also informed the Air Staff that he had reached "an informal understanding" with Vance that the Air Force would not attempt to deliver supplies to the Army by helicopter. The concession was made in the interest of preserving accord with Vance and Secretary of Defense, Robert S. McNamara, since the latter opposed an Air Force helicopter arm and had been twice challenged in force and budget actions earlier in the year. Thereafter, the Air Force advocated a limited helicopter role, although it continued to hope for the development of a vertical-flight, fixed wing craft. The Air Force's interim objectives included the development of new delivery modes for fixed wing transports such as a low-altitude parachute extraction system and the improvement of assault strip construction capability. Requesting the purchase of additional CH-3C's in November, the Air Force omitted reference to possible use of this aircraft in air supply operations for ground force support.

The outcome of these discussions was the official creation of the 20th Helicopter Squadron (USAF) at Tan Son Nhut on 8 October 1965. The unit was authorized a complement of 14 CH-3C's (reduced from 25 because of limited resources) and the aircraft were drawn mainly from the TAC unit at Eglin Air Force Base, FL, and from new production. The unit's mission, according to the Seventh Air Force (7AF), was:

> "To support various Air Force combat activities, such as the communications sites, Tactical Air Control System, air liaison officers, airfield construction, aeromedical evacuations, counterinsurgency operations, and to support/augment search and rescue forces in SEA [Southeast Asia] if required. The unit will also be respon-

sive to priority requirements of MACV."

Airlift activity commenced in December and sorties increased to a monthly average of 990 during the first three months of 1966. The CH-3Cs operated from the main base at Tan Son Nhut and from operating locations at Da Nang and Cam Ranh Bay (CRB). Operational control was initially vested in the local base support unit at each site, but shifted to the 14th Air Commando Wing at Nha Trang in early 1966. Planning and staff supervisory control was centered in the airlift branch of the 2nd Air Division. Control by the 315th Wing or within the airlift system was thus entirely absent, which was consistent with the clarification of roles.

The unit was soon occupied in tasks beyond its mission statement. Responding to a Marine request in January 1966, the 20th enlarged its Da Nang detachment to eight aircraft. For two months, the Air Force helicopters performed medium lift support for Marine operations south of Chu Lai, completing nearly 600 varied cargo and troop lifts. Six of the Da Nang aircraft returned to Nha Trang in March, promptly commencing extensive support of U.S. Army operations west of Tuy Hoa. Tasks authorized by the 2nd Air Division were limited to displacement and resupply of artillery elements, loads beyond the capability of available Army helicopters, and the transport of heavy items such as ammunition, rations, and water. The Nha Trang flight flew nearly 400 sorties in March in behalf of the Army, including retrieval of two downed UH-1's. Meanwhile, the Tan Son Nhut CH-3Cs served successfully in Operation MASTIFF,[170] and in April the Military Advisory Command Vietnam arranged with 7AF that first priority for use of these ships would be support of ground force operations, pending arrival of additional CH-47 Chinook helicopters. In June, General Westmoreland requested a specific allocation of CH-3C flying hours for the same purpose.

The critical shortages of CH-47 Chinooks temporarily ended doctrinal rigidity. The trend toward using them in air supply and troop movements with the Army ended, however, upon transfer of the 20th to Nha Trang in June and employment of the unit in unconventional warfare roles. Guidance from Air Force headquarters at the beginning of 1967 reconfirmed the Air Force position that its helicopters should not compete with Army helicopters, but should plainly establish their role in special air warfare.

Equally sensitive was the issue of the Army's fixed wing Caribou fleet. In a letter to Westmoreland dated 7 April 1965, Maj. Gen. Joseph H. Moore, commander of 7AF, renewed the proposal that the two companies of CV-2 Caribous then in Vietnam should be employed under the Southeast Asia Airlift System, promising better customer services and reduced aerial port duplication. Moore envisioned no major basing changes, but recommended scheduling by the airlift control centers under MACV priorities. Westmoreland, having requested an additional three Caribou companies in July for the Phase I expansion to raise the total to six,[171] rejected the idea of centralized control and indicated that each company was to support either a Corps area, the Special Forces, or MACV. The Air Force raised no opposition to the augmentation, appreciating that more Caribous were needed. The first of the three companies arrived in November and at the end of 1965 Caribou strength in Vietnam was 88 craft. Although General McConnell renewed the question of placing the Caribou force under the airlift system's control, agreement was limited to a MACV proviso that Caribou pilots should advise Air Force aerial ports when unused cargo or passenger space was anticipated. The Air Force meanwhile held firmly against a new Army proposal to procure 120 CV-7 Buffalo aircraft.[172] The Air Force viewed the turboprop aircraft as a costly duplication of the jet-modified C-123.

In late 1965, private negotiations began between Generals McConnell and Johnson over the transfer of Caribou and Buffalo aircraft to the Air Force. These were encouraged by the Chairman of the Joint Chiefs of Staff, General Earle Wheeler, who wished to avoid involving the Secretary of Defense, Robert McNamara, or the Joint Chiefs of Staff (where the other two services might exert their influence).

Negotiations resulting in the transfer of all Caribou and Buffalo aircraft to the Air Force was managed privately by the two chiefs of staff. McConnell had begun his tenure determined to do something about service differences on tactical aviation, and he later remembered that his observations on the Army's low usage rate of the Caribou became the catalyst for their discussions. Private conversations with Army Chief of Staff, General Harold K. Johnson, began in late 1965. Brig. Gen. Richard A. Yudkin, Deputy Director of Plans for Advanced Planning, who assisted McConnell in preparing the negotiating sessions, had the impression that the meetings were encouraged by the influence of Joint Chiefs Chairman Wheeler and by his desire to avoid resolution of the matter by the Secretary of Defense or by the Joint Chiefs of Staff (where the other services could exert influence).

McConnell and Johnson met frequently, but according to their own schedules, and they exchanged memoranda sometimes through handwritten notes. After each session McConnell "debriefed" a small number of Air Staff officers, informing them of the decisions reached or the direction being taken. The chief rarely asked for substantive advice although Yudkin and his associates prepared backup data for each meeting, and on one occasion produced eight different texts for a possible agreement, each carefully analyzed in its individual folder. At one point, Johnson charged that the airlift system lacked responsiveness in meeting emergency airlift requests. To this the Air Force replied on 9 March 1966, by offering: (1) to place liaison officers as low as battalion level if necessary, (2) to institute a system of emergency requests using the tactical air control system net, and (3) to accept the idea of ground force mission control under temporary circumstances. The Air Staff on the same date cautioned officers in the Pacific to avoid actions which might stiffen Westmoreland against a Caribou transfer. McConnell and Johnson drafted the final agreement in pencil in the latter's office. McConnell remembered that both chiefs informed their staffs that only constructive comments were wanted, and that "if anyone attempted to change the meaning of what we agreed to, he was fired." The imminence of final agreement became clear when on March 25 Vance advised the Joint Chiefs that any Caribou and Buffalo aircraft to be procured in the future would be assigned to the Air Force.

The formal agreement was signed by McConnell and Johnson on 6 April 1966. Its main provision was that the Army would transfer all Caribous and Buffalos to the Air Force by 1 January 1967, and relinquish its claims for future fixed wing tactical airlift craft. Johnson, in turn, gained assurance that the Army would be consulted in future force structure and developmental decisions and that Air Force Caribou, Buffalo, and C-123 aircraft might be "attached" to Army divisions or subordinate commands. The Air Force made a final renunciation of its helicopter supply role, but reserved the right to operate helicopters for rescue and special air warfare. Both services agreed to continue joint development of vertical takeoff craft.

For some Army officers, the loss of the Caribous in return for empty guarantees of the status quo in helicopters was a bitter defeat. A current of opinion resisted the claim of the superiority of the heavier C-130 for supply work in a combat zone. Of some consolation was the promise of easement in the Army's shortage of pilots. Nor did the Air Force, which had long challenged the usefulness of the Caribou, now receive the agreement with enthusiasm, appreciating the manpower and functioning resources the new Caribou squadrons would require. Yudkin legalistically felt it was unwise for the Air Force to renounce any air vehicle (i.e., the helicopter) needed for a military task. Both chiefs merit credit for enforcing a sensible agreement on their luke-warm subordinates and for creating a climate of cooperation during the transfer period which followed. Final resolution as to how the Air Force Caribou arm in Vietnam was to be used – whether under central control or "attached" to particular users – remained to be determined.

The implications of the agreement reached years into the future and influenced the history of airlift in Southeast Asia as well as that of the whole military airlift establishment. Given the climate of opinion in the Office of the Secretary of Defense, it is difficult to see how McConnell, as the advocate of the Air Force positions, could have achieved more. Army ownership of the medium helicopters in Vietnam appeared to be working well, exploiting fully the capabilities of those vehicles. The idea of placing some of these craft within the Southeast Asia Airlift System, while still appealing to airlifters, remained beyond consideration. At the least, McConnell kept open the path for future Air Force ownership of vertical and short field transports. Beyond this, assessment of the wisdom of the Caribou transfer awaited the performance of the Air Force in its utilization of these craft in the months and years to come.

The key points of the agreement formally signed by McConnell and Johnson on 6 April 1966,[173] read:

a. The Chief of Staff, US Army, agrees to relinquish all claims for CV-2 and CV-7 aircraft and for future fixed wing aircraft designed for tactical airlift. These assets now in the Army inventory will be transferred to the Air Force. (CSA and CSAF agree that this does not apply to the administrative mission support fixed wing aircraft.)

b. The Chief of Staff, US Air Force, agrees:

To relinquish all claims for helicopters and follow-on rotary wing aircraft which are designed and operated for intra-theater movement, fire support, supply and resupply of Army Forces and those Air Force control elements assigned to a Direct Air Support Center (DASC) and subordinate thereto.

To retain the CV-2 and CV-7 aircraft in the Air Force structure and to consult with the Chief of Staff, US Army, prior to changing the force levels of, or replacing these aircraft.

c. The Chief of Staff, US Army, and the Chief of Staff, US Air Force, jointly agree:

To revise all Service doctrinal statements, manuals, and other material in variance with the sub-stance and spirit of this agreement.

That the necessary actions resulting from this agreement will be completed by 1 January 1967.

Army Caribou at Fort Benning, GA
(Copyright © 2014 A. J. Stinson Family)

USAF Caribous on Ramp at Vung Tau (Copyright © 2014 Bill Craig)

Appendix II: 1969 Chronology

Date   **Event**

January

1   Head count of troops in Vietnam: US 536,040; RVN 826,500; ROK 50,003; AU 7,661; NZ 516; Thai 6,005; Phil 1,576

12   Can Tho attacked with B-40 rockets, 60 mm mortar, satchel charges, and automatic weapons.

19   Negotiating teams meet in Paris for more than 5 hours for procedural discussions.

20   Richard Nixon sworn in as President.

21   USS Ron Green County (LST-1559) hit by 122 mm rocket at Vung Tau.

25   First substantive talks held in Paris.

29   Stand-down for Tet announced for 150700 to 220700 February.

February

15   Vietnamese Marine Corps find arms cache 10 km NW of Minh Thanh – largest cache to date by Vietnamese Armed Forces.

23   Enemy launches indirect fire harassing attacks on more than 100 cities and bases.

25   Captured letter from VC cadre labels enemy's present activities as an "all-out offensive and uprising."

26   Fifty locations attacked by indirect, harassing fire.

28   Elements of 9th Regiment, 3rd Marine Division find two caches of weapons 50 miles SW of Quang Tri City (350 tons, mostly new weapons and munitions) – largest quantity captured in any one area to date.

28   Head count: US 541,847.

March

1   1,005 Hoi Chanh ("Open Arms" defectors) for week ending 1 March, largest one week total since March 1967

1   3rd Battalion, 503rd Airborne Infantry find cache of 346 tons of rice 23 km SSE of Bao Loc, Lam Dong Province.

3   Ben Het CIDG camp attacked by 10 USSR PT-76 tanks with 6 trucks in support. Two tanks and 6 vehicles destroyed. First use of armor by enemy in II Corps Tactical Zone since 7 Feb. 1968.

16   Sixty-five mortar and rockets strike military installations and population centers – highest number of attacks since start of current offensive, seven 122 mm rockets land in Saigon area.

29   US KIAs surpass Korean War KIA total of 33,629.

Date	Event
March	
31	Head count: US 540,306
April	
1	Secretary of Defense announces B-52 strikes reduced from 1800 to 1600 per month due to reduced defense spending.
11	MACV and USA SF compounds in Tay Ninh City receive 40 107 mm rockets.
19	Royal Khmer Government (Cambodia) rejects US initiative to reestablish diplomatic relations.
27	Grass fire at Amphibious Support Base #1, Da Nang spreads to main ammunition area, more than 39,000 tons of unserviceable ammunition destroyed.
30	Head count: US 543,482
May	
6	CH-47 crashes 3 miles SW of Phuoc Binh, 32 ARVN soldiers KIA, 34 injured; 2 US KIA, 1 injured.
12	159 indirect fire harassing attacks during night of 11-12 May.
31	Head count: US 540,429.
June	
2	Hoi Chanh for 1969 equals 18,748, greater than the 18,171 in 1968.
10	Nixon announces redeployment of 25,000 US troops.
18	B-52's end fourth year of participation in Vietnam War.
26	Ben Het shelled (1,539 rounds) for 26th consecutive day. Enemy soldier states intentions are to destroy camp to support the Paris peace conference.
29	Pressure continues on Ben Het, intensity decreases, 21 rounds of 75 mm recoilless fire kills 3 Allied soldiers and wounds 3.
30	Five AC-47 Spooky gunships turned over to VNAF as part of the Improvement and Modernization Program.
30	Head count: US 538,714
July	
8	3rd Battalion, 60th Infantry, 2nd Brigade, 9th Infantry Division departs for Fort Lewis, WA (first of the 25,000 man reduction).
11	Government of Vietnam President, Nguyen Van Thieu, calls for national vote to settle the war, offering participation to all political parties and groups if they renounce violence and pledge to accept election results.
13	9th Regimental Landing Team (USMC) begins redeployment to Okinawa (part of the 25,000 man reduction).

Date	Event

July

31   Head count: US 537,914

August

7   Satchel charges placed by enemy infiltrating over the beach detonate in Army convalescent hospital at Cam Ranh Bay. Two US KIA and 98 wounded, one ward destroyed, three heavily damaged.

12   149 attacks by fire around the country, 68 significant.

25   Mobile Riverine Force is disestablished, mission assumed by Vietnamese Navy Amphibious Task Force 211.

27   Hoi Chanh in 1969 exceeds 30,000.

31   Head count: US 509,569

September

3   Ho Chi Minh dies.

16   Nixon announces 35,000 more troops will be redeployed, beginning immediately, authorized reduce to 484,000.

30   Head count: US 510,530

October

2   Department of Defense announces US casualties for 21-27 September are lowest in more than 2 years, with 95 KIA.

9   US casualties for 28 September to 4 October lowest in nearly 3 years, with 64 KIA.

15   Vietnam War Moratorium (marches, rallies, vigils) held throughout US, Geneva, Paris, Rome, other capitals.

16   US casualties for 5-11 October include 82 KIA.

21   Hoi Chanh for 12-18 October are 1,310 – highest weekly total of the program.

21   US KIAs are 78.

22   6,000th aircraft lost (combat and non-combat, fixed- and rotary-wing)

23   Head count: US 497,300, lowest since 17 February 1969

25   US KIAs are 102.

27   NVA delegate in Paris announces "extremely important information on US POWs will be released"

31   Head count: US 496,274

November

3   US KIAs are 83 for 26 October to 1 November.

12   First AC-119K *Shadow* gunships arrive to replace AC-47 *Spooky* aircraft.

Date	Event

November

12	Republic of Philippines announces 1,500 man PHILCAGV will be withdrawn.
13	US KIAs are 97
15	Anti-war demonstrations in US (second in series).
20	Last National Guard (NG) unit leaves (Co. D, 151th Infantry Regiment, Indiana NG)
21	Ambassador Henry Cabot Lodge, US representative to Paris Peace Talks, announces resignation effective 8 December.
24	1/Lt. Calley to be tried by court-martial for killing of 109 Vietnamese in March 1968 at My Lai.
25	Last of 3rd Marine Division redeploys to Okinawa after 5 years and 120 major operations.
27	List of 59 US POWs released in Chicago by R.C. Davis (anti-war leader). List came from a member of NVN Paris Delegation.
30	Head count: US 478,701

December

4	Nguyen Van Thieu announces 24-hour cease fire on Christmas and New Year's Days.
14	Nixon announces third redeployment will be 50,000 by 15 April 70.
23	Secretary of State announces infiltration down about 60% compared with 1968.
23	Anti-war movement Madeline Duckles and Cora Weiss turn over to State Department a list of US POWs held by NVA (only four new names).
26	115 enemy violations of 24-hour Christmas truce.
31	Hoi Chanh for 1969 = 47,023 vs. 18,171 in 1968
31	End of year head count: US 483,326; RVN 969,256; Korea 48,869; Australia 7,672; New Zealand 552; Thailand 11,568; Philippines 189.
31	US casualties since 1961 exceed the Korea KIA total of 32,270.

GIẤY THÔNG-HÀNH

SAFE-CONDUCT PASS TO BE HONORED BY ALL VIETNAMESE GOVERNMENT AGENCIES AND ALLIED FORCES
이 안전보장패쓰는 월남정부와 모든 연합군에 의해 인정된 것입니다.
รัฐบาลเวียตนามและหน่วยพันธมิตร ยินดีให้เกียรศิแกผู้ถือบัตรผ่านปลอดภัยนี้.

"Blood Chit" (Copyright © 2014 Frank Pickart)

Maintenance Stand (Copyright © 2014 Bill Craig)

Bou on Ramp at CRB (Copyright © 2014 Tom Koza)

Air Force Cross

Silver Star

DFC

Air Medal

Appendix III: Awards

Rank	Last Name	First Name	MI	Award	Date	Location	Unit
CPT	Allison	Max	L	AM	13-Jun-69	Ben Het	537
TSG	Anderson	John	A	DFC	19-Nov-69		457
1LT	Anderson	Ray	W	DFC	29-Apr-69		459
TSG	Aust	James	H	DFC	20-Jul-69	RVN	457
TSG	Babcock	Edward	P	DFC	27-Nov-69		458
CPT	Bailey	Richard	W	DFC	05-Nov-69		535
MAJ	Baird	Richard	L	DFC	28-Mar-69	Ben Het/Dak Pek	457
MSG	Barber	John	E	DFC	25-Jul-69	RVN	457
TSG	Barker	Robert	L	DFC	13-May-69		536
MSG	Bartlett	Milford	S	DFC	30-Oct-69		458
SSG	Bednarski	Don	R	BS	15-Jan-69	Bu Krak	483
TSG	Bell	Lawrence	L	DFC	23-Apr-69		536
TSG	Berger	Morris	C	DFC	01-Apr-69	RVN	459
MAJ	Berggren	Richard	W	DFC	24-Nov-69		457
SGT	Berry	Perry	J	DFC	02-Jul-69	RVN	458
1LT	Bick	Bernard	F	DFC	03-May-69	RVN	459
MAJ	Biggins	Robert	B	DFC	25-Nov-69	Bu Dop	483
CPT	Bissinger, Jr	Harry	R	DFC	05-Nov-69		535
MAJ	Black	John	W	AM	13-Jun-69	Ben Het	537
1LT	Blinn	Roger	K	DFC	07-May-69	RVN	536
1LT	Boston	Douglas	M	DFC	30-Mar-69	Phouc Vinh	458
1LT	Boswell	Lance		DFC	28-Nov-69	near Bien Hoa	536
1LT	Bowling	David	B	PH	26-Dec-69	Tien Phuoc	459
1LT	Bowling	David	B	DFC	12-Aug-69	Tra Bong	459
SGT	Boylan	Frank		DFC	29-May-69	RVN	537
CPT	Brandl	Jimmie	R	DFC	12-Aug-69	Tra Bong	459
MAJ	Brennan	Richard	S	DFC	19-Jul-69	RVN	458
CPT	Brethouwer	Richard	L	DFC	21-Jun-69	Ben Het	537

Appendix III: Awards (cont.)

Rank	Last Name	First Name	MI	Award	Date	Location	Unit
TSG	Broussard	Emile	P	DFC	13-Jun-69	Ben Het	537
TSG	Brownfield	Donald	L	DFC	21-Jun-69	Ben Het	537
TSG	Callier	Roy	L	AM	11-Oct-69	Pleiku	459
CPT	Carlson	Edward	A	DFC	05-May-69	RVN	536
MAJ	Castles	John	H	DFC	27-Nov-69		536
TSG	Chasteen	Ralph	E	AM	26-Sep-69	Ben Het	537
1LT	Clancey, Jr	Daniel	J	DFC	08-Sep-69	Thien Ngon	535
1LT	Clark	Gary	L	AM	11-Oct-69	Pleiku	459
1LT	Cobbs, Jr	Leonard	W	DFC	08-Nov-69		535
CPT	Cocking	Duane	F	DFC	30-Mar-69		535
CPT	Cogley, III	Jesse	W	DFC	03-May-69	RVN	535
1LT	Cohen	Barry	L	DFC	23-Mar-69		535
1LT	Cohen	Barry	L	DFC	11-Apr-69		535
1LT	Cormack	David	E	DFC	09-May-69	RVN	458
1LT	Cowee	Bruce	T	DFC	29-Apr-69	RVN	458
MAJ	Cowell	Roger	T	DFC	10-Aug-69	RVN	459
SSG	Crafton	Stuart	B	DFC	06-Oct-69	RVN	537
SSG	Crocker	Dewey	L	DFC	14-Jun-69		457
1LT	Dana	Donald	G	DFC	05-May-69	RVN	459
1LT	Davis, Jr	Herbert	C	DFC	19-Aug-69	RVN	536
CPT	DeGroot, Jr	John	P	DFC	12-May-69	RVN	459
1LT	Dellamea	Vincent	E	DFC	08-May-69	RVN	458
1LT	Dennison, Jr	Charles	M	DFC	12-Sep-69	RVN	457
1LT	Denton	Dan	C	DFC	11-Nov-69		458
1LT	Depner	Deibert	A	DFC	15-Jun-69	RVN	536
CPT	Dickerson	Ivan	W	DFC	10-Dec-69		458
MSG	Dickman	Roy	C	DFC	13-Aug-69		536
1LT	Dijanni	Joseph	J	DFC	19-Aug-69	RVN	536
1LT	Dilley	Jerry	L	DFC	02-May-69	RVN	535

Appendix III: Awards (cont.)

Rank	Last Name	First Name	MI	Award	Date	Location	Unit
SSG	Dodds	John	L	DFC	24-Jun-69		536
1LT	Dodson, Jr	Claude	B	DFC	23-Aug-69	RVN	457
1LT	Dokken	Dennis	A	DFC	26-Dec-69	Tien Phuoc	459
MSG	Doyle	Vic	C	DFC	20-Aug-69	RVN	483
1LT	Drury	Jon	E	DFC	12-May-69	RVN	537
MAJ	Dugan	Robert	H	AM	21-Jun-69	Ben Het	537
TSG	Echols	Veries		DFC	31-Oct-69		458
TSG	Edwards	Fred	A	DFC	06-Nov-69		458
1LT	Erickson	Charles	R	DFC	07-Nov-69		535
MAJ	Evalenko	William	A	SS	13-Jun-69	Ben Het	537
CPT	Fadden	Michael	G	DFC	13-Oct-69		535
CPT	Farr	Howard	L	DFC	10-Sep-69	RVN	457
CPT	Findlay	William	R	DFC	16-Dec-69		535
1LT	Fischer	Curt		DFC	20-Jun-69	Ben Het	457
CPT	Fisher	Bobbie	D	DFC	13-Mar-69	RVN	457
MAJ	Fitzpatrick	Richard	L	DFC	22-Nov-69		459
1LT	Fong	Gerald	W	DFC	20-Nov-69		457
1LT	Fox, Jr	Richard	A	DFC	18-Sep-69	Mai Loc	458
LTC	Frazee	Donald	W	DFC	23-Feb-69		459
MSG	Fuhler	Donald	R	DFC	08-Sep-69		535
SSG	Fuller	Ralph	L	DFC	11-Apr-69		458
CPT	Furchak	Edward	L	DFC	12-Nov-69		537
CPT	Furchak	Edward	L	DFC	21-Jun-69	Ben Het	537
CPT	Garner, Jr	Hugh	T	DFC	12-Aug-69	near Duc Hue	535
TSG	Gill	Donald	M	PH	17-Jun-69	Phu Cat	483
CPT	Girod	Alan	L	DFC	26-Jun-69	Ben Het	537
TSG	Godek, Jr	Franklin	F	AM	31-Dec-69	Tien Phuoc ???	537
LTC	Gordon	Mitchell	K	AM	31-Dec-69		537
1LT	Gould	Michael	D	DFC	03-Dec-69	Bu Dop	535

327

Rank	Last Name	First Name	MI	Award	Date	Location	Unit
SGT	Grady	Robert	E	PH	17-Jun-69	Phu Cat	459
1LT	Grant	William	N	DFC	20-May-69	RVN	537
1LT	Greinke	Neil	N	PH	11-Sep-69	Plei Djereng	537
1LT	Greinke	Neil	N	DFC	17-Jun-69	Ben Het	537
CPT	Griffith	Charles	S	DFC	16-Aug-69		535
CPT	Grigg	Dale		AM	13-Jun-69	Ben Het	537
CPT	Gunkel	James	R	DFC	28-Apr-69	RVN	535
MAJ	Gutierrez	Julius	C	DFC	27-Apr-69	RVN	536
1LT	Guzman	Philip	M	DFC	24-Aug-69	RVN	457
TSG	Hafner	Andrew	W	DFC	24-Nov-69		457
TSG	Hames	George	W	DFC	02-Dec-69		537
MSG	Hamilton	Thomas	R	DFC	20-Dec-69		458
MAJ	Hamrin	Robert	S	DFC	13-Feb-69		536
MAJ	Hanavan, Jr	E. Patrick		BS	15-Jan-69	Bu Krak	535
1LT	Hardenburger	Robert	R	DFC	17-Jun-69	Ben Het ?	457
MAJ	Hardie	Charles	W	DFC	21-Jun-69	Ben Het	457
CPT	Haseltine	John	E	DFC	06-May-69	RVN	459
1LT	Hasley, Jr	Richard	L	DFC	17-Aug-69	RVN	457
1LT	Hassett	Steven	J	DFC	24-Aug-69	Moc Hoa	458
LTC	Hastings	Edgar	A	DFC	21-Jul-69	RVN	537
TSG	Hatcher	James	E	DFC	23-Feb-69		459
1LT	Hatcher, III	Walter	T	DFC	15-Aug-69		459
1LT	Havins, Jr	Felton	H	DFC	03-Jul-69	Ben Het	537
TSG	Hayes	Maurice	C	DFC	21-Jun-69	Ben Het ?	537
1LT	Herrell	Dennis	E	DFC	25-Jul-69	RVN	536
MAJ	Herrington	Felix	R	DFC	27-Aug-69	That Son	535
1LT	Hertel	Harris	C	DFC	17-Jul-69	RVN	459
SGT	Higgins	William	R	DFC	30-Jan-69	RVN	459
TSG	Hill	Robert	B	DFC	21-Jun-69	Ben Het	537

Appendix III: Awards (cont.)

Rank	Last Name	First Name	MI	Award	Date	Location	Unit
1LT	Hocutt	James	K	DFC	22-Nov-69	Bu Dop	458
CPT	Hudson, II	Robert	E	DFC	23-Sep-69		536
LTC	Hurley	Vincent	J	DFC	16-Jun-69	RVN	459
1LT	Hutton	William	E	DFC	12-Aug-69	RVN	459
SSG	Jackson	James	L	DFC	29-Jun-69	RVN	535
CPT	Jacobowitz	Leonard		DFC	14-Jun-69	RVN	536
SGT	Jaderberg	Albert		DFC	20-Jul-69	RVN	536
SSG	James, Jr	Donald		DFC	17-Aug-69		457
CPT	Jardine	Randy	B	DFC	05-Mar-69		458
TSG	Johnson	Travis	O	DFC	02-May-69		458
1LT	Jones	Dwight	B	DFC	16-Nov-69		458
TSG	Jones	Herman	D	DFC	15-Nov-69		537
1LT	Kassen	William	C	DFC	20-Nov-69		535
SSG	Kelley	Robert	G	DFC	11-Nov-69		457
CPT	Kelly	Joseph	M	DFC	28-Aug-69		458
TSG	Kern	Richard	L	DFC	23-Oct-69		535
SSG	Kimball	Manfred	W	DFC	31-Jul-69	RVN	536
MSG	Klang	William	L	DFC	23-Mar-69		459
LTC	Kozey, Jr	John		DFC	13-Jul-69		459
TSG	Kruse	Gerald	F	DFC	24-Nov-69		457
CPT	Lanoue	Richard	R	DFC	20-Nov-69	Duc Lap	459
MAJ	Lantz	Richard	M	DFC	27-Jun-69	RVN	458
TSG	Lara	Armand		DFC	12-Aug-69		459
MSG	Larkins	Earl	L	DFC	21-Jul-69	RVN	457
1LT	Larson	David	E R	DFC	27-Nov-69	Song Mao	457
LTC	Laughlin	Ronald	L	DFC	16-Feb-69		535
1LT	Lavelle	Michael	P	DFC	08-May-69	RVN	535
TSG	Lebrun	Charles	W	DFC	20-Nov-69		459
MSG	Lemmon	David	L	DFC	23-Feb-69		457

Appendix III: Awards (cont.)

Rank	Last Name	First Name	MI	Award	Date	Location	Unit
MAJ	Lockwood	Delbert	D	SS	13-Jun-69	Ben Het	537
MAJ	Lockwood	Delbert	D	DFC	24-Feb-69	Ben Het	537
MAJ	Lockwood	Delbert	D	PH	13-Jun-69	Ben Het	537
1LT	Loose	Chester	S	DFC	13-May-69	RVN	535
1LT	Loughran	John	T	DFC	20-Nov-69		458
LTC	MacFarren	Donald	J	DFC	26-Jun-69	Ben Het	537
LTC	MacFarren	Donald	J	AM	10-Jun-69	Ben Het	537
CPT	Marlin	Paul	R	DFC	25-Apr-69	RVN	535
SGT	Marrotte	Norman	A	DFC	15-Aug-69	Tra Bong?	459
1LT	Mascaro	Kenneth	E	DFC	11-Dec-69	Duc Phong	535
SGT	Matiash	Michael		PH	17-Jun-69	Phu Cat	459
MSG	Matthews	Otis	M	DFC	29-Oct-69	???	457
CPT	McClure	Spencer	F	DFC	11-Nov-69	Chu Lai	459
CPT	McElroy	Peter	A	DFC	10-May-69	RVN	536
MAJ	McKenzie	Christy	D	DFC	27-Jan-69	RVN	535
SMS	McWhorter	Charles	L	DFC	25-May-69		535
SSG	Mellert	John	D	DFC	10-Jun-69	Ben Het	537
1LT	Melton	Edgar	R	DFC	26-Sep-69		535
TSG	Merrill	David	D	BS	15-Jan-69	Bu Krak	483
TSG	Metrolis, Jr	Frank	J	DFC	15-Sep-69	RVN	457
CPT	Mickley	Jon	E	DFC	15-Dec-69	Bu Dop	535
1LT	Milazzo	Robert	P	DFC	29-Nov-69		535
1LT	Miles	David	A	AM	31-Dec-69		537
MSG	Miller	Robert	W	DFC	29-Oct-69		457
1LT	Miller	Gary	L	DFC	25-Jul-69	RVN	536
1LT	Miller	Arthur	L	DFC	12-May-69		459
TSG	Miller	Raymond	W	DFC	24-Oct-69	RVN	457
SGT	Miller	John	T	DFC	16-Jun-69		457
1LT	Mitchell	Harry	R	DFC	23-Jul-69	RVN	536

Appendix III: Awards (cont.)

Rank	Last Name	First Name	MI	Award	Date	Location	Unit
MAJ	Monroe	Kent	M	DFC	22-Jun-69	Ben Het	537
1LT	Mood, Jr	John	D	DFC	28-Jun-69	Ben Het	457
1LT	Mosher	Walter	L	DFC	11-Nov-69	Bu Dop	535
1LT	Muffley	Gary	S	DFC	27-May-69		535
CPT	Murphey, II	Thomas	G	DFC	24-May-69	RVN	458
1LT	Murphey, II	Thomas	G	BS	15-Jan-69	Bu Krak	458
MAJ	Murphy	Michael		AM	14-Jun-69	Ben Het	537
CPT	Murphy	Kevin	J	DFC	30-Nov-69		535
TSG	Myers	James	D	DFC	27-Nov-69	Bu Dop	458
LTC	Myers	Clem	B	DFC	24-Jun-69		535
CPT	Nafziger	Paul	A	DFC	19-Apr-69	RVN	459
1LT	Nelson	Randall	W	DFC	26-Aug-69		459
1LT	Nevins	Christopher	F	DFC	04-Dec-69	Bu Dop	458
TSG	Newport	Harold	M	DFC	04-Nov-69		535
SSG	Nickerson	Gilbert	M	DFC	26-Dec-69	Tien Phuoc	459
MAJ	Noren	Clinton	L	DFC	25-Oct-69	Ben Het	457
TSG	Norum	Russell	V	DFC	11-Dec-69	Duc Phong	535
MSG	Obets	Richard	C	DFC	27-Jun-69	RVN	536
TSG	Omyer	Morris	W	DFC	27-Nov-69		458
LTC	Osborn	James	R	SS	03-Jun-69	RVN	537
A1C	Osborne, Jr	William		BS	15-Jan-69	Bu Krak	483
TSG	Overcash	Hugh	M	DFC	14-Jun-69	Ben Het	537
TSG	Owen	Billy	P	DFC	22-Jun-69	Ben Het	537
TSG	Owens	Tom	M	DFC	23-Dec-69	Song Be	458
MSG	Paramore	Travis	M	DFC	13-Nov-69		457
1LT	Pavolko, Jr	George	J	DFC	22-Jun-69	RVN	459
TSG	Pearce	Joseph	P	DFC	13-Aug-69	Bu Dop	458
LTC	Pennington	Lawrence	E	DFC	11-Aug-69	RVN	459
LTC	Peterson	Vernon	L	DFC	02-Nov-69		457

331

Appendix III: Awards (cont.)

Rank	Last Name	First Name	MI	Award	Date	Location	Unit
CPT	Pettit, Sr	Eli	M	DFC	25-Sep-69		459
LTC	Piercy	Jeff	J	DFC	16-Nov-69	Bu Dop	458
TSG	Pierre	Robert	S	Airman's Medal	21-Apr-69		535
TSG	Piontek, Jr	Stanley	J	DFC	10-Apr-69	RVN	459
MAJ	Proctor	Lowell	T L	DFC	15-Dec-69		458
MAJ	Pulse, II	Paul	F	AM	17-Apr-69		537
TSG	Quarles	John	W	DFC	26-Jun-69	Ben Het	537
1LT	Quinn, Jr	William	F	PH	13-Jun-69	Ben Het	537
1LT	Quinn, Jr	William	F	DFC	13-Jun-69	Ben Het	537
SGT	Reynen	Leonard	M	DFC	24-Dec-69	Cau Mau	536
MAJ	Richardson, Jr	Nathan	T	DFC	11-Nov-69	Bu Dop	457
MSG	Richey	Moses	A	DFC	28-Aug-69		458
TSG	Rollin, Sr	Peter	R	DFC	08-Sep-69		535
1/L	Rollins	James	B	AM	11-Oct-69	Pleiku	459
1LT	Rosenquist	Parker	W	DFC	07-Jul-69	RVN	458
2LT	Ross	Charles	B	PH	11-Sep-69	Plei Djereng	537
2LT	Ross	Charles	B	DFC	11-Sep-69	Plei Djereng	537
LTC	Rossing	Arthur	T	AM	25-Sep-69		459
1LT	Safford	Steven	J	DFC	12-Aug-69		459
CPT	Sample, Jr	Robert	W	DFC	13-Apr-69	RVN	536
TSG	Scarborough	Donald	D	DFC	04-Jul-69	RVN	457
SGT	Schaeffer	John	E	DFC	13-Jul-69	RVN	536
MSG	Schmidtke	Roger	L	DFC	05-Nov-69	Bu Dop/Bunard	535
MAJ	Schultz	Andrew	M	DFC	07-Jun-69		458
TSG	Schultz	Earl	E	DFC	20-Dec-69		536
CPT	Scobee	Francis	R	DFC	10-Apr-69	RVN	535
TSG	Scott, Jr	Harry	A	DFC	08-Nov-69		535
1LT	Seavey	Derrill	V	DFC	04-Nov-69		458
CPT	Seymour	Ronald	D	DFC	10-May-69	RVN	459

Appendix III: Awards (cont.)

Rank	Last Name	First Name	MI	Award	Date	Location	Unit
MAJ	Shade	John	E	DFC	28-Aug-69		458
TSG	Shaw	Donald	F	DFC	25-Jun-69	RVN	536
SSG	Shepherd	William	L	DFC	25-Jun-69	Ben Het	537
CPT	Shoun	John	W	DFC	23-Oct-69		535
1LT	Sidwell	Larry	W	DFC	11-Jun-69	RVN	457
1LT	Siler, III	Maynard	D	AM	07-Oct-69	near Saigon	458
SSG	Sitzenstock, Jr	Charles	H	AM	25-Sep-69	North Vietnam	459
SSG	Sitzenstock, Jr	Charles	H	DFC	07-Feb-69	Phu Cat	459
1LT	Smith	William	D	DFC	25-Jun-69		535
CPT	Smith, Jr	Josh	M	DFC	20-Oct-69	Bu Krak	537
CPT	Sonick	Robert	L	DFC	27-Nov-69	Bu Dop	458
A1C	Sorenson	Thomas	C	Airman's Medal	21-Apr-69		535
SSG	Spence	Norman		DFC	03-May-69	RVN	457
TSG	Stafford	Edward	E	DFC	15-Aug-69		459
LTC	Stalk	George		DFC	12-Aug-69	Tra Bong	459
MSG	Stevenson	George	R	BS	15-Jan-69	Bu Krak	483
1LT	Stone	Michael	C	DFC	15-May-69	RVN	536
SSG	Sutterfield	Donald	V	DFC	19-Jan-69		458
MSG	Swaim	Walter	R	DFC	13-Nov-69		457
1LT	Sweatland	Keith	K	DFC	09-Nov-69		457
1LT	Tatum	Gail	F	DFC	21-Nov-69		457
LTC	Taylor	Robert	H	DFC	03-Jun-69	Ben Het	537
TSG	Taylor	Jake	M	DFC	15-Feb-69		458
LTC	Thielen	Edward	J	DFC	29-Sep-69	RVN	459
TSG	Thomas	Robert	F	DFC	28-May-69		458
TSG	Thomas, Jr	John	L	DFC	27-Jun-69	Ben Het	537
CPT	Tost	Charles	L	DFC	12-May-69	RVN	537
SSG	Turney	William	C	DFC	02-Jul-69		458
LTC	Tyler	Clifford	E	DFC	14-Jul-69	RVN	536

Appendix III: Awards (cont.)

Rank	Last Name	First Name	MI	Award	Date	Location	Unit
CPT	Underwood	Gary	R	DFC	15-Aug-69		459
MAJ	Vanness	Charles	R	DFC	17-Nov-69	Bu Krak	537
TSG	Verastro	Vincent	A	BS	15-Jan-69	Bu Krak	483
TSG	Vittorio	Wayne	F	DFC	28-Nov-69		536
MAJ	Vondersmith	William	M	DFC	21-Dec-69	Tien Phuoc	459
CPT	Wade	James	W	DFC	11-Sep-69	RVN	457
MAJ	Walker	Alvin	L	DFC	03-Nov-69		457
LTC	Walker	Melvin	K	DFC	19-Nov-69		457
TSG	Wall	James	D	PH	17-Jun-69	Phu Cat	483
1LT	Wansack	James	K	DFC	21-Oct-69		536
TSG	Wars, Jr	James	L	DFC	12-Aug-69		459
LTC	Watkins	Eugene	C	DFC	14-Aug-69	RVN	458
TSG	Welch, Jr	E	J	DFC	26-Dec-69	Tien Phuoc	459
LTC	White	Dawson	N	DFC	13-Nov-69	Bu Dop	457
TSG	White, Jr	John	E	PH	13-Jun-69	Ben Het	537
1LT	Wiesneth	Robert	P	PH	11-Sep-69	Plei Djereng	537
1LT	Wiesneth	Robert	P	DFC	25-Apr-69	Nhon Co	537
MAJ	Wigington	John	H	AM	13-Jun-69	Ben Het	537
SSG	Wilhelm	Frederick		PH	11-Sep-69	Plei Djereng	537
SSG	Wilhelm	Frederick		DFC	12-Jun-69	Ben Het	537
1LT	Wilks	Phillip	G	DFC	11-Aug-69	RVN	458
1LT	Williams	John	B	DFC	18-Dec-69		457
TSG	Wilson	Joseph	H	DFC	15-Nov-69		535
CPT	Wilson	Luther	R	DFC	15-Nov-69		459
CPT	Wilson	Luther	R	AM	25-Sep-69		459
1LT	Wilson	Clyde	M	DFC	26-Jun-69	Ben Het	537
1LT	Wisch	Roger	L	DFC	15-Jun-69	RVN	536
1LT	Witzig	William	L	DFC	26-Jun-69	Ben Het	537
1LT	Wohrer	James	F	DFC	22-Jun-69	Ben Het	537

Appendix III: Awards (cont.)

Rank	Last Name	First Name	MI	Award	Date	Location	Unit
MAJ	Wolpert	Donald	G	DFC	09-Nov-69		459
MAJ	Wright	Larry	D	SS	30-Oct-69		458
MAJ	Wright	Larry	D	DFC	29-Nov-69		458
SSG	York	Jerry	A	DFC	16-Jun-69	RVN	537
MAJ	Yost	Daniel	C	DFC	17-May-69	RVN	537
MAJ	Zachary	Daniel	L	DFC	23-Sep-69		536

335

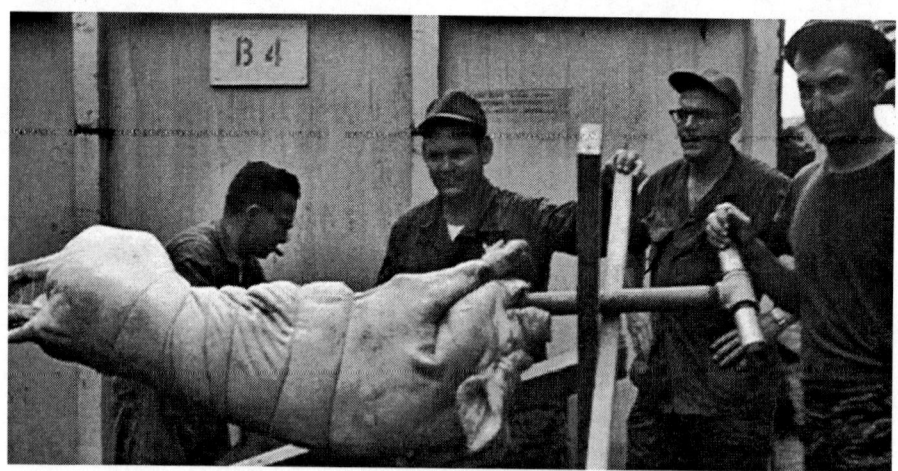

Hog Roast (Copyright © 2014 Ken Synco)

Appendix IV: Citations

Distinguished Flying Cross

"**Staff Sergeant Charles H. Sitzenstock, Jr.** distinguished himself by extraordinary achievement while participating in aerial flight as a Flight Engineer at Phu Cat Air Base, Republic of Vietnam on 7 February 1969. On that date, Sergeant Sitzenstock encountered a gear malfunction on his aircraft. Through his personal bravery and energetic application of his knowledge and skill, a successful gear-up landing was made with little damage to his aircraft and no personal injuries to the crew or passengers. The professional competence, aerial skill and devotion to duty displayed by Sergeant Sitzenstock reflect great credit upon himself and the United States Air Force." [1]

"**First Lieutenant Douglas M. Boston** distinguished himself by extraordinary achievement while participating in aerial flight as an Aircraft Commander at Phuoc Vinh, Republic of Vietnam on 30 March 1969. On that date, Lieutenant Boston loaded combat troops and took off while the airfield was under a rocket attack from hostile forces. Lieutenant Boston made two more trips into Phuoc Vinh to airlift combat troops needed at Minh Thanh. The professional competence, aerial skill and devotion to duty displayed by Lieutenant Boston reflect great credit upon himself and the United States Air Force." [2]

"**First Lieutenant Robert P. Wiesneth** distinguished himself by *heroism* while participating in aerial flight as a Copilot of a C-7A Aircraft near the Special Forces Camp at Nhon Co, Republic of Vietnam on 25 April 1969. On that date he flew an Emergency Resupply Mission in direct support of the besieged camp. With complete disregard for his personal safety he flew through extremely heavy hostile automatic weapons fire to successfully air drop vitally needed supplies without which the camp may have been overrun. The outstanding heroism and selfless devotion to duty displayed by Lieutenant Wiesneth reflect great credit upon himself and the United States Air Force." [3]

"**Staff Sergeant John D. Mellert** distinguished himself

by extraordinary achievement while participating in aerial flight as a Flight Engineer of a C-7A Aircraft near the Special Forces Camp at Ben Het, Republic of Vietnam on 10 June 1969. On that date Sergeant Mellert elected to fly an Emergency Resupply Mission in direct support of the besieged camp. With complete disregard for his personal safety he flew through hostile fire to successfully air drop vitally needed supplies without which the camp may have been overrun. The professional competence, aerial skill, and devotion to duty displayed by Sergeant Mellert reflect great credit upon himself and the United States Air Force." [4]

"**Staff Sergeant Frederick Wilhelm** distinguished himself by *heroism* while participating in aerial flight as a Flight Engineer of a C-7A Aircraft near the Special Forces Camp at Ben Het, Republic of Vietnam on 12 June 1969. On that date Sergeant Wilhelm flew an Emergency Resupply Mission in direct support of the besieged camp. With complete disregard for his personal safety he flew through extremely heavy hostile automatic weapons fire to successfully air drop vitally needed supplies without which the camp may have been overrun. The outstanding heroism and selfless devotion to duty displayed by Sergeant Wilhelm reflect great credit upon himself and the United States Air Force." [5]

"**First Lieutenant Neil N. Greinke** distinguished himself by *heroism* while participating in aerial flight as a Copilot of a C-7A Aircraft near the Special Forces Camp at Ben Het, Republic of Vietnam on 17 June 1969. On that date Lieutenant Greinke flew an Emergency Resupply Mission in direct support of the besieged camp. With complete disregard for his personal safety he flew through extremely heavy hostile automatic weapons fire to successfully air drop vitally needed supplies without which the camp may have been overrun. The outstanding heroism and selfless devotion to duty displayed by Lieutenant Greinke reflect great credit upon himself and the United States Air Force." [6]

"**First Lieutenant Curt Fischer** distinguished himself by extraordinary achievement while participating in aerial flight as a C-7A Copilot near the Special Forces Camp at Ben Het, Republic of Vietnam on 20 June 1969. On that date, Lieutenant Fischer volunteered to fly an Emergency Resupply airdrop mission to the besieged camp personnel who were critically low on supplies and in imminent danger of being overrun. With complete disregard for his personal safety, Lieutenant

338

Fischer flew through extremely heavy hostile ground fire at low altitude to successfully airdrop urgently needed supplies to the camp defenders. The professional competence, aerial skill and devotion to duty displayed by Lieutenant Fischer reflect great credit upon himself and the United States Air Force." [7]

"**Major Charles W. Hardie** distinguished himself by extraordinary achievement while participating in aerial flight as Flight Examiner in a C-7A aircraft near the Special Forces Camp at Ben Het, Republic of Vietnam, on 21 June 1969. On that date, Major Hardie flew an emergency resupply airdrop mission to the besieged Special Forces camp personnel who were in need of fresh supplies of food, water and ammunition. Realizing the inherent dangers involved with low altitude, slow airspeed airdrops and intense hostile ground fire, Major Hardie voluntarily completed the hazardous mission and helped to prevent the overrun of the camp. The professional competence, aerial skill, and devotion to duty displayed by Major Hardie reflect great credit upon himself and the United States Air Force." [8]

"**Captain Richard L. Brethouwer** distinguished himself by extraordinary achievement while participating in aerial flight as a Copilot of a C-7A aircraft near the Special Forces Camp at Ben Het, Republic of Vietnam on 21 June 1969. On that date Captain Brethouwer flew an Emergency Resupply Mission in direct support of the besieged camp. With complete disregard for his personal safety he flew through extremely heavy hostile fire to successfully air drop vitally needed supplies without which the camp may have been overrun. The professional competence, aerial skill, and devotion to duty displayed by Captain Brethouwer reflect great credit upon himself and the United States Air Force." [9]

"**Technical Sergeant Billy P. Owen** distinguished himself by extraordinary achievement while participating in aerial flight as Flight Engineer of a C-7A Aircraft near the Special Forces Camp of Ben Het, Republic of Vietnam on 22 June 1969. On that date Sergeant Owen elected to fly an Emergency Resupply Mission in direct support of the besieged camp. With complete disregard for his personal safety he flew through hostile fire to successfully air drop badly needed supplies without which the camp may have been overrun. The professional competence, aerial skill and devotion to duty displayed by Sergeant Owen reflect great credit upon himself and the United States Air

Force." [10]

"**Technical Sergeant John W. Quarles** distinguished himself by extraordinary achievement while participating in aerial flight as a Flight Engineer of a C-7A aircraft near the Special Forces Camp at Ben Het, Republic of Vietnam, on 26 June 1969. On that date, Sergeant Quarles elected to fly an Emergency Resupply Mission in direct support of the besieged camp. With complete disregard for his personal safety he flew through extremely heavy hostile automatic weapons fire to successfully air drop the vitally needed supplies without which the camp may have been overrun. The professional competence, aerial skill, and devotion to duty displayed by Sergeant Quarles reflect great credit upon himself and the United States Air Force." [11]

"**First Lieutenant William L. Witzig** distinguished himself by extraordinary achievement while participating in aerial flight as a Copilot of a C-7A aircraft near the Special Forces Camp of Ben Het, Republic of Vietnam on 26 June 1969. On that date his mission, *Soul 455*, was shuttling as required from Pleiku Air Base. The camp at Ben Het in the Central Highlands had been under siege for several weeks and was in danger of being overrun. Lieutenant Witzig, with deep concern for his fellow man and with great risk to his own life, volunteered to fly an Emergency Resupply mission to the camp, and was able to successfully complete the low airspeed, low altitude air drop in the face of heavy hostile fire. The professional competence, aerial skill and devotion to duty displayed by Lieutenant Witzig reflect great credit upon himself and the United States Air Force." [12]

"**Technical Sergeant John L. Thomas, Jr.** distinguished himself by extraordinary achievement while participating in aerial flight as a Loadmaster of a C-7A Aircraft near the Special Forces Camp at Ben Het, Republic of Vietnam on 27 June 1969. On that date, Sergeant Thomas elected to fly an Emergency Resupply mission in direct support of the besieged camp. With complete disregard for his personal safety, he flew through hostile fire to successfully air drop vitally needed supplies without which the camp may have been overrun. The professional competence, aerial skill and devotion to duty displayed by Sergeant Thomas reflect great credit upon himself and the United States Air Force." [13]

"**First Lieutenant John D. Mood** distinguished himself by extraordinary achievement while participating in aerial flight as Copilot of a C-7A Aircraft near the Special Forces Camp at Ben Het, Republic of Vietnam on 28 June 1969. On that date, Lieutenant Mood made an Emergency Resupply airdrop to the besieged Special Forces Camp personnel who were in need of fresh supplies of food, water and ammunition. Realizing the inherent danger involved with low altitude, slow airspeed airdrops and intense hostile fire, Lieutenant Mood voluntarily completed the hazardous mission and helped to prevent the overrun of the camp. The professional competence, aerial skill and devotion to duty displayed by Lieutenant Mood reflect great credit upon himself and the United States Air Force." [14]

"**First Lieutenant David B. Bowling** distinguished himself by extraordinary achievement while participating in aerial flight as a Pilot at Tra Bong, Republic of Vietnam on 12 August 1969. On that date, Lieutenant Bowling delivered a load of ammunition to a Special Forces Camp which was under heavy attack. In spite of hazardous terrain and the constant threat of hostile ground fire, he superbly accomplished this highly intricate mission in support of free world forces combating aggression. The professional competence, aerial skill and devotion to duty displayed by Lieutenant Bowling in the dedication of his service to his country reflect great credit upon himself and the United States Air Force." [15]

"**Captain Hugh T. Garner, Jr.** distinguished himself by extraordinary achievement while participating in aerial flight as Aircraft Commander of a C-7A Aircraft near the Duc Hue Special Forces Camp, Republic of Vietnam on 12 August 1969. On that date Captain Garner flew a Combat Essential resupply mission to the remote insecure airstrip which began to receive hostile fire while his cargo was being off-loaded. After delivering the cargo of critically needed supplies Captain Garner completed the hazardous mission despite the fact that his aircraft was damaged by hostile fire prior to takeoff from the 1500 foot airstrip. The professional competence, aerial skill and devotion to duty displayed by Captain Garner reflect great credit upon himself and the United States Air Force." [16]

"**Technical Sergeant Joseph P. Pearce** distinguished himself by extraordinary achievement while participating in aerial flight as a Flight Engineer at Bu Dop Special Forces camp, Republic of Vietnam on 13 August 1969. On that date, while carrying munitions to Bu Dop, Sergeant Pearce's aircraft encountered a rocket attack while taxiing to the off-load area. Despite the hazards involved, Sergeant Pearce quickly rigged and speed off-loaded the cargo enabling the aircraft to become airborne without extensive damage. The professional competence, aerial skill, and devotion to duty displayed by Sergeant Pearce reflect great credit upon himself and the United States Air Force." [17]

"**First Lieutenant Steven J. Hassett** distinguished himself by extraordinary achievement while participating in aerial flight as a C-7A Aircraft Commander at Moc Hoa Special Forces Camp, Republic of Vietnam on 24 August 1969. On that date, Lieutenant Hassett flew vitally needed fuel into Moc Hoa, a landing strip that had been so badly damaged by enemy rocket attack that only one thousand feet of runway was available. Although at maximum gross weight and landing at a minimal airstrip, Lieutenant Hassett elected to fly two resupply missions into Moc Hoa, executing tactical approaches and short field landings into the insecure and damaged airstrip. The professional competence, aerial skill and devotion to duty displayed by Lieutenant Hassett reflect great credit upon himself and the United States Air Force." [18]

"**First Lieutenant Manard D. Siler, III** distinguished himself by extraordinary achievement while participating in aerial flight as an Aircraft Commander near Saigon, Republic of Vietnam on 7 October 1969. On that date, Lieutenant Siler experienced an overspeed of his right engine which necessitated the shutdown of that engine. Because altitude and airspeed could not be maintained, Lieutenant Siler ordered the jettisoning of the load, after he had maneuvered his aircraft away from the city of Saigon to an unpopulated area. Lieutenant Siler then made a single engine landing at Ton Son Nhut Air Base. The fast and correct decisions of Lieutenant Siler enabled the safe return of the aircraft and crew. The professional competence, aerial skill, and devotion to duty displayed by Lieutenant Siler reflect great credit upon himself and the United States Air Force." [19]

"**Captain Josh M. Smith, Jr.** distinguished himself by extraordinary achievement while participating in aerial flight as an Aircraft Commander of a C-7A aircraft near the Special Forces Camp at Bu Krak, Republic of Vietnam, on 20 October 1969. On that date Captain Smith volunteered to qualify two student pilots and deliver combat necessary ammunition to the camp which had been under siege for several days. Contact was made with the camp and it was learned that the area around the camp was saturated with hostile forces. Captain Smith was able to successfully complete two missions to the camp under the cover of air strikes and bombing raids without sustaining aircraft damage or aircrew injury. The professional competence aerial skill and devotion to duty displayed by Captain Smith reflect great credit upon himself and the United States Air Force." [20]

"**Master Sergeant Roger L. Schmidtke** distinguished himself by extraordinary achievement while participating in aerial flight as Flight Engineer of a C-7A aircraft at Bu Dop and Bunard Special Forces Camps, Republic of Vietnam on 5 November 1969. At both camps the aircraft had made a successful tactical approach but just prior to touch down the fields came under intense hostile fire. During the ensuing go-arounds Sergeant Schmidtke insured that the cargo was secure and surveyed the aircraft for possible damage. The professional competence, aerial skill, and devotion to duty displayed by Sergeant Schmidtke reflect great credit upon himself and the United States Air Force." [21]

"**First Lieutenant Charles R. Erickson** distinguished himself by extraordinary achievement while participating in aerial flight as a Pilot of a C-7A aircraft in the Republic of Vietnam on 7 November 1969. Lieutenant Erickson was on a return mission when his plane encountered intense ground fire, inflicting numerous hits upon his aircraft which resulted in the loss of one engine and most of his fuel. With the possibility of fire due to fuel leaks, and other unknown damage to the aircraft, Lieutenant Erickson was able to navigate his aircraft and make a successful landing at home base without further incident. The professional competence, aerial skill, and devotion to duty displayed by Lieutenant Erickson reflect great credit upon himself and the United States Air Force." [22]

"**Captain Spencer F. McClure** distinguished himself by extraordinary achievement while participating in aerial flight as an Instructor Pilot at Chu Lai Air Base, Republic of Vietnam on 11 November 1969. On that date, Captain McClure's plane experienced an engine failure just after takeoff, while carrying a heavy load of cargo. Through his personal bravery and energetic application of his knowledge and skill, he was able to avert a possible major aircraft accident. The professional competence, aerial skill and devotion to duty displayed by Captain McClure reflect great credit upon himself and the United States Air

Force." [23]

"**Major Nathan T. Richardson, Jr.** distinguished himself by extraordinary achievement while participating in aerial flight as a C-7A Instructor Pilot near the Special Forces Camp at Bu Dop, Republic of Vietnam, on 11 November 1969. On that date, Major Richardson flew a Combat Essential Mission into the beleaguered Special Forces Camp. With complete disregard for his personal safety, Major Richardson landed his aircraft while the landing strip was under attack and off-loaded the cargo under heavy hostile fire. His determination and superior airmanship enabled him to skillfully deliver the vitally needed cargo to the camp defenders. The professional competence, aerial skill, and devotion to duty displayed by Major Richardson reflect great credit upon himself and the United States Air Force." [24]

"**First Lieutenant Walter L. Mosher** distinguished himself by extraordinary achievement while participating in aerial flight as Pilot of a C-7A aircraft at Bu Dop, Republic of Vietnam, on 11 November 1969. Lieutenant Mosher, flying a combat resupply mission, was advised of hostile activity at the camp but was able to make a successful approach and landing. While off-loading, however, the camp came under a heavy attack at which time Lieutenant Mosher made an immediate takeoff and tactical departure thereby evading the hostile fire. The professional competence, aerial skill and devotion to duty displayed by Lieutenant Mosher reflect great credit upon himself and the United States Air Force." [25]

"**Lieutenant Colonel Dawson N. White** distinguished himself by extraordinary achievement while participating in aerial flight as a C-7A Instructor Pilot at Bu Dop, Republic of Vietnam on 13 November 1969. On that date, Colonel White flew on a Combat Essential mission to deliver urgently needed supplies. Despite marginal weather conditions and the threat of hostile fire, Colonel White courageously accomplished the vital airlift mission without loss of personnel or equipment. The professional competence, aerial skill and devotion to duty displayed by Colonel White reflect great credit upon himself and the United States Air Force." [26]

"**Lieutenant Colonel Jeff J. Piercy** distinguished himself by extraordinary achievement while participating in aerial flight as a C-7A Aircraft Commander at Bu Dop Special Forces Camp, Republic of

Vietnam, on 16 November 1969. On that date Colonel Piercy delivered essential supplies to the camp which was under heavy hostile attack and which required Forward Air Controller coverage and fighter protection for all cargo missions. On the initial approach, the fighter protection was diverted requiring superior airmanship to avoid hostile ground fire, to make a safe approach and landing, and to speed off-load of the critically needed cargo. The professional competence, aerial skill, and devotion to duty displayed by Colonel Piercy reflect great credit upon himself and the United States Air Force." [27]

"**Major Charles R. Vanness** distinguished himself by extraordinary achievement while participating in aerial flight as an Aircraft Commander of a C-7A aircraft at Bu Krak Special Forces Camp on 17 November 1969. On that date Major Vanness elected to fly a Combat Essential resupply mission in direct support of the besieged camp. In an extremely hostile environment and under very marginal weather conditions Major Vanness was able to complete two on-target air drops into the camp. The professional competence, aerial skill, and devotion to duty displayed by Major Vanness reflect great credit upon himself and the United States Air Force." [28]

"**First Lieutenant William C. Kassen** distinguished himself by extraordinary achievement while participating in aerial flight as pilot of a C-7A aircraft at Thien Ngon, Republic of Vietnam, on 20 November 1969. Following a safe tactical approach and landing, hostile forces launched a ground attack against the airfield while Lieutenant Kassen's aircraft was off-loading cargo. Lieutenant Kassen coordinated the crew's actions, completed the cargo off-load and affected a safe, expeditious takeoff and tactical departure, sustaining no damage to aircraft or aircrew. The professional competence, aerial skill, and devotion to duty displayed by Lieutenant Kassen reflect great credit upon himself and the United States Air Force." [29]

"**Captain Richard R. Lanoue** distinguished himself by extraordinary achievement while participating in aerial flight as an Instructor Pilot at Duc Lap, Republic of Vietnam, on 20 November 1969. On that date Captain Lanoue delivered a critically needed load of rations and ammunition to the Special Forces camp which was surrounded and under attack from an unknown size hostile force. Through his personal bravery and energetic application of his knowledge and skill, he significantly furthered the goal of the United States in Southeast Asia. The professional competence, aerial skill, and devotion to duty displayed by Captain Lanoue reflect great credit upon himself and the United States Air Force." [30]

"**First Lieutenant James K. Hocutt** distinguished himself by extraordinary achievement while participating in aerial flight as a C-7A Aircraft Commander at Bu Dop Special Forces Camp, Republic of Vietnam on 22 November 1969. On that date, Lieutenant Hocutt was carrying sorely needed rations and key replacement personnel destined for Bu Dop, which was receiving intense mortar fire at that time. Lieutenant Hocutt's skill in making tactical approaches and departures from the hostile area resulted in saving the aircraft and the lives of the crew. The professional competence, aerial skill, and devotion to duty displayed by Lieutenant Hocutt reflect great credit upon himself and the United States Air Force." [31]

"**Captain Robert L. Sonick** distinguished himself by extraordinary achievement while participating in aerial flight as a C-7A Aircraft Commander at Bu Dop Special Forces camp, Republic of Vietnam on 27 November 1969. On that date, hostile fire had destroyed the loading ramp at Bu Dop, increasing the ground time required for off-loading. After the aircraft landed, the camp came under attack and two mortars hit within 100 yards of the aircraft. Despite the hostile fire, Captain Sonick continued off-loading the aircraft and delivered the vital cargo to the ground forces. The professional competence, aerial skill, and devotion to duty displayed by Captain Sonick reflect great credit upon himself and the United States Air Force." [32]

"**First Lieutenant David E. R. Larson** distinguished himself by extraordinary achievement while participating in aerial flight as Aircraft Commander of a C-7A aircraft at Song Mao airfield, Republic of Vietnam on 27 November 1969. Lieutenant Larson flew a critically needed flight test crew from Cam Ranh Bay Air Base to the Song Mao airfield to effect the recovery of a damaged aircraft engine and the maintenance personnel who performed an engine change. During the night recovery operation at the small insecure airfield, Lieutenant Larson exposed himself to hostile small arms fire and successfully completed the hazardous mission without the loss of personnel or equipment. The professional competence, aerial skill, and devotion to duty displayed by Lieutenant Larson reflect great credit upon himself and the United States Air Force." [33]

"**First Lieutenant Michael D. Gould** distinguished himself by extraordinary achievement while participating in aerial flight as pilot of a C-7A aircraft at Bu Dop, Special Forces camp, Republic of Vietnam on 3 December 1969. The camp had been subjected to such extensive hostile fire and activity that it was necessary to provide a forward air controller and fighter coverage for the mission. However, by close crew coordination and Lieutenant Gould's skillful maneuvering of the aircraft throughout a tactical approach and departure, needed medical supplies and equipment were delivered with minimum exposure to ground fire. The professional competence, aerial skill, and devotion to duty displayed by Lieutenant Gould reflect great credit upon himself and the United States Air Force." [34]

"**First Lieutenant Christopher F. Nevins** distinguished himself by extraordinary achievement while participating in aerial flight as a C-7A Aircraft Commander at Bu Dop Special Forces camp, Republic of Vietnam on 4 December 1969. On that date, Lieutenant Nevins was flying Combat Essential missions to Bu Dop which had seen extensive hostile activity for several days. Despite concentrations of unfriendly troops near the perimeter and the presence of antiaircraft weapons one-half mile off the end of the runway, Lieutenant Nevins made three shuttles to the Camp without suffering any damage to his aircraft. The professional competence, aerial skill, and devotion to duty displayed by Lieutenant Nevins reflect great credit upon himself and the United States Air Force." [35]

"**First Lieutenant Kenneth E. Mascaro** distinguished himself by extraordinary achievement while participating in aerial flight as pilot of a C-7A aircraft at Duc Phong Airfield, Republic of Vietnam, on 11 December 1969. Lieutenant Mascaro briefed the crew on his intended tactical approach and landing to include evasive action in event hostile fire was encountered. Upon landing, the airfield came under an intense hostile mortar attack, at which time he quickly repositioned the aircraft for takeoff while the cargo was speed off-loaded, and continued a safe tactical departure without incident. The professional competence, aerial skill, and devotion to duty displayed by Lieutenant Mascaro reflect great credit upon himself and the United States Air Force." [36]

"**Captain Jon E. Mickley** distinguished himself by extraordinary achievement while participating in aerial flight as pilot of a C-7A aircraft at Bu Dop Special Forces camp, Republic of Vietnam, on 15 December 1969. Captain Mickley, flying a combat resupply mission, was advised of hostile activity at the camp, but was able to make a successful tactical approach and landing. While off-loading, the camp came under a heavy ground attack, at which time he made an immediate tactical take off and departure thereby evading the hostile fire. The professional competence, aerial skill, and devotion to duty displayed by Captain Mickley reflect great credit upon himself and the United States Air Force." [37]

"**Major William M. Vondersmith, Jr.** distinguished himself by extraordinary achievement while participating in aerial flight as an Aircraft Commander at Tien Phuoc Special Forces camp, Republic of Vietnam on 21 December 1969. On that date, Major Vondersmith made numerous flights into an artillery outpost that was surrounded by hostile forces and was known to be an extremely high threat area. Through his personal bravery and energetic application of his knowledge and skill, he significantly furthered the goal of the United States in Southeast Asia. The professional competence, aerial skill, and devotion to duty displayed by Major Vondersmith reflect great credit upon himself and the United States Air Force." [38]

"**Technical Sergeant Tom M. Owens** distinguished himself by extraordinary achievement while participating in aerial flight as a Flight Engineer at Song Be, Republic of Vietnam on 23 December 1969. On that date, Sergeant Owens. As a C-7A crew member, had landed at Song Be, completed the cargo off-load and was waiting for the outbound load when the field came under mortar attack. Several rounds exploded close to the aircraft and put what was later determined to be thirty-seven holes in the aircraft. Sergeant Owens made a quick external inspection, assessed the damage and recommended to the Aircraft Commander that they take off to save the aircraft from destruction. The crew took off and made an uneventful flight back to Bien Hoa Air Base saving the crew and aircraft. The professional competence, aerial skill, and devotion to duty displayed by Sergeant Owens reflect great credit upon himself and the United States Air Force." [39]

"**Sergeant Leonard M. Reynen** distinguished himself by extraordinary achievement while participating in aerial flight as a C-7A Flight Engineer at Ca Mau, Republic of Vietnam on 24 December 1969. On that date, Sergeant Reynen flew a mission transporting critically needed fuel to the base of Cau Mau. Upon landing, the field came under hostile fire. By the time the aircraft had completed its ground roll, Sergeant Reynen had the load prepared for speed off-loading and the pilot was able to make a 180 degree turn and take off with less than two minutes of ground time accrued. The professional competence, aerial skill, and devotion to duty displayed by Sergeant Reynen reflect great credit upon himself and the United States Air Force." [40]

"**First Lieutenant Dennis A. Dokken** distinguished himself by extraordinary achievement while participating in aerial flight as copilot at Tien Phuoc, Republic of Vietnam on 26 December 1969. On that date, Lieutenant Dokken, as a C-7A crewmember, flew Tactical Emergency missions into Tien Phuoc airfield, where on 26 December a C-7A crew was shot down, killing the pilot and engineer and severely injuring the copilot. With Forward Air Controller and fighter support and under sporadic ground fire, Lieutenant Dokken and his crew continued for three days to deliver their cargo into the airfield. The professional competence, aerial skill, and devotion to duty displayed by Lieutenant Dokken reflect great credit upon himself and the United States Air Force." [41]

"**Staff Sergeant Gilbert Nickerson** distinguished himself by extraordinary achievement while participating in aerial flight as a C-7A Flight Engineer at Tien Phuoc, Republic of Vietnam on 26 December 1969. On that date, Sergeant Nickerson completed three sorties into Tien Phuoc in adverse weather carrying vitally needed ammunition. The base was under intense hostile fire, but off-loading was accomplished in minimum time due to the precise performance of Sergeant Nickerson. The professional competence, aerial skill, and devotion to duty displayed by Sergeant Nickerson reflect great credit upon himself and the United States Air Force." [42]

Air Medal (One Day Mission)

"**Captain Max L. Allison** distinguished himself by meritorious achievement while participating in aerial flight over Southeast Asia [Special Forces camp at Ben Het] on 13 June 1969. On that date, he superbly accomplished a highly intricate mission to support Free World forces that were combating aggression. His energetic application of his knowledge and skill were significant factors that contributed

349

greatly to furthering United States goals in Southeast Asia. His professional skill and airmanship reflect great credit upon himself and the United States Air Force." [43]

"**Major Michael Murphy** distinguished himself by meritorious achievement while participating in aerial flight over Southeast Asia [Ben Het] on 14 June 1969. On that date, he superbly accomplished a highly intricate mission to support Free World forces that were combating aggression. His energetic application of his knowledge and skill were significant factors that contributed greatly to furthering United States goals in Southeast Asia. His professional skill and airmanship reflect great credit upon himself and the United States Air Force." [44]

"**Staff Sergeant Charles H. Sitzenstock, Jr.** distinguished himself by meritorious achievement while participating in aerial flight over Southeast Asia on 25 September 1969. On that date, he superbly accomplished a highly intricate mission to support Free World forces that were combating aggression. His energetic application of his knowledge and skill were significant factors that contributed greatly to furthering United States goals in Southeast Asia. His professional skill and airmanship reflect great credit upon himself and the United States Air Force." [45]

"**First Lieutenant Gary L. Clark** distinguished himself by meritorious achievement while participating in aerial flight over Southeast Asia on 11 October 1969. On that date, he superbly accomplished a highly intricate mission to support Free World forces that were combating aggression. His energetic application of his knowledge and skill were significant factors that contributed greatly to furthering United States goals in Southeast Asia. His professional skill and airmanship reflect great credit upon himself and the United States Air Force." [46]

End Notes: Appendix IV (Citations)

[1] 7AF Special Order G-2166, dated 15 May 1970
[2] 7AF Special Order G-2165, dated 15 May 1970
[3] National Personnel Records Center query report 1-10014886386
[4] 7AF Special Order G-2166, dated 15 May 1970
[5] 7AF Special Order G-3912, dated 27 September 1969
[6] 7AF Special Order G-3909, dated 27 September 1969
[7] 7AF Special Order G-2165, dated 15 May 1970
[8] 7AF Special Order G-2556, dated 6 June 1970

[9] 7AF Special Order G-2137, dated 15 May 1970
[10] 7AF Special Order G-2166, dated 15 May 1970
[11] 7AF Special Order G-5224, dated 22 December 1969
[12] 7AF Special Order G-5285, dated 20 November 1970
[13] 7AF Special Order G-2166, dated 15 May 1970
[14] 7AF Special Order G-5284, dated 20 November 1970
[15] 7AF Special Order G-0149, dated 10 January 1970
[16] 7AF Special Order G-0122, dated 14 January 1971
[17] 7AF Special Order G-2166, dated 15 May 1970
[18] 7AF Special Order G-2633, dated 22 August 1971
[19] 7AF Special Order G-2143, dated 15 May 1970
[20] 7AF Special Order G-5284, dated 20 November 1970
[21] 7AF Special Order G-4440, dated 6 October 1970
[22] 7AF Special Order G-3182, dated 14 July 1970
[23] 7AF Special Order G-2215, dated 19 May 1970
[24] 7AF Special Order G-0502, dated 31 January 1970
[25] 7AF Special Order G-2165, dated 15 May 1970
[26] 7AF Special Order G-0617, dated 27 February 1971
[27] 7AF Special Order G-5284, dated 20 November 1970
[28] 7AF Special Order G-2556, dated 6 June 1970
[29] 7AF Special Order G-4138, dated 17 September 1970
[30] 7AF Special Order G-3182, dated 14 July 1970
[31] 7AF Special Order G-3182, dated 14 July 1970
[32] 7AF Special Order G-2556, dated 6 June 1970
[33] 7AF Special Order G-2557, dated 6 June 1970
[34] 7AF Special Order G-4440, dated 6 October 1970
[35] 7AF Special Order G-3182, dated 14 July 1970
[36] 7AF Special Order G-5284, dated 20 November 1970
[37] 7AF Special Order G-4806, dated 26 October 1970
[38] 7AF Special Order G-3182, dated 14 July 1970
[39] 7AF Special Order G-1941, dated 18 June 1971
[40] 7AF Special Order G-3799, dated 24 August 1970
[41] 7AF Special Order G-1940, dated 18 June 1971
[42] 7AF Special Order G-0386, dated 3 February 1971
[43] 7AF Special Order G-0786, dated 20 February 1970
[44] 7AF Special Order G-0992, dated 6 March 1970
[45] 7AF Special Order G-4923, dated 1 December 1969
[46] 7AF Special Order G-5139, dated 16 December 1969

Appendix V: Ben Het Report

DEPT. OF THE AIR FORCE
537TH TAS (PACAF)
APO SAN FRANCISCO

REPLY TO
ATTN OF: 537TAS (C)   7 July 1969
SUBJECT: Operations at Ben Het

TO: 483 TAW (C)

The 537th TAS played an active and vivid part in the 36 day siege of the Ben Het Special Forces Camp. The squadron conducted frequent C-7A Caribou missions into the Ben Het Airfield from early May through late May. The threat of enemy ground fire and enemy artillery being fired into the base camp was ever present. Many times our aircraft were turned away by the Special Forces Advisors because of intense incoming rounds. Several times our aircraft were subjected to enemy mortar rounds while unloading supplies and personnel at Ben Het. On one occasion an aircraft was hit by mortar fragments.

The airfield was declared closed in early June at which time the 537th TAS started making drops into the camp. A total of 10 drops were made from the 3rd through the 8th of June without an incident. However, on 30 June, six drops were made and all the aircraft commanders reported intense ground fire in spite of FAC support and armed helicopters operating in the area. No hits were received.

On 18 June another single C-7A aircraft free fall drop was scheduled in the morning. The tight ring and large number of enemy on all sides of the Ben Het Camp became quite apparent when the aircraft commander had to make two successive passes over the camp. No drop was made on the first pass because the camp did not pop smoke and there appeared to be people on the drop zone. The aircraft received very intense automatic weapons and 30 cal. fire on the run-ins to the drop zone and during the climb outs. The crew reported that they received in excess of 300 rounds of fire during these two passes over the camp. The FAC also reported heavy ground fire. The aircraft was not hit; however, Special Forces personnel later stated that considering the amount of fire received the crew was extremely fortunate.

The aircraft commander reported and discussed the incident with the C-7A Duty Officer at the 834th Air Div ALCC (Airlift Control Center). He stated to him that the condition at Ben Het was extremely dangerous for the C-7A on an airdrop without adequate fire suppression support. It was further stated that if we did not get support we were going to lose an aircraft. As the result of this, the afternoon drops were provided with a FAC and two armed helicopter gunships as direct support. Three ships in trail dropped in 2-5 minute intervals that afternoon — all three aircraft were hit by enemy ground fire. On 13 June, two drops made: a single aircraft and a four aircraft mission. A FAC, A-1E's, and armed helicopters supported these missions. Two of the aircraft in the four aircraft drop mission were hit by automatic weapons and 30 cal. ground fire. An aircraft commander and flight engineer were wounded on one aircraft and the co-pilot on the other. On 14 June one drop mission was flown with two aircraft, one of the two aircraft was hit by ground fire. One aircraft made a drop on 15 June with A-1E's providing suppression fire and a smoke screen, and the aircraft commandeer reported intense ground fire. From 17 June to 30 June all drop missions were receiving fighter (F-4, F-100, or A-37) fire suppression passes prior to the air drops and were escorted during the drops by A-1E's and once by F-100's. Also, the A-1's were providing smoke screens. Only one aircraft was hit by ground fire after 17 June (hit on 20 June) in spite of the intense ground fire received throughout the period.

A meeting was held on 21 June 1969 between the agencies concerned at TACC-Alpha to establish connection between fighter strikes, artillery, fighter escort, and airdrop mission aircraft at Ben Het. As the result of this meeting, a Time Over Target (TOT) was officially established for each drop. These TOTs were included in subsequent mission frags and were used to provide better coordination of activities.

Although additional fighter suppression support did much toward helping to alleviate the number of aircraft hit by ground fire after 17 June 1969, the incorporation of established procedures with the adoption of the drop procedures peculiar to the Ben Het situation by the 537th TAS also played an important part. Early drops were made in a more conventional tactical pattern with a single aircraft at a time. The intervals between aircraft varied from 2-5 minutes. In order to minimize the effectiveness of enemy ground fire and to better utilize the FAC, fighter, and armed helicopter support available, some general and flexible procedures for air drops were developed. These included the use of in-trail formations of two to six aircraft, Time Over Target (TOT) for planning purposes, best approach corridor to the Initial Point (IP) and drop zone (DZ), rapid in-trail formation descent to the IP at 20-30 second intervals, sharp turn at the IP to lower airspeed and a minimum run at drop altitude to the DZ, and, finally, a hard breaking turn after the drop with maximum power climb-out.

Weather was a factor in all missions from takeoff to landing at Pleiku AB. Some of the airdrops during this period were made under adverse weather conditions, which necessitated extreme pilot skill and caused additional exposure to enemy ground fire while maneuvering individually, or in a formation, for proper Initial Point position and for drop alignment and target area departure.

During the siege period of 10 June through 30 June 1969 the 537th TAS participated in 67 airdrops. A grand total of 87 airdrops were made by the 537th into Ben Het Special Forces Camp from 3 June through 3 July 1969. Seven of the squadron aircraft were hit by enemy ground fire with a total of 10 hits – three of which were 50 caliber rounds. Three squadron personnel on the different aircraft were wounded [Maj Delbert D. Lockwood, Lt William F. Quinn, and TSgt John E. White]. Of the seventy flying crew members in the squadron during the action from 3 June through 3 July, all but eight participated in one or more missions over Ben Het.

All aircraft were staged out of Pleiku AB for the drop missions. Pleiku ALCE provided mission coordination and ground loading support with the aid of the 5th Special Forces personnel and the Pleiku Aerial Port Detachment. 537th TAS maintenance personnel on temporary duty at Pleiku provided maintenance and cargo handling assistance. During the aforementioned aerial resupply activities, air crews of the 483rd Tactical Airlift Wing and the 457th and 458th Tactical Airlift Squadrons at Cam Ranh Bay also participated in the airdrop missions. Their missions are not included in the 537th TAS summaries or total figures.

GEORGE C. MARVIN
Lt. Col., USAF

Author's Note: Some sources believe that the North Vietnamese Army (NVA) used the lessons learned at Ben Het about Caribou drop tactics to plan the ambush at Dak Seang in April 1970.

Many awards (there may be others) were received by Caribou perconnel for Ben Het missions during the siege:

Silver Star:
Delbert D. Lockwood, William A. Evalenko

DFC:
Richard L. Brethouwer, Emile P. Broussard, Donald L. Brownfield, Curt Fischer, Edward L. Furchak, Alan L. Girod, Neil N. Greinke, Charles W. Hardie, Felton H. Havins, Robert B. Hill, Delbert D. Lockwood. Donald J. MacFarren, John D. Mellert, Kent M. Monroe. John D. Mood, Hugh M. Overcash. Billy P. Owen, John W. Quarles, William F. Quinn, William L. Shepherd, Robert H. Taylor, John L. Thomas, Frederick Wilhelm, Clyde M. Wilson, William L. Witzig. James F. Wohrer

Purple Heart:
Delbert D. Lockwood, William F. Quinn, John E. White

Air Medal (single mission): Max L. Allison, John W. Black, Robert H. Dugan, Dale Grigg, Donald J. MacFarren, Michael Murphy, John H. Wigington

Special Forces SP5 John Shaw During C-7A Drop at Ben Het
(Copyright © 1969 USAF)

Appendix VI: Airdrop Procedure

Operating Procedures for Airdrop Missions into Ben Het

GENERAL: Continued airdrops into Ben Het have necessitated the establishment of some general procedures. It is recognized that these procedures must be flexible and subject to change in order to adjust to the many variables (weather conditions, tactical situation, fighter support, etc.)

1. Pre-Flight Procedures:

a. Flight Make-up: When possible, flight should consist of a maximum of three aircraft. We must have previous Ben Het drop experience. When more than three aircraft were scheduled on one TOT (Time Over Target), is best to drop as elements of three aircraft, with approximately one minute between elements. If more than three aircraft were involved at one time, the problems of spacing and exposure to enemy fire are greatly magnified.

b. Loading: Pleiku ALCE and the aircraft flight engineers are responsible for loading. Aircraft not from the 537 TAS should bring their own drop kit. If a load consists of heavy bundles and light bundles, it is best to have a light bundles in the middle or apt to obtain best release.

c. Fighter Support: Pleiku ALCE makes all arrangements for FAC and fighter support, including a briefing. They will also provide mission radio frequencies.

d. Fuel: Fuel loading must necessarily vary with the weight of the load and the maximum ACL of individual aircraft. However, as much fuel as possible (2000 pounds is the recommended minimum) should be carried in case of enroute delays.

e. Briefing:

(1) ALCE personnel will provide a brief weather and tactical briefing.

(2) Flight lead will brief engine start time, takeoff and climb out procedures, proposed altitudes and airspeeds enroute, frequencies, run-in heading, IP, drop heading/altitude, breakaway procedures (direction of turn and heading), and recovery procedures.

f. Radio Procedures: Flight of aircraft will be called SOUL Flight for simplicity. Individual aircraft will be Lead, 2, 3, etc. Lead will handle all radio calls and will relate necessary information through interplay and frequencies. The rest of the flight will monitor frequencies as directed by Lead. The interplay and frequency presently in use is VHF 123.40. FAC and fighters are normally on UHF 255.1 or 312.0. however, the FAC can direct other frequencies in case of congestion, radio difficulties, etc.

g. Timing: All timing will be based on TOT. Enroute time is approximately 25 minutes. For planning purposes, timing should be approximately:

> (1) Loading complete – TOT minus 1 hour 30 minutes.
> (2) Engine start   – TOT minus 45 minutes.
> (3) Takeoff   – TOT minus 30 minutes.

2. Takeoff/Enroute:

a. VFR: Lead will request in-trail formation takeoff and obtain priority (CE, ER). Lead will climb to 1500 AGL at METO, then go to climb power. As the flight joins up in staggered in-trail formation with 2000 feet nose-to-tail separation, each aircraft will reduce to climb power. At level off, Lead will maintain 110 Knots IAS.

b. IFR: Lead will request minimum separation IFR takeoff as single ships, with radar vectors to VFR on top. As aircraft reach VFR on top, they will join up at the briefed altitude on the 340° radial Channel 107. Lead will maintain 100 knots at level off until joined up is complete. Then the flight will go to 110 knots.

c. Radio Calls:

> (1) Pre-drop report relayed through Pleiku ALCE, or *Hilda* (Lead for flight).

> (2) Lead will contact Artys enroute to determine best route area. *Tollhouse Lima* will be advised of intended drop for check-fire between Dak To and Ben Het.

> (3) Lead will call drop check warnings – 20 minutes, 10 minutes, etc., based on TOT. The one minute warning will be initiated when the flight is cleared in.

> (4) As soon as possible, Lead will establish contact with the FAC and determine working frequencies, wind and weather conditions, tactical situation, and expected time that the flight will be cleared in. He will also obtain the recommended post-drop turnout direction.

> (5) Post-drop report to Pleiku ALCE, or *Hilda* (Lead for flight).

3. Drop:

a. Legal advise flight when cleared in and begin approach at 5000 to 6000 feet near the bridge in the approach corridor. Flight will take up 20 second spacing. If more than three ships are involved, the second element should take one minute spacing behind the first element. At two miles from the IP, heading 290° - 300°, the set is initiated. Lead will obtain and maintain 160-170 knots until IP, power off (RPM 1500-2000). Other aircraft will maintain spacing. (As the run-in progresses, there is a tendency to bunch up, requiring the rare aircraft slowdown to maintain spacing).

At the IP, 2700 foot MSL, a level turn to final is initiated and airspeed allowed to decrease. Pilot advises crew "10 seconds," and copilot increases RPM to 2700. At release point, pilot calls "Green Light, Green Light, Green Light," pulls firmly up, and advances to maximum power. Climb out at 95 knots. As soon as the load is clear, and immediate 30-40° breaking turn will be made. Maximum power is left on until 4000 feet MSL.

b. If the breakaway will take aircraft in the clouds, the following procedure will be used:

(1) Left Break: Lead rolls out on 120° heading, #2 on 140°, and #3 on 160° and climb at METO power to VFR and rejoin.

(2) Right Break: All aircraft turn to 360° for one minute, then Lead climbs out on 090°, #2 on 070°, and #3 on 050° to VFR and rejoin.

(3) If more than one element is involved, repeat the above procedure with each element.

4. Recovery: Recovery will depend on whether. In VFR, in-trail recovery to Pleiku, with a normal downwind entry is recommended.

NOTE

1. These procedures are based on the present tactical situation at Ben Het, and the following currently existing conditions are:

a. All areas south and west of the camp are extremely hostile with possible large caliber fire. Area North of camp in north of the highway has dense small arms activity very close to the perimeter.

b. Aircraft are subject to intense ground fire from 4000 MSL down, so the time below this altitude must be minimized. Ground fire can be expected from just before the IP, throughout the drop, and during turnout.

c. Hostile gunners can accurately lead the C-7A when it is in the 100-120 knots range.

d. Suppression by fighters can be greatly enhanced if drop aircraft can indicate when and where they are receiving ground fire. For simplicity simply state "Receiving fire, 3 o'clock," for example.

2. If delayed in excess of one (1) hour after takeoff, make OPS NORMAL report to *Hilda* or Pleiku ALCE.

3. The Post Drop Report (483 TAW Form 14) will be submitted by Lead at Phu Cat.

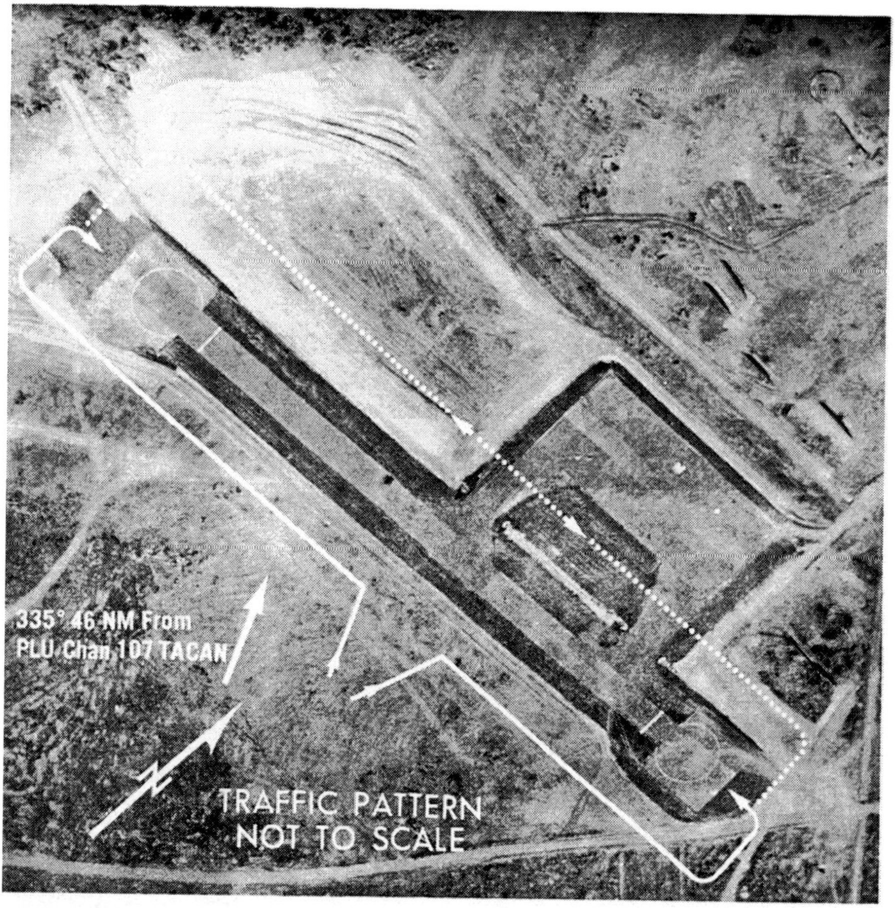

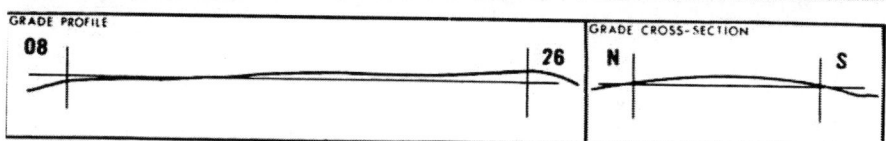

GRADE PROFILE

08   26

GRADE CROSS-SECTION

N   S

BEN HET, VIETM   YB872252   14°41'N   107°40'E
A   2230   15(M8A1)   60   08-26   Type 2 C7

AERODROME REMARKS - For Security ctc 5th S.F. Nha Trang. 100' ovrn W end, 57' ovrn E end, laterite ASP treated. 150' X 150' turnaround ea end. Two 50' wide access twys to 450' X 200' prkg area. Windsock N of midfield. End and 200' touchdown mkrs. HAZARDS - 6" lip btwn ovrn and Rwy 08 thld. Road crosses E ovrn.
RADIO - Ctc as per SF SOI

Bomb Shackle for LAPES Drop (Copyright © 2014 USAF)

Approaching the Drop Zone (Copyright © 2014 Dana Kelly)

Appendix VII: Awards Criteria

Background

The Distinguished Flying Cross was authorized by an Act of Congress of July 2, 1926. The medal is awarded to any officer or enlisted person of the Armed Forces of the United States who shall have distinguished herself/himself in actual combat in support of operations by heroism or extraordinary achievement while participating in an aerial flight, subsequent to November 11, 1918.

The "standard" wording of the DFC citation included the following phrases:

> "...distinguished himself by extraordinary achievement while participating in aerial flight...professional competence, aerial skill, and devotion to duty displayed by..."

or

> "...distinguished himself by heroism in aerial flight... outstanding heroism and selfless devotion to duty displayed by..."

Secretary of the Air Force, Dr. James G. Roche, authorized use of the "V" device, to represent valor, on Distinguished Flying Crosses awarded for heroism. The decision was intended to clearly distinguish and denote a DFC awarded for heroism. It allows any Reserve, Guard, or active duty Airman or Air Force DFC recipient honored for heroism on or after September 18, 1947 to wear the "V" device on the DFC. [published on June 30, 2004]

The Air Medal was established by Executive Order 9158 on May 11, 1942 and amended by Executive Order 9242 on Sept. 11, 1942.

It is awarded to U.S. military and civilian personnel for single acts of heroism or meritorious achievements while participating in aerial flight and foreign military personnel in actual combat in support of operations. Required achievement is less than that required for the Distinguished Flying Cross, but must be accomplished with distinction above and beyond that expected of professional airmen.

It is not awarded for peace time sustained operational activities and flights. Approval or disapproval authority is delegated to major command commanders or vice commanders for military and secretary of the Air Force for civilians and foreign military personnel. MAJCOMs will identify the missions and positions that qualify for this award. HQ USAF/XO must certify MAJCOM criteria.

Situation

The Vietnam War reached a crescendo in 1968, with more American troops on the ground in Vietnam and more casualties than ever before or after. On 31 October 1968, President Lyndon Johnson announced in a televised address to the nation that, based on developments in the peace talks in Paris, he had ordered an end to "all air, naval, and artillery bombardment of North Vietnam." Effective on 1 November, the USAF stopped OPERATION ROLLING THUNDER, the bombing of North Vietnam.

Records

Review of the over 21,000 Special Orders issued by 7AF between 1 July 1966 and 31 March 1972 discovered 1131 DFCs for C-7A crew members. The individuals were recognized as 483 TAW personnel by decoding his PAS identifier on the order. The PAS identifier specified the recipient's base of assignment and organization. There were probably many DFCs missed by this review, which was done during fourteen week-long visits to the Air Force Historical Research Agency (AFHRA) at Maxwell AFB, AL over a period of three years.

Of these 1131 DFCs for C-7A crew members found in the archives of the AFHRA, 82 were "End-of-Tour" awards covering action over a range of dates, with a "Start" date and an "End" date in the order, not for action on a single date. Two other DFCs were for time periods during Project Red Leaf. All of the other "End-of-Tour" DFCs had end dates in 1969, with the earliest end date being 27 January 1969 and the latest one being 24 October 1969. One can infer from this data that during the first 10 months of 1969, DFCs were awarded using different criteria than those for the time frames before or after that date range.

Distinguished Flying Crosses (All)

	1967	1968	1969	1970	1971	1967-1971
457 TAS	17	24	45	50	75	211
458 TAS	23	49	45	51	53	221
459 TAS	17	67	45	33	1	163
535 TAS	9	9	44	50	61	173
536 TAS	37	27	33	27	34	158
537 TAS	38	19	39	76	33	209
Total	141	195	251	287	257	1131

Distinguished Flying Crosses (End-of-Tour)

	1967	1968	1969	1970	1971	1967-1971
457 TAS	0	0	16	0	0	16
458 TAS	0	0	10	0	0	10
459 TAS	0	0	16	0	0	16
535 TAS	0	0	11	0	0	11
536 TAS	0	0	20	0	0	20
537 TAS	0	0	9	0	0	9
Total	0	0	82	0	0	82

These "End-of-Tour" DFCs were not confined to the 483 TAW. Aircrew members from many different Air Force units in SEA were awarded these unusual DFCs. They were unusual because the concept of a DFC awarded for actions over a period of time are not in concert with the spirit and wording of the governing regulations. The widespread use of this approach to the awarding of DFCs was clearly approved and/or directed by higher headquarters, probably 7AF itself, since 7AF was the major command authorized to award the DFC.

The citation for some DFCs was prepared by "filling in the blanks" of a standard, pre-printed form. Only the individual's name, date, and location were personalized in the citation. The end result was a bland, matter-of-fact repetition of a few sentences. A typical citation like this for an Air Medal was:

> "< name > distinguished himself by meritorious achievement while participating in aerial flight over Southeast Asia on < date >. On that date, he superbly accomplished a highly intricate mission to support Free World forces that were combatting aggression. His energetic application of his knowledge and skill were significant factors that contributed greatly to furthering United States goals in Southeast Asia. His professional skill and airmanship reflect great credit upon himself and the United States Air Force."

This was a lazy and shameful way of recognizing the service of a combat veteran who flew in harm's way each day to support his brothers-in-arms in the camps, landing zones, and bases of Vietnam.

One C-7A squadron commander expressed openly to his crews that awarding a DFC for tactical airlift operations in Vietnam was inappropriate and "diminished the value of DFCs for service during WW II." In lieu of the existing Air Force directives, he established his own criterion for recommending a DFC for approval by 7AF. His criterion

Name	10-30 Jun	2-3 Jul	Third Pilot (orientation)
Allison, Max L	3	1	
Berta, William C	2		
Black, John W	4	1	
Brethouwer, Richard L	5		
Broussard, Emile P	9	1	
Brownfield, Donald L	2		
Chasteen, Ralph E	3	1	
Cope, Jesse M	6		
Crafton, Stuart B	2	1	
Croach, Robert E	4		1
Davenhall, Kenneth L	6		
Davis, James H	4		1
Donovan, Steven R	4		1
Dugan, Robert H	2		
Evalenko, William A	6	1	
Fletchall, Albert E	8	1	
Furchak, Edward	6		
Girod, Allan L	2		
Greinke, Neil N	2		
Grigg, Dale	4	1	
Grimsley, Joe W	1		
Hammond, Charles K Jr,	3		
Harmon, George L	2		
Havins, Felton H	3	1	
Hayes, Maurice C	3		
Hill, Robert E	3		
Holdener, Irwin K	4		
Houghtling, Donald H	3	1	
Ketring, Charles E	5	1	
Koshko, Kent D	2		
Lockwood, Delbert D	8		

Sorties to Ben Het

Name	10-30 Jun	2-3 Jul	Third Pilot (orientation)
Maki, Dennis A	4	1	
Marshall, Lyle B	1		
Marvin, George C	6		
Mellert, John D	3		
Miles, David A			1
Monroe, Kent M	5	1	
Murphy, Michael	5		
Obermiller, Terry L	2	2	
Overcash, Hugh M	2	1	
Owen, Billy P	3		
Poland, Robert F	5		
Prescott, Calgen A	1	1	
Quarles, Jown W	4		
Quinn, William F	4	1	
Riess, Michael T	3	1	
Rodda, Allen J	2		
Ryland, William K	1	1	
Selbe, George G	8		
Shepherd, William L	2		
Smolinski, Jerome P	1		
Spurger, George A		1	
Taylor, Charles C Jr		1	2
Taylor, Robert. H		2	
Thomas, John L	1	1	
Vanness, Charles R	3		
White, John E Jr	2	1	
Wigington, John H	6		
Wilhelm, Frederick	1	1	
Wilson, Clyde M	3		
Wohrer, James F	4	2	

Sorties to Ben Het

was "four combat air drops." Despite opposition from his aircrew members, he persisted in applying his own criterion. As a result, 39 pilots and Flight Engineers of his squadron received the DFC for four or more combat airdrops at Ben Het, but many others did not. Eight individuals received an Air Medal rather than a DFC. At least six individuals met the "four combat air drops" criteria, but received neither a DFC nor an Air Medal. They were 1/Lt. Robert E. Croach, 1/Lt. James H. Davis, 1/Lt. Steven R. Donovan, 1/Lt. Robert F. Poland, 1/Lt. Michael T. Riess, TSgt. Kenneth L. Davenhall, and SSgt. Jesse M. Cope.

After a new squadron commander assumed command on 14 November 1969, the new leadership of the squadron made an effort to correct the earlier errors of omission. Many personnel were approved for awards, but some of these awards were not properly recorded in the personnel records or were never presented to the recipients. Some special orders are in the AFHRA records, but were not received by the individuals, especially in cases where the individual separated from the Air Force upon return to the CONUS.

Sadly, the records at the AFHRA are missing a significant number of 7AF Special Orders dated between 6 May and 8 June 1970. This block of orders is when many of the "missing" awards would have been recorded and corrective action could be taken by the affected individuals.

In the third quarter of 1969, many changes occurred in the Awards and Decorations (A&D) program of the Wing. Among these was a new A&D Officer for the 483 TAW and new, more stringent, requirements on eligibility for award of the Distinguished Flying Cross (DFC). These included a single-event narrative for an End-of-Tour DFC and a tighter system of suspenses for all award recommendations submitted. In an effort to eliminate common problems, the Wing A&D Officer met with awards representatives of each of the seven squadrons on 4 September. Many problem areas were discussed and it was agreed that action was needed to reduce the requirements for the eligibility for End-of-Tour DFCs. Representatives from the CBPO, Personal Affairs Branch, also attended the meeting.

A critically needed [537 TAS] squadron policy statement on the receiving of awards[1] came down from the Squadron Commander on 2 March [1970]. It stated that, "deserving personnel receive recognition appropriate to their level of responsibility and performance." However, the commander also pointed out that the policy "is not to be construed that any award is automatic." The intent of the policy, according to Lt Peter S. Neff, Squadron Awards and Decorations Officer, was to maintain the integrity of medals received for service in the Republic of Vietnam. By requiring written justification of awards, the "automatic atmosphere surrounding the Distinguished Flying Cross and other associated awards of merit should be removed."

The letter was addressed to all 537 TAS personnel and it read:

"1. The 537 TAS policy on awards and decorations is that deserving personnel receive recognition appropriate to their level of responsibility and performance. This is not to be construed that any award is automatic.

2.   The Air Medal for sustained activity will continue to be submitted by the Awards and Decorations Office. All other awards will be recommended to the Awards and Decorations Office by the Commander, 537 TAS. This recommendation will be by letter and will contain proper justification for the award.

3.   The policy for the end-of-tour Distinguished Flying Cross is as follows:

'All squadron crew members will submit a resume of the mission they desire to use as justification for the award. Forms are available through the Awards and Decorations Office and will be submitted to the Commander for approval. Though the award is not automatic, all crew members will be recommended and the recommendation forwarded to 7th Air Force for approval.' "

End Notes: Appendix VII Awards Criteria
[1] 197001-19700331 537 TAS history

"Blood, Sweat & Tears" (Copyright © 2014 Tom Finkler)

Appendix VIII: Aircraft Performance

1969	CRB			Vung Tau		
	O/R	NORM	NORS	O/R	NORM	NORS
Jan	67.2	30.5	2.3	80.8	16.7	2.5
Feb	80.2	18.5	1.3	82.1	15.8	2.1
Mar	82.2	15.6	2.2	81.1	14.5	4.4
Apr	81.8	17.3	0.9	85.5	11.4	3.1
May	85.6	13.7	0.7	84.9	13.0	2.1
Jun	82.9	16.0	1.1	89.4	9.5	1.1
Jul	80.9	18.0	1.1	84.1	13.5	2.4
Aug	79.7	18.8	1.5	82.0	15.2	2.8
Sep	78.8	18.3	2.9	82.8	15.1	2.1
Oct	78.9	16.9	4.2	78.1	16.0	5.9
Nov	75.1	21.4	3.4	82.1	14.1	3.8
Dec	73.6	23.2	3.2	79.1	12.8	8.1

1969	Phu Cat			Wing		
	O/R	NORM	NORS	O/R	NORM	NORS
Jan	87.1	12.9	0.0	78.4	20.0	1.6
Feb	87.7	12.3	0.0	83.3	15.6	1.1
Mar	86.1	13.1	0.8	83.1	14.4	2.5
Apr	86.2	12.5	1.3	84.4	13.8	1.8
May	85.4	14.3	0.3	85.3	13.7	1.0
Jun	86.7	13.1	0.2	86.2	13.0	0.8
Jul	85.6	14.3	0.1	83.5	15.3	1.2
Aug	85.5	14.0	0.5	82.3	16.0	1.7
Sep	82.8	15.8	1.4	81.5	16.4	2.1
Oct	82.5	14.7	2.8	79.8	15.9	4.3
Nov	81.3	16.7	2.0	79.6	17.3	3.1
Dec	82.2	14.9	2.9	78.0	17.2	4.8

Col. LaRue was DCM until March when Lt. Col. William A. Ulrich took over as DCM.

Maintenance Reliability

	Initial Launch		
	Reliability	Delays	Hours
January	98.2%	28	36.2
February	99.3%	10	7.5
March	99.3%	10	9.9
April	99.5%	7	4.8
May	99.4%	9	7.6
June	99.9%	1	0.7
July	99.8%	4	3.4
August	99.7%	5	7.3
September	99.8%	17	14.5
October	97.8%	33	40.0
November	98.7%	19	22.0
December	97.8%	33	10.0

	Enroute		
	Reliability	Delays	Hours
January	98.2%	274	471.6
February	98.3%	250	416.8
March	98.5%	239	392.0
April	98.6%	218	331.4
May	98.6%	214	312.0
June	99.0%	214	214.5
July	98.4%	223	344.6
August	98.9%	160	257.1
September	98.4%	204	349.1
October	98.4%	227	465.0
November	98.3%	199	423.0
December	98.3%	223	354.0

Appendix IX: Airlift Accomplishments

1969	457 TAS	458 TAS	459 TAS	537 TAS	535 TAS	536 TAS	Monthly Subtotal
Sorties							
Jan	2,518	2,426	2,201	3,265	2,856	2,287	15,553
Feb	2,266	2,110	2,231	2,893	2,692	2,240	14,432
Mar	2,624	2,330	2,433	3,360	2,930	2,432	16,109
Apr	2,459	2,267	2,156	3,213	3,022	2,282	15,399
May	2,400	2,301	2,314	3,183	3,132	2,200	15,530
Jun	2,146	2,093	2,309	2,989	2,721	1,888	14,146
Jul	2,256	2,158	2,303	3,107	2,744	1,653	14,221
Aug	2,370	2,295	2,678	3,063	2,709	2,084	15,199
Sep	2,107	2,017	1,926	2,770	2,571	1,724	13,115
Oct	2,270	???	1,994	???	???	???	14,514
Nov	2,296	???	1,756	???	???	???	13,634
Dec	2,501	???	1,735	???	???	???	14,785
Hours							
Jan	1808.8	1789.1	1597.5	1616.0	1648.6	1639.3	10,099.3
Feb	1661.6	1658.6	1622.2	1480.6	1534.4	1530.4	9,487.8
Mar	1916.8	1825.5	1863.4	1735.1	1738.2	1702.8	10,781.8
Apr	1850.8	1721.8	1680.8	1628.5	1681.4	1628.7	10,192.0
May	1784.6	1718.2	1692.4	1675.5	1757.9	1595.4	10,224.0
Jun	1709.1	1642.1	1589.9	1628.5	1650.5	1473.8	9,693.9
Jul	1830.5	1747.9	1682.1	1670.2	1742.3	1410.5	10,083.5
Aug	1880.5	1740.0	1792.2	1638.6	1718.8	1625.9	10,396.0
Sep	1745.0	1601.8	1496.5	1546.7	1635.8	1442.2	9,468.0
Oct	1785.2	1666.8	1531.8	1710.1	1795.9	1511.8	10,001.6
Nov	1742.4	1509.0	1422.5	1663.5	1844.5	1593.9	9,775.8
Dec	1828.0	1685.0	1445.9	1766.0	1944.0	1635.9	10,304.8

1969 USAF totals were 176, 637 sorties and 120,508.5 hours.
1968 USAF totals were 174,702 sorties and 119,184.1 hours.
1967 USAF totals were 155,938 sorties and 100,230.8 hours.
1966 USAF totals were 129,324 sorties and 87,125.0 hours.

1969	457 TAS	458 TAS	459 TAS	537 TAS	535 TAS	536 TAS	Monthly Subtotal
Cargo (tons)							
Jan	1336.2	1439.0	1963.3	1279.6	1299.2	1577.1	8,894.4
Feb	1185.1	1331.0	2031.4	1113.4	1255.9	1627.1	8,543.9
Mar	1374.6	1481.3	1997.5	1306.9	1415.3	1765.0	9,340.6
Apr	1251.2	1287.3	1790.9	1248.5	1379.6	1705.3	8,662.8
May	1317.2	1296.3	2019.5	1085.2	1271.0	1596.1	8,585.3
Jun	1076.2	1068.1	2003.4	967.0	994.9	1469.5	7,579.1
Jul	1123.0	1140.4	1751.7	1011.5	1088.5	1210.9	7,326.0
Aug	1228.8	1207.6	2393.7	1093.2	1121.3	1397.6	8,442.2
Sep	912.4	1058.6	1485.1	888.8	1090.9	1275.2	6,711.0
Oct	879.0	1559.2	1530.7	621.8	1411.5	1438.8	7,441.0
Nov	765.0	1099.0	1259.3	1094.5	1440.8	1352.4	7,011.0
Dec	952.0	1163.0	1360.4	1198.9	1665.0	1533.7	7,873.0

	457 TAS	458 TAS	459 TAS	537 TAS	535 TAS	536 TAS	Monthly Subtotal
Passengers							
Jan	18,061	13,165	7,285	32,732	25,522	10,199	106,964
Feb	15,224	8,924	6,837	29,194	22,953	8,667	91,799
Mar	18,220	12,466	10,306	33,215	22,162	10,925	107,294
Apr	16,384	12,951	9,758	31,848	22,532	8,868	102,341
May	12,918	11,897	6,513	30,773	23,732	8,981	94,814
Jun	12,820	12,063	6,540	30,405	21,920	6,166	89,914
Jul	13,657	11,929	8,689	30,686	22,306	5,758	93,025
Aug	12,831	14,505	7,246	27,976	18,069	7,543	88,170
Sep	10,865	11,343	5,401	24,350	15,657	5,986	73,602
Oct	13,327	13,935	6,040	25,754	12,512	4,732	76,300
Nov	14,645	10,858	4,641	22,312	11,409	5,237	69,102
Dec	13,337	11,631	4,165	21,527	12,180	4,353	67,193

1969 USAF totals were 96,410.3 tons and 1,060,518 passengers.
1968 USAF totals were 104,225.8 tons and 1,308,259 passengers.
1967 USAF totals were 95,320.1 tons and 1,081,629 passengers.
1966 USAF totals were 89,010.0 tons and 822,432 passengers.

Appendix X: Personnel Authorized/Assigned

1969

	Authorized				Assigned			
	Q1	Q2	Q3	Q4	Q1	Q2	Q3	Q4
457 TAS								
officers	*	*	*	*	*	*	*	*
airmen	*	*	*	*	*	*	*	*
civilians	*	*	*	*	*	*	*	*
458 TAS								
officers	51	51	51	51	38	50	47	42
airmen	137	86	86	85	84	89	89	71
civilians	0	0	0	0	0	0	0	0
459 TAS								
officers	54	*	54	54	47	*	47	47
airmen	250	*	311	313	217	*	277	262
civilians	0	0	0	0	0	0	0	0
535 TAS								
officers	55	55	50	54	50	51	50	44
airmen	161	161	151	151	169	154	151	136
civilians	54	46	0	0	51	43	0	0
536 TAS								
officers	51	51	51	51	49	43	44	40
airmen	80	80	80	80	91	82	73	65
civilians	0	0	0	0	3	3	0	0
537 TAS								
officers	51	51	51	51	49	49	41	*
airmen	80	82	81	*	75	75	64	*
civilians	0	0	0	0	0	0	0	0

* Squadron did not report this data.

Appendix XI: Aircraft Authorized

	First Quarter 1969	Second Quarter 1969	Third Quarter 1969	Fourth Quarter 1969
Authorized				
457 TAS	16	16	16	16
458 TAS	16	16	16	16
459 TAS	16	16	16	15
535 TAS	16	16	16	16
536 TAS	16	16	16	16
537 TAS	16	16	16	16
Possessed				
457 TAS	15	15	14	15
458 TAS	15	15	14	15
459 TAS	14	14	14	12
535 TAS	14	14	16	14
536 TAS	13	13	16	16
537 TAS	16	15	15	15
Combat Ready				
457 TAS	14	13	14	14
458 TAS	15	15	15	15
459 TAS	13	15	16	14
535 TAS	10	14	15	15
536 TAS	11	15	12	12
537 TAS	15	15	13	15

459 TAS Flight Engineers - 1969 (Copyright © 2014 Bill Falconer)

459 TAS Pilots - 1969 (Copyright © 2014 Bill Falconer)

Appendix XII: Acronyms

1Cav	1st Cavalry
12AF	12th Air Force
12 CSG	12th Combat Support Group
457 TAS	457th Tactical Airlift Squadron
458 TAS	458th Tactical Airlift Squadron
459 TAS	459th Tactical Airlift Squadron
535 TAS	535th Tactical Airlift Squadron
536 TAS	536th Tactical Airlift Squadron
537 TAS	537th Tactical Airlift Squadron
483 TAW	483rd Tactical Air Wing
516 TAW	516th Tactical Airlift Wing
5SFG	5th Special Forces Group
6483 TGP	6483th Tactical Group Provisional
7AF	7th Air Force
9AF	9th Air Force
834AD	834th Air Division
AAA	Anti-Aircraft Artillery
ACL	Allowable Cabin Load
ADF	Automatic Direction Finder
ADIZ	Air Defense Identification Zone
AFC	Air Force Cross
AFHRA	Air Force Historical Research Agency
AFLC	Air Force Logistics Command
AFSC	Air Force Specialty Code
AGE	Aerospace Ground Equipment
AGL	Above Ground Level
AID	Agency for International Development (also USAID)
ALCC	Airlift Control Center
ALCE	Airlift Control Element
ALO	Air Liaison Officer
ALOREP	Air Liaison Officer Reporting System
AM	Air Medal
APG	Airplane General
APR	Airman Performance Report
ARVN	Army of Republic of Vietnam
ASC	Allowance Source Code
ATCO	Air Transportation Coordinating Office
AVGAS	Aviation Gas

AvCo	Aviation Company (U.S. Army)
AWM	Awaiting Maintenance
AWP	Awaiting Parts
BEMO	Base Equipment Management Office
BHP	brake horsepower
BOQ	Bachelor Officer's Quarters
CAMS	Consolidated Aircraft Maintenance Squadron
CBPO	Consolidated Base Personnel Office
CCTS	Combat Crew Training Squadron
CCTW	Combat Crew Training Wing
CDC	Career Development Courses
CE	Combat Essential
CES	Civil Engineering Squadron
CG	Center of Gravity
CIDG	Civilian Irregular Defense Group
CONEX	Container, Express
CONUS	Continental United States
CORDS	Civil Ops. and Rural Development Support
CQ	Charge of Quarters
CRB	Cam Ranh Bay Air Base
CSA	Chief of Staff, Army
CSAF	Chief of Staff, Air Force
CSG	Combat Support Group
DAAR	Daily Air Activity Report
DASC	Direct Air Support Center
DCM	Deputy Commander, Materiel
DCO	Deputy Commander, Operations
DEROS	Date of Estimated Return from Overseas
DFC	Distinguished Flying Cross
DIFM	Due In From Maintenance
EAID	Equipment Authorization Inventory Data
EDCSA	Estimated Date of Change of Station Accountability
EUR	Emergency Unsatisfactory Report
FAC	Forward Air Controller
FCF	Functional Check Flight
FE	Flight Engineer or Flight Examiner
FM	Frequency Modulation (as in FM radio)
FMS	Field Maintenance Squadron
FOB	Forward Operating Base
FOD	Foreign Object Damage
FOL	Forward Operating Location

FSN	Federal Stock Number
FTD	Field Training Detachment
FY	Fiscal Year
GCA	Ground Controlled Approach
GCI	Ground Controlled Intercept
GRADS	Ground Radar Aerial Delivery System
GSE	Ground Support Equipment
GVN	Government of the Republic of Vietnam
HE	Heavy Equipment
Hq.	Headquarters
IFFV	First Field Force Vietnam
IIFFV	Second Field Force Vietnam
III MAF	Third Marine Amphibious Force
IFR	Instrument Flight Rules
IG	Inspector General
ILS	Instrument Landing System
IOC	Integral Oil Control
IP	Instructor Pilot
IRAN	Inspection and Repair As Necessary
ISSL	Initial Spares Support List
JP-4	Jet Propellant 4
JUSMAG	Joint United States Military Assistance Group
KIA	Killed In Action
LAPES	Low Altitude Parachute Extraction System
LPO	Local Purchase Order
LZ	Landing Zone
MACTHAI	Military Assistance Command, Thailand
MACV	Military Assistance Command, Vietnam
MDR	Material Deficiency Report
METO	Maximum Except for Takeoff
MOI	Maintenance Operating Instruction
MOB	Main Operating Base
MOI	Maintenance Operating Instruction
MSEP	Maintenance Standardization and Evaluation Program
NCO	Non-Commissioned Officer
NCOIC	Non-Commissioned Officer in Charge
NORM	Not Operationally Ready due to Maintenance [230]
NORM-G	NORM, Grounding condition
NORS	Not Operationally Ready due to Supply [231]
NORS-G	NORS, Grounding condition
NOTAM	Notice to Airmen

NRTS	Not Repairable This Station
	Code 1 – Repair Not Authorized
	Code 2 – Not Repairable due to lack of equipment, tools, or facilities
	Code 6 – Not Repairable due to lack of technical data
	Code 9 – Condemned
NVA	North Vietnamese Army
NVN	North Vietnam
OER	Officer Effectiveness Report
OHR	Operational Hazard Report
OIC	Officer In Charge
OJT	On-the-Job-Training
OLAA	Operating Location A (Phu Cat)
OLAB	Operating Location B (Vung Tau)
OMS	Organizational Maintenance Squadron
OOI	Office Operating Instruction
OpOrder	Operations Order
OpPlan	Operations Plan
ORI	Operational Readiness Inspection
PACAF	Pacific Air Forces
PAD	Program Action Directive
PCS	Permanent Change of Station
PIF	Pilot Information File
PIREP	Pilot Report
PMEL	Precision Measurement Equipment Laboratory
POL	Petroleum, Oil, Lubricants
PRIDE	Personal Responsibility In Daily Effort
PSP	Pierced Steel Planking
QCDR	Quality Control Deficiency Report
QDR	Quality Deficiency Report
R&R	Rest and Relaxation
RAM	Rapid Area Maintenance
RED HORSE	Rapid Engineer Deployable Heavy Operational Repair Squadron (Engineer)
ROK	Republic of Korea
R/T	Receiver/Transmitter
RVN	Republic of Vietnam
SEA	Southeast Asia
SEAOR	Southeast Asia Operational Requirement
SKT	Specialty Knowledge Test
SOI	Squadron Operating Instruction

SS	Silver Star
TAC	Tactical Air Command
TACAN	Tactical Air Navigation
TALAR	Terminal Approach Landing Aid
TALO	Tactical Air Liaison Officer
TAS	Tactical Airlift Squadron
TASK	Turn Around Support Kit
TAW	Tactical Airlift Wing
TCS	Troop Carrier Squadron
TCW	Troop Carrier Wing
TCTO	Time Compliance Technical Order
TDY	Temporary Duty
TFW	Tactical Fighter Wing
TMA	Traffic Management Agency
TOC	Tactical Operations Center
TOT	Time Over Target
TTB	Tactical Training Bundle
UHF	Ultra High Frequency
UMD	Unit Manning Document
UPT	Undergraduate Pilot Training
UR	Unsatisfactory Report
USAID	United States Agency for International Development
USARV	United States Army Vietnam
VC	Viet Cong
VDM	Vehicle Deadlined for Maintenance
VDP	Vehicle Deadlined for Parts
VFR	Visual Flight Rules
VOCO	Vocal Order of the Commander
VOR	Very High Frequency Omnidirectional Range
WAPS	Weighted Airman Promotion System
WRAMA	Warner Robins Air Materiel Area (AFLC)
WSSLO	Weapon System Support Logistics Officer

Road from Vung Tau AB to Town (Copyright © 2014 Bill Craig)

Water Buffalo for Air Drop (Copyright © 2014 Denny Dillon)